**W9-ANJ-459**

# Style Differences in Cognition, Learning, and Management

# Routledge Series in Management, Organization and Society

This series presents innovative work grounded in new realities, addressing issues crucial to an understanding of the contemporary world. This is the world of organized societies, where boundaries between formal and informal, public and private, local and global organizations have been displaced or have vanished, along with other nineteenth century dichotomies and oppositions. Management, apart from becoming a specialized profession for a growing number of people, is an everyday activity for most members of modern societies.

Similarly, at the level of enquiry, culture and technology, and literature and economics, can no longer be conceived as isolated intellectual fields; conventional canons and established mainstreams are contested. Management, Organization and Society addresses these contemporary dynamics of transformation in a manner that transcends disciplinary boundaries, with books that will appeal to researchers, student and practitioners alike.

**Turning Words, Spinning Worlds**
Chapters in Organizational Ethnography
Michael Rosen

**Breaking Through the Glass Ceiling**
Women, power and leadership in
agricultural organizations
Margaret Alston

**The Poetic Logic of Administration**
Styles and changes of style in the art
of organizing
Kaj Sköldberg

**Casting the Other**
Maintaining gender inequalities in the
workplace
Edited by Barbara Czarniawska and
Heather Höpfl

**Gender, Identity and the Culture of
Organizations**
Edited by Iiris Aaltio and Albert J. Mills

**Text/Work**
Representing organization and
organizing representation
Edited by Stephen Linstead

**The Social Construction of
Management**
Texts and identities
Nancy Harding

**Management Theory**
A critical and reflexive reading
Nanette Monin

# Style Differences in Cognition, Learning, and Management

Theory, Research, and Practice

**Edited by Stephen Rayner
and Eva Cools**

Routledge
Taylor & Francis Group
New York   London

First published 2011
by Routledge
270 Madison Ave, New York, NY 10016

Simultaneously published in the UK
by Routledge
2 Park Square, Milton Park, Abingdon, Oxon OX14 4RN

*Routledge is an imprint of the Taylor & Francis Group, an informa business*

Typeset in Sabon by IBT Global.

*Library of Congress Cataloging in Publication Data*
    Style differences in cognition, learning, and management : theory, research, and practice / edited by Stephen Rayner and Eva Cools.
        p. cm. — (Routledge studies in management, organizations, and society ; 10)
    Includes bibliographical references and index.
    1. Cognitive styles.   2. Learning, Psychology of.   3. Management — Psychological aspects.   I. Rayner, Stephen.   I. Cools, Eva, 1977–
    BF318.S82 2011
    153 — dc22
    2010013710

ISBN13: 978-0-415-80199-7 (hbk)
ISBN13: 978-0-203-84185-3 (ebk)

*To all style scholars and practitioners who contribute(d) to the European Learning Styles Information Network (ELSIN) since its origin in 1996*

# Contents

## PART II
## Personal Diversity: Style Differences in Thinking, Learning, and Knowledge Acquisition

## PART III
## Personal Diversity: Style Differences in Lifelong Learning and Workplace Contexts

## PART IV
## Summing Up: The Journey Continues . . .

# Foreword
## Reports of a Death Greatly Exaggerated

It is a great privilege for me to be able to write a foreword to a book compiled of the work of many of the leading scholars in styles research. I will begin by stating the obvious: styles research and practice has been criticized, sometimes severely, in recent years. In the wake of these critiques, one might be excused for thinking that styles research was in a state of terminal decline, spiraling downwards into a morass of unreliable and unvalidated measures and untested interventions without the safety net of a convincing and compelling theoretical architecture. Indeed, the high-profile nature of some of the criticisms in the UK at least might lead hard-pressed practitioners, many of whom are swamped on an almost daily basis by a plethora of fads and fashions and exhortations from managers and policymakers to raise their game, to a negative evaluation of styles. This would be regrettable, because as readers of this book will discover, not only are reports of the death of styles greatly exaggerated; style has much to contribute to the continuous improvement of teaching and learning practices in a way that is intellectually rigorous and satisfying.

It is true that styles research faces a number of significant challenges, both theoretical and methodological, but any field of inquiry that is utterly de-problematized is severely lacking one of the fundamental attributes of scientific endeavor—that of uncertainty. Indeed, one of the distinctive and laudable features of styles is that its researchers have, in the main, openly accepted that the field is problematic and have often eagerly embraced uncertainty. One might even argue that styles researchers have at times been rather too willing to lie down, roll over, and accept uncritically the critiques leveled both from inside and outside the field. The chapters in this book clearly demonstrate that styles research is not only alive and well but kicking back, and much of this has been achieved within the vibrant community of scholars that comprise the European Learning Styles Information Network (ELSIN).

Singling out themes is almost as hazardous as singling out contributions; I will risk the former, and leave the latter to reviewers and readers. Amongst the newer applications of styles for teaching and research, this book provides leading-edge contributions in relation to working in inclusive educational settings and improving access to learning for students with learning difficulties, and exciting new applications associated with Web-based digital technologies and virtual worlds. Theoretically and methodologically, the book signals movements toward consensual understandings of, and theoretical bases for, the psychology of individual differences in style, and the development of longitudinal and mixed methodologies leading to deeper understandings of styles across a range of tasks and in a variety of contexts, and going beyond descriptive and correlational analyses. For me the underlying theme of the book is an underscoring of the vital importance of knowledge and consequent regulation of cognition and learning: this is metacognition. As this book amply demonstrates, styles and metacognition are umbilically attached. From the perspective of cognitive style, metacognition may be defined as a self-aware and intentional orientation to the representation and processing of information during learning, thinking, problem solving, and decision making; hence knowledge of styles is a necessary (but not sufficient) condition for metacognition. As witnessed in the diversity of contributions to this book, from an applied perspective across multiple domains, styles and metacognition are not only intertwined but vitally important for several reasons: firstly, self-awareness of cognitive styles is a prerequisite for metacognition; secondly, educator awareness of styles increases the likelihood of the incorporation of style-related factors into the design of educational programs and curricula; thirdly, styles research has considerable but underexploited potential to contribute to evidence-based educational and training practices for developing learners' metacognitive knowledge and skill; and fourthly, the latter has the power to equip individuals for productive and satisfying roles as mentally self-governing, lifelong learners in the knowledge-based economies of the information age.

This book, along with other recently published volumes as well as the steady stream of papers on the subject in academic journals and conference activity, clearly demonstrates that reports of the death of styles are not only greatly exaggerated but that we may be witnessing a resurgence of a field that has emerged from a period of critical self-examination refreshed and with sounder theoretical and methodological bases, and knowing which are the important questions to ask. Uncertainty, framed within and with respect for a research tradition that has already achieved much over the best part of a century, is a healthy attribute of styles research, and the willingness to be open to criticism and to critically self-reflect bodes well for a surer-footed reemergence. As every competent and experienced educational practitioner knows, 'one size does not fit all' and in this regard there is no other field of educational research that has the degree of unrealized potential that styles possesses to contribute to improved educational practice. This book is a foundational work of theory and evidence for researchers and practitioners who wish to not only understand individual differences in learning and thinking but also acknowledge and accommodate the diversity that exists amongst learners and which educational practice has a professional duty to address.

*Eugene Sadler-Smith*
*School of Management, University of Surrey, UK*

# Figures

# Tables

# 1 Setting the Scene
## The Journey toward a Paradigm Shift

*Stephen Rayner and Eva Cools*

## INTRODUCTION: SETTING THE SCENE

This book was originally proposed to honor fifteen years of contributions to the field of style research in cognition and learning presented at the annual conference of the European Learning Styles Information Network (ELSIN) (http://www.elsinnews.com/); it was founded in 1996 as a multidisciplinary community of scholars and practitioners in the domain of strategies and styles of thinking and learning. Our intention, however, quickly turned to a more ambitious project involving a wish to create a collection of chapters offering leading-edge research, theory, and practice in the field of style differences across a range of domains. This idea was felt to be all the more urgent given the contemporary publication of several widely acclaimed critical texts rejecting some of the major work in the field of cognitive and learning styles, and more generally, a practitioner-inspired questioning of the relevance in style research for the applied fields of education and workplace training. A widespread opinion, furthermore, expressed time and again by both critics and proponents of style theory, has been the need for a more clearly stated, reliable, and coherent articulation of the state of the science in the field of style research. This is exactly our intention. We hope this book will represent a timely step toward realizing greater levels of shared clarity and relevance in style research, providing both a purpose and rationale for this collection of work.

Moreover, to realize this aim, we agreed from the outset to observe one of the founding principles of ELSIN and deliberately seek to bring established and new researchers together in an effort to further nurture synergy and knowledge creation in the research community. A cursory glance at the various contributors to this book will confirm the presence of new researchers together with well-known leading researchers in the field (see Appendix 1A to this chapter). Original pioneering work in style, for example, is widely associated with David Kolb, Richard Boyatzis, Robert Sternberg, Lifang Zhang, Jan Vermunt, and Rita Dunn. The mix of more recently established researchers adds new perspective and together with more established scholars deepens our understanding of the knowledge domain. Finally, it is useful in this respect to take a historical perspective and acknowledge the work of these leading researchers over a fifty-year period. In particular, we would like to celebrate the work of a colleague, Rita Dunn, who has recently died. Indeed, the work of 'Dunn and Dunn' has played an influential and central part for more than fifty years in developing the field. Since what appears to have been a busy and exciting time in the days of the seminal North American Secondary School Project led by James Keefe (1985), to continuing work and development of their learning style model at St John's University, New York, during the latter part of the 20th century, Rita Dunn enthusiastically, energetically, and conscientiously advanced the theory and implementation of style-led curriculum differentiation in the work of schools and colleges in the US and later across the globe. She also presented a memorable keynote lecture at the ELSIN conference in 2003, stirring vigorous debate and adding to the growing need for further understanding and development of style theory and its application in learning and teaching across the workplace. It truly goes without saying that her death is a loss to the field and that the chapter co-written with Andrea Honigsfeld for this book is probably one of the last pieces of work to be completed by Rita. We are honored to include it in this book.

It is not surprising, then, that our approach to researchers, of combining the new with the established, places a particular value upon the doctoral degree and the research student as well as research practitioners from a range of applied disciplines such as medicine, social sciences, and education. It is particularly pleasing to look back at fifteen years of such development and witness an evolving synergy of research between these different groups within the ELSIN community. This activity is firstly evidenced by the continuing presence of students in ELSIN engaged in a PhD study, and secondly, by the growing number of citations of research reported in various proceedings of the annual ELSIN conference, in a range of articles published in peer-reviewed academic publications. These contributions have added to the work of the wider style research field, which is a complex mix of interdisciplinary and global groups made up of academics from several subject domains including education, psychology, business, computer science, information systems, management, human resources, and other related fields.

It is important, however, in spite of all of this emphasis upon interdisciplinarity, to stress that style research should be understood as both a distinct and diverse field of research. The interdisciplinary, international, and multiverse structure of this field is reflected in the composition of the ELSIN community and the range of delegates who attend its annual conference. ELSIN conferences, for example, have repeatedly drawn an international body of researchers from different European countries and yet even further afield including Iran, Japan, China, Taiwan, Australia, New Zealand, Canada, Mexico, the US, China, Israel, Nigeria, Hong Kong, South Africa, and the Philippines. Unsurprisingly, then, the field is diverse and complex. Intellectually, it is in itself a knowledge domain characterized by a number of different and conflicting theories, models, and terminology. The field of style research, moreover, has been criticized for the following shortcomings:

- persistent lack of research rigor, applicability, and relevance in working with contexts of practice (Coffield, Moseley, Hall, & Ecclestone, 2004a, 2004b);
- the tendency to proliferate contested and conflicting forms of knowledge (Messick, 1994; Neisser et al., 1996; Reynolds, 1997); and
- weak theory in explaining the phenomena of cognitive style and learning styles (Furnham, 2001; Sternberg, 1997).

To the newcomer, the result is a body of knowledge comprising a plethora of assessment tools, competing claims for reliability and validity, and theory or research based upon and reflecting the traditional dominance of experimental design and positivist methodology. All of this can be bewildering and disappointing. For some, it is reason enough to dismiss the field as irrelevant and even dangerous insofar as it reflects outdated forms of psychology that prevent more relevant and appropriate ways of explaining and working with individual differences and diversity in the educational setting or the management of human performance in the workplace.

A favorite example of this position is the following sound-byte commentary composed by Frank Coffield in an article in the UK *Times Educational Supplement*. He stated, in a partisan-like dismissal of style, that:

> The field of learning styles suffers from almost fatal flaws of theoretical incoherence and conceptual confusion; for example, you can read about left-brainers versus right-brainers, pragmatists versus theorists, and globalists versus analysts. We collected thirty such pairings—the logo for the learning styles movement should be Dichotomies R Us. There is no agreed technical vocabulary and after thirty years of research, there is no consensus. (Coffield, 2005, p. 18)

For others, however, the state of the science in style research is a source of frustration and exasperation rather than compelling grounds for rejection or dismissal. It is arguably a lack of consensual theory that is preventing purposeful development of the domain and meaningful application of the construct as part of the work of practitioners in teaching, training, or management. There is a great deal of work to be done in the field if the situation is to be satisfactorily addressed, and those involved in the creation of new knowledge perhaps need to be tasked with further developing new paradigms underpinning the epistemology of style in thinking, learning, and behavior.

In setting up our own particular contribution to such work in the editing of this book, we began with an open call for chapters focusing upon 'leading research' in the style community. Around seventy scholars responded to this call for submission of a chapter proposal, and given the positive size and quality in response, selection of content was both challenging and difficult. It was, nonetheless, reassuring testimony that the international research community engaged in developing an understanding and application of style differences in human performance was alive and productive. It is, furthermore, evidence that this book might fairly claim to reflect leading-edge research, theory, and practice on style differences in human performance. It is our hope that the various perspectives reflected in a diverse range of international work throughout the book support and set out possibilities for a new and alternative research paradigm(s), focusing on facilitating revision and new consensus in the field of style differences and, in turn, the underpinning areas of differential and individual differences psychology (see Appendix 1A to this chapter). To this end, we have used a series of style-based titles to organize the structure of the book.

## PART I: THE THEORY OF STYLE DIFFERENCES

The first part of the book comprises work that relates to the theory of style differences, including research around developing and understanding the basis of psychometric assessment of style differences; the construction of models of style and their meaning; and the work of researching style in terms of developing methodology, epistemology, and paradigm shift. The direction for this work builds upon earlier efforts to strategically frame style research (see, for examples, various contributions in: Schmeck, 1988; Riding & Rayner, 2000; Sternberg & Zhang, 2001; Zhang & Sternberg, 2009). Important scholarly tasks identified in this section of the book include the need to further affirm the nature, structure, and function of the style construct in the psychology of the individual. Building upon some of the key themes originally identified by Curry (1983), Zhang and Sternberg (2005), Riding and Rayner (1998), and more recently articulated by Zhang and Sternberg (2009), we propose that more work is still needed to realize:

1. a consensual definition of cognitive styles, learning styles, and thinking styles ensuring clarity and coherence in describing the psychological construct of style;
2. verification that styles are either traits or states in the psychology of the individual; and
3. confirmation that styles are value-laden inferring potential for differential functioning in diverse contexts.

We would add to this list of controversial issues or needs a new and urgent focus on research examining the interaction between personal diversity (style, personality, and self-perception) and social diversity (culture, community, and organizational agency). The processes of learning and teaching overlay these twin aspects of diversity and in turn further impact upon individual performance across a wide range of activity. For practitioners, this is where the relevance of theories such as the 'matching hypothesis' and 'style flexing' are to be found, tried, and tested (Rayner, 2007a, 2007b).

We also propose taking this approach further to focus upon additional action-orientated themes in style research aimed at establishing a paradigm shift and the creation of new knowledge parameters in the field (see discussion on paradigms in the field of style research in Rayner & Peterson, 2009). These themes, which are reflected in the work reported in Part I and also throughout the rest of this book (see Appendix 1A to this chapter), include:

1. Recognizing a good style theory—reusing traditional recipes, scripts, and templates defining the nature and structure of style.
2. Extending a good style theory—using new recipes, scripts, and templates to challenge, revise, develop, and, when appropriate, integrate existing models of style.
3. Enabling theory building in styles research and applied practice—in particular assuring rigor and value in research projects and the wider field of style research.
4. Managing theory-building utilizing basic and applied research approaches across the domain and between communities of researchers.
5. Developing new forms of research methodology to enable greater synergy between basic and applied style research.

The contributions to Part I, as previously stated, reflect some or all of these themes and set out a new baseline for future work. In Chapter 2, Valentyna Moskvina and Maria Kozhevnikov use a historical approach to review the existing body of cognitive style research in order to reconstruct a general logic and development in the field, as well as determine directions for future research. Crucially, they assert that cognitive style is a complex variable with multiple dimensions, and that different styles can operate at different levels of information processing. John and Esther Roodenburg in Chapter 3 present an example of new research returning to the psychometric methods employed in style assessment with a focus upon the construct interrelationships between personality and style, a structure drawing upon Jungian psychology and originally mapped out by Myers-Briggs (1980), giving us the Myers-Briggs Type Indicator (MBTI). They argue that sidestepping epistemological conflict and carefully managing 'statistical gobbledygook' can lead to reestablishing construct validity from a classical test theory perspective. For Chapter 4, Li-fang Zhang and Weiqiao Fan further develop an integration of style models drawing upon Sternberg's theory of mental self-government. Utilizing the threefold framework of intellectual styles, the authors present the case for using this model as an encompassing term for such constructs as cognitive styles, learning styles, and thinking styles. In Chapter 5, Garima Sharma and David Kolb describe the concept of learning flexibility in Experiential Learning Theory and its relationship to integrative learning and adult development. The chapter provides an account of a research method integrating new and established psychometric approaches used to validate hypotheses about learning flexibility and adaptation to differing contexts of learning. Gert Vanthournout, Vincent Donche, David Gijbels, and Peter Van Petegem in the final chapter of this first section report on a systematic review of existing longitudinal research adopting the learning pattern framework devised by Vermunt (1996). This is in turn used to offer an integrative account of learning by bringing together four different learning components, namely processing strategies, regulation strategies, learning conceptions, and learning orientations.

## PART II: PERSONAL DIVERSITY: INDIVIDUAL DIFFERENCES IN THINKING, LEARNING, AND KNOWLEDGE ACQUISITION

The second part of our book examines the function and effect of style in the context of learning, knowledge acquisition, training and development, and pedagogy. A large number of studies have been conducted in this area, and style differences have been found to impact upon the way people learn, process knowledge, and develop (Hayes & Allinson, 1996, 1998; Messick, 1994, 1996; Rayner, 2000; Riding, 2001; Riding & Rayner, 1998; Saracho, 2000). The task identified here, then, is to ask what it is we should know and quite crucially, actually do with style theory, in educating professional practitioners for working with individual differences in their workplace.

Richard Boyatzis and Charalampos Mainemelis open this section in Chapter 7 with a consideration of the association between learning style as assessed in Kolb's model and adaptive styles of business and management students in an MBA program. They report upon a large-scale longitudinal research study, providing both an example of mixed-method survey over time and evidence-based insights into a pluralism of styles in MBA students, as well as significant associations between abstract learning styles and academic attainment. In Chapter 8, Patrícia Almeida, Helena Pedrosa de Jesus, and Mike Watts present research using models of style preference and learning strategy, respectively, that is, Kolb's LSI and the alternative tradition of orientation to study (Biggs, 2001; Entwistle & Peterson, 2004; Vermunt, 1996), to identify undergraduate students' learning styles, types of questions, and approaches to learning. Their research reveals students exhibit both deep and surface approaches to learning, with evidence of an intermediate ('meso') approach between the two. The findings do not indicate a unique category of critical questions, but that criticality is clearly conditioned by the context. Chapter 9 contains an account of Ian Kinchin's research accessing student visualization using concept maps to investigate the interrelationship between individual differences and structures of knowledge, learning styles, and university teaching. Findings suggest that some approaches to teaching within the traditional lecture-based university course inhibit students from adopting their preferred learning style, channeling students towards strategies that are rewarded even when meaningful learning has not occurred.

Melodie and Sherman Rosenfeld in Chapter 10 argue the need to directly consider a paradigm shift in the researching and theory of style differences. They propose a deliberate approach to research based on reconstructing a complementary paradigm, one that gives voice to learners about their own styles based on self-reflection and self-regulation (Boekaerts & Corno, 2005). In Chapter 11, Elizabeth Peterson, Sarah Carne, and Sarah Freear also address the questions surrounding the key issue of theory into practice and the relevance of style in the professional education of teachers and trainers in work-based education. They report research investigating the effects of raising preservice secondary school teachers' awareness of style research and their perceptions of the relevance of styles to their teaching practice. They argue that, whereas styles may not have a major impact on academic outcomes, it is clearly relevant and useful for increasing teachers' appreciation of diversity in their classrooms, increasing teacher and learner self-awareness, and giving teachers tools to help engage their students in learning. Similarly in Chapter 12, Jan Vermunt, building upon seminal work in understanding student orientations to learning in university education, presents the case for more research investigating patterns in student and teacher learning. He offers an account of recent research investigating 'teacher learning' in the context of educational innovation. Findings reveal how basic learning patterns are similar for students and teachers, but the manifestation of these patterns in actual learning is different.

In the final chapter of this section, Carol Evans and Michael Waring investigate the important function of feedback in episodes of formative assessment and how this relates to style differences of students engaged in learning. The research reported reveals the importance of aligning feedback to the specific learning needs of individual student teachers, particularly in relation to developing self-regulation skills. Importantly, the authors argue for an explicit link between theory and practice. This is made by exploring the metacognitive potential of an understanding of cognitive styles as part of a developing model of applying style differences described as a 'Personal Learning Styles Pedagogy' (PLSP). The argument presented here is that adopting such an approach can very usefully inform the development and enhancement of feedback within initial teacher education (ITE).

## PART III: PERSONAL DIVERSITY: DIFFERENCES IN LIFELONG LEARNING AND WORKPLACE CONTEXTS

Part 3 draws upon work looking at how style differences impact upon human performance across lifelong learning and the workplace community. Personal diversity is reflected in the way individual differences feature in work related to decision-making behavior, conflict management, strategy development, and group processes (Leonard, Scholl, & Kowalski, 1999). Style differences are considered to be an important factor in individual performance within and across organizational settings, for instance, in the areas of selection, vocational and occupational preferences, team composition and performance, training and development, and organizational learning (Armstrong, 2000; Sadler-Smith, 1998, 2000). A key theme for this section is therefore the interaction between people and their environment and the underlying processes of community, culture, and personal diversity. A second key theme for this section is the development and application of Web-based learning and the opportunities offered in the advance of new technologies and media that are part of e-learning and the construction of new pedagogies and learning environments.

Glenn Hardaker, Annie Jeffery, and A'ishah Sabki (Chapter 14) provide us with a series of interesting insights into both of these key themes with a focus upon research and development of innovative pedagogies in the construction of e-learning. This chapter provides a pragmatic perspective on the application of learning style and personal pedagogy on what is called 'Second Life' as part of the adoption of more 'participative technologies', and an increasing need for educationists to generate personalized knowledge of the groups they are working with and the technologies they are being asked to use as tools for learning, teaching, and training.

Chapter 15, in turn, directly addresses the issue of context and a need to include culture as a variable when doing research in learning styles. Zarina Charlesworth draws on selected results from a multistage research project carried out with undergraduate students of diverse nationalities to show that culture has an influence on learning styles across a range of nationalities and international settings in education.

In Chapter 16, Nikos Tsianos, Panagiotis Germanakos, Zacharias Lekkas, and Costas Mourlas report on a continuing program of research and development in the area of Web-based learning. They focus on the nature of cognitive style in adaptive hypermedia environments, across two distinct domains: e-learning media and commercial websites. The results of experimental research are interpreted to show how style may be used in order to enhance the design of educational and commercial hypermedia content in a measurable and meaningful way.

In Chapter 17, Kristin Backhaus provides an alternative appraisal of situated practice in business and management education to elicit an educationist's perspective on the task of using style theories and assessment to succeed in the challenge of preparing a diverse population of students in a rapidly changing business environment. A framework for applying cognitive styles research to a set of four specific issues facing business educators is proposed and an argument made for building a style paradigm that can be used to directly inform teaching and learning.

The final two chapters in this section follow a similar theme, that is, a focus upon the practical uses of style, in particular with exceptional students in the setting of mainstream schooling. Both chapters examine the same key questions as identified in the previous chapter and which might be summed up in asking how we should use knowledge of style in practice. The bottom line here, it seems, is always the need to return to thinking through how an awareness of style can improve performance. It must feature in practice in a way that can deepen understanding, reinforce respect for personal perspective yet crucially always serve to enhance learning, teaching, and work-related tasks involving the individual, the group, and the organizational community.

In Chapter 18, Rita Dunn and Andrea Honigsfeld offer an overview of learning styles-based differentiating instruction for at-risk students. The authors place the Dunn and Dunn model of learning styles in the larger contexts of style research as well as educational practice to acknowledge and respond to the scholarly criticism of the Dunn and Dunn learning styles model. They conclude that many at-risk students might not need special education services if their diverse learning needs were more consistently accommodated. Tilly Mortimore in Chapter 19 provides a more sharply focused but complementary perspective on teachers working with students presenting special educational needs (SEN) and explores how teachers can further develop their own inclusive pedagogy to better meet the learning needs of all students in the classroom. A careful appraisal of the process of translating theory into practice is presented, giving practical insights into resolving the question of the practitioner critically exploiting theory to better apply style in developing school-based practices and a style-led pedagogy.

## PART IV: SUMMING UP: THE JOURNEY CONTINUES . . .

The long-standing $64 question facing us in this work is: what is the final balance in terms of new knowledge and intellectual profit realized at the end of this book project? Did we succeed in contributing to a paradigm shift? We think the answer is yes and no: yes when looking at the global perspective presented by the whole book (see Appendix 1A to this chapter); no when looking at each chapter in its own right. Every chapter focuses on a particular important aspect, as demonstrated in the preceding overview. In addition, as stated by Rayner and Peterson in the following assertion, a paradigm shift takes time and needs to be assessed in the long term. We are positive about theoretical, conceptual, empirical, methodological, and practical evolutions that have recently taken place in the style field, but there is still a way to go. In this sense, we deliberately set out in this book to stimulate theoretical debates and empirical studies that continue contributing to a process of paradigm shift.

> While a paradigm shift in the social sciences may not be as disruptive as that experienced in the natural sciences, the shift is likely to be a messier process, often proving to be slow and imprecise. The influences of prevailing orthodoxies rarely completely disappear but are eventually encompassed within a modified epistemology. Nonetheless, if we are seeking a paradigm shift in our thinking about researching and theorizing cognitive styles, this process of change needs to be deliberately stimulated as a way of creating new knowledge. It will not happen spontaneously or necessarily result in an instant transformation of knowledge. (Rayner & Peterson, 2009, p. 122)

The concluding chapter of our book brings together these key themes and our recommendations for the further development of the field, drawing upon the content of the book while also building upon lessons learned from the past fifteen years of style research in cognition and learning (as presented and discussed in the past annual ELSIN conferences). We reflect, in particular, on the advancement of the style field from three perspectives: theoretical and conceptual constructions, methodological and measurement evolutions, and applications of style.

## BIBLIOGRAPHY

Armstrong, S.J. (2000). Individual differences in cognitive style and their potential effects on organizational behavior: a summary of recent empirical studies. In R.J. Riding & S.G. Rayner (Eds.), *International Perspectives on Individual Differences. Volume 1: Cognitive Styles* (pp. 215–237). Stamford, CT: Ablex.

Biggs, J. (2001). Enhancing learning: a matter of style or approach? In R.J. Sternberg & L.F. Zhang (Eds.), *Perspectives on Thinking, Learning and Cognitive Styles* (pp. 73–102). Mahwah, NJ: Lawrence Erlbaum Associates.

Boekaerts, M., & Corno, L. (2005). Self-regulation in the classroom: a perspective on assessment and intervention. *Applied Psychology: An International Review, 54*, 199–231.

Coffield, F.C. (2005). Kinaesthetic nonsense. *Times Educational Supplement, 14*, January, 17–18.

Coffield, F.C., Moseley, D.V.M., Hall, E., & Ecclestone, K. (2004a). *Learning Styles and Pedagogy in Post-16 Learning: Findings of a Systematic and Critical Review of Learning Styles Models*. London: Learning and Skills Research Centre.

Coffield, F.C., Moseley, D.V.M., Hall, E., & Ecclestone, K. (2004b). *Should We Be Using Learning Styles? What Research Has to Say to Practice*. London: Learning and Skills Research Centre.

Curry, L. (1983). An organization of learning style theory and constructs. In L. Curry (Ed.), *Learning Style in Continuing Medical Education* (pp. 115–123). Halifax: Dalhouse University.

Entwistle, N., & Peterson, E.R. (2004). Learning styles and approaches to studying. In C. Spielberger (Ed.), *Encyclopedia of Applied Psychology* (pp. 537–542). New York: Academic Press.

Furnham, A. (2001). Vocational preference and P-O fit: reflections on Holland's theory of vocational choice. *Applied Psychology: An International Review, 50,* 5–29.

Hayes, J., & Allinson, C.W. (1996). The implications of learning styles for training and development: a discussion of the matching hypothesis. *British Journal of Management, 7,* 63–73.

Hayes, J., & Allinson, C.W. (1998). Cognitive style and the theory and practice of individual and collective learning in organizations. *Human Relations, 51,* 847–871.

Keefe, J.W. (1985). Assessment of learning style variables: the NASSP task force model. *Theory into Practice, 24,* 138–144.

Leonard, N.H., Scholl, R.W., & Kowalski, K.B. (1999). Information processing style and decision making. *Journal of Organizational Behavior, 20,* 407–420.

Messick, S. (1994). The matter of style: manifestations of personality in cognition, learning and teaching. *Educational Psychologist, 29,* 121–136.

Messick, S. (1996). Bridging cognition and personality in education: the role of style in performance and development. *European Journal of Personality, 10,* 353–376.

Myers-Briggs, I. (1980). *Gifts Differing: Understanding Personality Type.* Palo Alto, CA: Davies-Black Publishing.

Neisser, U., Boodoo, G., Bouchard, T.J., Jr., Boykin, A.W., Brody, B., Ceci, S.J., et al. (1996). Intelligence: knowns and unknowns. *American Psychologist, 51,* 77–101.

Rayner, S.G. (2000). Reconstructing style differences in thinking and learning: profiling learning performance. In R.J. Riding & S.G. Rayner (Eds.), *International Perspectives on Individual Differences. Volume 1: Cognitive Styles* (pp. 115–177). Stamford, CT: Ablex.

Rayner, S. (2007a). What next? Developing global research and applied practice the field of cognitive and learning styles. In L. Lassen, L. Bostrom, & H.K. Knoop (Eds.), *Laering og Laeringsstile. Om unikke of faelles veje I paedagogikken* (pp 165–183). Virum, Denmark: Dansk Psykologisk Forlag.

Rayner, S.G. (2007b). A teaching elixir, learning chimera or just fool's gold? Do learning styles matter? *British Journal of Support for Learning, 22,* 24–31.

Rayner, S., & Peterson, E.R. (2009). Reaffirming style as an individual difference: toward a global paradigm or knowledge diaspora? In L.F. Zhang & R.J. Sternberg (Eds.), *Perspectives on the Nature of Intellectual Styles* (pp. 107–137). Heidelberg: Springer.

Reynolds, M. (1997). Learning styles: a critique. *Management Learning, 28,* 115–133.

Riding, R. (2001). The nature and effects of cognitive style. In R.J. Sternberg & L.F. Zhang (Eds.), *Perspectives on Thinking, Learning, and Cognitive Styles* (pp. 47–72). Mahwah, NJ: Lawrence Erlbaum Associates.

Riding, R.J., & Rayner, S.G. (1998). *Cognitive Styles and Learning Strategies.* London: David Fulton.

Riding, R.J., & Rayner, S. (Eds.) (2000). *International Perspectives on Individual Differences. Volume 1: Cognitive Styles.* Stamford, CT: Ablex.

Sadler-Smith, E. (1998). Cognitive style: some human resource implications for managers. *International Journal of Human Resource Management, 9,* 185–202.

Sadler-Smith, E. (2000). Cognitive style and learning in organizations. In R.J. Riding & S.G. Rayner (Eds.), *International Perspectives on Individual Differences. Volume 1: Cognitive Styles* (pp. 181–213). Stamford, CT: Ablex.

Saracho, O.N. (2000). Framework for effective classroom teaching: matching teachers' and students' cognitive styles. In R.J. Riding & S.G. Rayner (Eds.), *International Perspectives on Individual Differences. Volume 1: Cognitive Styles* (pp. 297–314). Stamford, CT: Ablex.

Schmeck, R.J. (1988). *Learning Strategies and Learning Styles (Perspectives on Individual Differences)*. New York: Springer.

Sternberg, R.J. (1997). *Thinking Styles*. Cambridge: Cambridge University Press.

Sternberg, R.J., & Zhang, L.F. (Eds.) (2001). *Perspectives on Thinking, Learning and Cognitive Styles*. Mahwah, NJ: Lawrence Erlbaum Associates.

Vermunt, J. (1996). Metacognitive, cognitive and affective aspects of learning styles and strategies: a phenomenographic analysis. *Higher Education, 31*, 25–50.

Zhang, L.F., & Sternberg, R.J. (2005). A threefold model of intellectual styles. *Educational Psychology Review, 17*, 1–53.

Zhang, L.F., & Sternberg, R.J. (Eds.) (2009). *Perspectives on the Nature of Intellectual Styles*. Heidelberg: Springer.

*Appendix 1A.* Overview of Chapters in the Book

| | Author(s) | Origin authors[a] | Main field authors | Main focus chapter | Concept (Measure(s))[b] | Context | Major contribution to paradigm shift |
|---|---|---|---|---|---|---|---|
| 2 | Moskvina & Kozhevnikov | US | Psychology | Theoretical Conceptual | Cognitive style | Broad, unspecified | * Historical review<br>* Identification of gaps and avenues for further research |
| 3 | Roodenburg & Roodenburg | Australia | Psychology | Methodological Conceptual | Style | Broad, unspecified | * Overview of role of psychometrics in style research<br>* Methodological advices |
| 4 | Zhang & Fan | Hong Kong China | Education, Psychology | Theoretical Conceptual | Thinking style (TSI; TSI-R; TSI-R2; TSTI; PTSTI; PTSLI) | Broad, diverse | * Comprehensive review of conceptual and empirical contributions of the theory of mental self-government |
| 5 | Sharma & Kolb | US | Organizational Behavior | Conceptual Empirical | Learning style(KLSI; LFI) | Broad, diverse | * Development and validation of Learning Flexibility Index<br>* Case study as basis for self-development |
| 6 | Vanthournout, Donche, Gijbels, & Van Petegem | Belgium | Education | Theoretical Methodological | Learning pattern(ILS) | Higher education | * Methodological review<br>* Focus on longitudinal research designs |
| 7 | Boyatzis & Mainemelis | US Greece | Organizational behavior | Empirical Practical | Learning style(KLSI; ASI) | Management education | * Large-scale empirical study on distribution of learning and adaptive styles in management education<br>* Concrete and applicable advices for management educators |

*continued*

*Appendix 1A continued.* Overview of Chapters in the Book

| | Author(s) | Origin authors[a] | Main field authors | Main focus chapter | Concept (Measure(s))[b] | Context | Major contribution to paradigm shift |
|---|---|---|---|---|---|---|---|
| 8 | Almeida, Pedrosa de Jesus, & Watts | Portugal UK | Education | Empirical Methodological | Learning style (KLSI) | Higher education | * Mixed-method inquiry on the link between students' questions and their style<br>* Focus on (teaching) context |
| 9 | Kinchin | UK | Education | Conceptual Practical | Learning style | Higher education | * Model of student-centered learning from the perspective of knowledge structures<br>* Focus on (teaching) context |
| 10 | Rosenfeld & Rosenfeld | Israel | Education | Conceptual Methodological | Individual learning difference (KLSI; LCI; SOLAT; VAK; GEFT; 4-MAT; Triarchic Abilities Model) | Teacher education | * Model of student-centered learning from the perspective of increased teacher sensitivity to style preferences (on the basis of self-reflection and self-regulation, this is second-person perspective)<br>* Identification of avenues for further research |
| 11 | Peterson, Carne, & Freear | New Zealand | Psychology | Empirical Methodological | Style (different models, unspecified)[c] | Teacher education | * Model of student-centered learning of increased teacher awareness to style preferences<br>* Qualitative design |
| 12 | Vermunt | The Netherlands | Education | Theoretical Conceptual | Learning pattern(ILS) Teaching pattern | Higher education Teacher education | * Model of patterns in teacher learning in parallel to existing models of students' learning patterns<br>* Focus on (teaching) context |

*Appendix 1A  continued.* Overview of Chapters in the Book

| | Author(s) | Origin authors[a] | Main field authors | Main focus chapter | Concept (Measure(s))[b] | Context | Major contribution to paradigm shift |
|---|---|---|---|---|---|---|---|
| 13 | Evans & Waring | UK | Education | Empirical Methodological | Cognitive style (CSI) | Teacher education | * Mixed-method inquiry on the link between student teachers' feedback preferences and their style<br>* Concrete and applicable advices for teacher educators |
| 14 | Hardaker, Jeffery, & Sabki | UK US | Education Business & Management | Conceptual Methodological | Personal learning style | Higher education | * Model of personalized e-pedagogy in virtual worlds<br>* Case study research as illustration |
| 15 | Charlesworth | Switzerland | Education | Empirical Methodological | Learning style (LSQ) | Higher education | * Mixed-method inquiry on the link between students' cultural background and their style<br>* Focus on cultural context |
| 16 | Tsianos, Germanakos, Lekkas, & Mourlas | Greece Cyprus | Education Business & Management | Empirical Methodological | Cognitive style (CSA) | Higher education | * Experimental study on the effects of personalized e-learning environment |
| 17 | Backhaus | US | Business & Management | Theoretical Practical | Cognitive style | Management education | * Overview of relevant style-related findings for business education in the 21st century<br>* Concrete and applicable advices for management educators |

*continued*

Appendix 1A *continued.* Overview of Chapters in the Book

| | Author(s) | Origin authors[a] | Main field authors | Main focus chapter | Concept (Measure(s))[b] | Context | Major contribution to paradigm shift |
|---|---|---|---|---|---|---|---|
| 18 | Dunn & Honigsfeld | US | Education | Theoretical Practical | Learning style(ELSA; LS: CY†; LIVES) | Primary and secondary education | * Overview of conceptual and empirical contributions of Dunn and Dunn model of learning styles<br>* Concrete advices on how this model can be meaningfully applied for differentiating instruction for at-risk students |
| 19 | Mortimore | UK | Education | Theoretical Practical | Learning style | Secondary education | * Concrete advices on how style theory can be applied for the inclusion of vulnerable learners<br>* Focus on (teaching/learning) context |

Notes. [a]This refers to their affiliation at the moment of writing their chapters. [b]For the full references of these measures, see the respective chapters that used them: 4-MAT Model (McCarthy, 1980); ASI = Adaptive Style Inventory (Boyatzis & Kolb, 1993); CSA = Cognitive Style Analysis (Riding & Cheema, 1991); CSI = Cognitive Style Index (Allinson & Hayes, 1996; Hodgkinson & Sadler-Smith, 2003); ELSA = Elementary Learning Style Assessment (Dunn, Rundle, & Burke, 2007); GEFT = Group Embedded Figures Test (Witkin, Oltman, Raskin, & Karp, 1971); ILS = Inventory of Learning Styles (Vermunt, 1996); KLSI = Kolb's Learning Style Inventory (Kolb, 1976, 1999, 2007); LCI = Learning Combination Inventory (Johnston & Dainton, 1997); LFI = Learning Flexibility Index (Sharma & Kolb, Chapter 5, this volume); LIVES = Learning in Vogue: Elements of Style (Missere & Dunn, 2007); LS:CY! = Learning Style: The Clue to You! (Burke & Dunn, 1998); LSQ = Learning Style Questionnaire (Honey & Mumford, 1986; Lashley, 2002); PTSLI = Preferred Thinking Styles in Learning Inventory (Zhang, 2007); PTSTI = Preferred Thinking Styles in Teaching Inventory (Zhang, 2003); SOLAT = Your Style of Learning and Thinking Inventory (Torrance, 1980); TSI = Thinking Styles Inventory (Sternberg & Wagner, 1992); TSI-R = Thinking Styles Inventory – Revised (Sternberg, Wagner, & Zhang, 2003); TSI-R2 = Thinking Styles Inventory—Revised II (Sternberg, Wagner, & Zhang, 2007); TSTI = Teaching Styles in Teaching Inventory (Grigorenko & Sternberg, 1993); Triarchic Abilities Model (Sternberg, 1985); VAK = Visual/Auditory/Kinesthetic Modalities Inventory (Barsch, 1980). [c]More information on the used models and tests is available from the first author of this chapter.

# Part I

# The Theory of Style Differences

# 2 Determining Cognitive Styles
## Historical Perspective and Directions for Future Research

*Valentyna Moskvina and Maria Kozhevnikov*

## INTRODUCTION

Cognitive style historically refers to a psychological dimension representing consistencies in an individual's manner of cognitive functioning, particularly with respect to acquiring and processing information (Ausburn & Ausburn, 1978). Despite great popularity in the early 1950s, interest in cognitive style research began to decline in the 1970s. The field was left without a coherent theory and without a complete understanding of how cognitive styles were related to other psychological constructs. In this chapter, we will use a historical approach to review the existing body of cognitive style research in order to reconstruct the general logic and development of the field, as well as determine directions for future research. To facilitate following the major advances and accumulation of theoretical and experimental problems in cognitive style literature, discussion of the development of the field is divided into four main periods (see Figure 2.1), which will be elaborated further as the review of cognitive style studies progresses.

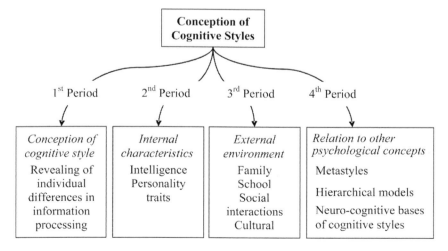

*Figure 2.1* The four main periods and their contribution to cognitive style research.

## HISTORICAL PERSPECTIVE ON THE DEVELOPMENT
## OF THE COGNITIVE STYLE CONSTRUCT

### First Period: Origins of Cognitive Style Research

The first period began in the 1940s and early 1950s, and it is characterized by experimental studies that revealed the existence of individual differences in perceiving information and performance on other cognitive tasks (Klein, 1951; Klein & Schlesinger, 1951; Witkin & Ash, 1948). Witkin and Ash (1948) reported significant differences in the ways individuals perceive an 'upright' orientation. In a famous psychological experiment investigating perceptual differentiation, some subjects perceived a rod as upright only when it was in alignment with the axes of the surrounding field, whereas other subjects were not influenced by characteristics of the field. At around the same time, Klein (1951) was studying how accurately people make judgments about changes in perceptual stimuli, and noted the existence of clear individual differences in subjects' performance. Klein presented his subjects with projected squares that constantly changed in size. He identified two types of individuals: individuals who tended to notice contrasts and had the ability to maintain a high degree of stimulus differentiation (designated 'sharpeners') and individuals who were most likely to notice similarities among stimuli and ignore the differences (designated 'levelers').

Despite their lack of theoretical approach, the main contribution of the studies of the first period, as shown in Figure 2.1, is that they were the first to recognize that individuals can differ not only in their overall level of task performance but in the ways of perceiving and solving cognitive tasks. Although the term 'cognitive style' had yet to be coined, the studies of the first period introduced the idea of cognitive style to psychological research.

### Second Period: The Proof of the Concept of Cognitive Style

The beginning of the second period of cognitive style studies dates back to the early 1950s. Klein (1951) was the first to describe cognitive styles (he called them 'perceptual attitudes') as patterns of adaptation to the external world that regulate an individual's cognitive functioning. To achieve equilibrium between an individual's inner demands and the external requirements of one's environment, an individual needs to develop special mechanisms, which constitute his or her 'ego control system'. In support of his theory, Klein reported a study in which he showed that in terms of personality, the leveler group exhibited a 'self-inwardness' pattern of behavior characterized by "avoidance of competition or any situation requiring active manipulation" (Klein, 1951, p. 339). Sharpeners, on the other hand, were more manipulative and active, having high needs for attainment and autonomy. Klein considered both poles of the leveling/sharpening dimension as equal in their adaptive value (i.e., both poles present a way for an individual to achieve a satisfactory equilibrium), but different in their repertoires of psychological functions.

At the same time, Witkin and colleagues (1954) conducted a large-scale study on field dependence, in which two main groups of subjects were distinguished: 'field-dependent' individuals who exhibited high dependency on the surrounding field and 'field-independents' who were characterized by low dependency on the surrounding field. There was also a significant relationship between subjects' performance on perceptual tests and their personalities. Field-dependent individuals made greater use of external social referents in ambiguous situations and were more attentive to social cues than field-independent people. However, field-independent subjects were characterized by better control over their own impulses and greater self-esteem (for a review, see also Witkin & Goodenough, 1981). Similarly to Klein (1951), Witkin and colleagues (1954) explained individual differences in perception as different modes of adjustment to the world, because both field-dependent and field-independent groups have specific characteristics that are adaptive to particular situations.

In the 1950s, when ubiquitous use of intellectual ability assessments led individuals to a prescribed position in life, the idea of bipolarity (i.e., value-equal poles of cognitive style dimensions) spawned a great deal of interest, implying that individuals' abilities could be different, but allow equal degrees of success. As a result, a tremendous number of studies on 'style types' started to appear in the literature. Along with field-dependence/independence and leveling/sharpening, a large number of other dimensions were proposed, such as field articulation (element articulation versus form articulation, Messick & Fritzky, 1963), impulsivity/reflection (Kagan, 1966), breadth of categorization (Pettigrew, 1958) and many others. By the end of the 1970s, dozens of cognitive style dimensions were described. In attempts to integrate these dimensions, Messick (1976) proposed a list of nineteen cognitive styles and Keefe (1988) synthesized a list of forty separate styles (for a review, see Kozhevnikov, 2007).

Overall, the main schema of experimental studies on cognitive styles in the second period was as follows: a simple cognitive task with two or more possible and usually equally efficient solutions was offered to a subject. Because all solutions to the task were considered equal in value and adaptivity to the environment, it was assumed that subjects' chosen method revealed their preferences rather than abilities. As a consequence of such a general approach, as many different cognitive styles were proposed as cognitive tasks of which researchers could conceive. One of the main problems of these studies, as noted in many reviews (e.g., Kozhevnikov, 2007; Sternberg & Grigorenko, 1997), is the lack of a general theoretical approach that would lay the foundation for systematizing the numerous overlapping cognitive style dimensions. Another problem is in the concept of adjustment, proposed by Klein (1951) and Witkin and colleagues (1954), which was not concretized and operationalized in the context of the cognitive style studies. Although the concept of cognitive style had been introduced as value-free, the solutions to the cognitive tasks used in many studies were not always strictly comparable; one of the ways rather than the other was usually more efficient. This fact is especially apparent in the most commonly used instruments to measure cognitive styles deriving from this period, such as Witkin's Embedded Figure Test (Witkin et. al., 1954). Researchers consistently reported higher intelligence among individuals who prefer a field-independent style (e.g., MacLeod, Jackson, & Palmer, 1986; McKenna, 1984).

Because of the preceding problems, many of the promising benefits of studying individual cognitive styles were lost. Consequently, by the end of the 1970s, research into cognitive styles declined drastically. However, despite these problems, the second period made an important contribution to the understanding of the main characteristics of cognitive styles. The link drawn in Figure 2.1 between cognitive style and an individual's internal characteristics schematically represents the main idea of cognitive style research of the second period: cognitive style represents relatively stable differences in individuals' preferred ways of processing information and they are closely related to, and are developed experientially on the basis of, an individual's internal characteristics, such as abilities and personality traits.

## Third Period: Cognitive Styles in the Wider Context of Applied Fields

Although theoretical interest in cognitive style started to decline in the 1970s, interest in the relevance of cognitive styles to applied fields (e.g., education, psychotherapy, and management) has continued to increase, demonstrating the practical necessity of understanding individual differences in mechanisms of cognitive functioning. The main feature of these more recent studies has been their focus on styles related to complex cognitive tasks, such as problem solving or decision making (Agor, 1984; Kirton, 1989), learning styles (Dunn, Dunn, & Price, 1989; Gregorc, 1982; Kolb, 1984), and a variety of 'personal cognitive styles' and 'personal styles', such as optimistic/pessimistic, explanatory, anxiety-prone, and others (Alloy et al., 1999; Myers, 1976). In contrast to cognitive styles of the second period, which focused primarily on individual differences in perception and basic cognitive functions, these styles were based on complex cognitive tasks. For instance, Kirton (1976), working with management styles, introduced the adaptor/innovator dimension, which relates to different ways in which people approach problem solving, decision making, and creativity (Kirton, 1989). Adaptors approach problems within the current paradigm and accept generally recognized policies, whereas innovators challenge the existing paradigm and propose solutions for 'doing things differently'.

A problem with the third period is that it multiplied the already large number of proposed cognitive style dimensions by introducing the new terminology of learning styles, decision-making styles, and personal styles without clearly defining what these were and how they differed from other cognitive styles. Cognitive styles were closely related to personality traits and personality styles included a strong cognitive component. The set of theoretical questions concerning the mechanisms of cognitive styles and their relationship to other major psychological constructs remained unanswered. The significant contribution of the third-period research is that these studies expanded the view of cognitive styles, considering them as constructs that might operate not only at the level of solving simple cognitive tasks but can also be found in relation to more complex cognitive activities, such as problem solving, decision making, learning, and various other activities. Another significant contribution of the third period is the expansion of studies of individual cognitive styles to groups and organizations, and the examination of the interaction between the cognitive style of an individual and corresponding characteristics of the external environment. Throughout the third period, empirical support for the connection between an individual's cognitive style and the requirements of different kinds of social groups gradually accumulated (Agor, 1984; Kirton, 1989; Kolb, 1984). The conception of cognitive styles as adaptive patterns of adjustment to one's environment, suggested by Klein (1951) and Witkin and colleagues (1954), was expanded to include descriptions of particular requirements of certain social groups on an individual's cognitive functioning. One's cognitive style became thought of not only in terms of personality or abilities but also of social interactions regulating an individual's beliefs and value system. The link connecting the cognitive style construct with the external environment, drawn in Figure 2.1, represents this important contribution of the third period.

## Fourth Period: Recent Trends in Cognitive Style Research

Starting in the early 1980s, new trends in cognitive style research emerged. These can be roughly divided into three research themes: the splitting trend, the unifying trend, and examining styles from a cognitive/neurological perspective.

### Splitting Trend

The splitting trend reflects the tendency to analyze in depth the performance of individuals on a certain task within a group representing a single pole of a particular style dimension. The impulsivity/reflectivity dimension, which represents the preference for making responses quickly versus pausing in order to decrease the amount of errors in problem-solving situations, has been one of the first cognitive styles where the splitting tendency has emerged. In addition to the traditional groups of 'reflective' (slow-accurate) and 'impulsive' (fast-inaccurate) individuals, two other subgroups were identified: the 'fast-accurate' and the 'slow-inaccurate' (Eska & Black, 1971; Keller & Ripoll, 2001). The researchers came to the conclusion that reflective individuals might better be viewed not only as those who are slow and accurate, but also as those who can adapt their response time to the context and thus become more mobile and efficient (i.e., faster and accurate) in problem solving.

Similar results demonstrating the existence of individuals capable of adjusting their cognitive styles (mobile individuals) were obtained for other cognitive style dimensions. Niaz (1987) identified four groups of participants on the basis of field-dependence/independence and intelligence measures: 'mobile field-independent', 'mobile field-dependent', 'fixed field-independent', and 'fixed field-dependent'. Research showed that the fixed field-independent group of students received the highest intelligence scores among all the groups. At the same time, mobile individuals (both field-dependent and field-independent) performed significantly better than all other groups in three college courses (chemistry, mathematics, and biology). Furthermore, Kholodnaya (2002) conducted an empirical study in which the subjects were administered a number of different traditional cognitive style and intelligence tests. Using cluster analysis, she demonstrated that each of the cognitive style dimensions (field dependence/independence, constricted/flexible cognitive control, impulsivity/reflexivity, and narrow/wide range of equivalence) could be split further along a mobile versus fixed subdimension. Niaz (1987) and Kholodnaya (2002) concluded that mobile individuals can spontaneously regulate their intellectual activities and effectively resolve cognitive conflicts by using metacognitive abilities, whereas fixed functioning would imply a certain degree of inflexibility in information processing.

In conclusion, the results of the splitting trend suggest that individuals differ in the extent to which they exhibit flexibility and self-monitoring in their choice of cognitive styles. More recently, Kozhevnikov (2007) suggested that the splitting tendency can be viewed as a result of the existence of a superordinate mobility-fixity metastyle dimension, which serves as a control structure for other subordinate cognitive styles. That is, the metastyle represents the extent to which metacognitive mechanisms are formed in a particular individual, and which govern an individual's flexibility in the use of subordinate styles depending on the requirements of a task. The significant contribution of the splitting trend is that it introduced metacognition as an important element of cognitive style research, showing that metacognitive processes can control an individual's current preferred way of thinking.

## Unifying Trend

The unifying trend involves studies that attempt to unite existing models of style into a unifying theory with a limited number of central dimensions.

One of the first attempts to organize a considerable array of cognitive style dimensions was made by Allinson and Hayes (1996), who asked whether cognitive style is a complex or unitary construct and whether all the varieties of cognitive styles are simply different facets of an analytical/intuitive dimension (i.e., preference to process information analytically versus applying a holistic and more intuitive approach). However, their empirical data have not consistently confirmed their hypothesis about the unitary nature of cognitive style, casting doubt on the idea that all cognitive style dimensions can be conceptualized as one analytical/intuitive dimension. Other researchers have argued that cognitive style can be conceptualized as consisting of two orthogonal dimensions (e.g., Hodgkinson & Sadler-Smith, 2003; Riding & Cheema, 1991). For instance, Riding and Cheema (1991) proposed that the vast variety of cognitive styles could be reduced to two major independent dimensions: holistic/analytic (i.e., the tendency to process information in wholes versus part-by-part) and verbalizer/imager (i.e., the tendency to represent information verbally versus visually). Still other researchers (e.g., Leonard, Scholl, & Kowalski, 1999) reported correlations between the various subscales of widely used cognitive style instruments and showed empirically that, although many of the measures seem to overlap conceptually, no simple, strong interrelationships were found among them, suggesting that cognitive style is a more complex variable with multiple dimensions.

There have also been several attempts to build multilevel hierarchical models of styles and relate cognitive style to other psychological constructs and processes (e.g., Miller, 1987, 1991; Nosal, 1990; see also Kozhevnikov, 2007 for a review). For instance, Miller (1987) proposed a hierarchical model of cognitive style, in which a vertical dimension was added to the horizontal analytical/holistic dimension to represent different stages in information processing, such as perception, memory (representation, organization, and retrieval), and thought. According to Miller's model, different cognitive styles can be identified at different stages of information processing, for instance, field-dependence/independence at the perceptual level, conceptual complexity at the memory level, and serial versus holistic at the thought level. Later, Nosal (1990) introduced a model of cognitive style with four main levels of information processing: perception, concept formation, modeling (i.e., schema generation and reorganization of information), and program (i.e., metacognition). Similar to Miller's model, Nosal suggested that different cognitive styles might be identified at each level of information processing, for instance: field-dependence/independence represents style operating at the perceptual level, whereas mobility/fixity is a style operating at the program level.

Overall, the studies of a unifying trend endeavored to systematize in some way the variety of cognitive styles and establish a possible relationship among them. The contribution of the unifying trend is that it empirically confirmed that cognitive styles are neither based on a single underlying dimension nor operating in isolation, but that there is a structural relation among them. Hierarchical models of cognitive style provided a theoretical basis for a hierarchical classification of cognitive styles according to the level of information processing at which they operate (from simple perceptual decision to complex problem-solving behavior and self-monitoring functioning; see Figure 2.1).

## Cognitive Style from Cognitive/Neurological Perspective

As previously mentioned, one of the most serious problems in the field of cognitive style research has been the tendency to consider cognitive styles as isolated from the context of other psychological concepts and theories. The third trend of this period is comprised of a limited number of studies carried out to clarify the mechanisms of cognitive styles from a cognitive/ neurological perspective.

Results from the early studies of the relationship between field-dependent/independent cognitive style dimension and brain functioning suggest that the differences between field-dependent and field-independent individuals are more than just general deficiencies or preferences based in one or the other of the hemispheres (e.g., Garrick, 1978; Pizzamiglio & Carli, 1974; see also Tinajero, Paramo, Cadaveira, & Rodriguez-Holguin, 1993 for a review). In general, the results of these studies showed that field-dependent individuals exhibit greater between-hemisphere coherence, suggesting their less pronounced hemispheric differentiation (O'Connor & Shaw, 1977; Oltman, Semple, & Goldstein, 1979). Several researchers also suggested that cognitive styles might reflect variations in the efficiency of cognitive processes associated with frontal lobe systems (for a review, see also Globerson, 1989). These data provided empirical support for the idea, first proposed by Klein (1951), that cognitive styles play a regulatory function: from automatic data encoding as in the case of the field-dependence/ independence dimension to conscious allocation of mental resources as in the case of mobility/fixity dimension.

More recently, several neurophysiological studies reported different neural activity in subjects of different cognitive styles in the absence of any differences in their behavioral performance, pointing out the clear difference between cognitive style and the ability to perform a particular task. For instance, Gevins and Smith (2000) examined the electroencephalogram (EEG) of subjects who preferred verbal versus nonverbal cognitive styles while subjects performed a spatial working memory task. Although the subjects' behavioral performance did not differ significantly, subjects who preferred a verbal style exhibited greater reduction of alpha signals in the left hemisphere, whereas subjects who preferred a nonverbal style displayed greater alpha reduction in the right hemisphere. Furthermore, in a functional magnetic resonance imaging (fMRI) study conducted by Motes, Malach, and Kozhevnikov (2008), spatial visualizers (i.e., individuals who tend to think in schematic and spatial images) and object visualizers (i.e., individuals who tend to think in pictures and colorful detailed images) were administered the embedded picture task. Whereas there were no differences in subjects' behavioral performance, spatial and object visualizers showed differential activation in regions in the dorsal and ventral processing pathways, related to spatial and pictorial visual processing, respectively.

Overall, these and similar studies provided insights into the specific neural mechanisms underlying particular cognitive styles and how they differ between individuals. Such studies can be considered the first serious attempts to relate cognitive style to theories and concepts in modern cognitive psychology and neuroscience, and thus integrate the study of cognitive style into the main body of psychological science research.

## DETERMINING COGNITIVE STYLE AND
## DIRECTION FOR FUTURE RESEARCH

So far, we have reviewed the four main periods of cognitive style research. The first period revealed that individuals use different approaches to solve perceptual and cognitive tasks. The second period revealed that preferences for these approaches are quite stable and related to intelligence and personality characteristics. The studies of the third period acknowledged that cognitive style had practical implications in applied fields. This period made clear that cognitive styles are determined not only by the internal characteristics of an individual, but also by external requirements (i.e., social, educational, professional). The splitting trend in the fourth period introduced the importance of metacognition in cognitive style research, showing that metacognitive processes can determine the preferred way of thinking, allowing an individual to employ different styles depending on the requirements of a given situation. The unifying trend suggested that cognitive style is a complex variable with multiple dimensions and that different styles can operate at different levels of information processing. In addition, the studies of the fourth period attempted to relate cognitive style to distinct patterns of neural activity in the absence of differences in behavioral performance. Overall, the fourth period showed that there should be a close connection between the concept of cognitive style and other psychological constructs of contemporary psychology.

Returning to Figure 2.1 and summarizing cognitive style characteristics suggested by research from all four periods, we propose that cognitive style represents relatively stable patterns in an individual's manner of information processing, which can be conceptualized as distinctive adaptations to the world. These patterns develop slowly and experientially as a result of the interplay between basic individual characteristics (i.e., general intelligence, personality) and long-term external requirements (i.e., education, formal/informal training, professional requirements, cultural and social environment). In terms of their functions, cognitive styles are responsible for the control and regulation of an individual's cognitive activity, and they can be organized into a hierarchical structure according to the level at which they operate, with the perceptual level lowest and the metacognitive level highest.

The historical analysis of the cognitive style field has shown the necessity of studying cognitive style not only as a set of particular features but rather as the integrated outcome of the interaction between one's intellectual abilities, personality traits, and the external environment. Along with the need to study cognitive style as an integral system mediating the relationship between environmental requirements and the idiosyncratic features of an individual, it is also necessary to organize different styles into coherent dimensions in the context of the recent theories of cognitive science. In this respect, Nosal's model is one of the most promising existing models of cognitive style, because it demonstrates that it is possible to systematize different style dimensions in a hierarchical fashion. Such an approach, relating information-processing theories and intelligence components to different cognitive style dimensions, could provide a general research model that could be more fully adapted by researchers concerned with the role of learning, memory, and attention in cognitive style. Also, employment of the most recent theories about brain structure as well as advanced neuroimaging methods such as functional magnetic resonance imaging (fMRI) or event-related potential (ERP) recordings opens up a wide range of possibilities for further investigation of information-processing differences between individuals of different cognitive styles in terms of hemispheric lateralization or cerebral specialization. Research in this direction should provide valuable data for improving our understanding both of the nature of cognitive styles and their biological base.

Furthermore, knowing how the formation of cognitive style depends on an individual's learning environment would be extremely valuable for educators. Exploring different influences on cognitive style formation, as well as development of improved measures of cognitive style, will allow better identification and, if necessary, correction of the influence of (inappropriate) cognitive styles on problem solving in a variety of applied fields, from public education to individual consulting in management and politics.

A second equally important research direction is to consider how cognitive style might affect the efficacy of various modes of communication and media technology. Awareness about the existence of different cognitive styles is essential for effective communication in personal, business, and mass-media settings. With the rapid development of communication media technologies, along with the growth of international business, the importance of being able to effectively communicate with individuals from different learning environments increases tremendously. Because cognitive styles can be seen as adaptations of an individual's information-processing system to particular environmental requirements (cultural, professional, social, interpersonal), better understanding of the factors that influence the development of certain cognitive styles and how cognitive style might affect individuals' understanding of various media will help to build a much more effective communication process in multiple domains. With these growing academic and societal needs to understand cognitive style, now is the time to research cognitive style anew and generate a theoretical framework that could integrate the concept of cognitive style into mainstream of psychology.

## BIBLIOGRAPHY

Agor, W.H. (1984). *Intuitive Management*. Englewood Cliffs, NJ: Prentice Hall.

Allinson, J., & Hayes, C. (1996). The Cognitive Style Index: a measure of intuition-analysis for organizational research. *Journal of Management Studies, 33*, 119–135.

Alloy, L.B., Abramson, L.Y., Whitehouse, W.G., Hogan, M.E., Tashman, N.A., Steinberg, D.L., et al. (1999). Depressogenic cognitive styles: predictive validity, information processing and personality characteristics, and developmental origins. *Behavior Research and Therapy, 37*, 503–531.

Ausburn, L.J., & Ausburn, F.B. (1978). Cognitive styles: some information and implications for instructional design. *Educational Communication and Technology, 26*, 337.

Dunn, R., Dunn, K., & Price, G.E. (1989). *Learning Styles Inventory*. Lawrence, KS: Price Systems.

Eska, B., & Black, K.N. (1971). Conceptual tempo in young grade-school children. *Child Development, 42*, 505–516.

Garrick, C. (1978). Field dependence and hemispheric specialization. *Perceptual and Motor Skills, 47*, 631–639.

Gevins, A., & Smith, M. (2000). Neurophysiological measures of working memory and individual differences in cognitive ability and cognitive style. *Cerebral Cortex, 10*, 829–839.

Globerson, T. (1989). What is the relationship between cognitive style and cognitive development. In T. Globerson & T. Zelniker (Eds.), *Cognitive Style and Cognitive Development* (pp. 71–85). Norwood: N.J. Ablex.

Gregorc, A.F. (1982). *Gregorc Style Delineator*. Maynard, MA: Gabriel Systems.

Hodgkinson, G.P., & Sadler-Smith, E. (2003). Complex or unitary? A critique and empirical re-assessment of the Allison-Hayes Cognitive Style Index. *Journal of Occupational and Organizational Psychology, 76*, 243–268.

Kagan, J. (1966). Reflection-impulsivity: the generality and dynamics of conceptual tempo. *Journal of Abnormal Psychology, 71*, 17–24.

Keefe, J.W. (1988). Development of the NASSP learning style profile. In J.W. Keefe (Ed.), *Profiling and Utilizing Learning Style* (pp. 1–28). Reston, VA: National Association of Secondary School Principals.

Keller, J., & Ripoll, H. (2001). Reflective-impulsive style and conceptual tempo in a gross-motor task. *Perceptual and Motor Skills, 92*, 739–749.

Kholodnaya, M.A. (2002). *Kognitiivnii stili: o prirode individual'nogo uma* [*Cognitive styles: About the nature of individual's mind*]. Moscow: PER SE.

Kirton, M.J. (1976). Adaptors and innovators: a description and measure. *Journal of Applied Psychology, 61*, 622–629.

Kirton, M.J. (Ed.) (1989). *Adaptors and Innovators*. London: Routledge.

Klein, G.S. (1951). A personal world through perception. In R.R. Blake & G.V. Ramsey (Eds.), *Perception: An Approach to Personality* (pp. 328–355). New York: The Ronald Press Company.

Klein, G.S., & Schlesinger, H.J. (1951). Perceptual attitudes toward instability: I. Prediction of apparent movement experiences from Rorschach responses. *Journal of Personality, 19,* 289–302.

Kolb, D.A. (1984). *Experiential Learning: Experience as a Source of Learning and Development.* Englewood Cliffs, NJ: Prentice Hall.

Kozhevnikov, M. (2007). Cognitive styles in the framework of modern psychology: toward an integrated framework of cognitive style. *Psychological Bulletin, 133,* 464–481.

Leonard, N.H., Scholl, R.W., & Kowalski, K.B. (1999). Information processing style and decision making. *Journal of Organizational Behavior, 20,* 407–420.

MacLeod, C.M., Jackson, R.A., & Palmer, J. (1986). On the relation between spatial ability and field dependence. *Intelligence, 10,* 141–151.

McKenna, F.P. (1984). Measures of field dependence: cognitive style or cognitive ability? *Journal of Personality and Social Psychology, 47,* 593–603.

Messick, S. (1976). Personality consistencies in cognition and creativity. In S. Messick (Ed.), *Individuality in Learning* (pp. 4–23). San Francisco: Jossey-Bass.

Messick, S., & Fritzky, F.J. (1963). Dimension of analytic attitude in cognition and personality. *Journal of Personality, 31,* 346–370.

Miller, A. (1987). Cognitive styles: an integrated model. *Educational Psychology, 7,* 251–268.

Miller, A. (1991). Personality types, learning styles, and educational goals. *Educational Psychology, 11,* 217–238.

Motes, M.A., Malach, R., & Kozhevnikov, M. (2008). Object-processing neural efficiency differentiates object from spatial visualizers. *NeuroReport, 19,* 1727–1731.

Myers, I.B. (1976). *Introduction to Type.* Palo Alto, CA: Consulting Psychologist Press.

Niaz, M. (1987). Mobility-fixity dimension in Witkin's theory of field-dependence-independence and its implication for problems solving in science. *Perceptual and Motor Skills, 65,* 755–764.

Nosal, C.S. (1990). *Psychologiczne modele umyslu [Psychological models of mind].* Warszawa: PWN.

O'Connor, K., & Shaw, J.C. (1977). Field dependence, laterality and EEG. *Biological Psychology, 6,* 93–109.

Oltman, P.K., Semple, C., & Goldstein, L. (1979). Cognitive style and interhemispheric differentiation in EEG. *Neuropsychologia, 17,* 699–702.

Pettigrew, T.F. (1958). The measurement of category width as cognitive variable. *Journal of Personality, 26,* 532–544.

Pizzamiglio, L., & Carli, R. (1974). Visual, tactile and acoustic embedded figures test with patients with unilateral brain damage. *Cortex, 10,* 238–247.

Riding, R., & Cheema, I. (1991). Cognitive styles—an overview and integration. *Educational Psychology, 11,* 193–216.

Sternberg, R.J., & Grigorenko, E.L. (1997). Are cognitive styles still in style? *American Psychologist, 52,* 700–712.

Tinajero, C., Paramo, M.F., Cadaveira, F., & Rodriguez-Holguin, S. (1993). Field dependence-independence and brain organization: the confluence of two different ways of describing general norms of cognitive functioning? A theoretical review. *Perceptual and Motor Skills, 77,* 787–802.

Witkin, H.A., & Ash, S.E. (1948). Studies in space orientation: IV. Further experiments on perception of the upright with displaced visual field. *Journal of Experimental Psychology, 43,* 58–67.

Witkin, H.A., & Goodenough, D.R. (1981). *Cognitive Style: Essence and Origins.* New York: International Universities Press.

Witkin, H.A., Lewis, H.B., Hertzman, M., Machover, K., Bretnall, P.M., & Wapner, S. (1954). *Personality through Perception.* New York: Harper and Brothers Publishers.

# 3 Basic Psychometrics for Model Building and the Validation of Cognitive Style

*John Roodenburg and*
*Esther M. Roodenburg*

## INTRODUCTION

The style domain has been widely recognized as frustrated by a plethora of disparate conceptualizations and theoretical perspectives well summarized in the literature, most recently by Peterson, Rayner, and Armstrong (2009). This chapter aims to help scholars in the style domain understand psychometrics and how these can contribute to furthering consensus in future research by outlining some of the basic ways in which it can help by defining, refining, and validating a disparate domain. While appreciated in the operationalization of theories, psychometrics has much more to offer to the validation of individual theories as well as the validation of the domain as a whole. We explain how some of the statistical routines used by psychometricians are far more 'rubbery' as flexible tools than is often realized and why statistics working together with substantive theory is so important in practical research.

Importantly, before we move on we want to refer to two issues to put the remainder of the chapter in the right perspective. First, whereas our primarily understanding of style comes from cognitive style, we use the term 'style' to indicate that we consider what we outline to be relevant to the style domain in general. Secondly, whereas qualitative and quantitative researchers in the past have seen their epistemologies as competing, the fairly recent development of mixed-method research paradigms reflects the recognition that they are complementary. For style research we need both a qualitative and a quantitative perspective working within a mixed paradigm.

To realize our objective, we will focus on the following four key aspects: (1) what psychometrics is and has to offer as a significant player in refining and unifying the style field, including overcoming epistemological conflict and *gobbledygook* (see Pedhazur & Schmelkin, 1991); (2) the role of statistical modeling underpinning psychometrics; (3) the role and benefits of some of the most relevant statistical routines; and (4) the contributions of psychometric reliability and validity for building a more coherent domain. In this process, we set into context notions of quantitative research complementing qualitative research, and classical test theory and its implications. In addition, we consider the implications of understanding style as one aspect of individual differences along with abilities and personality traits. Finally, we make a number of important distinctions, such as between test operationalization and nomological net, experimental and correlational designs, and exploratory and confirmatory statistics.

## PSYCHOMETRICS: MEASURING AND EXPLAINING STYLE?

As background to considering what psychometrics has to offer to style research methodology, we note that style is conceptually a third domain in the psychological study of individual differences, the poor cousin of abilities and personality traits (Jonassen & Grabowski, 1993). Individual differences are core business for psychometricians. As such, style researchers can learn from the successful way psychometrics has been used in defining, refining, and validating its cousins' successful universal models and allow for theoreticians with competing epistemologies. In personality, for example, we now have the Big Five Personality factors (De Raad, 2000), also known as the Five Factor Model (Costa & McCrae, 1992) and reflected somewhat in Eysenck's giant Three (Eysenck & Eysenck, 1975) and Cattell's 16PF (Cattell, 1989). In cognition, the study of differential abilities, Gf-Gc theory, now more commonly now known as the Cattell-Horn-Carroll (CHC) model, has given us a table of abilities akin to the periodic table in chemistry (McGrew, 2005). To fully appreciate what psychometrics has to offer style in the same way, we need to understand the function of psychometrics in psychology.

Psychometrics is a branch of psychology concerned with psychological measurement. In a sense, psychometrics offers to style what engineering offers to construction: a well-defined approach to understand how things in the field work and interact. Statistics should not be confused with psychometrics. Statistics are basic tools used by psychometricians just as mathematics is a fundamental tool for engineers. Combined with experience, the application of statistics involves well-established protocols and rules of thumb. Attesting to a substantive discipline, there are numerous textbooks on psychological testing and assessment that outline fundamental constructs.

## Classical Test Theory

Psychometrics is generally understood as test construction, which to the novice researcher can appear to be a simple straightforward matter of framing the right questions. Psychometricians, however, have established that there is considerable science around ensuring that test and questionnaire items actually measure what is intended. The most widely used approach is known as the 'classical test theory' (DeVellis, 2003), in which any one test or questionnaire item is considered to only partly measure 'true score' (intended construct), but typically also includes other irrelevant constructs as well as random data.

In terms of the classical test theory, the task of test developers is to devise items that maximize true score. In general, operationalization requires generating a pool of items based on some theoretical criteria and in one way or another determines how these items cluster around underlying constructs. Items that fail or are only weakly associated can be removed or amended. Rules of thumb have been established that suggest that each particular construct measured should preferably be indicated by at least three items. Importantly, such operationalization depends on the veracity of a particular theoretical model on which the items have been based. If there are many different models and theories as in style, such endeavor simply results in a disparate range of instruments measuring quite different types of constructs, with little to offer to any unification of the domain as a whole.

However, as with research in the domains of ability and personality, psychometrics has much more to offer to style than simply the method for the operationalization of individual theories. The discipline has established various criteria for ascertaining the validity of specific constructs as well as theory more broadly. The most relevant ones for style are briefly outlined in the final section of this chapter. Prior to considering these, we examine various statistical approaches to building models for individual theories or integrating constructs from across a range of origins. Various validity criteria are no less relevant to such more complex models.

## Psychometrics, Epistemological Conflicts, and Gobbledygook?

As human beings, researchers and theoreticians are far less dispassionate than we would like to think. Epistemological preferences can become well-defended, especially when we experience difficulty perceiving from an alternative perspective. Royce and Powell (1983) have suggested that a preference for a particular theoretical orientation most likely reflects a conflation of personality, experience, ability, and style factors conceptualizing differing epistemological styles, including rational and empirical. From a rationalist perspective, style is validated by logical relationships with a founding theory. Take, for example, proponents of the Myers-Briggs Type Indicator (MBTI; Myers & McCaulley, 1985) and their understanding of extraversion: Jung's theory of psychological type (Jung, 1971) is the ultimate criteria and any failings of the instrument are routinely considered an artifact of inadequate operationalization or understanding of the theory, not the theory itself (Geyer, 1997). With such a disparate field of theoretical perspectives in style, the vexed question from a principally rationalist approach is philosophical: which theory should be the leading or defining theory?

Psychometrics assumes a simple grounded empirical and positivist epistemology that is not in conflict with any of the many varied theoretical perspectives in style. From an empirical realistic point of view, validation of the constructs requires grounding by establishing objectively identifiable concrete (optimally denotative) characteristics. More abstract connotative terms (psychometrically known as latent variables) should be related in some way to one or other such denotative characteristics (Copi, 1968). Ideally, such an empirical approach should facilitate the ascertainment of common meaning of connotative terms (statistically identified as 'communality', that is, common true score) without alliances to any one specific conceptual theory or epistemology.

Such grounding is important for the formation of a common style terminology as well as overcoming gobbledygook. For a meaningful discourse we need to speak the same language; we need to understand substantially the same meaning by each word, which is why disciplines typically develop their own technical language. Warning against vague terms with the internal consistency of a marshmallow, Pedhazur and Schmelkin (1991) cogently illustrate the pitfalls with their Gobbledygook Generator. This comprises a table of three columns of words where you simply choose a random three-figure number and combine the corresponding word from each column to generate highfaluting titles such as, for example, 637 = 'Optimal Reciprocal Projection'. Hypnotherapists and inspirational speakers often use such open language to good effect: everyone can project their own desires and idiosyncratic meaning into the script giving a sense of full agreement, but with what?

The most significant initiative to establish a common terminology and unifying structure in style is the work of Riding and his associates that categorized a wide range of cognition-centered styles across two dimensions: holistic/analytic and verbalizer/imager, operationalized in the cognitive Styles Analysis (Riding, 1991). This model is, however, confined to cognition-centered style that focuses on performance under *test* conditions as in ability assessment. It did not include personality-centered style that differs in being ascertained by *questionnaires* akin to personality assessment. These two types of style reflect the conceptualization of style as a conflation of or interface between abilities and personality.

A study of whiskey (the stuff many enjoy drinking) offers a fascinating example of how psychometrics may facilitate a common style lexicon. Wishart (2006) surveyed expert whiskey tasters from around the world, each using their own idiosyncratic terms and language to describe a comprehensive set of whiskeys. Using some of the statistical routines outlined and recommended for style later in this chapter, he used communalities to ascertain a common flavor vocabulary around twelve factors. Two important aspects characterize the soundness of his study. In the design, Wishart used experts with considerable experience in discriminating differences. In the validation, he relates the classifications to the theory and various processes of whiskey making.

Hence, to fill the gap left by Riding's research, Roodenburg (2003) applied a similar methodology to that of Wishart (2006) to develop a common vocabulary for personality-centered style. To ensure a personality-centered approach, he adapted the psycho-lexical method originally developed for building the Big Five personality trait model (De Raad, 2000). The psycho-lexical approach is based on the observation that important differences become encoded in language. Roodenburg surveyed the language of a sample of Australian schoolteachers ($N$ = 690) for describing differences between the ways that senior students think. The resulting lexicon was subjected to various types of modeling to ascertain an optimum set of key words. The benefits of using different modeling techniques are evident from the results of modeling the key words in an arrangement around a circle known as a circumplex (standard psycho-lexical practice). The circular arrangement clearly reflected the hexagon structure of Holland's Occupational Interests (Roodenburg & Roodenburg, 2009). Such parallel modeling provides an opportunity for a convincing form of *convergent validity* known as the Multi-Trait Multi-Method (MTMM) espoused by Campbell and Fiske (1959). This also serves to validate style within individual differences. A further advantage of methods used by Wishart (2006) and Roodenburg (2003) is that a lexical process ensures comprehensiveness and balance in sampling a domain in a way that is unrestricted or unduly influenced by any particular theory. This ameliorates two potentially serious threats to validity that are explained later on in the chapter: construct underrepresentation and bloated specificity. Importantly, whereas psychometric analysis based on global methods such as the lexical approach is unifying, microlevel applications of analysis *within* a range of definitions or specific theories also remain equally legitimate for validating central constructs. We move now to consider the types of statistical modeling available for developing style.

## STATISTICAL MODELING

We can think about the tasks of psychometrics as achieving two distinct goals. As already mentioned, there is test construction. Alternatively, once reasonable variables representing key constructs have been established, it is time to ascertain the nomological net, which is the lawful or stable relationships of these variables with other variables mainly outside the domain. This serves to establish construct utility. To understand which statistics help to achieve these two goals, it is important to recognize that there are two statistical camps: the experimental and the correlational. This situation is reflected in Cronbach's description of researching individual differences.

> Individual differences have been an annoyance rather than a challenge to the experimenter. The correlational psychologist is in love with just those variables, the experimenter left home to forget. (Cronbach, 1957, p. 674)

Experimental research attempts to manipulate variables singly, preferably in a controlled environment and in an ordered manner, employing univariate statistics in procedures such as *t* tests and analysis of variance (ANOVA). Experimental research can contribute piecemeal to building a nomological net, but has little to offer building complex integrated models or ascertaining underlying factorial structures. Test construction and model building is best achieved by multivariate statistics in correlational designs. At the basis of all of these routines is little more than the simple idea of forming groups around concepts, that is, correlation.

Factor analysis remains the ubiquitous approach to determining underlying structure. It offers relatively rigid simple hierarchical structures assuming *simple structure* on the grounds of parsimony. McKnight (2005), at a recent conference on individual differences, likened the effects of such assumptions to that of baking tins on shaping cakes. There is equally a case to suggest that the real world is not that simple. Individual differences interact and overlap. No doubt the argument for simple structure was attractive when computing was costly, difficult, and limited. With improved computing power and the development of more user-friendly interfaces, many and varied alternative statistical routines now offer intriguing flexibility, allowing more complex model building. Some of the more popular alternatives include principal components analysis, circumplex modeling, cluster analysis, smallest-space analysis, and structural equation modeling (SEM). Probably the only remaining obstacle is a widespread angst shared by many researching practitioners for using and understanding statistics. As we review some of these basic routines in more detail, we encourage the quantitatively challenged reader to remember that despite its formidable title, multivariate statistics are basically about multiple associations known as correlation.

Moreover, just as we have mixed methods referring to a complementary integration of qualitative and quantitative perspectives, the adoption of multimethod statistical modeling of structure and relationships with different statistical routines is useful because the various routines impress their own potentially restrictive shape on any structure. In the following section we review underlying concepts, benefits, and limitations of key statistical routines that we consider to have particular relevance to style research. Operational details have been left to the many excellent statistical textbooks and monographs.

## AN OUTLINE OF KEY STATISTICAL ROUTINES

### Correlation

We have established that correlation is the fundamental measure of statistical association that conceptually lies at the heart of theory building, as theory building is about groupings and generalizations. Correlation can only describe simple associations, the degree to which change in one variable is accompanied by change in another.

## Multiple Regression: Moderation and Mediation

Multiple regression contributes substantially to the essential nomological net by allowing the exploration of more than simple direct relationships between variables. There have been several methods developed around multiple regression that determine quite complex relationships, including moderation and mediation (Holmbeck, 2002). Moderation is an analytical process that allows us to study the interaction between two variables in producing or affecting a third. For example, a particular style may not directly impact on well-being. However, particular levels of the style may interact with an ability to enhance that ability's impact on well-being. This is distinct from mediation, where the relationship between two constructs is explained in part by a third construct. For example, anxiety leading to depression may be explained in part by the negative beliefs (mediator) of more anxious people.

## Factor Analysis

Factor analysis is the dominant statistical routine that has been developed for reducing numerous variables into groups known as factors. We now more specifically examine some of the characteristics of factor analysis that have implications for shaping style research.

### *Exploratory or Theory Driven?*

Factor analysis is generally regarded as exploratory as it does not require any prior specification of relationships, depending purely on numerically defined associations (correlations) evaluated only by a series of mathematical algorithms. As one quantitatively challenged undergraduate student asked recently in a class: "How do the thingies in the program know the meaning in order to organize the items into factors?" They don't! The programs are completely blind to any meaning or theory. The initial factors are often assumed to indicate an absolute structure but the statistical routines alone cannot determine a preferred rotation. Groupings are only meaningful if interpretable in terms of some substantive theory. In fact, optimal factor arrangements indicating substantive factors (latent constructs) are usually the result of running the analysis many times and making numerous theory-guided tweaks (a process known as 'iteration'). Each iteration should progress to a structure that makes better sense in terms of extant theory with more interpretable factors.

Far from impartial, this process is as much art as science. Not only does factor analysis impress its own form on the data, but as with all statistics, the quality of output is entirely dependent on the quality of input: 'junk in, junk out'. Input must be guided by the best theory available. It is not only the quality of what is included, but because factor analysis takes no account of meaning, output can be seriously distorted by a lack of balance between, or inclusion of, items. These problems are recognized as bloated specificity (Nesselroade & Cattell, 1988), that is, too many items about the same thing are included; or construct underrepresentation is allowed, involving absence of items describing an important aspect. These two problems can also misinform the criteria concerning the optimum number of factors to extract; this is because when factor analysis establishes the first group around a factor (the most dominant cluster), this cluster sets the compass for subsequent groups as they are organized to be optimally unrelated.

### Procrustes—From Exploration to Confirmation

There is a special adaptation that attempts to address the problem of lack of meaning guiding factor analysis, known as Procrustes rotation. This allows the arrangement of the factors (preferred rotation) to be guided by specifying the dominant factor on the basis of extant theory. In that sense it is no longer purely exploratory, introducing us to the increasingly popular area of setting up an a priori model and checking it out. In contrast to an exploratory approach, this is known as confirmatory analysis.

There should be some caution in applying a priori determinants without first establishing generalizability. In personality research, for example, extraversion is known to be a well-validated factor, the first and dominant component in Western applications (De Raad, 2000). However, personality is influenced by culture. In non-Western applications, Big Five factors can emerge differently, as in a study of English speaking Singaporean of Chinese ethnicity (Teo, 2006). Here, agreeableness and not extraversion came first, creating a somewhat different organization that reflected the influence of the Chinese interpersonal relatedness constructs of Ren Qing and Harmony (Cheung, Cheung, Wada, & Zhang, 2003), which concern family relations or friends.

## Spatial Modeling

Style is much more disparate and possibly complex than either personality or abilities. Yet, even with the limits of factorial structures for reflecting the complexities of personality, some researchers have sought to develop more spatial forms of representation. Taking smallest space notions such as the circumplex, research in the Netherlands, modeling the Big Five (Hendriks, 1997), has spatially represented the results of Procrustes rotations. A lexicon of key words has been used in this work to form the required item pool.

The two highest loadings of each item are plotted as coordinates in a series of binary factor arrangements so as to create a series of circumplex maps of all the items in factor space. This allows for much greater complexity in clustering, facilitating what is now established as a balanced comprehensive trait model.

However, this modeling by the previously mentioned 'Big Five' researchers has still incorporated a form of factor analysis known as principal components analysis. These represent smallest space and proximity data analysis processes that are more distinct (Kruskal & Wish, 1978). Whereas mostly developed in social research to identify groups of individuals, cluster analysis can be applied to variables instead of individuals to give confirmatory groupings. Many such alternative methods have advantages enabling smaller samples and less regular distribution of data. Such procedures can also be more qualitative friendly in an allowance of detail and context.

## Modeling Structure: Structural Equation Modeling (SEM)

Anyone who can conceive and draw relationships between measurable items and latent constructs, no matter how quantitatively challenged, can profit from structural models for their theories. Although running an analysis may require a fair degree of understanding and skill (and this should be both conceptual *and* psychometric) and SEM programs may be somewhat technical, output is as easy to understand as the diagrams for input. Provide data and SEM is applied by simply turning these relationships into a series of equations. Output tells the user three important results: effect size, model fit, and model modification.

### Effect Sizes

The program estimates the sizes of the various relationships plus what is not accounted for, and calling the latter 'error'. The advantage of all variables being considered simultaneously is that we can suggest quite complex models that would otherwise require numerous hypotheses and inevitably an extensive series of factor analyses and regression routines. A SEM model overcomes the problem of double counting.

### Model Fit

The output evaluates how well the model fits the data provided with a series fit indices that are relatively easy to interpret using well-established rules of thumb available in most beginners SEM books. The comparative fit of models across groups or time can also be evaluated by a version of fit indices. This is known as model invariance and is an effective way to estimate generalizability across populations and change over time.

*Model Modification*

In addition to indicating how well models fit, programs can be asked to suggest changes that may significantly improve fit. These suggested changes are reported as modification indices that specify the additions or deletions of relationships most likely to significantly improve the model. If theoretically meaningful, these changes can be made and the adjusted model rerun. For researchers who know their field well, this can be exciting, as among other things these results can suggest previously unidentified factors hidden among the errors. There are pitfalls, however, especially when individuals are driven by the mathematics instead of balanced interpretive theory, and these are now well outlined in a number of texts about SEM, our preferred being that of Kline (2005). If a new theoretically justified model emerges, a powerful way of validating the changes is by using the program's capacity for comparing fit across groups.

With regard to 'bloated specificity', SEM can be very effectively used to overcome an imbalance among variables of a style model or between models of style. In this process, single factors can first be modeled individually in what has been called single-factor congeneric modeling (Macdonald, 1981) to ensure unifactorial items, then pair-wise to ensure minimum overlap, and finally by entering a structural model for an entire instrument (Hattei, 1985).

## PSYCHOMETRIC VALIDITY

Over the last half century in particular, psychometricians have developed a substantial array of validity constructs, some of which overlap, some specific, and some more general. The qualities that mark validity in one way or another have been systematized by two definitive articles: the classic paper by Cronbach and Meehl (1955) and the more recently expanded conceptualization by Messick (1995).

Importantly, before the validity of any construct can be considered, the reader is reminded that we need measures that give consistent results, known as reliability. Reliability is handled well in just about any basic text on testing, with standard routines available in most common statistical computer packages.

## A More Coherent Approach

Traditional psychometric conceptualizations of validity were developed in the first half of the 20th century when the experimental paradigm was in ascendancy and psychometricians considered optimum measurement required laboratory conditions. Our university department, for instance, is housed in a building that was originally designed in the 1970s without windows for the objective scientific study of exceptional children. The sustained critique that science alone may be too artificial for studying human beings has seen a drive for more ecologically based real-life assessments (Jensen & Bourgeron, 2001).

In this regard, Messick's (1995) more inclusive approach has been timely, although not unchallenged. He sees traditional validity as mainly content and effect oriented, and classical validity as criterion related. In proposing what he calls a new unified model of validity, he suggests that to be comprehensive, test validity should include political as well as scientific factors; it should also take into account the socially beneficial as well as harmful potential of score interpretation and use. Messick advocates that more than being a property inherent in the test itself, validity rests with a test administrator. Utility of a test is dependent on a sound appreciation of the diagnostic and predictive relationships of the underlying constructs with other constructs (nomological net). Sound individual interpretation depends on an insightful person evaluating the results in the light of perceptions gained from a firsthand experience of the respondent.

Having established that validity goes well beyond any instrument itself, to both the domain as a whole and the people who use particular instruments, consideration is given to some key validities which are generally assessed by examining relationships between items, factors, and other constructs using correlation, various types of regression, factor analysis, and structural modeling. For style, the following validities may be particularly pertinent. These factors should all resonate with the points that have been made in this chapter about the usefulness of psychometrics for theory building and unification in the style domain.

## Theoretical Validity

In the first place, any domain or area of a domain needs to have a recognized set of defining parameters. Such definition is best achieved through a consensus of expert judgment, as carried out in the study already mentioned by Peterson and colleagues (2009). Researchers, practitioners, and naïve respondents can also be consulted in terms of evaluating potential questionnaire items to improve face validity. Whereas most items are designed by experts with a particular construct in mind using well-honed questionnaire construction methods (DeVellis, 2003), there are alternative methods that can define content such as those already mentioned using the psycho-lexical method.

## Invalidity

Invalidity is usually the result of random error or noise, or the presence of extraneous or unidentified factors across items (construct irrelevant variance). These may include factors such as readability, for example. Invalidity can also include acquiescence and social desirability. If unaccounted for, the variance of such factors across items can be reflected in correlations that create their own factors, factors that can be easily misidentified (Hofstee, Ten Berge, & Hendriks, 1998). Whereas irrelevant variance not related to base theory can confound a factor extraction in factor analysis, in SEM there is an opportunity for identifying the unaccounted variance associated with each variable or construct, and playing with it through modification indices to identify the variance related or extraneous to the domain.

## Meaning

In terms of classical test theory, the preferred item measures a single construct. Such items are unifactorial in that they show a high (primary) loading on only one factor and minimal loadings on other factors. The process outlined earlier of refining these using SEM to evaluate single-factor congeneric models through to evaluating these within complex models can be used to ensure *convergent* and *discriminant validities*. These validities require items and constructs that measure the same thing to be optimally related, and quite distinct from what they are not supposed to be related to, respectively.

There is a need, however, for caution. With this form of validity for style, there may be alternative arrangements, that is, rotational positions of factors or overlapping factors that are equally legitimate, especially if a primary concern is utility. Consider, for example, 'Creative', 'Verbal', and 'Spatial' as representing three distinct style factors. Let us assume that extraverted thinking (ET) includes scoring more highly as verbal and less as creative. Whereas ET may therefore be regarded as less desirable being multifactorial, it may be more useful when used, for example, to assess the need for individuals to be active in problem solving in group work.

## Consequential Validity

Overall, the breadth of Messick's review of validity can be fully appreciated when considering such constructs as consequential validity. This implies that validity includes the effects of an instrument and its constructs. For example, the terminology used in reporting results to clients may include information that is disturbing or open to misinterpretation. Tests may reveal information that is unacceptable or injurious in some way. Thus, Messick recognizes that validity is not entirely 'objective' but needs to take into account subjective, cultural, and individual values.

## CONCLUSION

In this chapter, we have acknowledged that style as a theory and a construct of psychology is a 'cousin' of abilities and personality, thereby locating it within the domain of individual differences. We have outlined how on this basis psychometrics can be used to facilitate an inclusive unifying framework, and within which various statistical routines can refine and validate the frameworking of theory. We have reviewed the ways key relevant statistics are much more 'rubbery' and 'dynamic' than often appreciated, implying a much greater need for iterative interplay between theory and statistics and thereby offering opportunity for mixing method in a relationship with qualitative approaches.

In acknowledging the fundamentals of classical test theory in defining basics such as item true score and item clustering, we have suggested how the use of multiple statistical routines can validate one another, and how various routines can be used in more creative ways to advance style in the future. We have outlined how psychometrics also offers a body of distinct evaluative criteria for validity. Again, these expanded criteria imply the need to integrate qualitative theory with quantitative methods. We also realize how much broader psychometrics is than mere quantification of data when it includes ethics and the social context.

As a general overview, we have not reviewed psychometrics in terms of specific style theories other than to recognize that there are two types of cognitive style, personality-centered and cognition-centered. This chapter has aimed to facilitate a broader understanding of what psychometrics has to offer style, hopefully encouraging qualitative scholars to collaborate with quantitative researchers in multimethod approaches and development of the research field.

## BIBLIOGRAPHY

Campbell, D.T., & Fiske, D.W. (1959). Convergent and discriminant validation by the multitrait-multimethod matrix. *Psychological Bulletin, 56*, 81–105.

Cattell, H.B. (1989). *The 16PF: Personality in Depth*. Champaign, IL: Institute for Personality and Ability Testing.

Cheung, F.M., Cheung, S.F., Wada, S., & Zhang, J.X. (2003). Indigenous measures of personality assessment in Asian countries. *Psychological Assessment, 15*, 280–289.

Copi, I.M. (1968). *Introduction to Logic* (3rd ed.). New York: Macmillan.

Costa, P.T., & McCrae, R.R. (1992). *The NEO Personality Inventory (Revised) Manual*. Odessa, FL: Psychological Assessment Resources.

Cronbach, L.J. (1957). The two disciplines of scientific psychology. *American Psychologist, 12*, 671–684.

Cronbach, L.J., & Meehl, P.E. (1955). Construct validity in psychological tests. *Psychological Bulletin, 52*, 281–302.

De Raad, B. (2000). *The Big Five Personality Factors: The Psycholexical Approach to Personality*. London: Hogrefe & Huber.

DeVellis, R.F. (2003). *Scale Development: Theory and Applications* (2nd ed.). Thousand Oaks, CA: Sage Publications.

Eysenck, H.J., & Eysenck, S.B.G. (1975). *Manual of the Eysenck Personality Questionnaire*. Sevenoaks, Kent: Hodder & Stoughton.

Geyer, P. (1997). Typetexts and materials. *Australian Journal of Psychological Type, 6*, 40–42.

Hattei, J. (1985). Methodology review: assessing unidimensionality of tests and items. *Applied Psychological Measurement, 9,* 139–164.

Hendriks, A.A. (1997). *The Construction of the Five-Factor Personality Inventory (FFPI).* Unpublished doctoral thesis, Rijksuniversiteit Groningen, Groningen, The Netherlands.

Hofstee, W.K.B., Ten Berge, J.M.F., & Hendriks, A.A.J. (1998). How to score questionnaires. *Personality and Individual Differences, 25,* 897–909.

Holmbeck, G.N. (2002). Post-hoc probing of significant moderational and mediational effects in studies of pediatric populations. *Journal of Pediatric Psychology, 27,* 87–96.

Jensen, M.E., & Bourgeron, P.S. (2001). *A Guidebook for Integrated Ecological Assessments.* New York: Springer-Verlag.

Jonassen, D.H., & Grabowski, B.L. (1993). *Handbook of Individual Differences, Learning and Instruction.* Hillsdale, NJ: Lawrence Erlbaum Associates.

Jung, C.G. (1971). *Psychological Types* (Vol. 6). Princeton: Princeton University Press.

Kline, R.B. (2005). *Principles and Practice of Structural Equation Modelling* (2nd ed.). New York: Guilford Press.

Kruskal, J.B., & Wish, M. (1978). *Multidimensional Scaling.* Newbury Park, CA: Sage Publications.

Macdonald, R.P. (1981). The dimensionality of tests and items. *British Journal of Mathematical and Statistical Psychology, 34,* 100–117.

McGrew, K.S. (2005). The Cattell-Horn-Carroll (CHC) theory of cognitive abilities: past, present, and future. In D.P. Flanagan & P.L. Harrison (Eds.), *Contemporary Intellectual Assessment: Theories, Tests, and Issues* (2nd ed.). New York: Guilford Press.

McKnight, P. (2005). *Distinguishing between Poor Models and Poor Data: What Do We Learn from This?* Paper presented at the International Society for the Study of Individual Differences, Adelaide, South Australia.

Messick, S. (1995). Validity of psychological assessment: validation of inferences from persons' responses and performances as scientific inquiry into score meaning. *American Psychologist, 50,* 741–749.

Myers, I.B., & McCaulley, M. (1985). *Manual: A Guide to the Development and Use of the Myers-Briggs Type Indicator.* Palo Alto, CA: Consulting Psychologists Press.

Nesselroade, J.R., & Cattell, R.B. (eds.) (1988). *Handbook of Multivariate Experimental Psychology* (2nd ed.) New York, NY: Plenum.

Pedhazur, E.J., & Schmelkin, L.P. (1991). *Measurement, Design, and Analysis: An Integrated Approach.* Hillsdale, NJ: Lawrence Erlbaum Associates.

Peterson, E., Rayner, S., & Armstrong, S. (2009). Researching the psychology of cognitive style and learning styles: is there really a future? *Learning and Individual Differences, 19,* 518–523.

Riding, R.J. (1991). *Cognitive Styles Analysis.* Birmingham, England: Learning and Training Technology.

Roodenburg, J. (2003). Cognitive style: a psycholexically derived personality-centred model. *European Journal of Personality, 17,* 119–141.

Roodenburg, J., & Roodenburg, E.M. (2009). *Occupational interests and personality centered cognitive style.* Paper presented at the 8th Industrial and Organisational Psychology Conference. Retrieved from http://www.allworthjuniper.com.au/8th_IOP_Conference_Proceedings.pdf at March 18, 2010.

Royce, J.R., & Powell, A. (1983). *Theory of Personality and Individual Differences: Factors, Systems, and Processes.* Englewood Cliffs, NJ: Prentice Hall.

Teo, P.S.G. (2006). *Cross-Cultural Generalizability of Big Five Model Indicators.* Unpublished minor research project, Monash University, Melbourne.

Wishart, D. (2006). *Whiskey Classified* (rev. ed.). London: Pavion Books.

# 4 The Theory of Mental Self-Government Grows Up
## Where Has It Led the Field after 21 Years?

*Li-fang Zhang and Weiqiao Fan*

## INTRODUCTION

Much knowledge about thinking styles as defined in Sternberg's theory of mental self-government (1988, 1997) has been accumulated over the past decade. Furthermore, Sternberg's theory as well as the work based on it has been a major force in advancing the field of intellectual styles. Yet, there is not a single piece of work that documents such knowledge and advancement. This chapter is intended to be a comprehensive review of the work derived from Sternberg's theory of mental self-government. It is divided into five sections. First, the theory and the research tools used to operationalize the theory are introduced. Second, major research findings, especially those that speak to the three controversial issues over the nature of styles (i.e., styles as traits versus states, styles as value-laden versus value-free, and styles as different constructs versus similar constructs with different labels), are presented. The third section presents one particularly unique product of the theory of mental self-government—the threefold model of intellectual styles (an encompassing term for such constructs as cognitive styles, learning styles, and thinking styles). The fourth section elaborates the threefold model's contributions to the field and its practical significance for education and beyond. Finally, some conclusions are drawn.

## THE THEORY OF MENTAL SELF-GOVERNMENT AND ITS RESEARCH TOOLS

As one of the most recent theories of styles, Sternberg's (1997) theory stated that just as there are different ways of governing a society, there are different ways that people prefer to use their abilities, that is, thinking styles. According to Sternberg, there are thirteen thinking styles that fall into five dimensions: functions, forms, levels, scopes, and leanings. Based on empirical data and on the value dimension concerning the nature of thinking styles, Zhang (2002) reconceptualized the thirteen styles into three types.

Type I thinking styles (including the legislative, judicial, global, hierarchical, and liberal styles) tend to be more creativity-generating and they denote higher levels of cognitive complexity. These styles are considered as carrying more adaptive values because they are strongly related to desirable human attributes such as higher levels of cognitive development (Zhang, 2002) and the openness personality trait (Fjell & Walhovd, 2004). Type II styles (including the executive, local, monarchic, and conservative styles) suggest a norm-favoring tendency and they denote lower levels of cognitive complexity. These styles are considered as carrying less adaptive values because they are strongly associated with undesirable attributes such as lower levels of cognitive development and neuroticism. Type III styles (including the oligarchic, anarchic, internal, and external styles) may manifest the characteristics of either Type I or Type II thinking styles. These styles are regarded as value-differentiated. Consider the internal style (preference for working independently), a style that is classified as a Type III style. One may work independently but creatively (thus, showing the characteristics of Type I styles). However, one could also work independently but in a norm-conforming manner (thus, showing the characteristics of Type II styles).

Although various research methods (e.g., questionnaire survey, interview, and experiment) have been used to study thinking styles, four main inventories have been responsible for generating the bulk of the literature on thinking styles. These are: (1) the Thinking Styles Inventories, (2) the Teaching Styles in Teaching Inventory, (3) the Preferred Thinking Styles in Teaching Inventory, and (4) the Preferred Thinking Styles in Learning Inventory. All four inventories are composed of statements that require the respondents to rate the degree to which they agree (or disagree) with what is described in each statement (see Sternberg & Wagner, 1992; Sternberg, Wagner, & Zhang, 2003, 2007; Zhang, 2003a; Zhang & Sternberg, 2009a).

## MAIN RESEARCH FINDINGS

Research findings on thinking styles were first documented in 1995 when Sternberg and Grigorenko published a series of studies of school students and teachers in the United States. Yet, it was Zhang and Sachs' (1997) study of Hong Kong university students that heralded hundreds of studies of thinking styles among various populations across the globe. Needless to say, testing the validity of the theory in different cultural contexts has been one of the major research endeavors (e.g., Fer, 2007). Moreover, given that whether or not styles contribute to academic achievement is one of the initial questions that motivated the work on styles, a number of studies investigated the contributions of thinking styles to academic achievement (e.g., Tsagaris, 2007). This research suggests that Sternberg's theory is one that can be applied to various cultures and that thinking styles do make a difference in academic achievement. Going beyond the aforementioned types of research, scholars have also ventured a wide range of investigations that yielded findings that have contributed significantly to our understanding of the nature of intellectual styles, particularly concerning the three aforementioned controversial issues. In the reminder of this part, we highlight findings that shed light on the three controversial issues.

## Styles as Traits versus States

Research suggests that thinking styles largely represent states because they are malleable. Such malleability is manifested in three types of research. The first focuses on the relationship between thinking styles and demographic variables. The second concerns the study of style match. The third examines the effects of instructions on styles.

### Thinking Styles and Demographics

When proposing his theory, Sternberg (1997) made an explicit argument for the malleability of thinking styles. He contended that at least seven socialization variables are likely to affect the development of thinking styles. These are culture, gender, age, parental style, religious upbringing, schooling, and occupation. Thus far, except for the variable religious upbringing, all other variables have been tested with thinking styles. This research lent strong support to Sternberg's argument.

To date, although only less than a handful of studies of thinking styles set their major research objective as identifying style differences based on culture in its traditional sense (i.e., national or ethnic culture), all existing studies suggest that culture does make a difference in people's thinking styles. For example, Tang (2004) concluded that the thinking styles of Chinese Canadians differed significantly from those of the Hong Kong samples, with the former scoring significantly higher on two of the Type I styles as well as on two of the Type II styles than did the latter. Further empirical evidence supporting the effect of cultural orientations can be found in more recent work (Tsagaris, 2007; Zhang, Fu, & Jiao, 2008).

Age and gender are two variables that have been addressed in many studies of thinking styles (e.g., Fer, 2007; Tsagaris, 2007). Although the particular thinking styles associated with age and gender were not consistent across all studies, general trends are clear. That is, older participants generally preferred Type I thinking styles more than did younger participants. Males usually scored higher on Type I styles than did females. Zhang and Sternberg (2006) explained that the positive correlation between age and Type I styles is consistent with the notion that, as people get older, their thinking tends to become more complex, at least to a certain point. They attributed gender differences in thinking styles to the stereotypical gender role orientation that men tend to be the rule makers and that women tend to be the rule followers.

Socioeconomic status (SES) has also been examined with thinking styles in a number of studies in different cultural settings. Early in 1995, Sternberg and Grigorenko found that students from higher SES families scored higher on the legislative thinking style (a Type I style) but lower on the local and conservative (Type II) styles. Similarly, among Hong Kong secondary school students, Ho (1998) found that students from higher SES families scored higher on the judicial style (also a Type I style) but lower on the local and conservative styles. Similar findings have been obtained in mainland China and Taiwan (see Zhang & Sternberg, 2006). The finding that students from higher SES families used Type I styles more often was not obtained coincidentally. For example, students from higher SES families are often exposed to more situations that are intellectually stimulating. Such stimulation may be conductive to the development of Type I styles.

The argument that thinking styles can be socialized has also been supported by research findings obtained from studies that examined styles of people from different occupations. For example, Kaufman (2001) found that journalists scored higher on the executive style than did creative writers, whereas creative writers scored higher on the legislative style than did journalists. Hommerding (2003) asserted that there was an apparent influence of the library world upon the thinking styles of public library directors. As a final example, Gridley (2007) concluded that artists were more legislative, anarchic, and internal in their thinking styles, whereas engineers were more hierarchical and executive in their thinking styles.

### Matching of Thinking Styles

Results from several studies examining the issue of style match also tell a similar story about the modifiability of styles. Sternberg and Grigorenko (1995) found that teachers' thinking styles tend to match the stylistic ideology of their schools. It is possible that teachers tend to gravitate toward schools that fit them ideologically. It is also possible that they tend to become alike and fit into the institution in which they teach. Either way, socialization seems to have played a role in the formation of teachers' thinking styles. In a similar way, Zhang (2003b) concluded that there were significant correlations in data from the assessment of children's and parents' thinking styles. This suggests that children's styles might have been socialized through interacting with their parents. As a final example, He's (2007) analysis of interview data suggested that students did make conscious efforts in matching their own learning styles with their teachers' teaching styles. Moreover, students of Type I styles reportedly made more efforts than did students of Type II styles.

*Effects of Instructions on Styles*

At present, only Fan's (2008) study of the change of thinking styles can be classified as being experimental. Results revealed that students in the hypermedia learning environment increased in their liberal style, whereas students in the traditional learning environment decreased in their legislative and global thinking styles. Moreover, at the end of the semester, students who studied in the traditional learning environment scored significantly higher than did students who studied under the hypermedia condition on three of the four Type II thinking styles: executive, conservative, and monarchic.

## Styles as Value-Laden Versus Value-Free

Findings from several lines of investigations are in favor of the position that styles are value-laden, with Type I thinking styles being more adaptive than are Type II styles. These include the studies of styles with (1) perceptions of work environments, (2) cognitive and affective development, (3) psychosocial development, (4) personality traits, and (5) teaching and learning behaviors. Some of these studies have been reviewed elsewhere (see Zhang & Sternberg, 2006, 2009a). In this context, we put more emphasis on new research evidence.

### Perceptions of Work Environments

Several studies have been carried out to examine the relationships between thinking styles and people's perceptions of their work environments. For example, Zhang and Sternberg (2002) found that Hong Kong schoolteachers who reported more frequent use of Type I teaching styles tended to perceive their work environments more positively, including their career prospect, autonomy at work, and the quality of their students. Comparable results were obtained among Hong Kong kindergarten teachers (Lee, 2002).

Studies conducted in nonacademic settings provided similar evidence. A series of three studies (for a summary, see Higgins & Zhang, 2009) consistently showed that positive perceptions of one's abilities and of one's work environments contributed to Type I thinking styles. In contrast, negative perceptions contributed to Type II styles.

### Cognitive and Affective Development

Research on the relationships of thinking styles to cognitive and affective development suggests that Type I styles are more adaptive because they are significantly associated with positive cognitive and affective development. For instance, Zhang (2002) concluded that, in general, students who reasoned at higher levels of cognitive development reported the use of a wider range of thinking styles, in particular, Type I styles, whereas students who reasoned at lower levels of cognitive development reported the use of Type II styles only.

Thinking styles have been examined with several variables that fall within the domain of affective development: self-esteem (Zhang & Postiglione, 2001), emotions (Zhang, 2008a), achievement motivation (Fan & Zhang, 2009), and mental health (Chen & Zhang, 2009). Type I styles significantly predicted higher levels of self-esteem and achievement motivation to approach success among university students, as well as lower levels of depression and hostility, and lower scores on role insufficiency and psychological strain among academics. By contrast, Type II thinking styles significantly contributed to lower levels of self-esteem and a tendency to display the achievement motivation to avoid failure among university students, as well as to higher scores on phobic anxiety, obsessive-compulsiveness, and psychoticism among academics (see Zhang & Sternberg, 2009a for details).

### Psychosocial Development

The nature of thinking styles as it pertains to their value has also been revealed in studies that placed their emphasis on the relationship between thinking styles and psychosocial development as defined by Chickering (1969). In general, Type I thinking styles significantly contributed to students' sense of identity and of vocational purpose and Type II styles did so negatively (Zhang, 2004, 2008b). Recently, Zhang (2009a) found that Type I styles positively contributed to psychosocial development as defined in Erikson's (1968) theory, while Type II styles did so negatively.

### Personality Traits

Thinking styles have been examined with at least three types of personality traits. Between 2001 and 2003, several studies (e.g., Zhang & Huang, 2001) examining the relationships between thinking styles and the Big Five personality traits (Costa & McCrae, 1992) in Hong Kong and mainland China consistently indicated that Type I thinking styles were positively related to such adaptive personality traits as openness and conscientiousness, whereas Type II styles were positively related to neuroticism, a personality trait often regarded as undesirable. Subsequently, this finding was supported by studies conducted in the United States, Norway, and Iran (see Zhang & Sternberg, 2009a for details).

Recently, Palut (2008) concluded that all five Type I thinking styles were negatively associated with higher levels of externality, a personality trait often shown to be correlated with less adaptive attributes such as school discipline problems and task postponement. Finally, Zhang's (2009b) study showed that, in general, Type I styles and the external style were negatively related to anxiety, whereas the conservative style was positively related to anxiety.

### Teaching and Learning Behaviors

The value-laden nature of thinking styles is also revealed by findings concerning students' learning behaviors and teachers' teaching behaviors. Studies of secondary school and university students in Hong Kong, mainland China, and the United States consistently suggested that students prefer that their teachers teach in Type I teaching styles, and not Type II teaching styles. Complementarily, both school and university teachers preferred that their students use Type I learning styles (see Zhang & Sternberg, 2009a).

Moreover, that Type I styles carry more positive value was also shown in findings indicating that Type I teaching styles are significantly associated with teaching behaviors that are more conducive to effective learning. For example, studies of both kindergarten and secondary schoolteachers in Hong Kong showed that teachers higher on Type I teaching styles reported more frequent use of the conceptual-change teaching approach, whereas teachers higher on Type II teaching styles reported more frequent use of the knowledge-transmission teaching approach (Lee, 2002).

Chen (2007) concluded that Type I teaching styles were strongly associated with the affiliative and self-enhancing humor styles—commonly perceived as beneficial, whereas Type II teaching styles were significantly related to the aggressive and self-defeating humor styles. As a final example, Yeh (2007) found that Taiwanese preservice teachers with the legislative or judicial thinking style were more analytical, mindful, and reflective in their teaching practices.

## Styles as Different Constructs versus Similar Constructs with Different Style Labels

This issue has been addressed by studies examining if style constructs from different theoretical models overlap. These style constructs are from all three traditions in studying styles (Grigorenko & Sternberg, 1995): cognition-centered as represented by modes of thinking (Torrance, 1988), personality-centered as represented by career personality types (Holland, 1994) and personality types (Myers & McCaulley, 1985), and activity-centered as represented by learning approaches (Biggs, 1992). This research was mainly conducted in Hong Kong, Turkey, mainland China, and the United States. All existing studies concluded that thinking styles shared large amounts of variance with other style constructs. These amounts ranged from 19% to 76%, with the majority being above 60% (Zhang & Sternberg, 2005).

## FROM THE THEORY OF MENTAL SELF-GOVERNMENT
## TO THE THREEFOLD MODEL OF INTELLECTUAL STYLES

One of the motivations for Sternberg to construct the theory of mental self-government was to provide a theoretical framework that is more general and that could bring together existing works on styles that were in disarray. This intention has been well achieved. Seventeen years after the publication of the theory of mental self-government, the threefold model of intellectual styles came into being. The threefold model is deeply rooted in empirical findings centered on the theory of mental self-government (see Zhang & Sternberg, 2005).

The threefold model has two major accomplishments. First, adopting an open system and cutting across individual models (e.g., Witkin's [1964] field-independent and field-dependent styles are classified into two different style types, rather than into the same tradition/approach), it harnesses existing styles into one of three types: Type I, Type II, and Type III intellectual styles. For the first time, the term 'intellectual styles' was used to represent all existing style labels. As such, the model has not only built a common language and conceptual framework for styles but also moved styles from theory to practice, enabling people to understand their own or others' intellectual styles in terms of five easy-to-monitor dimensions of preferences. These are one's preference for high degrees of structure versus low degrees of structure, for cognitive simplicity versus cognitive complexity, for conformity versus nonconformity, for authority versus autonomy, and for group versus individual work (see Zhang & Sternberg, 2005 for details).

As a second accomplishment, the model is the first that takes an explicit stand on the three long-standing controversial issues in the field. The model affirms that most styles are value-laden rather than value-free; that they have both trait-like and state-like aspects, but for the most part are malleable and hence more state-like; and that they overlap highly across theories.

## THE THREEFOLD MODEL: FURTHER CONTRIBUTIONS

As previously noted, the threefold model has theoretically brought together the once fragmented work in the field. However, the question concerns the degree to which advancement has been made based on the threefold model. In the following, we discuss the model's contributions to the field of styles and its practical significance for education.

### Contributions to the Field of Intellectual Styles

Although it has only been published in 2005, the threefold model has generated much interest in the scholarly community. Empirical studies reported in several doctoral dissertations (Fan, 2008; He, 2007; Tsagaris, 2007) and a great number of research articles (Betoret, 2007; Sun & Hu, 2008) have been conceptualized within the context of the threefold model. Still, the most focused discussion centered on this model is found in Zhang and Sternberg's (2009b) edited book *Perspectives on the Nature of Intellectual Styles*. The threefold model enabled the contributors in this book to converse with a common language and within a general conceptual framework for styles. Likewise, the positions regarding the nature of intellectual styles described in the threefold model have stimulated much debate in Zhang and Sternberg's (2009b) book. Contributors in this book mainly agreed that styles are not value-free, that they are essentially malleable, and that they overlap highly across theoretical models; achieving complete harmony on these issues seems to be remote.

Take the case of the general perception that styles are value-laden. The shared view among all contributors is that styles are value-differentiated. That is, context influences the effectiveness of a style. However, within this common understanding, contributors' opinions varied vis-à-vis which types of styles carry more positive value. For instance, in elucidating the relationship between creativity and intellectual styles, Kaufman and Baer (2009) clearly spelled out the advantages of Type I styles over Type II styles. Similarly, Zhang and Sternberg (2009a) presented numerous findings demonstrating that Type I styles are associated with a wide range of attributes normally considered positive. Zhang and Sternberg also noted that although these empirical findings suggested that Type I styles should be encouraged, Type I styles are often stifled in reality, as in the case of students' being tested for their memorization. Likewise, Sadler-Smith (2009) contended that much of education and training is directed more toward the development of the analytic mode (Type II styles) than toward the intuitive mode (Type I styles) of processing. He called for more attention being paid to the intuitive mode. Jablokow and Kirton (2009), on the other hand, argued that too much importance was already placed on Type I styles.

Concerning the state-versus-trait dispute, the majority of contributors in Zhang and Sternberg's (2009b) book were in favor of the notion that styles are malleable. There is also a consensus that styles overlap highly across theories. For instance, Evans and Waring (2009) accredited the overlapping nature of styles with the idea of a hierarchy of interrelated cognitive style dimensions. Renzulli and Sullivan (2009) demonstrated overlaps among styles by elaborating on two of the most recent integrative style models: Riding and Cheema's (1991) wholistic/analytic and verbal/imagery style dimensions and Zhang and Sternberg's (2005) three types of intellectual styles. Rayner and Peterson (2009) alluded to the overlapping nature of various styles by noting the confusion over definitions of and terminologies for different styles.

As a final example, in constructing his duplex model of cognitive style, Sadler-Smith (2009) used two modes (analytic and intuitive) and one style (versatile) to encapsulate the many previously proposed style labels. More recently, in an attempt to bring further unity to the field, Verdurmen and Van Petegem (2009) proposed what they called 'a complementary model'. The authors demonstrated how the complementary model could be established by integrating aspects of Coffield and colleagues' (2004) stability taxonomy into the threefold model. The authors reaffirmed the heuristic value of the threefold model for continuing advancement of the field.

## Practical Significance for Education and Beyond

Apart from having contributed to the advancement of the field of styles, the threefold model also has practical implications for various parties in education and beyond. These implications can be discussed in view of the two major accomplishments of the threefold model of intellectual styles as discussed earlier.

### From the Perspective of Three Types of Styles along Five Dimensions of Preferences

The fact that the threefold model classifies all styles into three categories based on people's preferences along five major dimensions makes it possible that educational practitioners attend to three broad types of styles, rather than to the particular styles in the plethora of existing individual style models. Here are two examples:

First, the threefold model can help to address one of the major concerns often expressed by people to whom the notion of styles is novel. For instance, teachers often ask: " . . . there are many different styles . . . How could our teaching accommodate so many different styles?" The threefold model would say that, in general, teachers need only to attend to the three broad types of intellectual styles by addressing the five basic dimensions of preferences underlying intellectual styles. For example, teachers could target meeting students' needs for complex cognitive tasks, autonomy, or working with peers. They could also aim at addressing students' needs for teachers' provision of structure and for working on one's own. These strategies can also be applied well in management in business settings.

Second, the threefold model provides a practical framework for educational practitioners in their efforts of fostering student development in multiple dimensions: cognitive, affective, physiological, psychological, and sociological. Educational programs can be designed more systematically so that not only students' intellectual styles are taken into consideration but also their characteristics in other domains such as the five dimensions of preferences are taken into account, for intellectual styles are intricately entwined with these five dimensions. The same goes with effective human resource development in business settings.

## From the Perspective of Style Overlap, Style Malleability, and Style Value

The explicit position that the threefold model takes on each of the three controversial issues over the nature of styles has implications for practitioners in both academic and nonacademic settings.

First, the model's position that styles overlap highly across theories suggests that styles inventory givers could make use of the interrelationships among the intellectual styles in reducing the time spent on testing. For example, when time is limited, a test giver could use one or two inventories to identify students' intellectual styles, rather than administering a whole range of inventories. Subsequently, with reasonable confidence, one could estimate the test taker's scores on the scales in other style inventories based on the interrelationships among intellectual styles.

Second, the threefold model asserts that styles are malleable. Knowledge about the malleability of styles is also important for practitioners. Only when one believes that styles can be changed is one willing to make efforts to cultivate the styles desired. If styles are static, any effort in style modification would be in vain. Therefore, the threefold model offers people the confidence in deliberately strengthening or changing particular styles.

Finally, the threefold model suggests that styles are value-laden rather than value-free and that Type I styles generally carry more adaptive values than do Type II styles. This explicit position is also critical for practitioners to be aware of. Often, practitioners are encountered with the problem of not knowing what styles they should aim at cultivating among their clients (e.g., students). With strong research evidence revealing the adaptive value of Type I styles, practitioners should feel more comfortable in taking strategies to promote Type I styles.

## CONCLUSIONS

As the most recent and the most general model of styles, the theory of mental self-government has generated a tremendous amount of research interest in the scholarly community. Not only has it produced many empirical findings, but it also has laid the foundation for the construction of the most encompassing integrative model of styles in the present time—the threefold model of intellectual styles. The threefold model, in turn, has not only brought together the disparate work completed on styles in nearly the past six decades and, for the first time, taken unambiguous stands on some of the long-standing controversial issues in the field, but also inspired much debate over the nature of intellectual styles. Equally importantly, findings documented in this literature have their practical implications for education and beyond.

# BIBLIOGRAPHY

Betoret, F.D. (2007). The influence of students' and teachers' thinking styles on student course satisfaction and on their learning process. *Educational Psychology, 27*, 219–234.

Biggs, J.B. (1992). *Why and How do Hong Kong Students Learn? Using the Learning and Study Process Questionnaires*, Education Paper No. 14, Faculty of Education, The University of Hong Kong.

Chen, G.H. (2007). *University Teachers' Humor Production in the Classroom and Student Ratings of Teaching Effectiveness.* Unpublished dissertation, The University of Hong Kong.

Chen, G.H., & Zhang, L.F. (2009). *The Role of Thinking Styles in Mental Health.* Unpublished manuscript.

Chickering, A. (1969). *Education and Identity.* San Francisco: Jossey-Bass.

Coffield, F.C., Moseley, D.V.M., Hall, E., & Ecclestone, K. (2004). *Learning Styles and Pedagogy in Post-16 Learning: Findings of a Systematic and Critical Review of Learning Styles Models.* London: Learning and Skills Research Centre.

Costa, P.T., Jr., & McCrae, R.R. (1992). *The NEO-PI-R: Professional Manual.* Odessa, FL: Psychological Assessment Resources.

Erikson, E.H. (1968). *Identity: Youth and Crisis.* New York: W.W. Norton.

Evans, C., & Waring, M. (2009). The place of cognitive style in pedagogy: realizing potential in practice. In L.F. Zhang & R.J. Sternberg (Eds.), *Perspectives on the Nature of Intellectual Styles* (pp. 169–208). New York: Springer.

Fan, W. (2008). Thinking styles among university students in Shanghai: comparing traditional and hypermedia instructional environments. *Dissertation Abstracts International, Section A: Humanities and Social Sciences, 68* (7A), 2808.

Fan, W.Q., & Zhang, L.F. (2009). Thinking styles and achievement motivations. *Learning and Individual Differences, 19*, 299–303.

Fer, S. (2007). What are the thinking styles of Turkish student teachers? *Teachers College Record, 109*, 1488–1516.

Fjell, A.M., & Walhovd, K.B. (2004). Thinking styles in relation to personality traits: an investigation of the Thinking Styles Inventory and NEO-PI-R. *Scandinavian Journal of Psychology, 45*, 293–300.

Gridley, M.C. (2007). Differences in thinking styles of artists and engineers. *The Career Development Quarterly, 56*, 177–182.

Grigorenko, E.L., & Sternberg, R.J. (1995). Thinking styles. In D. Saklofske & M. Zeidner (Eds.), *International Handbook of Personality and Intelligence* (pp. 205–229). New York: Plenum.

He, Y.F. (2007). The roles of thinking styles in learning and achievement among Chinese university students. *Dissertation Abstracts International Section A: Humanities and Social Sciences, 67* (8A), 2879.

Higgins, P., & Zhang, L.F. (2009). The thinking styles of human resource practitioners. *The Learning Organization, 16*, 276–289.

Ho, H.K. (1998). *Assessing Thinking Styles in the Theory of Mental Self-Government: A Mini Validity Study in a Hong Kong Secondary School.* Unpublished manuscript, The University of Hong Kong.

Holland, J.L. (1994). *Self-Directed Search.* Odessa, FL: Psychological Assessment Resources.

Hommerding, L. (2003). Thinking style preferences among the public library directors of Florida. *Dissertation Abstracts International (Section B): The Sciences & Engineering, 63* (11B), 5545.

Jablokow, K.W., & Kirton, M.J. (2009). Problem solving, creativity, and the level-style distinction. In L.F. Zhang & R.J. Sternberg (Eds.), *Perspectives on the Nature of Intellectual Styles* (pp. 137–168). New York: Springer.

Kaufman, J.C. (2001). Thinking styles in creative writers and journalists. *Dissertation Abstracts International (Section B): The Sciences and Engineering*, 62 (3B), 1069.

Kaufman, J.C., & Baer, J.M. (2009). How are intellectual styles related to creativity across multiple domains? In L.F. Zhang & R.J. Sternberg (Eds.), *Perspectives on the Nature of Intellectual Styles* (pp. 87–106). New York: Springer.

Lee, K.L. (2002). *Thinking Styles and Approaches in Teaching among Hong Kong Kindergarten Teachers*. Unpublished manuscript, The University of Hong Kong.

Myers, I.B., & McCaulley, M.H. (1985). *Manual: A Guide to the Development and Use of the Myers-Briggs Type Indicator*. Palo Alto, CA: Consulting Psychologists Press.

Palut, B. (2008). The relationship between thinking styles and level of externality: a study of Turkish female preschool student teachers. *Social Behavior and Personality*, 36, 519–528.

Rayner, S., & Peterson, E.R. (2009). Reaffirming style as an individual difference: toward a global paradigm or knowledge diaspora? In L.F. Zhang & R.J. Sternberg (Eds.), *Perspectives on the Nature of Intellectual Styles* (pp. 107–134). New York: Springer.

Renzulli, J.S., & Sullivan, E.E. (2009). Learning styles applied: harnessing students' instructional style preferences. In L.F. Zhang & R.J. Sternberg (Eds.), *Perspectives on the Nature of Intellectual Styles* (pp. 209–231). New York: Springer.

Riding, R.J., & Cheema, I. (1991). Cognitive styles—an overview and integration. *Educational Psychology*, 11(3 & 4), 193–215.

Sadler-Smith, E. (2009). A duplex model of cognitive style. In L.F. Zhang & R.J. Sternberg (Eds.), *Perspectives on the Nature of Intellectual Styles* (pp. 3–28). New York: Springer.

Sternberg, R.J. (1988). Mental self-government: a theory of intellectual styles and their development. *Human Development*, 31, 197–224.

Sternberg, R.J. (1997). *Thinking Styles*. New York: Cambridge University Press.

Sternberg, R.J., & Grigorenko, E.L. (1995). Styles of thinking in the school. *European Journal for High Ability*, 6, 201–219.

Sternberg, R.J., & Wagner, R.K. (1992). *Thinking Styles Inventory*. Unpublished test, Yale University.

Sternberg, R.J., Wagner, R.K., & Zhang, L.F. (2003). *Thinking Styles Inventory— Revised*. Unpublished test, Yale University.

Sternberg, R.J., Wagner, R.K., & Zhang, L.F. (2007). *Thinking Styles Inventory— Revised II*. Unpublished test, Tufts University.

Sun, D., & Hu, Y. (2008). A threefold model of intellectual styles: the more integrated theory of cognitive style. *Psychological Science*, 31, 169–172.

Tang, J.M. (2004). Are Asian thinking styles different? Acculturation and thinking styles in a Chinese Canadian population. *Dissertation Abstracts International*, 65 (3-B), 1573.

Torrance, E.P. (1988). *SOLAT (Style of Learning and Thinking) Manual*. Bensenville, IL: Scholastic Testing Service.

Tsagaris, G.S. (2007). The relationships between thinking style preferences, cultural orientations and academic achievement. *Dissertation Abstracts International Section A: Humanities and Social Sciences*, 67 (9A), 3290.

Verdurmen, C., & Van Petegem, P. (2009). Portraying the scenery of intellectual styles. What's in a name? *Proceedings of the 14th annual conference of the European Learning Styles Information Network* (pp. 21–27). Bulle-en-Guyère, Switzerland: Les Roches Guyère, University of Applied Sciences.

Witkin, H. A. (1964). Origins of cognitive style. In C. Sheerer (Ed.), *Cognition, Theory, Research, Promise* (pp. 172–205). New York: Harper & Row.

Yeh, Y.C. (2007). Aptitude-treatment interactions in pre-service teachers' behavior change during computer-simulated teaching. *Computers & Education, 48,* 495–507.

Zhang, L.F. (2002). Thinking styles and cognitive development. *The Journal of Genetic Psychology, 163,* 179–195.

Zhang, L. F. (2003a). *The Preferred Thinking Styles in Teaching Inventory.* Unpublished test, The University of Hong Kong, The University of Hong Kong.

Zhang, L.F. (2003b). Are parents' and children's thinking styles related? *Psychological Reports, 93,* 617–630.

Zhang, L.F. (2004). Contributions of thinking styles to vocational purpose beyond self-rated abilities. *Psychological Reports, 94,* 697–714.

Zhang, L.F. (2007). *Preferred Thinking Styles in Learning Inventory.* Unpublished test, The University of Hong Kong.

Zhang, L.F. (2008a). Thinking styles and emotions. *The Journal of Psychology, 142,* 497–515.

Zhang, L.F. (2008b). Thinking styles and identity development among Chinese university students. *The American Journal of Psychology, 121,* 255–271

Zhang, L.F. (2009a). *Thinking Styles and the Eriksonian Stages: A Triadic Investigation.* Unpublished manuscript.

Zhang, L. F. (2009b). Anxiety and thinking styles. *Personality and Individual Differences, 47,* 347–351.

Zhang, L.F., Fu, H., & Jiao, B. (2008). Accounting for Tibetan university students' and teachers' intellectual styles. *Educational Review, 60,* 21–37.

Zhang, L.F., & Huang, J.F. (2001). Thinking styles and the five-factor model of personality. *European Journal of Personality, 15,* 465–476.

Zhang, L.F., & Postiglione, G.A. (2001). Thinking styles, self-esteem, and socioeconomic status. *Personality and Individual Differences, 31,* 1333–1346.

Zhang, L.F., & Sachs, J. (1997). Assessing thinking styles in the theory of mental self-government: A Hong Kong validity study. *Psychological Reports, 81,* 915–928.

Zhang, L.F., & Sternberg, R.J. (2002). Thinking styles and teacher characteristics. *International Journal of Psychology, 37,* 3–12.

Zhang, L.F., & Sternberg, R.J. (2005). A threefold model of intellectual styles. *Educational Psychology Review, 17,* 1–53.

Zhang, L.F., & Sternberg, R.J. (2006). *The Nature of Intellectual Styles.* Mahwah, NJ: Lawrence Erlbaum Associates.

Zhang, L.F., & Sternberg, R.J. (2009a). Revisiting the value issue in intellectual styles. In L.F. Zhang & R.J. Sternberg (Eds.), *Perspectives on the Nature of Intellectual Styles* (pp. 63–85). New York: Springer.

Zhang, L.F., & Sternberg, R.J. (Eds.) (2009b). *Perspectives on the Nature of Intellectual Styles.* New York: Springer.

# 5   The Learning Flexibility Index
## Assessing Contextual Flexibility in Learning Style

*Garima Sharma and David A. Kolb*

## INTRODUCTION

Experiential learning theory (ELT; Kolb, 1984) draws on the work of prominent 20th-century scholars who gave experience a central role in their theories of human learning and development to develop a dynamic, holistic model of the process of learning from experience and a multilinear model of adult development. ELT is a dynamic view of learning based on a cycle of learning with four learning modes—Concrete Experience (CE), Reflective Observation (RO), Abstract Conceptualization (AC), and Active Experimentation (AE). It is a holistic theory that defines learning as the major process of human adaptation involving the whole person. As such, ELT is applicable not only in the formal education classroom but in all areas of life. For forty years, research based on ELT has been conducted all around the world supporting the applicability of the model in different cultures, educational specializations, and life contexts. The 2009 Experiential Learning Theory Bibliographies (Kolb & Kolb, 2009a, 2009b) include over 3,000 research studies.

Most style typologies in cognition, learning, and personality conceive of styles as fixed traits or preferences that vary little from situation to situation or over time. The learning style concept in ELT is different in that learning style is not conceived as a fixed trait but a dynamic state. This dynamic state arises from an individual's preferential resolution of the dual dialectics of the experiential learning cycle—experiencing/conceptualizing (AC-CE) and acting/reflecting (AE-RO). Nine distinct learning styles have been identified that can be portrayed on a two-dimensional learning space defined by AC-CE and AE-RO (Kolb & Kolb, 2005a; see also Figure 5.2).

The stability of learning style arises from consistent patterns of transaction between individuals and learning situations in their life. This process is called accentuation: the way we learn about a new situation determines the range of choices and decisions we see, the choices and decisions we make influence the next situation we live through, and this situation further influences future choices. Learning styles are thus specialized modes of adaptation that are reinforced by the continuing choice of situations where a style is successful (Kolb & Kolb, 2005b).

Different situations demand and reinforce the application of different learning styles. Because a specialized learning style represents an individual preference for only one or two of the four modes of the learning cycle, its effectiveness is limited to those learning situations that require these strengths. Learning flexibility indicates the development of a more holistic and sophisticated learning process. Following Jung's theory (1971) that adult development moves from a specialized way of adapting toward a holistic integrated way, development in learning flexibility is seen as a move from specialization to integration. Integrated learning is a process involving a creative tension among the four learning modes that is responsive to contextual demands. This is portrayed as an idealized learning cycle or spiral where the learner 'touches all the bases'—experiencing, reflecting, thinking, and acting—in a recursive process that is responsive to the learning context and what is being learned. The theory argues that this development in learning flexibility results from integration of the dual dialectics of conceptualizing/experiencing and acting/reflecting that allows the learner to move freely around the learning cycle using all four modes to learn from an experience.

In this chapter, we further develop the concept of learning flexibility in ELT. We introduce a new measure of learning flexibility—the Learning Flexibility Index (LFI)—an improvement over the measures of learning flexibility used earlier. We provide empirical construct validity evidence for the LFI and illustrate through a case study how learning style and learning flexibility influence individual learning.

## PREVIOUS ELT RESEARCH ON LEARNING FLEXIBILITY

Previous research on learning flexibility (previously named adaptive flexibility) was conducted with the Adaptive Style Inventory (ASI; Boyatzis & Kolb, 1993). The ASI was originally developed to assess individuals' level of integrative complexity as they progressed from the specialized to integrated stage of the ELT developmental model (Kolb, 1984). The instrument assessed adaptive flexibility by measuring how individuals change their learning style in response to different situational demands. It was based on the theory that if people show systematic variability in their response to different contextual learning demands, one could infer a higher level of integrative development because systematic variation would imply higher order decision rules or metacognitive processes (Kolb & Kolb, 2009c) for guiding behavior.

A number of researchers have found evidence to support the link between learning flexibility and integrative development. Early studies found that adaptive flexibility is positively related to higher levels of ego development on Loevinger's (1966) sentence completion instrument (Kolb, 1984; Kolb & Wolfe, 1981). Individuals with higher levels of adaptive flexibility perceived themselves to be more self-directed in their current life situation and to have greater flexibility. They had higher levels of differentiation in their personal relationships, and used more constructs to describe their life structure. In addition, they experienced less conflict and stress in their life despite experiencing their life to be more complex. Subsequent research on learning flexibility has replicated some of these findings. Perlmutter (1990) studied fifty-one medical professionals and found significant relationships between Loevinger's (1966) ego development instrument and adaptive flexibility. Thompson (1999), in a sample of fifty professionals from various fields, found that self-directed learners had higher levels of adaptive flexibility than learners who were not self-directed.

Another study, by Mainemalis, Boyatzis, and Kolb (2002), examined the relationship between learning style as measured with the Kolb Learning Style Inventory (KLSI; Kolb, 1999, 2007) and ASI adaptive flexibility. They tested the hypothesis that learners with equal preferences for dialectically opposed learning modes would be better able to integrate them into a flexible learning process. They proposed that a balanced learning style (as given by the absolute value for the dialectics of experiencing/conceptualizing and acting/reflecting adjusted for population mean) would be related to learning flexibility. In other words, the more an individual is balanced on the conceptualizing/experiencing and acting/reflecting dialectics, the more will he or she exhibit learning flexibility. This was supported for the dialectic of conceptualizing/experiencing. No significant result was found for the dialectic of acting/reflecting. However, they also found an equally strong relationship between learning flexibility and a preference for concreteness over abstraction, the KLSI AC-CE score. This raises the question whether learning flexibility is a function of balancing opposing learning modes or a function of contextual sensitivity, which is being more concrete in learning style. In her comprehensive review of ASI research, Bell (2005) reported other construct validity evidence but suggested a need for revision of the original instrument and the creation of new measures of adaptive flexibility.

Using an earlier version of the current LFI instrument, Akrivou (2008) found a relationship between learning flexibility and integrative development as measured by her Integrative Development Scale (IDS). She created this scale by identifying items that describe the integrative stage of adult development as defined in the works of Loevinger (1966, 1976; Loevinger, Hy, & Bobbitt, 1998), Rogers (1961), Perry (1970), Kegan (1982, 1994), and Kolb (1984, 1988, 1991). Another study by Moon (2008), using the early LFI, examined sales performance in financial services, finding that learning flexibility influenced sales success as measured by monthly volume of sales.

## CONSTRUCT VALIDATION OF THE LFI

Based on this previous work, we consider six hypotheses about the relationship of the LFI to variables comprising a nomological net of construct validity: the demographic variables of age, gender, educational level, and educational specialization as well as learning style and integrative development.

### Demographic Variables

These variables were chosen because of previous demonstrated relationships with learning style (Kolb & Kolb, 2005a). Whereas we have found no previous research on the relationship between flexibility in learning and demographic variables, other research on individual flexibility and related variables suggests the following hypotheses.

*Hypothesis 1: Learning flexibility will decrease with age.* Negative relationships have been found between age and cognitive flexibility (Collins & Tellier, 1994; Salthouse & Meinz, 1995) and the inability to deal with change and to shift sets in task accomplishment (Ridderinkhof, Span, & van der Molen, 2002).

*Hypothesis 2: Women will exhibit higher learning flexibility than men.* Women have been shown to have greater gender-role flexibility (Green, Bigler, & Catherwood, 2004; Levy, Taylor, & Gelman, 1995; Mendez & Crawford, 2002) and flexibility in coping with stressful life events like immigration (Remennick, 2005).

*Hypothesis 3: Higher levels of education will result in lower learning flexibility.*

*Hypothesis 4: Learning flexibility will be lower for individuals in educational specializations that emphasize abstraction.*

Hypotheses 3 and 4 are based on the positive relationship between educational level and the preference for the abstract learning style (Kolb & Kolb, 2005a) and the finding of Mainemelis and colleagues (2002) that abstract learning styles are less flexible on the ASI.

### Learning Style

ELT predicts relationships between learning style and learning flexibility. Specifically, it draws on Piaget's (1952) theory that learning requires a balance or equilibrium between accommodation, external adaptation through active involvement in experience (CE & AE), and assimilation, internal cognitive organization through reflective abstraction (RO & AC). "The 'accord of thought with things' and the 'accord of thought with itself' expresses this dual functional invariant of adaptation and organization" (Piaget, 1952, p. 8). Accommodative adaptation, therefore, incorporates novelty and variability whereas assimilative organization promotes stability and consistency. Learning flexibility is the result of the integration of these two processes. The Mainemalis et al. (2002) study mentioned earlier found some support (significant only on the AC/CE dimension) for the hypothesis that learning flexibility is related to a balance between these two processes but also found equal support for the hypothesis that accommodative learning styles were more flexible than assimilative learning styles. Thus, we propose to test two conflicting hypotheses to determine the relationship between assimilative and accommodative learning styles and learning flexibility:

> *Hypothesis 5a: A balance between an assimilative and accommodative learning style will be related to higher learning flexibility.*
> *Hypothesis 5b: A preference for the assimilative versus the accommodative learning style will be related to lower learning flexibility.*

## Integrative Development

Finally, as described earlier, learning flexibility is thought to be indicative of the higher order process-oriented thinking related to higher stages of adult development. This hypothesis will be tested by examining the relationship between learning flexibility and Akrivou's (2008) Integrative Development Scale.

> *Hypothesis 6: Learning flexibility is positively related to integrative development.*

## METHOD

### Samples

The primary sample for this study was obtained from the publisher of the Kolb Learning Style Inventory (KLSI), Hay Group Transforming Learning. This database comprises a large sample with diversity in gender, age, education, profession, country of residence and birth, and learning styles. For our study, we used a sample of 7,536 individuals from this database. This included all individuals who took the inventory between March 2008 and May 2009. From a sample of over 10,000, we used 7,536 after excluding those with missing data. We decided to use a large sample rather than selecting a smaller more homogeneous sample, recognizing that effect sizes were likely to be smaller due to greater error variance in the large heterogeneous sample but that these conservative estimates would be more generalizable. This sample was used for assessing the KLSI, the LFI, and demographic variables. The second sample was from Akrivou's (2008) study consisting of 169 individuals: 75% of whom are middle- and senior-level managers in three multinational companies and medium-sized organizations based in the Midwest of the United States.

The remaining individuals are managers or professionals in multinational or professional service firms (see Table 5.1).

## Measures

### *The Kolb Learning Style Inventory*

We used the Kolb Learning Style Inventory, Version 3.1 (KLST; Kolb, 2007). The KLSI contains twelve items that ask respondents to rank four sentence endings that correspond to the four learning modes—CE, RO, AC, and AE. The KLSI assesses six variables, four primary scores that measure an individual's relative emphasis on the four learning modes and two combination scores that measure an individual's preference for abstractness over concreteness (AC-CE) and action over reflection (AE-RO). To create a continuous variable to assess an individual's preference for the accommodative versus the assimilative learning style, a new combination score was created (this is used to test Hypotheses 5a and 5b): Accommodation/Assimilation = ((AE + CE)-(AC + RO)). This measure has been used in previous studies by Wierstra and de Jong (2002) and Allinson and Hayes (1996).

### *The Learning Flexibility Index*

The LFI is comprised of eight items that describe eight different learning contexts chosen to represent learning situations that emphasize different modes around the learning cycle. The situations 'starting something new' and 'influencing someone' emphasize AE and CE. 'Getting to know someone' and 'learning in a group' emphasize CE and RO. 'Planning something' and 'analyzing something' emphasize RO and AC, and 'evaluating an opportunity' and 'choosing between alternatives' emphasize AC and AE. The items are revisions of the original ASI in a ranking format similar to the KLSI. Respondents are asked to think of an example of each situation in their life and then to rank which of the four learning mode responses to the learning situation they tend to use. For example, for the item "When I start something new", the endings are "I rely on my feelings to guide me" (CE); "I imagine different possibilities" (RO); "I analyze the situation" (AC); and "I try to be practical and realistic" (AE). The LFI items follow the KLSI in the Hay online survey used in this research.

We introduced a new measure for calculating learning flexibility based on the Kendall's Coefficient of Concordance or W (Legendre, 2005), a nonparametric statistic typically used to measure the degree of agreement among judges. This measure represented an improvement over earlier measures of learning flexibility (e.g., Akrivou, 2008; Mainemalis et al., 2002; Moon, 2008) in that it took into account all of the variability in ranking across learning contexts without relying on difference scores which would be problematic in regression analysis. In the LFI, W is calculated for each individual by assessing the degree of agreement in their ranking of the four learning modes across the eight different learning contexts. A low W score for an individual indicates that the learner varies their ranking of learning modes across learning contexts, thus showing high learning flexibility.

W finds the deviation between the mean response ranking (by learning mode) and the grand mean of the ranking. This deviation is divided by the maximum possible sum of squares deviation. The coefficient varies from 0 to 1 with 1 denoting complete agreement (Sigler & Tallent-Runnels, 2006). We thus define the Learning Flexibility Index (LFI) as: LFI= 1-W. The modified formula for W is:

$$W = (12S - 3p^2n \ (n+1)^2))/p^2 \ (n^3-n)$$

$$S = \sum_{i=1}^{n} R_i^2$$

Where,
$p$ = number of learning contexts (= 8)
$n$ = number of learning modes (= 4)
R = row sum of ranks

### Demographic Variables

The variable for age comprised of seven ordinal categories from under 19 to over 65 years. This was transformed into a continuous variable from 1 to 7. Gender was coded as 1 for males and 0 for females. The five categories for education from primary school to doctoral degree were recoded into a continuous variable from 1 to 5. The different educational specializations from the database were ranked so that a lower rank indicated concrete contextual learning demands and a higher rank indicated abstract conceptual learning demands in the specialty based on data reported by Kolb (1984, pp. 126–127). For example, social work as a profession will have a lower rank, whereas mathematics will have a higher rank.

### Integrative Development Scale

The measure for this variable is from Akrivou's (2008) study. The following items were used from her scale: "My life's work is a deep expression of my principles, values and identity"; "In all my roles and relationships I am able to be authentic and express my true inner self"; "When it comes to life satisfaction the journey is as important as the destination"; "I feel I am the creator of my own life story"; and "I am committed to making the world a better place". The alpha reliability for this scale was 0.70.

## RESULTS

Table 5.1 gives the means and standard deviations for all variables and their intercorrelations. As predicted in Hypotheses 1–4, we see significant negative correlations of age, gender, educational level, and educational specialization with learning flexibility. Correlations of other variables with learning flexibility were also significant and in the hypothesized direction. The accommodative learning orientation and integrative development were positively related to learning flexibility. In addition, the correlation between age and integrative development in sample 2 (row 7 of Table 5.1) was significantly positive ($r = 0.16$, $p < 0.05$), the opposite of the relationship between age and learning flexibility in sample 1 ($r = -0.05$, $p < 0.01$).

Hypotheses 1 to 5 focused on the impact of age, gender, education, educational specialization, and accommodating/assimilating learning style on learning flexibility. To test Hypotheses 1–5 we ran hierarchical multiple regression (for the online sample with $N = 7,536$) in which age, gender, education, and educational specialization were entered in the first step, the KLSI variable accommodation/assimilation in the second step, and the square of this variable as the last step. Step 2 was added to test Hypothesis 5b that states that a preference for accommodation over assimilation will lead to higher learning flexibility. The square of this variable was entered

*Table 5.1* Means, Standard Deviations, and Correlations

| Variable | M | SD | 1 | 2 | 3 | 4 | 5 | 6 | 7 |
|---|---|---|---|---|---|---|---|---|---|
| 1. Learning Flexibility Index[a] | 0.71 | 0.17 | — | | | | | | |
| 2. Age[b] | 3.73 | 1.13 | -0.05** | — | | | | | |
| 3. Gender[c] | 0.47 | 0.50 | -0.08** | 0.08** | — | | | | |
| 4. Education[d] | 3.28 | 0.86 | -0.06** | 0.22** | 0.06** | — | | | |
| 5. Specialization[e] | 10.72 | 4.50 | -0.05** | -0.02 | 0.21** | 0.10** | — | | |
| 6. Acc-Assm[f] | 0.29 | 18.23 | 0.25** | -0.04** | -0.16** | -0.07** | -0.13** | — | |
| 7. Integrative development[g] | 19.42 | 3.48 | 0.23** | 0.16* | -0.14 | -0.00 | -0.07 | 0.07 | — |

**p < 0.01; * p < 0.05.

Notes: [a]N = 7,536 for Learning Flexibility Index; [b]for age: 1 = under 19, 2 = 19–24 years, 3 = 25–34 years, 4 = 35–44 years, 5 = 45–54 years, 6 = 55–64 years, 7 = 65 and over; [c]for gender: 1 = male, 0 = female; [d]for education: 1 = primary school, 2 = secondary school, 3 = university degree, 4 = master's degree, and 5 = doctoral degree; [e]for specialization in the increasing order of abstract conceptualization and decreasing order of concrete experience: 1 = fine and applied arts, 2 = humanities, 3 = literature, 4 = languages, 5 = social work, 6 = nursing, 7 = physical education, 8 = communications, 9 = business, 10 = social sciences, 11 = psychology, 12 = medicine, 13 = law, 14 = agriculture, 15 = accounting, 16 = engineering, 17 = computer science and information science, 18 = science and mathematics; [f]Acc-Assm = Accommodation-Assimilation = (AE + CE)-(AC + RO); [g]N = 169 for Integrative Development.

to test Hypothesis 5a, which states that a balance between assimilation and accommodation will lead to higher learning flexibility. The square term gives the equation an inverted-U form where as one moves along the accommodation-assimilation axis learning flexibility increases, peaking at the balance point and then decreases afterwards. Thus, the linear term is entered to test Hypothesis 5b whereas the square term tests Hypothesis 5a. These are entered in steps 2 and 3 of the regression to see their incremental effect in explaining learning flexibility (see Table 5.2).

When we entered the linear variable for accommodation-assimilation in Model 2, it significantly explains an additional 5% variance in learning flexibility ($F\Delta$ (7,530) = 104.48, $p < 0.001$) after that explained by age, gender, education, and educational specialization. Accommodation-assimilation is positively related to learning flexibility ($\beta = 0.24$, $p < 0.01$) implying that as preference for the assimilative learning style increases, learning flexibility decreases. This supports Hypothesis 5b.

In Model 3, in the regression we entered the square term for accommodation/assimilation. This variable significantly explains an additional 2% variance in learning flexibility ($F\Delta$ (7,529) = 116.60, $p < 0.001$) after accounting for the other variables. The significant and negative coefficient

*Table 5.2*   Regression for Learning Flexibility Index

| Variable | Learning Flexibility Index[a] | Integrative Development[b] | | |
|---|---|---|---|---|
| | Hyp1–4 | Hyp 5b | Hyp 5a | Hyp 6 |
| | Model 1[c] | Model 2 | Model 3 | Model 1 |
| Age | –0.03* | –0.02* | -0.02 | 0.18* |
| Gender | –0.07** | –0.04** | -0.04** | –0.18* |
| Education | –0.05** | –0.04** | –0.03** | 0.00 |
| Specialization | –0.03* | –0.01 | –0.02 | –0.03 |
| Acc-Assm[d] | | 0.24** | 0.23** | 0.01 |
| Square of Acc-Assm | | | –0.14** | |
| Learning Flexibility Index | | | | 0.25** |
| R | 0.11 | 0.25 | 0.29 | 0.36 |
| $R^2$ | 0.01 | 0.07 | 0.09 | 0.13 |
| Adj. $R^2$ | 0.01 | 0.06 | 0.08 | 0.10 |
| $R^2\Delta$ | 0.01** | 0.05** | 0.02** | 0.06** |

**$p < 0.01$; * $p < 0.05$.
Notes: [a]N = 7,536 for Learning Flexibility Index as the dependent variable. [b]For integrative development as the dependent variable N = 169. [c]Values are standardized regression coefficients. [d]Acc-Assm = Accommodation-Assimilation = (AE + CE)-(AC + RO).

for this variable ($\beta = -0.14$, $p < 0.01$) indicates an inverted-U shape between accommodation-assimilation and learning flexibility consistent with the balancing Hypothesis 5a.

To understand the findings in Model 2 and 3, we plotted the predicted value of learning flexibility controlling for the demographic variables against the variable accommodation-assimilation (see Figure 5.1). The conflicting linear and curvilinear relationships between accommodative-assimilative learning style and learning flexibility found by Mainemalis et al. (2002) are resolved by splitting the difference at the accommodative end of the learning style continuum. Both hypotheses agree at the assimilative end of the learning style continuum (that is, balanced learning style is related to higher learning flexibility and assimilative learning style results in lower learning flexibility) and are confirmed in the result shown in Figure 5.1. At the accommodative end, the relationship is neither linear nor curvilinear, declining from the balance point only slightly. This suggests that inflexibility in learning occurs primarily when the assimilative process of internally organizing thought is not counterbalanced by some external accommodative orientation. In other words, it is the assimilative learning style that is the most inflexible. Boyatzis and Mainemalis in Chapter 7 of this volume found similar results. In their sample of MBA students they found a high preference for abstraction and lower flexibility in learning from concrete experience, supporting our finding that it is the assimilative learning style that is the most inflexible.

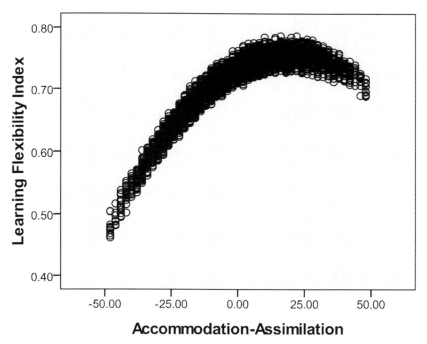

*Figure 5.1* Graph of predicted value of LFI from the regression and the variable for accommodation-assimilation.

To test Hypothesis 6, we ran a separate regression (on the sample with $N = 169$) with integrative development as the dependent variable. Hypothesis 6 predicted a positive relationship between learning flexibility and integrative development. Under the column for integrative development in Table 5.2, we see the results for this regression. After controlling for the demographic variables and learning style, learning flexibility is significantly and positively related to integrative development ($\beta = 0.25$, $p < 0.01$) explaining 6% of the variance in integrative development, supporting Hypothesis 6.

To test for discriminant validity of the LFI, we calculated Kendall's W using items from KLSI (items 1–12 that measure learning style). We then correlated the integrative development variable with both LFI and 1-Kendall's W from the KLSI items. LFI will have discriminant validity if the correlation of LFI with integrative development is significant whereas that of 1-Kendall's W from the LSI items is not. LFI and integrative development show a significant correlation ($r = 0.23$, $p < 0.01$), whereas 1-Kendall's W from the KLSI items does not show a significant correlation with integrative development ($r = 0.09$, $p = 0.22$). What these results show is that the LFI variability in response to different learning contexts that is hypothesized to relate to higher order decision rules for learning is related to integrative development; but the variability in response to general descriptions of oneself as a learner on the KLSI is not related to integrative development.

Whereas the first order correlations and regressions showed statistical confirmation of the hypothesized nomological net of construct validation for the LFI, effect sizes for the demographic variables are negligible, explaining less than 1% of the variance in each case. Effect sizes for the learning-style variable and the LFI were somewhat larger but still small (explaining 6% of the variance for the Model 2 and 8% for the Model 3 regression). For the correlation between LFI and IDS, 5.3% of the variance was explained and the R square for the regression indicated 10% of the variance explained. These small effect sizes indicate little utility of the results for such practical applications as using the LFI to predict levels of adult development, although they are still of value for confirming construct validity of the LFI. Construct validation is not focused on an outcome criterion, but on the theory or construct the test measures. Here the emphasis is on the pattern of convergent and discriminant theoretical predictions made by the theory. Failure to confirm predictions calls into question the test and the theory.

> However, even if each of the correlations proved to be quite low, their cumulative effect would be to support the validity of the test and the underlying theory.
>
> (Selltiz, Jahoda, Deutsch, & Cook, 1959, p. 160)

A primary practical use of the LFI lies in the analysis of individual patterns of contextual variability that individuals can use to understand how they learn in different situations in their life. Construct validation of the LFI lends credibility to the validity of these patterns. The following case study illustrates this practical application.

## USING THE LFI FOR PERSONAL DEVELOPMENT

In the preceding analysis we have shown nomothetic construct validation for the LFI across a large sample of diverse individuals. The LFI also provides an idiographic profile describing each individual's unique way of responding to the different learning contexts. By scoring a person's learning style in each of the eight learning contexts, we can create a picture of how flexibly they move around the regions of the ELT learning space. This information, coupled with one's learning style, can provide a fuller picture of how one learns in different life situations and identify developmental needs for flexible adaptation to different learning demands.

To illustrate, following we provide a profile of a person with a high LFI score along with excerpts from his self-analysis of how he learns (this report was written to describe the learning style results he was given and did not include his LFI score feedback). Figure 5.2 shows the LFI contextual learning style results for Mark, a mid-forties executive for an international nonprofit organization, who had a high LFI score at the 98th percentile. Mark's learning style on the KLSI was balancing and he used this style when *getting to know someone better*, *to plan*, and *to learn in a group*. In the *deciding between two alternatives* context he became more concrete, using the experiencing style. *To evaluate opportunities* and *start something new*, he changed his style to become accommodating, concrete, and active. *To influence someone*, he became more abstract and *to analyze something*, he adopted an abstract and reflective learning style. Thus, Mark shows flexibility in all four learning modes in response to the learning demands of different situations.

Mark's self-analysis provides support for this portrait of his learning flexibility. He mentions how taking the KLSI was difficult because his preference for all of the learning modes made ranking choices difficult: *I had a difficult time answering the LSI questions. I have had a difficult time with other types of indicators in the past, including the MBTI. I have wondered at times if maybe I don't know myself very well, but I prefer to think that I am a well-balanced person.*

He then describes how his educational experiences have shaped his ability to operate flexibly in all of the learning regions: *As I look back at my educational experience, I can see how I have grown toward the balancing style. My exposure to a wide variety of learning experiences strengthened my skills in the different learning styles over the years. I majored in civil engineering in college (converging skills). I was heavily involved in the campus retreat program and other faith-related activities, which placed*

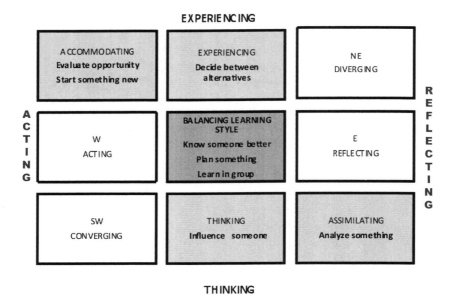

*Figure 5.2*  Example of movement in the learning space for a person with high learning flexibility.

*a strong emphasis on reflection and finding meaning in concrete personal experience (diverging skills). After college I volunteered for a year with Habitat for Humanity and learned to build houses exclusively through hands-on experience (accommodating skills). I earned a master's degree in Religion and Religious Education requiring a good deal of reading and research (assimilating skills).*

In his current career and personal life, Mark prefers variety rather than specialized mastery in one area: *I am most interested in a career that involves a variety of activities. I have a number of different functions in my current job, from one-on-one coaching to creating informational resources and developing training programs to facilitating trainings and planning meetings. In my life outside of work, I have numerous hobbies and interests. I love learning new things, and I look for new challenges, but it is the variety of activities that I enjoy. In the past I've wondered why I seem to lack the drive that others have to be the absolute best at one thing. Now I realize that my drive is just as strong, but different. I'm driven to pursue many different interests and learn in a variety of ways.*

The skills that Mark has developed in the different regions of the learning space enable him to adapt to different learning contexts and tasks: *I find that I am able to adapt my learning style to meet the demands of the task at hand. I tend to pick up new skills or concepts quickly. I have learned that if I give conscious thought to my learning processes and am deliberate about moving through the stages, from experience to reflection to thinking to acting, I will become a more proficient learner. I am able to take different perspectives and bridge differences between people with different styles. I do at times have difficulty making decisions because my ability to understand different perspectives often makes it challenging to commit to one of my own.*

The preceding case illustrates how the LFI contextual learning style analysis relates to the life of a high flexibility person. Coupled with learning style results, the LFI can give learners a rich portrait of how they learn in the many contexts of their life. By using the examples that they created to answer the LFI questions, individuals can plan strategies to deal with these real learning situations.

## CONCLUSION AND IMPLICATIONS

Thus far, we have described the development of the Learning Flexibility Index and a measure of learning flexibility based on the Kendall's W statistic. We have shown construct validity for the LFI measure by testing six hypotheses about the place of the LFI in a nomological net. The LFI is negatively related to age and educational level. Women and those in concrete professions tend to be more flexible. Individuals with an assimilating learning style tend to be less flexible. Learning flexibility is positively related to Akrivou's (2008) Integrative Development Scale. Finally, the case study of an individual with a high LFI score illustrates how learning style and learning flexibility can combine to produce unique patterns of adaptation to different learning contexts.

Whereas these results provide general support for the validity of the LFI in a large diverse sample, further research is needed to extend the LFI nomological net, particularly in more specific contexts. For example, building on Moon's (2008) study showing a relationship between learning flexibility and relationship sales of complex financial products, we would predict relationships between the LFI and performance in roles that involve multiple learning demands, for instance, managers of cross-functional teams or entrepreneurs. Similarly, learning flexibility may be related to performance in interdisciplinary educational programs. It might also be related to communicating effectively with persons whose learning style differs from one's own. Another important line of future research is the exploration of the relationship between learning flexibility and adult development, for instance, relating the LFI to measures of adult development stages in the theories of Loevinger, Perry, and Kegan.

Further refinements can be developed for LFI measurement. Whereas we have noted the methodological benefits of using Kendall's W to assess contextual differences in learning style, the index only gives an overall assessment of flexibility. It would be useful to develop quantitative indices of the specific ways an individual changes their style in different contexts as illustrated in the case study of Mark. Specifically, submeasures of flexibility in the four learning modes and indicators of whether the flexibility is toward or away from the learning demands of the context might be illuminating.

From a practical perspective, the results portray an interesting pattern. Individuals who are men, older, highly educated, and specialists in abstract, paradigmatic fields are more assimilative in learning style and have less learning flexibility. The results further suggest that it is the orientation toward abstraction and reflection characteristic of the assimilative learning style that lead to inflexibility. Because it is the assimilative style that is the most favored and most developed in formal education systems, we might ask if this abstract approach is producing the unintended negative consequence of learning inflexibility. Emphasis on conceptual learning at the expense of contextual learning may lead to dogmatic adherence to ideas without testing them in experience, what Whitehead called "the fallacy of misplaced concreteness". Contextual learning approaches like experiential learning (Kolb, 1984) and situated learning (Lave & Wenger, 1991) may help education to nurture integrated learners who are as sensitive to context as they are to abstract concepts.

A related issue concerns the priority placed on specialized as against integrative learning in education. Specialization in subject matter and the learning style most suited to learning it may well produce higher levels of specialized mastery. Mainemalis et al. (2002) found that specialized learning styles led to greater development of learning skills related to the specialization than did balanced learning styles. We saw how Mark in the earlier case study was concerned that his balance and flexibility in learning kept him from achieving mastery in one particular area. However, learning flexibility leads to integrative development and perhaps greater personal fulfillment, better work-life balance, and a broader, more tolerant and holistic perspective on the world. These too are important aims of education.

The LFI offers an important additional perspective in the ongoing debate about how to use learning style information to enhance learning. In chapter 11 of this volume, Peterson, Carne, and Freear describe the great emphasis placed on matching learning style and teaching style in order to increase student learning. This approach may well facilitate learning of specialized material. The concept of learning flexibility, however, shifts the focus from specialized style matching to the process of movement through all modes of the learning cycle. This holistic process-oriented approach that combines a matching strategy with a corresponding emphasis on increasing learning skills in nondominant learning styles may well prove to be the most effective educational strategy. Teachers can respond to the diversity of learning styles present in nearly every classroom by teaching around the cycle using approaches that fit with all four learning modes.

The Learning Flexibility Index provides a validated tool for investigating the important role that learning flexibility plays in education, management, and personal development. Even the most specialized educational program has a curriculum that requires learning subject matter with different learning style demands. When we consider liberal education and multidisciplinary programs, there are even greater demands for learning flexibility. In the contemporary management and leadership literature there are consistent calls for adaptability and flexibility in coping with the continually changing dynamics of the global community. Similarly, individuals throughout their lives face a multitude of learning and problem-solving tasks that require a flexible approach in learning how to deal with them. The LFI can provide a self-development tool for individuals to understand their learning flexibility in order to become more effective learners and progress from specialization to integration in adult development.

## BIBLIOGRAPHY

Akrivou, K. (2008). *Differentiation and Integration in Adult Development: The Influence of Self-Complexity and Integrative Learning on Self Integration.* Unpublished doctoral dissertation, Case Western Reserve University, Cleveland, OH.

Allinson, C.W., & Hayes, J. (1996). The Cognitive Style Index: a measure of intuition-analysis for organizational research. *Journal of Management Studies, 33*, 119–135.

Bell, A.A. (2005). *The Adaptive Style Inventory: An Assessment of Person-Environment Interactions.* Unpublished manuscript, Department of Educational Leadership, University of Connecticut.

Boyatzis, R.E., & Kolb, D.A. (1993). *Adaptive Style Inventory: Self Scored Inventory and Interpretation Booklet.* Boston, MA: Hay Transforming Learning.

Collins, B., & Tellier, A. (1994). Differences in conceptual flexibility with age as measured by a modified version of the Visual Verbal Test. *Canadian Journal on Aging, 13*, 368–377.

Green, V.A., Bigler, R., & Catherwood, D. (2004). The variability and flexibility of gender-typed toy play: a close look at children's behavioral response to counterstereotypic models. *Sex Roles, 51*, 371–386.

Jung, C.G. (1971). *Psychological Types* (Vol. 6). Princeton, NJ: Princeton University Press.

Kegan, R. (1982). *The Evolving Self.* Cambridge: Harvard University Press.

Kegan, R. (1994). *In Over Our Heads: The Mental Demands of Modern Life.* Cambridge, MA: Harvard University Press.

Kolb, A.Y., & Kolb, D.A. (2005a). *The Kolb Learning Style Inventory, Version 3.1: 2005 Technical Specifications.* Boston: Hay Resources Direct.

Kolb, A.Y., & Kolb, D.A. (2005b). Learning styles and learning spaces: enhancing experiential learning in higher education. *Academy of Management Learning and Education, 4*, 193–212.

Kolb, A.Y., & Kolb, D.A. (2009a). *Experiential Learning Theory Bibliography: 1971–2005.* Retrieved from www.learningfromexperience.com on January 10, 2010.

Kolb, A.Y., & Kolb, D.A. (2009b). *Experiential Learning Theory Bibliography: Recent Research 2005–2007.* Retrieved from www.learningfromexperience.com on January 10, 2010.

Kolb, A.Y., & Kolb, D.A. (2009c). The learning way: meta-cognitive aspects of experiential learning. *Simulation and Gaming: An Interdisciplinary Journal, 40*, 297–327.

Kolb, D.A. (1984). *Experiential Learning.* Upper Saddle River, NJ: Prentice Hall.

Kolb, D.A. (1988). Integrity, advanced professional development, and learning. In S. Srivastava (Ed.), *Executive Integrity: The Search for High Human Values in Organizational Life* (pp. 68–88). San Francisco: Jossey-Bass.

Kolb, D.A. (Ed.) (1991). *The Challenges of Advanced Professional Development.* Chicago: The Council for Adult and Experiential Learning (CAEL).

Kolb, D.A. (1999). *Learning Style Inventory Version 3.* Boston: Hay Transforming Learning. Retrieved from www.haygroup.com/tl on December 14, 2009.

Kolb, D.A. (2007). *The Kolb Learning Style Inventory, Version 3.1.* Boston: Hay Transforming Learning.

Kolb, D.A., & Wolfe, D.M. (1981). *Professional Education and Career Development: A Cross Sectional Study of Adaptive Competencies in Experiential Learning* (NIE No. NIG-G-77–0053). Department of Organizational Behavior, Case Western Reserve University (ERIC no. ED209493).

Lave, J., & Wenger, E. (1991). *Situated Learning.* Cambridge, England: Cambridge University Press.

Legendre, P. (2005). Species associations: the Kendall coefficient of concordance revisited. *Journal of Agricultural, Biological, and Environmental Statistics, 10*, 226–245.

Levy, G.D., Taylor, M.G., & Gelman, S.A. (1995). Traditional and evaluative aspects of flexibility in gender roles, social conventions, moral rules and physical laws. *Child Development, 66*, 515–531.

Loevinger, J. (1966). The meaning and measurement of ego development. *American Psychologist, 21*, 195–206.

Loevinger, J. (1976). *Ego Development: Conceptions and Theories.* San Francisco: Jossey-Bass.

Loevinger, J., Hy, L., & Bobbitt, K. (1998). Revision of the scoring manual. In J. Loevinger (Ed.), *Technical Foundations for Measuring Ego Development: The Washington University Sentence Completion Test.* Mahwah, NJ: Lawrence Erlbaum Associates.

Mainemelis, C., Boyatzis, R.E., & Kolb, D. (2002). Learning styles and adaptive flexibility: testing experiential learning theory. *Management Learning, 33*, 5–33.

Mendez, L.M.R., & Crawford, K.M. (2002). Gender-role stereotyping and career aspirations: a comparison of gifted early adolescent boys and girls. *Journal of Secondary Gifted Education, 13*, 96–107.

Moon, B.A. (2008). *Learning Style Influence on Relationship Sales Success.* Unpublished doctoral dissertation, Case Western Reserve University, Cleveland, OH.

Perlmutter, S. (1990). *Cognitive Complexity and Time Perspective in Hybrid Organizations.* Unpublished doctoral dissertation, Case Western Reserve University, Cleveland, OH.

Perry, W. (1970). *Forms of Intellectual and Ethical Development in College Years.* New York: Holt, Rinehart, & Winston.

Piaget, J. (1952). *The Origins of Intelligence in Children.* New York: International University Press.

Remennick, L. (2005). Immigration, gender, and psychosocial adjustment: a study of 150 immigrant couples in Israel. *Behavioral Science, 53*, 847–863.

Ridderinkhof, K.R., Span, M.M., & van der Molen, M. (2002). Perseverative behavior and adaptive control in older adults: performance monitoring, rule induction, and set shifting. *Brain and Cognition, 49*, 382–401.

Rogers, C.R. (1961). *On Becoming a Person*. Boston: Houghton Mifflin.

Salthouse, T.A., & Meinz, E.J. (1995). Aging, inhibition, working memory and speed. *Journals of Gerontology, 50,* 297–306.

Selltiz, C., Jahoda, M., Deutsch, M., & Cook, S.W. (1959). *Research Methods in Social Relations*. New York: Henry Holt & Company

Sigler, E.A., & Tallent-Runnels, M.K. (2006). Examining the validity of scores from an instrument designed to measure metacognition of problem solving. *The Journal of General Psychology, 133,* 257–276.

Thompson, L.M. (1999). *Love of Learning as the Driver for Self-directed Learning in the Workplace*. Unpublished doctoral dissertation, Case Western Reserve University, Cleveland, OH.

Wierstra, R.F.A., & Jong, F.P.C.M. (2002). A scaling theoretical evaluation of Kolb's Learning Style Inventory-2. In M. Valcke & D. Gombeir (Eds.), *Learning Styles: Reliability and Validity*. 7th annual ELSIN Conference, 26–28 June, Ghent, Belgium.

# 6 Further Understanding Learning in Higher Education

## A Systematic Review on Longitudinal Research Using Vermunt's Learning Pattern Model

*Gert Vanthournout, Vincent Donche, David Gijbels, and Peter Van Petegem*

### INTRODUCTION

Over the last few decades, a lot of research effort has been invested in exploring how students learn in higher education, what factors influence these processes, and whether these processes evolve over time or not. This research stems from a variety of research traditions (Biggs, 1993; Entwistle & McCune, 2004) and has evolved in different directions. The research field of interest here is that of the 'Students' Approaches to Learning' tradition (the SAL-tradition). Research in this tradition generally focuses on how students perceive their own study processes or learning strategies (Biggs, 2001; Schmeck, 1988). Some of the internationally acclaimed models in this tradition are based on the work by John Biggs and colleagues (Biggs, 2003) or by Noël Entwistle and colleagues (Entwistle & Ramsden, 1983), and more recently the framework on learning patterns developed by Jan Vermunt and colleagues (Vermunt & Verloop, 1999; Vermunt & Vermetten, 2004).

The latter model is used as the central framework for the research presented in this chapter. The aim of this chapter is more specifically to address the issues of stability and variability of learning in higher education by systematically reviewing longitudinal studies using the learning-pattern model and its accompanying Inventory of Learning Styles (ILS). This model was chosen as it has proven to be psychometrically sound (Boyle, Duffy, & Dunleavy, 2003; Coffield, Moseley, Hall, & Ecclestone, 2004), and provides an integrative framework by combining cognitive, metacognitive, and motivational aspects of learning (Vermunt, 1996). Moreover, the model takes into account dimensions that indicate problems in the learning process, such as students' lack of regulation. The chapter firstly describes the theoretical framework on learning patterns; secondly, the results of the systematic review on longitudinal research using this model are presented; and finally, conclusions are drawn, gaps in the current research are identified, and perspectives for future research are provided.

## THEORETICAL FRAMEWORK

### Learning Patterns

In his original framework, Vermunt (1996) introduced the notion of 'learning style' as an attempt to provide a more comprehensive and integrated account of learning by bringing together four different aspects of learning, namely: cognitive processing strategies, regulation strategies, conceptions of learning, and orientations to learning (Vermunt, 1998; Vermunt & Vermetten, 2004). Each of these components is comprised of several learning dimensions as is shown in Table 6.1. Utilizing factor analysis, Vermunt identified four learning styles that integrate dimensions from the different learning components: an *undirected style*, a *reproduction-directed style*, a *meaning-directed style*, and an *application-directed style*. Because the notion of learning styles is mostly associated with invariant personality characteristics and a more trait-like view on learning, Vermunt and colleagues started using the more neutral term 'learning patterns' in order to account for the modifiability of students' learning styles (Vermunt & Minnaert, 2003; Vermunt & Vermetten, 2004). The term 'learning patterns' will be used throughout this chapter.

### The Inventory of Learning Styles

The Inventory of Learning Styles (ILS) was devised to assess these four learning patterns and their related dimensions. This self-report

*Table 6.1*  Learning Components, Learning Dimensions, and Learning Patterns

|  | Meaning-directed | Reproduction-directed | Application-directed | Undirected |
|---|---|---|---|---|
| *Cognitive processing strategies* | Deep processing *Relating and structuring *Critical processing | Stepwise processing *Analyzing *Memorizing | Concrete processing | Little processing activities |
| *Regulation strategies* | Self-regulation | External regulation | Self-/External regulation | Lack of regulation |
| *Learning orientations* | Personal interest | Self-test oriented Certificate oriented | Vocation oriented | Ambivalent |
| *Conceptions of learning* | Construction of knowledge | Intake of knowledge | Use of knowledge | Cooperative learning Stimulating education |

*Note:* Based on Vermunt and Vermetten (2004).

questionnaire originally consisted of 120 statements, scored on a five-point Likert scale. It generated sixteen main and four subscales variables: four processing strategies, three regulation strategies, five conceptions of learning, and four learning orientations. In most studies using the ILS, only the sixteen main scales are used. Since the first development of the ILS, several authors have developed adaptations to the original questionnaire (e.g., Donche & Van Petegem, 2008; Lindblom-Ylänne & Lonka, 1999).

## Similarities and Differences with Approaches to Learning

It would be restrictive to dwell on the learning patterns without making reference to the related concept of approaches to learning. Generally, an approach to learning is described as how students perceive themselves going about learning in a specific learning situation. A distinction is usually made between a deep and a surface approach to learning (Biggs, 2003; Entwistle & Ramsden, 1983). The former is associated with students' intentions to understand and to engage in meaningful learning and using strategies that are appropriate for creating such meaning. The latter refers to students engaging in learning in an inappropriate, superficial way, based on motives or intentions that are extrinsic to the real purpose of the task (Biggs, 2001; Entwistle, 1991).

Although different terms are used to describe learning, similarities between both frameworks seem apparent at first sight, as also indicated by Vermunt (1998). Therefore, some authors have explicitly drawn conceptual lines between the deep learning approach and (parts of) the meaning-directed and application-directed patterns by Vermunt (Vermetten, Vermunt, & Lodewijks, 2001). Others have pointed to theoretical similarities between the surface approach and the reproduction-directed (Vermunt & Minnaert, 2003) or undirected patterns, respectively (Hoeksema, 1995). Richardson (2004), however, warns that conceptual similarities do not necessary result in high correlations between scales in instruments based on each model. In any case, from a viewpoint of high-quality learning, the meaning-directed and application-directed learning patterns or deep approach to learning are regarded as more desirable than the reproduction-directed and undirected pattern or surface approach (Vermunt & Vermetten, 2004).

## Theoretical Stance on Change and Stability in Learning Patterns

In the wider debate as to whether the way students learn is predominantly a 'state' (process or action) or a 'trait' (personal characteristic), the learning-pattern framework takes an in-between position. On the one hand, the model states that students have general preferences in learning or usual ways to go about learning (Vermunt, 1998), whereas, on the other hand, it acknowledges that students' learning processes can be influenced by the learning environment (Vermetten, Vermunt, & Lodewijks, 2002). In these viewpoints, Vermunt and colleagues concur with other models in the SAL-tradition. In addition, however, the Vermunt model also theorizes that some aspects of learning, such as learning conceptions or orientations, are more prone to change and partially regulate the other, more changeable aspects of learning, such as processing strategies or regulation strategies (Vermunt, 1998; Vermetten, Vermunt, & Lodewijks, 1999a).

## Research Aim: Empirical Evidence from Longitudinal Studies

Surprisingly, most findings on the changeability of learning stem from cross-sectional data (e.g., Vermetten, Vermunt, & Lodewijks, 1999b, 2002). Longitudinal research designs, however, provide the possibility to explore this subject more thoroughly (Bijleveld, van der Kamp, & Mooijaart, 1998). Although the plea for more longitudinal designs in learning styles research has been issued over twenty years ago (e.g., Watkins & Hattie 1985), not many actual studies have been undertaken in the SAL-tradition (Gordon & Debus, 2002; Wilson & Fowler, 2005). The current study aims at providing a systematic review of the longitudinal research that applied the learning-pattern model. The following research questions are addressed: (1) Do students' learning patterns or their constituting dimensions evolve throughout higher education and if yes, in what way? (2) What contextual and individual factors are found to be related to these developments?

## METHOD

### Criteria for Inclusion and Search Procedures

The SAL-tradition is characterized by a tangle of related and partially overlapping concepts, sometimes leading to a misuse of terminology. Therefore, a range of key words was used for the literature search. It was decided to use the key words 'learning strategies', 'approaches to learning/studying', 'study approaches', 'learning orientations', 'processing strategies', 'learning patterns', and 'learning styles' in combination with 'longitudinal' and 'higher education'. No date restrictions were applied.

For a study to be included in the research synthesis, the following criteria had to be met:

- systematic report on the gathering and analysis of empirical data;

- explicit reference to learning-pattern framework as a research model and/or use (a part of) the ILS;
- students in higher education as research participants;
- data gathering on students' learning with the same students for at least two times and with an interval of at least five months (one semester);
- at least one research question on the development of learning.

Between January and September 2009, the electronic databases ERIC, Academic Search Elite, E-journals, and PsycINFO were searched. This resulted in ninety-seven citations, with considerable overlap between search results for different keywords. After cross-referencing the results and assessing the abstracts with the inclusion criteria in mind, nine studies were retained. In addition, review articles and theoretical overviews were consulted. Studies were also sought after by going through the references of each of the articles, starting with the most recent one (snowball method). Google Scholar was used to search the Internet and to look for research that cited the studies from the initial searches (using the 'cited in' function in Google Scholar). Finally, particular authors were contacted to provide studies that were hard to find. These additional searches yielded five unique, new studies. In one case, two different versions of the same study were found (Vermetten, Lodewijks, & Vermunt, 1997; Vermetten et al., 1999b). For this review, this study was considered only once. Two studies (Coertjens, Donche, & Van Petegem, 2009; Donche, Coertjens, & Van Petegem, in press) applied different data-analysis techniques to the same data. Only complementary results from these studies will be treated separately. In the end, thirteen articles were included in our analysis, investigating a total of fifteen cohorts.

## Synthesizing the Studies

The next step involved ordering and then synthesizing information with which the studies could be compared. This was extracted from the selected articles (see the synthesis portrayed in Table 6.2). The following information was included: first author and the year of publication; study domain; number of subjects; focus of the study; variables; number of measurements; duration; data-analysis techniques; main findings; and reported effect sizes.

The focus of each study identified was coded as follows: studies concerning a specific course unit or module were categorized as course-specific (CS), whereas research on an entire course or curriculum was labeled as general (G). Outcomes were coded as follows: significant increases in scores on learning-pattern dimensions were coded with a +, significant decreases were labeled with a −, and not-significant changes are not reported. To label the magnitude of reported effect sizes, conventional cutoffs were used. $D$ values of 0.2, 0.5, and 0.8 were interpreted as small-, medium-, and large-effect sizes, respectively, whereas for $\eta^2$, cutoffs of 0.01, 0.06, and 0.14 were applied (Green & Salskind, 2003).

*Table 6.2* Literature Matrix

| | Study | Domain | N | Focus Variables | Measurements | Duration | Analysis | Findings | Effect sizes |
|---|---|---|---|---|---|---|---|---|---|
| 1 | Busato et al. (1998) | Psychology | S1: 32 S2: 26 | G | Learning patterns | 23 | 1 year 2 years | Paired sample t-tests Repeated-measures MANOVA | Study 2: Meaning oriented + | Small |
| 2 | Coertjens et al. (2009) | 8 professional bachelor programs | 254 | G | Processing strategies Regulation strategies Initial learning pattern | 3 | 3 years | (Multivariate) multilevel analysis | Deep processing + Self-regulation + Lack of regulation – | |
| 3 | Donche et al. (submitted) | 8 professional bachelor programs | 254 | G | Processing strategies Regulation strategies Learning conceptions Initial learning pattern | 3 | 3 years | Repeated-measures MANOVA Paired sample t-tests | Relating and structuring + Critical processing + Memorizing – Concrete processing + Self-regulation + External regulation – Lack of regulation – Intake – Construction + Stimulating education – | |

*continued*

*Table 6.2 continued*  Literature Matrix

| Study | Domain | N | Focus Variables | Measure-ments | Duration | Analysis | Findings | Effect sizes |
|---|---|---|---|---|---|---|---|---|
| 4  Donche & Van Petegem (2009) | Teacher education | 236 | G | Processing strategies Regulation strategies Learning conceptions Initial learning pattern | 2 | 3 years | Paired sample t-tests Effect sizes | Deep processing + Concrete processing + Self regulation + Lack of regulation – Intake – Construction + Stimulating education – | Medium Large Medium Small Large Small Small |
| 5  Donche (2005) | Teacher education | 115 | G | Processing strategies Regulation strategies Learning orientations Learning conceptions | 2 | 8 months | Paired sample t-tests | Deep processing + Concrete processing + Self regulation + | |
| 6  Nieminen et al.(2004) | Pharmacy | 66 | G | Regulation strategies Learning conceptions | 2 | 3 years | Repeated-measures ANOVA Effect sizes | Intake – External regulation – Lack of regulation – | Medium Medium Medium |

*continued*

Table 6.2 *continued*  Literature Matrix

| Study | Domain | N | Focus Variables | Measure-ments | Duration | Analysis | Findings | Effect sizes |
|---|---|---|---|---|---|---|---|---|
| 7 Marambe (2007) | Medical education | S1: 144 S2: 92 | G | Processing strategies Regulation strategies Learning orientations Learning conceptions | 2 | 9 months 20 months | Paired sample t-test | Relating and structuring – (S1) Critical processing – (S1) Memorizing – (S1 + S2) Analyzing – (S1 + S2) Self regulation – (S1 + S2) External regulation (S2) Lack of regulation + (S1) – (S2) Construction – (S2) Intake – (S2) Use – (S2) Stimulating education + (S1) – (S2) Personal interest – (S1 + S2) Self-test – (S2) Vocation – (S2) Ambivalent + (S1) | |
| 8 Severiens et al. (2001) | Tertiary technical colleges | 271 | G | Processing strategies Regulation strategies | 3 | 9 months | Repeated-measures ANOVA | Stepwise processing – Deep processing + Concrete processing + External regulation – Self regulation + | |

*continued*

*Table 6.2 continued*  Literature Matrix

| Study | Domain | N | Focus | Variables | Measure-ments | Duration | Analysis | Findings | Effect sizes |
|---|---|---|---|---|---|---|---|---|---|
| 9 Smith et al. (2007) | Pharmacy | 521 | CS | Learning patterns | 2 | 5 months | Repeated-measures ANOVA | Meaning oriented – / Reproduction oriented – / Application directed – | |
| 10 Stromsø et al. (2004) | Medicine | 61 | CS | Regulation strategies Learning conceptions | 2 | 5 months | Paired sample t-test | No significant changes | |
| 11 Van der Veken et al. (2009) | Medicine | S1: 34 S2: 30 | G | Processing strategies Regulation strategies Learning orientations Curriculum type | 3 | 3 years | Paired sample t-test Repeated measures ANOVA Effect sizes | Structuring + (S2 only) / Critical processing + / Expressing + / Relating + / Vocation orientation + | Small / Medium / Small / Medium / Medium |
| 12 Vermetten et al. (1999b) | Economy Law Social sciences Arts | 276 | G | Processing strategies Regulation strategies Learning orientations Learning conceptions Departments | 2 | 2 years | Test-retest correlations Paired sample t-tests Effect sizes | Deep processing + / Concrete processing + / Self-regulation + / Certificate orientation – / Vocational orientation + / Personal interest + / Intake – | Small / Small / Small / Small / Small / Small / Small |
| 13 Vermunt & Minnaert (2003) | Social sciences | 244 | G | Processing strategies Regulation strategies Learning orientations Learning conceptions | 2 | 9 months | Effect sizes | Deep processing + / Concrete processing + / Stepwise processing + / Self-regulation + / Intake – | Small / Small / Small / Small / Small |

RESULTS

## Change and Stability

In researching change and stability in learning, studies took different perspectives, both in the focus and duration of the research and in the learning components they explored. Half of the studies investigated the development of learning over a period of one year or longer (one year or more = six studies, less than one year = six studies). One study combined both time frames (study 7). Research predominantly focused on general changes in learning (G = eleven studies) using two measurements in time (two moments = eight studies; three moments = four studies; combination = one study). Eleven studies explored changes in some or all learning dimensions, whereas only two investigated changes in complete learning patterns.

### Change and Stability in Learning Dimensions

Of the studies investigating changes in learning dimensions, mostly applied are paired sample *t* tests (studies 4, 5, 7, 10, 12) or repeated measures of analysis of variance (in studies 3, 6, 8, 11). In one case, a multilevel approach was carried out (study 2).

All studies on developments in deep *processing strategies* report a significant increase in this strategy (studies 2, 4, 5, 8, 12). In addition, with three cohorts of students a significant increase in the subscales of the deep processing dimensions was found (studies 3, 11). Only one single study, using first-year students, reported a significant decrease in both the relating and structuring and the critical processing scales (study 7). This seems to be in line with the results of a recent study (Donche et al., in press), based on three measurement moments, indicating that the increase in deep processing occurs predominantly in the senior years of higher education. Concrete processing strategies are found to increase in most of the studies (5/7; studies 3, 4, 5, 8, 12), whereas not a single study reports a decrease in this scale. Most studies on stepwise processing (0/7) or its subscales (2/5; study 11) reported no significant changes. A study by Severiens, Ten Dam, and Van Hout Wolters (2001), however, found a significant decrease in stepwise processing strategies, whereas Marambe (2007) reported significant decreases in the subscales for stepwise processing both with first- and third-year students. Donche and Van Petegem (2009), however, found this decrease only with senior students.

Eleven studies explored developments in *regulation strategies*. Five of these studies showed a significant increase in self-regulation, whereas only one reported a decrease, albeit with two cohorts (study 7). Most studies (7/11; studies 2, 4, 5, 8, 10, 11, 12) found no significant changes in external regulation strategies, whereas not a single increase in this strategy was reported. A small majority of the research (6/11; studies 5, 8, 10, 11, 12) found no significant changes in lack of regulation, whereas results of four studies indicated a decrease in this scale (studies 3, 4, 6, 7). Coertjens and colleagues (2009) found this decrease to be stronger in the senior years. In one study, again with 'freshmen', a significant increase was reported (study 7).

Eight studies explored the development of students' *learning conceptions,* although not all studies incorporated all of the constituting scales. Nieminen, Lindblom-Ylänne, and Lonka (2004) more specifically used only the scales that investigated the concept of learning as the intake or the construction of knowledge. Predominantly, scales showed no significant changes, with one exception. A majority of studies (5/8; studies 3, 4, 6, 7, 12) found that students endorsed the view of learning as the intake of knowledge significantly less throughout higher education. This was, however, rarely combined with an increase in other conceptions such as learning as constructing (2/8; studies 3, 4) or using knowledge (0/8). Some studies (3/8; studies 3, 4, 7) also found students' need for stimulating education to decrease over time.

Six studies questioned students on *learning orientations.* Similar to learning conceptions, few significant changes were found. Only a significant increase in vocation orientation was reported in half of the studies (studies 11, 12).

### Change and Stability in Learning Patterns

Two studies investigated the development of *learning patterns.* Busato, Prins, Elshout, and Hamaker (1998) only found one significant trend across a period of two years, namely an increase of the meaning-directed pattern. However, the results of this study have to be interpreted with caution because of the small sample sizes used in this study ($N < 40$). Smith and colleagues (2007) explored the development of learning patterns with four cohorts over a period of one year using a cross-sectional, repeated measures design. Meaning-directed and reproduction-directed scores declined significantly in the sample of the first-year students. There were no significant changes in the students' scores on any of the learning patterns for the students enrolled in the second year. For students in years three and four, scores on the application-directed pattern declined significantly over time. In contrast to the previous study, the results of this research did not appear to provide evidence of any significant developments towards a deeper way of learning.

### Practical Relevance of Changes Investigated Through Effect Sizes

Six studies report effect sizes to investigate the practical significance of changes (studies 1, 4, 6, 11, 12, 13). Results indicate that, apart from the studies by Donche and Van Petegem (2009), Van der Veken, Valcke, De Maeseneer, and Derese (2009), and Nieminen and colleagues (2004), most effect sizes were small. The outcomes of the first study stated medium-effect sizes for deep processing strategies and self-regulation strategies and even large-effect sizes for concrete processing and intake of knowledge (Donche & Van Petegem, 2009). The second study reported medium effects for critical processing, relating, and vocation orientation (Van der Veken et al., 2009), whereas Nieminen and colleagues (2004) found a medium-effect size for external regulation. No particular learning dimension comes out on the right side across all these studies.

## Conclusions on Change and Stability of Learning

Based on the results of these thirteen studies, it can be concluded that students' learning patterns do change throughout higher education and that students predominantly evolve toward a more meaning-oriented or application-oriented way of learning and away from an undirected pattern. From the viewpoint of high-quality learning, these results are promising. However, it also has to be mentioned that, despite promising results for the nature of change in learning, reported effect sizes in most studies only seem to indicate a small to moderate impact.

Outcomes of these studies also predominantly support the theoretical learning-pattern model as learning conceptions and orientations appear to be less prone to change. However, studies investigating learning developments over a longer period of time (more than one year) show that even these components can change. For instance, students became more vocation-oriented throughout higher education.

It also has to be noted that some learning and regulation strategies, such as stepwise processing and especially external regulation, seem highly resilient to changes, especially in the first year of higher education. These results point towards the functional value of these strategies, be it as crucial and necessary strategies throughout all of higher education or as a survival strategy in the freshmen year. Some evidence for both explanations could be found in our review.

On the one hand, some studies found no decline in stepwise processing or only in the memorizing subscale. It might therefore be oversimplifying to treat stepwise processing strategies as solely a superficial way of learning, as has also been stated by Haggis (2003). Vermetten and colleagues (2001), for instance, suggest that the adoption of stepwise strategies might also reflect the hardworking, conscientious side of the study process in higher education. Others argue that students need to combine both insights and the skill to thoroughly process large quantities of information to be successful in higher education (Donche & van Petegem, 2009; Meyer & Shanahan, 2003). However, some authors have pointed towards factors in the learning environment and foremost to assessment practices to explain why these strategies are maintained (for an overview, see Kyndt, Baeten, Struyven, & Dochy, 2009).

On the other hand, however, some studies in our review reported a decline in stepwise processing in the senior years, indicating that, at least for some students, memorizing might be a survival strategy to cope with the uncertainty of new (learning) situations (Gijbels, Coertjens, Vanthournout, Struyf, & Van Petegem, 2009). Once these students are accustomed to the new learning environments, they will adapt their learning patterns to its expectations. Additional studies using more measurement moments over a longer period of time could provide a more decisive answer on this point.

Mastering and adapting to expectations of changing learning environments might also explain why students gradually less endorse the view of learning as solely the intake of knowledge. It might, however, take more time for the 'new' learning strategies to root in and change students' learning conceptions towards a more constructive view on learning. Alternatively, parallel to the fact that students perceive both deep and stepwise strategies as crucial, they could also be developing a 'moderate' or 'mixed' conception of learning as the combination of first taking in a knowledge base and then applying this or constructing new meaning with it. It would be interesting to investigate this hypothesis, for instance through qualitative research.

To summarize, the studies in our review mostly confirmed the theoretical learning pattern as developed by Vermunt (1998). However, the model might be partially amended by the aforementioned differences in changeability *within* the learning components. It seems that the boundaries of change and stability not only run between but also across learning components.

Finally, it is noteworthy that learning patterns as a whole seem more resilient to change. This is possibly due to the fact that the notion is a compound concept, in which more stable components mask evolutions in changeable aspects, possibly rendering it difficult to pinpoint why expected changes do not occur. This might explain why a striking number of studies in our review opted to incorporate the learning dimensions instead of the entire range of learning patterns. Therefore, for the future, the value of concept of learning *patterns* might predominantly lie in the fact that it outlines relations between learning components, rather than in the fact that it subsumes these components under four higher order concepts, as initially defined by Vermunt (1998).

## Relationship with Personal and Contextual Factors

### Relationship with Personal Factors

Although there is some research on the relationship between learning dimensions and student characteristics (e.g., overviews by Kyndt et al., 2009; Richardson, 1994), there are very few studies on the impact of those characteristics on the development of learning (Vanthournout, Donche,

Gijbels, & Van Petegem, 2009; Wilson & Fowler, 2005). Only three studies have attempted to integrate student characteristics by taking their initial learning patterns into account and exploring differential developments in learning for different patterns (studies 2, 3, 4).

Using cluster-analysis techniques, all studies identified three subgroups of students with similar learning patterns, namely a reproductive/undirected pattern, a flexible pattern, and a meaning-oriented pattern. Subsequently, analyses were carried out on the learning-pattern dimensions for each of the clusters to investigate whether differential effects for these subgroups occurred. All three studies agree students' initial learning patterns evolve differently throughout higher education, although they also acknowledge that all subgroups generally seem to evolve towards a more meaning-oriented way of learning.

## Relationship with Contextual Factors

Parallel to findings on the personal factors, very few studies using the learning-pattern model explicitly incorporate contextual factors or investigate their relationship with learning patterns to search for reasons why students' learning dimensions or patterns change. Only two studies try to empirically shed some light on factors in the learning environment influencing the development of processing and regulation strategies (studies 11, 12).

In a conference paper, preceding the article published in 1999 (Vermetten et al., 1999b), Vermetten and colleagues (1997) explored the development of learning dimensions within several departments. Results indicated some differences in learning-patterns development between these courses. All other studies in this review were set in a single educational context or no attempts were made to compare between courses.

Generally, studies using the Vermunt model report little detail on the educational context in which they were set. Only Van der Veken and colleagues (2009) explored the impact of an innovative medical curriculum—centered within a more integrated and contextual approach—on the students' learning patterns. They found out that students in the new curriculum were significantly better in structuring and using resources in their studies than their counterparts in the previous year. They also exhibited less lack of regulation from the third year on. All other studies in the review implicitly seem to assume that the learning environments students experienced during their investigation did not differ from the 'usual learning environments' students come across when progressing through higher education.

## Conclusions about Influencing Factors

Based on the studies in our review, we can conclude that only little is known about the factors influencing learning-pattern development. The scarce studies looking into this question pointed towards differential effects for student characteristics (initial learning patterns) and contextual factors (major, quality of the learning environment), but due to the limited number of studies, no (strong) conclusions can be drawn at this point. More research is certainly needed on this topic.

A possible explanation for this lack of research might be that the learning-pattern model's strong point lies in mapping the general and complex development of learning across and apart from learning environments or study years. Pinpointing specific factors in the learning environment that influence this development—as has been done with the approaches to learning (e.g., Biggs, 2003; Kyndt et al., 2009)—might prove to be a daunting task.

However, one could hypothesize that there are student factors that influence learning that are not context-dependent, such as students' personality traits or socioeconomic state. In a similar way, contextual factors could be considered. The school's general culture or its assessment policy, for instance, or the faculty's general views on innovating teaching methods or the predominant teaching style in an institution could all be conceived as factors that influence the way students go about their learning, independent of specific course modules. Up to now, the influence of these factors remains mostly underexposed in the approaches to learning research. The general and complex nature of the Vermunt model could be well suited in 'capturing' these course-independent influences.

## GAPS AND FUTURE DIRECTIONS

Longitudinal research on the development of learning patterns is still in its infancy, as can be witnessed in the fact that since the development of the learning-patterns model in the nineties, only thirteen longitudinal studies were executed. Half of these were published or presented after 2005, possibly indicating a growing interest in the use of this model for longitudinal research. The nature of research questions that these studies explored has been subject to change as well as the methodologies adopted. For instance, it has become apparent that scholars using the Vermunt model are only just starting to look into the relationship with contextual and personal factors. Hopefully, in the future, more quasi-experimental designs and studies across longer periods of time will be carried out.

With regard to data-analysis techniques, there seems to be a tendency towards more complex designs over a longer period with multiple measurement moments and more advanced techniques such as multilevel analysis. There is, however, still room for methodological improvements. For instance, whereas all but one study (Van der Veken et al., 2009) provides information on nonresponse, none explicitly tries to tackle the question of 'selection effects' or dropout throughout the duration of the study. There is in most studies, however, a significant group of students who participated in the pretest but not in the posttest. Simply ignoring the learning patterns of students who did not participate in the posttest, whatever their reason may be, might result in a partial picture. Finally, some of the studies based conclusions on a relatively small group of respondents (less than fifty). This raises questions around the validity of the conclusions and should be addressed more explicitly.

Insight into students' learning patterns could almost certainly benefit from more qualitative and mixed-method designs. These, too, might shed more light on the question: 'Why do (parts) of students' learning patterns change and others remain stable?' It is striking that the SAL-tradition in general and Vermunt's model in particular are both founded on qualitative research (Vermunt, 1996), yet make so little use of it in contemporary studies.

In the end, the question needs to be raised: 'Did our study really review longitudinal studies?' This depends, of course, upon how longitudinal research is defined and what criteria are applied. This in itself remains a scientific discussion (Menard, 2002). Narrow definitions point towards criteria such as 'repeated-measurements' (at least three waves) and 'an extended period of time' (Singer & Willet, 2003). Other authors provide a broader definition. According to Menard (2002), for instance, longitudinal research is characterized by (a) data collection for two or more time periods, (b) in which the subjects are the same, and (c) the analysis involves some comparison between the collected data. Although we used this broader definition for this review, it should not avert researchers from setting more stringent criteria for their studies. It has to be noted that some of the most recent studies (studies 2, 3, 11) have started to pay more attention to this vulnerability by incorporating more than two waves in their data collection. This certainly seems a way forward in understanding learning-pattern development.

To conclude, the statement that Watkins and Hattie (1985) made over twenty years ago regarding the learning-styles field that 'longitudinal research is scarce' generally still holds true for learning patterns, although we might now add that preliminary results indicate that '(aspects) of learning patterns are changeable' and 'students in higher education generally evolve towards more meaning-oriented or application-oriented learning patterns'. We hope that this chapter has succeeded in providing some initial insight in developmental trends in learning patterns and by doing this will inspire others to carry out more longitudinal research in the learning-styles field.

## BIBLIOGRAPHY

Biggs, J. (1993). What do inventories of students' learning processes really measure? A theoretical review and clarification. *British Journal of Educational Psychology, 63,* 3–19.

Biggs, J. (2001). Enhancing learning: a matter of style or approach. In R.J. Sternberg & L.F. Zhang (Eds.), *Perspectives on Thinking, Learning, and Cognitive Styles* (pp. 73–103). London: Lawrence Erlbaum Associates.

Biggs, J. (2003). *Teaching for Quality Learning at University.* Buckingham: The Society for Research into Higher Education.

Bijleveld, C., van der Kamp, L., & Mooijaart, A. (1998). *Longitudinal Data Analysis: Design, Models and Methods.* London: Sage Press.

Boyle, E., Duffy, T., & Dunleavy, K. (2003). Learning styles and academic outcome: the validity and utility of Vermunt's inventory of learning styles in a British higher education setting. *British Journal of Educational Psychology, 73,* 267–290.

Busato, V., Prins, F., Elshout, J., & Hamaker, C. (1998). Learning styles: a cross-sectional and longitudinal study in higher education. *British Journal of Educational Psychology, 63,* 427–442.

Coertjens, C., Donche, V., & Van Petegem, P. (2009). A longitudinal view on the development of learning patterns throughout higher education. *Paper presented at the 14th annual conference of the European Learning Styles Information Network,* Bulle-en-Gruyère, June 17–19.

Coffield, F., Moseley, D., Hall, E., & Ecclestone, K. (2004). *Learning Styles and Pedagogy in Post-16 Education.* London: Learning and Skills Research Centre.

Donche, V. (2005). *Leren, onderwijzen en leren onderwijzen: onderzoek naar opvattingen en handelingen van studenten en docenten [Learning, Teaching and Learning how to Teach: Research into the Conceptions and Behaviour of Students and Teachers].* Antwerp: Academia Press.

Donche, V., Coertjens, L., & Van Petegem, P. (in press). The development of learning patterns throughout higher education. *Learning and Individual Differences.*

Donche, V., & Van Petegem, P. (2008). The validity and reliability of the short inventory of learning patterns. In E. Cools, H. Van den Broeck, C. Evans & T. Redmond (Eds.), *Style and Cultural Differences: How Can Organisations, Regions and Countries Take Advantage of Style Differences? Proceedings of the 13th Annual Conference of the European Learning Styles Information Network* (pp. 49-59). Gent, Belgium: Vlerick Leuven Gent Management School.

Donche, V., & Van Petegem, P. (2009). The development of learning patterns of student teachers: a cross-sectional and longitudinal study. *Higher Education, 57,* 463–475.

Entwistle, N. (1991). Approaches to learning and perceptions of the learning environment. *Higher Education, 22,* 205–227.

Entwistle, N., & McCune, V. (2004). The conceptual bases of study strategy inventories. *Educational Psychology Review, 16,* 325–345.

Entwistle, N., & Ramsden, P. (1983). *Understanding Student Learning.* London: Croom Helm.

Gijbels, D., Coertjens, L., Vanthournout, G., Struyf, E., & Van Petegem, P. (2009). Changing students' approaches to learning: a two-year study within a university teacher training course. *Educational Studies, 35,* 503–513.

Gordon, C., & Debus, R. (2002). Developing deep learning approaches and personal teaching efficacy within pre-service education context. *British Journal of Educational Psychology, 72,* 483–511.

Green, S., & Salskind, N. (2003). *Using SPSS for Windows and Macintosh.* Upper Saddle River, NJ: Prentice Hall.

Haggis, T. (2003). Constructing images of ourselves? A critical investigation into 'approaches to learning' research in higher education. *British Educational Research Journal, 29,* 89–104.

Hoeksema, L. (1995). *Learning Strategy as a Guide to Career Success in Organizations*. Leiden: DSWO Press.

Kyndt, E., Baeten, M., Struyven, K., & Dochy, F. (2009). Approaches to learning in higher education: from student and context to outcome. A review of research. *Paper presented at the biannual meeting of the European Association on Learning and Instruction*, Amsterdam, The Netherlands. August 25–29.

Lindblom-Ylänne, S., & Lonka, K. (1999) Individual ways of interacting with the learning environment are they related to study success? *Learning and Instruction, 9*, 118.

Marambe, K. (2007). *Patterns of Student Learning in Medical Education—A Sri Lankan Study in a Traditional Curriculum*. Unpublished doctoral dissertation, University of Maastricht, Maastricht, Netherlands.

Menard, S. (2002). *Longitudinal Research*. Thousand Oaks, CA: Sage.

Meyer, J.H.F., & Shanahan, M.P. (2003). Dissonant forms of 'memorising' and 'repetition'. *Studies in Higher Education, 28*, 5–20.

Nieminen, J., Lindblom-Ylänne, S., & Lonka, K. (2004). The development of study orientations and study success in students of pharmacy. *Instructional Science, 32*, 387–417.

Richardson, J. (1994). Mature students in higher education: I. A literature survey on approaches to learning. *Studies in Higher Education, 19*, 309–326.

Richardson, J. (2004). Methodological issues in questionnaire-based research on student learning in higher education. *Educational Psychology Review, 16*, 347–358.

Schmeck, R. (1988). An introduction to strategies and styles of learning. In R. Schmeck (Ed.), *Learning Strategies and Learning Styles* (pp. 3–20). New York: Plenum Press.

Severiens, B., Ten Dam, G., & Van Hout Wolters, B. (2001). Stability of processing and regulation strategies: two longitudinal studies on student learning. *Higher Education, 42*, 437–453.

Singer, J., & Willett, J. (2003). *Applied Longitudinal Data Analysis. Modelling Change and Event Occurrence*. Oxford: University Press.

Smith, L., Saine, B., Krass, I., Chen, T., Bosnic-Anticevich, S., & Sainsburry, E. (2007). Pharmacy students' approaches to learning in an Australian university. *American Journal of Pharmaceutical Education, 71*, 1–8.

Strømsø, H., Grøttum, P., & Hofgaard Lycke, K. (2004). Changes in student approaches to learning with the introduction of computer-supported problem-based learning. *Medical Education, 38*, 390–398.

Van der Veken, J., Valcke, M., De Maeseneer, J., & Derese, A. (2009). Impact of the transition from a conventional to an integrated contextual medical curriculum on students' learning patterns: a longitudinal study. *Medical Teacher, 31*, 433–441.

Vanthournout, G., Donche, V., Gijbels, D., & Van Petegem, P. (2009). Alternative data-analysis techniques in research on student learning: illustrations of a person-oriented and developmental perspectives. *Reflecting Education, 5*, 35–51.

Vermetten, Y., Lodewijks, H., & Vermunt, J. (1997). *Change and Stability in Learning Strategies During the First Two Years at the University*. Paper presented at the annual meeting of the American Educational Research Association, Chicago, March 24–28.

Vermetten, Y., Vermunt, J., & Lodewijks, H. (1999a). Consistency and variability of learning strategies in different university courses. *Higher Education, 37*, 1–21.

Vermetten, Y., Vermunt, J., & Lodewijks, H. (1999b). A longitudinal perspective on learning strategies in higher education: different viewpoints towards development. *British Journal of Educational Psychology, 69*, 221–242.

Vermetten, Y., Vermunt, J., & Lodewijks, H. (2001). The role of personality traits and goal orientations in strategy use. *Contemporary Educational Psychology, 26*, 149–170.

Vermetten, Y., Vermunt, J., & Lodewijks, H. (2002). Powerful learning environments? How do students differ in their response to instructional measures. *Learning and Instruction, 12*, 263–284.

Vermunt, J. (1996). Metacognitive, cognitive and affective aspects of learning styles and strategies: a phenomenographic analysis. *Higher Education, 31*, 25–50.

Vermunt, J. (1998). The regulation of constructive learning processes. *British Journal of Educational Psychology, 68*, 149–171.

Vermunt, J., & Minnaert, A. (2003). Dissonance in student learning patterns: when to revise theory? *Studies in Educational Evaluation, 28*, 49–61.

Vermunt, J., & Verloop, N. (1999). Congruence and friction between learning and teaching. *Learning and Instruction, 9*, 257–280.

Vermunt, J., & Vermetten, Y. (2004). Patterns in student learning: relationships between learning strategies, conceptions of learning and learning orientations. *Educational Psychology Review, 16*, 359–384.

Watkins, D., & Hattie, J. (1985). A longitudinal study of the approaches to learning of Australian tertiary students. *Human Learning, 4*, 127–141.

Wilson, K., & Fowler, J. (2005). Assessing the impact of learning environments on students' approaches to learning comparing conventional and action learning designs. *Assessment and Evaluation in Higher Education, 30*, 87–101.

# Part II
# Personal Diversity

Style Differences in Thinking,
Learning, and Knowledge Acquisition

# 7 Assessing the Distribution of Learning and Adaptive Styles in an MBA Program

*Richard E. Boyatzis and Charalampos Mainemelis*

## INTRODUCTION

Whether discovered through empirical study, personal reflection, or the musing of an educator as we ponder why different students respond to the same material in various ways, a common statement in higher education is that students learn in different ways. As the diversity of students in our MBA classes and programs increases (Friga, Bettis, & Sullivan, 2003), one consequence is that we can expect the diversity of their approaches to learning to increase. Therefore, to create an environment that enhances sustained learning of all or even most MBA students, we must engage a wider variety of teaching methods and pedagogy than the typical curriculum contains (Kolb & Kolb, 2005; Vermunt, Chap. 12 in this volume). Yet, a commonly used practice is to design curricula and deliver courses with a 'one size fits all' assumption (Kolb, Boyatzis, & Mainemelis, 2001).

Attempts at innovation in management education have come in frequent waves since Porter and McKibbin (1988) articulated the shortcomings of MBA graduates. Schools have experimented with competency-based or skill-building courses; integrated core curriculum; internationalization of the curriculum; information systems; ethics; service learning; action learning; and e-commerce. The objective is typically to increase the MBA's development of knowledge, capability, and attitudes that enable them to move toward their personal dreams, effectively serve and lead organizations, and contribute to society. As Pfeffer and Fong (2002) and Mintzberg (2004) reported, MBAs do not appear to be learning what they need to be effective managers and leaders. But to move beyond the self-justifying illusion that these innovations are effective, a question must be posed: are these innovations serving students with the diverse approaches to learning equally?

In this chapter we present data collected over a period of nine years from 1,358 full-time and part-time MBA students on their preferred learning styles and adaptive styles. Because there is no published, large-scale report of the distribution of learning and adaptive styles among MBA students, and especially their relation to salient selection and performance criteria like GMAT scores and GPA, we wanted to establish the empirical basis for the belief that students learn in different ways, even for the subset of students enrolled in an MBA program. Drawing on the results of our study, we discuss implications for the current curriculum design and pedagogy as well as the challenge of responding to the pluralism of learning and adaptive styles in graduate management education.

## STUDENTS LEARN IN DIFFERENT WAYS

Building on the previous works of Dewey, Piaget, and Lewin, David Kolb (1984) developed the Experiential Learning Theory (ELT) suggesting that a person learns through four primary modes, which represent the two dialectical tensions we experience in learning. One dialectical tension regards two ways of *grasping* experience: apprehension and comprehension. Kolb's theory tells us that we learn from Concrete Experience (CE) as the primary mode of apprehension, and Abstract Conceptualization (AC) as the primary mode of comprehension. The other dialectical tension is between extension and intention, two ways for *transforming* experience. Kolb claims that we learn from Active Experimentation (AE) as the primary mode of extension and Reflective Observation (RO) as the primary mode of intention (see Figure 7.1, and also Sharma & Kolb, Chap. 5 in this volume).

These modes form a recursive cycle that describes the learning process. When engaged in learning, a person moves through CE (i.e., experiencing and sensing) to RO (i.e., observing, reflecting upon the experience, and trying to make sense out of it). Then the learner moves through AC (i.e., building a model or framework with which to understand the phenomenon) to AE (i.e., trying or implementing some new thought or behavior to examine this framework or concept).

Thirty years of research on Kolb's experiential learning theory by many scholars has established that people prefer to learn through certain 'learning styles' (for an overview of 1,000 studies on ELT, see Kolb et al., 2001). This research shows that when people are using their preferred learning style they learn more effectively, are more excited and engaged, enjoy the process more, and apply the learning more than when using styles other than their preferred one (Lennick-Hall & Sanders, 1997).

Each of these learning styles is typically a combination of two or three of the primary modes mentioned earlier. There are four learning styles that specialize in two modes and underdevelop the other two. These learning styles, shown in Figure 7.1, are known as Accommodator, Diverger, Assimilator, and Converger. An Accommodator has a preferred learning style in which Active Experimentation and Concrete Experience are used as their primary sources of learning activity. Research has shown that people with this style learn better through hands-on experience, projects, feedback from peers, small-group discussions, active cooperation with other people, and active involvement in the task (i.e., internships, action projects, etc.; Kolb, 1984).

A Diverger uses Concrete Experience and Reflective Observation and learns better through careful observation, brainstorming, peer feedback, working with others, and personal experience. An Assimilator uses Reflective Observation and Abstract Conceptualization. People with this style learn better through logical analysis of ideas and facts, theory readings, case studies, creating or building theories and frameworks, books and lectures, and so forth. A Converger uses Abstract Conceptualization and Active Experimentation and, as research has shown, people with this style learn better through experimenting with new ideas, simulations, laboratory assignments, and practical application (Kolb, 1984, 1999; Kolb et al., 2001).

Sometimes a person integrates one of the dialectical dimensions of the learning process, therefore using three of the primary modes. This pattern of learning styles can be described in terms of a compass position—Northerner, Southerner, Easterner, and Westerner learning styles, as shown in Figure 7.1. In this way, a person using Active Experimentation, Concrete Experience, and Reflective Observation may be labeled a Northern learning style. Similarly, an Eastern learning style incorporates Concrete Experience, Reflective Observation, and Abstract Conceptualization. A Southern learning style incorporates Reflective Observation, Abstract Conceptualization, and Active Experimentation. A Western learning style incorporates Abstract Conceptualization, Active Experimentation, and Concrete Experience. These four second-order learning styles combine the characteristics of the two first-order styles (described earlier), which they integrate (Abbey, Hunt, & Weiser, 1985; Hunt, 1987; Sharma & Kolb, Chap. 5 in this volume). Another learning style describes those people who are balanced in their preferences, that is, they integrate all four modes of the learning process (Mainemelis, Boyatzis, & Kolb, 2002).

Kolb and his colleagues explored how people respond when faced with situations that do not arouse and engage their preferred learning style. In other words, they examined how people adapt to learning (Boyatzis & Kolb, 1993; Kolb, 1984; Kolb & Wolfe, 1981; Mainemelis et al., 2002). When placed in situations that emphasize certain modes in the way they stimulate engagement of people, offer cues and rewards, people may not be able to use their preferred learning style. Can they respond to the cues and stimuli in the situation? Can they adapt and be flexible in learning from the situation or are they inhibited or demotivated in such situations and therefore show an inflexibility to learn in this type of situation?

In addition to understanding a person's preferred learning style, we can more fully understand their capability and willingness to learn by also knowing about their adaptive styles which describe their learning flexibility and inflexibility. The adaptive styles carry the same names as the learning styles, but instead of measuring learning preference they measure the degree to which people change their preferred learning style to adapt to and extract learning from varied situations which pose different learning demands.

## Consequences of Graduate Students' Diverse Approaches to Learning

If students learn in a variety of ways, then the diversity of approaches will affect the degree of learning, and in particular the amount of sustained learning. In various studies, it has been shown that students do better (i.e., get better grades) and feel better about their academic experience (i.e., more content, more involved with their peers, and perceive the workload as lighter) when there is a congruence between their personal learning style and that promoted by the faculty and curriculum of the department in which they are studying (Kolb & Kolb, 2005; Lennick-Hall & Sanders, 1997). When there is lack of congruence between their personal learning style preference and that of the department, students tend to report more anomie, alienation, and shift closer to their preferred learning styles in activities following graduation, including in selection of majors for master's and other graduate work (Kolb, 1984).

Whereas management appears to involve all aspects of the learning cycle, certain management jobs appear to emphasize some learning styles over others. For example, an Accommodative learning style appears characteristic of people in sales and marketing management jobs, whereas a Divergent learning style appears characteristic of people in human resource management jobs. An Abstract learning style appears characteristic of people in finance management jobs, whereas a Convergent learning style appears characteristic of people in accounting management (Kolb, 1984). This is important given that research has shown that learning styles differentially affect the development of interpersonal, information, analytical, and behavioral skills in MBA programs (Mainemelis et al., 2002).

If MBA students have a variety of learning styles (i.e., preferences) and adaptive styles (i.e., learning flexibility and inflexibility), then the efficacy of various innovations, not to mention the original curriculum, will vary among the students as a function of their learning and adaptive styles (Boyatzis, Cowen, & Kolb, 1995). Assuming that 'one size fits all' in terms of learning styles may result in 'misdiagnosis' of a student as lacking seriousness or intellectual power when we are witnessing the negative impact of diverse approaches to learning. Following this logic, we would expect that the best design of curriculum and pedagogy to increase the sustained learning of the graduates would be one that addresses and engages the diverse approaches to learning of our MBA students (Kolb & Kolb, 2005).

On the other hand, there does appear to be a bias of faculty in research universities toward Assimilative learning styles (Kolb, 1984). In analyzing the emphasis of faculty members for each of their MBA courses, Boyatzis (1991) reported a bias toward Abstract and Reflective learning styles when the composite of the faculty emphasis and intent for all of the MBA courses were combined.

## Hypotheses

On the basis of our experiences in teaching and earlier studies we expect that, when compared with the normative standards of a large and diverse sample, the learning styles of the MBA students in our sample will show a high degree of pluralism (i.e., the sample will show all nine styles). We also expect that the sample will show a preference for AC and AE, which is common among graduate students. In addition, we expect that the sample will show an inflexibility toward learning in each of the four modes. A specific hypothesis is that one's preference for Abstract Conceptualization (AC) will correlate with one's verbal, quantitative, and total GMAT scores. Further, one's preference for abstract conceptualization will also correlate with one's MBA GPA.

## METHOD

An empirical study was designed to assess the pluralism of learning and adaptive styles among MBA students, as well as their relation to GMAT scores and MBA GPA. The study was part of a projected, fifty-year longitudinal research study of student learning, managerial careers, and lifelong competency development. For the purposes of the current study, we used data collected over a period of nine years from 1,358 MBA full-time and part-time students at a Midwestern private research university.

## Sample

Due to differences in the program duration and work experiences during the MBA, we divided our sample into full-time and part-time students. The full-time sample consisted of 627 students who entered the MBA program between 1990 and 1997. The average age at entry into the program was 26.7, 65% of the students were male, and 20% were nonnative English speakers. The students completed a battery of learning instruments during a required MBA course called Managerial Assessment and Development (Boyatzis et al., 1995; Boyatzis & Saatcioglu, 2008; Boyatzis, Stubbs, & Taylor, 2002). At the conclusion of the required course, all students are asked to give their written consent for their data to be used in various research studies. An average of 89% of the students each year gave their permission for continued use of their data in research.

For those who granted permission to use their information in research, random samples were studied at graduation. For this subset of the sample, other data were collected including their final MBA GPA. This subset sample consisted of 230 full-time students who entered the program between 1990 and 1994, and graduated between 1992 and 1995. The average entering age of this subset of the sample was 26.8, and 62% of them were male.

The part-time sample consisted of 704 students who entered the MBA program between 1990 and 1994. The average age was 27.7, 32% of the students were female, and less than 1% were nonnative English speakers. For the samples of students studied at graduation, we also collected MBA GPA data. This subset sample consisted of eighty-four students who entered the part-time program between 1990 and 1993, and graduated between 1991 and 1996. The average entering age of this subset of the sample was 27.7, and 32% of them were female.

## Measures

Demographic data, GMAT scores, and MBA GPA were obtained from the students' files at the university. Data about students' learning and adaptive styles were collected with the Learning Style Inventory (LSI; Kolb, 1999) and the Adaptive Style Inventory (ASI; Boyatzis & Kolb, 1993; Kolb, 1984) in the required MBA course described earlier.

### *Learning Style Inventory*

The Learning Style Inventory (LSI; Kolb, 1999) is the first and most widely used learning styles instrument in research and practice. It consists of twelve questions which ask individuals to force-rank their preferred modes of learning: Conceptualizing (AC), Experiencing (CE), Acting (AE), and Reflecting (RO). Another two scores measure one's relative preference for one or the other end of the two dialectical dimensions—Conceptualizing/Experiencing (AC-CE) and Acting/Reflecting (AE-RO).

Individual learning styles are determined based on the (AC-CE) and (AE-RO) scores. The lower third ($\leq$–1) of the (AC-CE) LSI normative sample distribution (Kolb, 1999) are people who show a preference toward CE, those in the upper third ($\geq$ 12) show a preference toward AC, whereas the middle third are balanced in their AC/CE preferences. Similarly, the lower third ($\leq$–1) of the (AE-RO) LSI normative sample distribution are people who show a preference toward RO, whereas the upper third ($\geq$ 12) show a preference for AE; the middle third consist of individuals who balance their preferences for AE and RO. A cross tabulation of the recoded variables (i.e., the AC-CE and AE-RO scores) divides the topographical LSI space into nine equal rectangular areas that correspond to the nine learning styles described earlier (Figure 7.1). For example, individuals with balanced preferences in both the AC/CE and AE/RO dimensions will score in the middle thirds of both the AC-CE and AE-RO scores, and, after the cross tabulation, their scores will fall into the central rectangle which belongs to the balanced learning style (see Figure 7.1). To determine the learning styles of the students in our samples we recoded into the thirds their AC-CE and AE-RO scores using the cut-points of the LSI normative sample distributions (i.e., lowest to –1, 0 to 11, and

12 to highest). In this way, we are analyzing the pluralism of learning styles among MBA students with the pluralism of styles found in a large, national, and ethnically diverse sample.

### Adaptive Style Inventory

The Adaptive Style Inventory (ASI; Boyatzis & Kolb, 1993; Kolb, 1984) uses a paired-comparison method to rank learning preferences for the four learning modes in eight personalized learning contexts. The ASI measures adaptive flexibility in learning, the degree to which one changes learning style to respond to different learning situations in their life. The ASI was designed to be theoretically commensurate with the LSI whereas methodologically diverse in order to reduce spurious common method variance among the two instruments (Kolb et al., 2001; Mainemelis et. al., 2002).

Like the LSI, the ASI produces four mode scores (AC, CE, AE, RO) and two dimensional scores (AC-CE and AE-RO). As mentioned earlier, these six scores are comparable to the commensurate LSI scores (Mainemelis et al., 2002). More interestingly, however, the ASI also produces vector scores, which are used to compute the nine adaptive styles. In the ASI, individuals are invited to select eight personalized learning contexts, two for each of four diverse learning situations (i.e., valuing, thinking, deciding, and acting). For each one of these eight items, the respondents have to describe the way they adapt by selecting six sentences from six sets of paired sentences. Choice is limited to one sentence per pair (e.g., one should choose between "I rely on what feels right to me" and "I establish criteria for evaluating"). Because the paired sentences correspond to the dialectical learning modes (i.e., three pairs for AC/CE and three pairs for AE/RO), there are two possible vectors per dimension for each item. These vector scores are used to compute the nine adaptive styles. In this study, we used the two vector formulae introduced by Mainemelis and colleagues (2002) to compute the adaptive flexibility/inflexibility on the AC/CE and AE/RO dimensions. The two vector scores are normally distributed and their cross-tabulation produces nine equal areas in the topographical ASI space, corresponding to the nine adaptive styles.

### RESULTS

The mean LSI scores per program type, gender, and age are shown in Table 7.1. Part-time students show a significantly stronger preference for AC ($t = -4.42$, $p < 0.001$, power = 86%) and the AC end of the AC/CE dimension ($t = -5.34$, $p < 0.001$, power > 95%) than full-time students, whereas the latter show a significantly stronger preference for CE ($t = 4.62$, $p < 0.001$, power > 88%) than part-time students. Male students have a significantly stronger preference for AC ($t = -6.60$, $p < 0.001$, power > 99%) and the AC end of the AC/CE dimension ($t$ = −5.95, $p$ < 0.001, power > 99%) than female students, whereas the latter show a significantly stronger preference for CE ($t$ = 3.26, $p$ < 0.01, power > 82%) than men. Women also have a significantly stronger preference for AE ($t$ = 3.58, $p$ < 0.001, power > 87%) than men. There were no significant differences between the two age groups. Further, there were no significant differences between program types, genders, and age groups in terms of their mean ASI scores.

The distribution of the 1,286 learning styles is shown in Figure 7.1. There is pluralism of styles among MBA students, but the distributions show a significant bias toward AC. In the full-time program, the percentage of students in each cell ranged from 7% to 16% (11.11% was the expected value for each cell). The chi-square statistic was significant ($\chi^2$ = 20.43, $N$ = 607, $df$ = 4, $p$ < 0.001), showing a significant bias toward the AC mode. Assimilators (16.3%), Southerners (13.8%), and Westerners (12.7%) are the most frequent styles among the full-time students, and Divergers (7.1%) are the least frequent. In the part-time program, the percentage of students in each cell ranged from 3% to 20%, and the chi-square test was significant ($\chi^2$ = 25.50, $N$ = 679, $df$ = 4, $p$ < 0.001). The most frequent styles in the part-time sample are the Southerner (19.7%), the Converger (16.6%) and the Assimilator (15.8%), with the Diverger style being the least frequent (3.4%).

The distribution of the 925 adaptive styles is also shown in Figure 7.1. Here too the results show a pluralism of styles, but also a stronger preference for AC. Most MBA students in the full-time and part-time programs have a Southerner (22% and 28%, respectively), Assimilator (20% and 18%), or Converger (16% and 19%) adaptive style, with Divergers (4% and 3%) and Easterners (6% and 4%) being the least frequent adaptive styles. In the full-time program, the percentage of students in each cell ranged from 4% to 20%, and the chi-square statistic was marginally significant ($\chi^2$ = 9.58, $N$ = 396, $df$ = 4, $p$ < 0.05). In the part-time program, the percentage of students in each cell ranged from 3% to 28%, and the chi-square was significant ($\chi^2$ = 19.45, $N$ = 529, $df$ = 4, $p$ < 0.001).

Analysis of the distribution suggests that there is pluralism of learning styles and adaptive styles among both the full-time and the part-time MBA students, but there is a strong bias for AC over CE which is more pronounced in the part-time sample. Thirty-eight percent in the full-time sample (53% in the part-time) have an AC learning preference, and only 26% (17%) have a CE preference, as shown in Figure 7.2. On the other hand, and contrary to our expectations, the samples appear balanced with regard to their AE and RO preferences: 32% and 34%, respectively, in the full-time sample, and 30% and 33% in the part-time sample.

Figure 7.2 also shows pluralism with regard to learning inflexibility. There is an important degree of inflexibility in the AE (30% of the full-time and 25% of the part-time students) and RO (33% and 38%, respectively) modes. As we predicted, learning inflexibility is much higher with regard to concrete learning: 58% of the full-time students and 65% of the part-time

*Table 7.1*   LSI and ASI Mean Scores per Program Type, Gender, and Age at Entry

| | Program | | Gender | | Entering age | |
|---|---|---|---|---|---|---|
| | Full-time | Part-time | Men | Women | < 27 | > 27 |
| *LSI scores* | (*n* = 607) | (*n* = 679) | (*n* = 865) | (*n* = 430) | (*n* = 682) | (*n* = 589) |
| Conceptualizing (AC) | 32.89 | 34.69 | 34.75 | 31.95 | 33.78 | 33.80 |
| Experiencing (CE) | 25.41 | 23.68 | 24.04 | 25.38 | 24.29 | 24.82 |
| Acting (AE) | 33.26 | 34.25 | 33.32 | 34.82 | 34.06 | 33.55 |
| Reflecting (RO) | 28.45 | 27.38 | 27.89 | 27.86 | 27.88 | 27.83 |
| AC-CE | 7.48 | 11.01 | 10.71 | 6.57 | 9.49 | 8.98 |
| AE-RO | 4.82 | 6.87 | 5.43 | 6.97 | 6.18 | 5.72 |
| *ASI scores* | (*n* = 396) | (*n* = 529) | (*n* = 627) | (*n* = 308) | (*n* = 504) | (*n* = 404) |
| Conceptualizing (AC) | 13.83 | 14.23 | 14.06 | 14.12 | 14.08 | 14.05 |
| Experiencing (CE) | 10.06 | 9.51 | 9.54 | 10.09 | 9.98 | 9.54 |
| Acting (AE) | 11.84 | 12.09 | 12.03 | 11.94 | 12.03 | 11.89 |
| Reflecting (RO) | 12.26 | 12.14 | 12.35 | 11.82 | 11.88 | 12.50 |
| AC-CE | 3.77 | 4.72 | 4.52 | 4.03 | 4.10 | 4.51 |
| AE-RO | −0.43 | −0.05 | −0.32 | 0.12 | 0.15 | −0.61 |

**CE**

| | | |
|---|---|---|
| Accommodators | Northerners | Divergers |
| LSI: FT: 65 (10.7%), PT: 65 (9.6%) | LSI: FT: 49 (8.1%), PT: 28 (4.1%) | LSI: FT: 43 (7.1%), PT: 23 (3.4%) |
| ASI: FT: 35 (8.8%), PT: 46 (8.7%) | ASI: FT: 30 (7.6%) PT: 25 (4.7%) | ASI: FT: 16 (4.0%), PT: 15 (2.8%) |

**AE**                                                                                                   **RO**

| | | |
|---|---|---|
| Westerners | Balanced | Easterners |
| LSI: FT: 77 (12.7%), PT: 97 (14.3%) | LSI: FT: 70 (11.5%), PT: 61 (9.0%) | LSI: FT: 69 (11.4%), PT: 51 (7.5%) |
| ASI: FT: 31 (7.8%), PT: 43 (8.1%) | ASI: FT: 32 (8.1%), PT: 39 (7.4%) | ASI: FT: 22 (5.6%), PT: 23 (4.4%) |

| | | |
|---|---|---|
| Convergers | Southerners | Assimilators |
| LSI: FT: 51 (8.4%), PT: 113 (16.6%) | LSI: FT: 84 (13.8%), PT: 134 (19.7%) | LSI: FT: 99 (16.3%), PT: 107 (15.8%) |
| ASI: FT: 64 (16.2%), PT: 98 (18.5%) | ASI: FT: 87 (22.0%), PT: 146 (27.6%) | ASI: FT: 79 (19.9%), PT: 94 (17.8%) |

**AC**

*Notes:* [a] LSI: FT = Full Time, N = 607; PT = Part Time, N = 679. [b] ASI: FT = Full Time, N = 396; PT = Part Time, N = 529.

*Figure 7.1* Distribution of 1,286 MBA student LSI learning styles[a] and 925 MBA student ASI adaptive styles[b].

students show a learning inflexibility when it comes to learning through CE (i.e., direct experience, sensing, and interpersonal relations). The inflexibility is much smaller in the AC mode (21% and 17%), which, as we explained earlier, is emphasized more by MBA programs.

One of our hypotheses in this study was that the AC bias found in MBA programs is present not only in the curriculum but also in the admission selection process. As shown in Table 7.2, in the full-time sample the correlation between AC and the AC end of the AC/CE dimension, on the one hand, and the GMAT scores, on the other hand, is significant for the

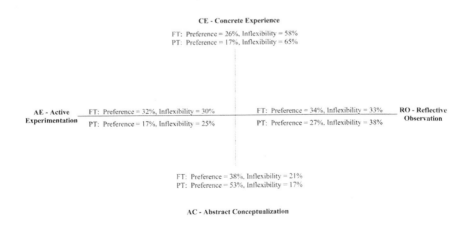

**CE - Concrete Experience**
FT: Preference = 26%, Inflexibility = 58%
PT: Preference = 17%, Inflexibility = 65%

**AE - Active Experimentation**
FT: Preference = 32%, Inflexibility = 30%
PT: Preference = 17%, Inflexibility = 25%

FT: Preference = 34%, Inflexibility = 33%
PT: Preference = 27%, Inflexibility = 38%
**RO - Reflective Observation**

FT: Preference = 38%, Inflexibility = 21%
PT: Preference = 53%, Inflexibility = 17%

**AC - Abstract Conceptualization**

*Note:* FT = Full-time, N = 607; PT = Part-time, N = 679

*Figure 7.2* Distribution of learning preference and inflexibility by mode.

quantitative and total scores ($r$'s range from 0.15 to 0.23, $p < 0.001$, and power $> 95\%$). The same pattern of results is observed in the part-time sample ($r$'s range from 0.19 to 0.21, $p < 0.001$, power $> 99\%$), but here some correlations of lower significance are also shown in the verbal scores. We conclude that our hypothesis is supported for the quantitative and total GMAT scores in both samples, but not for the verbal scores. The results show some significant negative correlations between GMAT scores and the other three modes (CE, RO, AE). As we expected, only the AC mode shows consistent and positive correlations with GMAT scores.

Also in Table 7.2 is the correlation between AC and the GPA, which is significant. An unexpected finding is the negative correlation of RO with MBA GPA. None of these findings was confirmed, however, for the two-dimensional AC/CE and AE/RO scores. A similar pattern of results as far as AC is concerned is observed in the part-time sample where MBA GPA correlates both with the AC and the AC end of the AC/CE dimension. We conclude that our hypothesis, that the AC bias found in MBA programs is shown also in the way we commonly judge progress or performance in the MBA program, finds some modest support, particularly in the part-time subsample.

## DISCUSSION

To summarize the results, MBA students in a full-time program show a pluralism of learning style preferences and adaptive styles, with a bias toward abstract conceptualization adaptive styles. MBA students in a part-time program show a pluralism of learning style preferences and adaptive styles, with a somewhat larger bias toward abstract learning and adaptive styles. The combination of these distributions suggests that for any method of teaching or learning activity, a substantial percentage of MBA students will find the process appealing in that it invokes and corresponds to their preferred learning style. But another percentage of MBA students, which varies more than the learning preference, will find that particular method of teaching or learning activity to be boring, irrelevant, or demotivating. When this negative reaction is evoked, it is likely that they will not sustain or retain the learning, even if it has been demonstrated once in an exam or through a paper.

When the distribution shown in Figure 7.2 is examined, it reveals that whereas about one fourth of the MBA students will prefer a concrete learning activity, about half will be inflexible. This may come in their comments as to lack of relevance, or accusations of it being 'soft' or merely the usual evidence of less interest, boredom, and spending their time on other courses or activities better suited to their learning preference and/or flexibility. About one third of the MBA students will prefer an abstract learning activity; only about one fifth will be inflexible and therefore 'turned off' to it.

Table 7.2   Correlations and Power Statistic for LSI Scores, GMAT Scores, and MBA GPA

| LSI scores | GMAT verbal[a] | | GMAT quantitative[a] | | GMAT total[a] | | MBA GPA[b] | |
|---|---|---|---|---|---|---|---|---|
| | Pearson r | Power >[c] | Pearson r | Power > | Pearson r | Power > | Pearson r | Power > |
| **Full-time sample** | | | | | | | | |
| Conceptualizing (AC) | 0.03 | — | 0.17*** | 98% | 0.23*** | 99% | 0.24*** | 94% |
| Experiencing (CE) | -0.02 | — | -0.08 | — | -0.03 | — | 0.10 | — |
| Acting (AE) | -0.02 | — | -0.06 | — | -0.12** | 84% | -0.07 | — |
| Reflecting (RO) | 0.01 | — | -0.04 | — | -0.09* | 58% | -0.24*** | 95% |
| AC-CE | 0.03 | — | 0.15*** | 95% | 0.16*** | 96% | 0.10 | — |
| AE-RO | -0.02 | — | -0.01 | — | -0.02 | — | 0.11 | — |
| **Part-time sample** | | | | | | | | |
| Conceptualizing (AC) | 0.15*** | 96% | 0.21*** | 99% | 0.21*** | 99% | 0.31** | 75% |
| Experiencing (CE) | -0.02 | — | -0.13** | 92% | -0.10* | 72% | -0.19 | — |
| Acting (AE) | -0.02 | — | -0.02 | — | -0.02 | — | -0.15 | — |
| Reflecting (RO) | -0.10* | 71% | -0.06 | — | -0.09* | 60% | 0.01 | — |
| AC-CE | 0.10* | 70% | 0.21*** | 99% | 0.19*** | 99% | 0.29* | 70% |
| AE-RO | 0.05 | — | 0.02 | — | 0.04 | — | -0.09 | — |

$* p < 0.05$; $** p < 0.01$; $*** p < 0.001$.

Notes: [a]$N = 576$ for the full-time and $N = 313$ for the part-time sample. [b]$N = 215$ for the full-time and $N = 72$ for the part-time sample. [c]Power analysis is performed at $\alpha = 0.05$, two-sided.

About one third of the MBA students will prefer an active learning activity and about one third will be inflexible and therefore 'turned off' to it. About one third of the MBA students will prefer a reflective learning activity and about one third will be inflexible and therefore 'turned off' to it.

Many of the recent innovations in MBA programs are more concrete and active than the traditional methods of lecture, case analysis, recitation through problem analysis, and exams. They add face validity to the MBA student and perceived 'real-world' relevance of their programmatic activities. Innovations such as service learning and action learning invoke active experimentation and concrete experience styles. A competency assessment and development course is likely to invoke more concrete and reflective learning, whereas development of a learning plan will invoke more active learning than the traditional curriculum components (Leonard, 2008). Attempting to expose MBAs to international issues has been approached with more varied pedagogy (Friga et al., 2003). International trips and visits provide stimulation for the active and concrete learners, whereas studying international cases and special topics like currency fluctuations provides stimulation for the abstract learners.

Whereas we can criticize most traditional university curriculum for placing too much emphasis on the abstract and reflective, it has also been noted that the more active learning methods often fail to complete the learning cycle, and therefore do not engage or stimulate the reflective learners (Mainemelis et al., 2002). In other words, insufficient time is spent in reflecting and processing experiences and making sense of them for students engaged in internships, service learning, and action learning projects to maximize the amount of sustained learning from these experiences.

Whereas many of the recent wave of innovations will help to redress the current imbalance implicit in the typical MBA curriculum, it will still run the risk of turning off as many students as those who are motivated or inspired by the learning activity.

The results also indicate that full-time MBAs and female MBAs will want a broader distribution of teaching methods to engage their learning styles. The part-time MBAs and the male MBAs, with their bias toward abstract learning styles, will be happier and show evidence of learning with traditional lecture, recitation, and case study methods than will the full-time or female MBAs as a whole. The difficulty of making the curriculum more 'female friendly' and less gender biased has been noted in a recent *Financial Times* survey and research articles seeking to explain why so few females apply to and/or complete an MBA (Case & Thompson, 1995; see also Friga et al., 2003). The lack of pluralism in the teaching methods may be a major contributor.

An interesting question about the effectiveness of distance learning, electronically delivered and Internet-based courses and programs may also be dramatically affected by the learning styles engaged and used in such courses and programs. An Internet-based course using electronic lecture, recitation, and case study will be geographically convenient but will have the same learning style bias as a live course using these methods. The challenge to those designing these programs is the same as for the live delivery MBA programs—you must engage all of the learning styles!

There is also an association of preferred abstract learning styles to one of the admissions screening tools, the GMAT. Emphasis on this screening tool and its use in prominent rankings of programs have incited many schools to look for ways to increase their entering students' GMAT scores. Given these forces in our environment, it is likely that the curriculum of most MBA programs will continue to have a bias toward abstract learning and adaptation. When we add the association of grades in the part-time MBA program with abstract learning styles, we continue to create the syllogistic loop of justifying the curriculum methods by showing high grades of students, which overemphasizes abstract learning and adaptive styles. This bias will exaggerate the prominent criticism of MBA programs that we teach students 'to analyze the hell out of anything' but do not teach them how to lead and work with others to solve problems (Andrews, 2004; Boyatzis et al., 1995; Mintzberg, 2004; Pfeffer & Fong, 2002; Porter & McKibbin, 1988; Tyson, 2005).

A major implication of these findings is that we recognize and appreciate the significance of the commonly held belief that 'students learn in different ways'. Faculty and administrators should exam their curriculum, teaching methods, and pedagogy for implicit bias. Once and if such bias is observed, then either change or rearrange the curriculum components to invoke and stimulate the pluralism of learning styles and minimize the arousal of the inflexibility of MBA's adaptive styles. The redesign of the curriculum in an MBA should emphasize all of the learning styles and therefore invoke all of the adaptive styles, minimizing the inflexibility. In other words, does the curriculum move a student through all four modes of the learning cycle? Is this movement regular and reasonable even in the time devoted to each mode, or does the unevenness reflect the faculty learning preference and disciplinary bias rather than the learning style of the students and needs of management jobs?

In addition to the overall curriculum, each semester can be examined for the same concern about equal emphasis on the entire learning cycle. Each course can be examined, as well as each class, for the same consideration. The class, course, and semester are fractals of the curriculum, and as such should stand the test of pluralism in their appeal to and stimulation of all approaches to learning.

On the basis of the distributions shown in Figures 7.1 and 7.2, the following principles can be used in the design and delivery of MBA curricula and programs.

Principle 1. Educators should design increased pluralism into learning activities.

1a. There should be more of a focus on each of the learning styles in each class, each course, each term, and the overall program.

1b. The design of a class, a course, and the program should reflect the rhythm, as well as intellectual and emotional flow of the learning cycle (see Sharma and Kolb's chapter in this volume for more specific examples).

Principle 2. Educators should promote application through Active Experimentation once concepts, theories, and observations are identified.

Principle 3. Educators should extract more learning from active and concrete activities.

3a. Given the majority of learning styles of MBAs, all concrete or active learning, such as action learning, field projects, internships and service learning, should be followed with more time devoted to reflecting on the experiences.

3b. All concrete or active learning should be followed by more time and coaching devoted to interpreting the meaning and possible learning from each activity.

3c. As a rule of thumb, time for reflection and interpretation should be equal to the time spent in the activity itself.

In this manner (see, for example, Friga et al., 2003; Vermunt, Chap. 12 in this volume), we have an increasing hope of creating a student-focused motivating environment in which all, or almost all, students will be excited about learning and sustain the ideas, knowledge, perspectives, and capability learned during an MBA program for years into their lives and careers.

## BIBLIOGRAPHY

Abbey, D.S., Hunt, D.E., & Weiser, J.C. (1985). Variations on a theme by Kolb: a new perspective for understanding counseling and supervision. *The Counseling Psychologist, 13*, 477–501.

Andrews, N. (2004). Global business capabilities. *Business Strategy Review, 15*, 4–10.

Boyatzis, R.E. (1991). Faculty intent and student outcome in graduate management education. In J.D. Bigelow (Ed.), *Managerial Skills: Explorations in Practical Knowledge* (pp. 90–102). Newbury Park, CA: Sage Publications.

Boyatzis, R.E., Cowen, S.S., & Kolb, D.A. (Eds.) (1995). *Innovation in Professional Education: Steps in a Journey from Teaching to Learning.* San Francisco: Jossey-Bass.

Boyatzis, R.E., & Kolb, D.A. (1993). *Adaptive Style Inventory: Self Scored Inventory and Interpretation Booklet.* Boston: TRG Hay/McBer, Training Resources Group.

Boyatzis, R.E., & Saatcioglu, A. (2008). A twenty year view of trying to develop emotional, social and cognitive intelligence competencies in graduate management education. *Journal of Management Development, 27*, 92–108.

Boyatzis, R.E., Stubbs, L., & Taylor, S. (2002). Learning cognitive and emotional intelligence competencies through graduate management education. *Academy of Management Journal on Learning and Education, 1,* 150–162.

Case, S., & Thompson, L. (1995). Gender differences in student development: examining life stories, career histories, and learning plans. In R.E. Boyatzis, S. Cowen, & D.A. Kolb (Eds.), *Innovation in Professional Education: Steps in a Journey from Teaching to Learning* (pp. 135–160). San Francisco: Jossey-Bass.

Friga, P.N., Bettis, R.A., & Sullivan, R.S. (2003). Change in graduate management education and new business school strategies for the 21st century. *Academy of Management Learning and Education, 2,* 233–249.

Hunt, D.E. (1987). *Beginning with Ourselves.* Cambridge, MA: Brookline.

Kolb, A.Y., & Kolb, D.A. (2005). Learning styles and learning spaces: enhancing experiential learning in higher education. *Academy of Management Learning and Education, 4,* 193–212.

Kolb, D.A. (1984). *Experiential Learning: Experience as the Source of Learning and Development.* Upper Saddle River, NJ: Prentice-Hall.

Kolb, D.A. (1999). *Learning Style Inventory—Version 3: Technical Specifications.* Boston: TRG Hay/McBer, Training Resources Group.

Kolb, D.A., Boyatzis, R.E., & Mainemelis, C. (2001). Experiential learning theory: previous research and new directions. In R.J. Sternberg & L.F. Zhang (Eds.), *Perspectives on Thinking, Learning, and Cognitive Styles* (pp. 227–247). Mahwah, NJ: Lawrence Erlbaum Associates.

Kolb, D.A., & Wolfe, D. (1981). *Professional Education and Career Development: A Cross-Sectional Study of Adaptive Competencies in Experiential Learning.* Final report NIE grant no. NIE-G-77-0053, ERIC no. ED 209 493 CE 030 519.

Lennick-Hall, C.A., & Sanders, M.M. (1997). Designing effective learning systems for management education: student roles, requisite variety, and practicing what we teach. *Academy of Management Journal, 40,* 1334–1368.

Leonard, D. (2008). The impact of learning goals on emotional, social and cognitive competency development. *Journal of Management Development, 27,* 109–128.

Mainemelis, C., Boyatzis, R.E., & Kolb, D.A. (2002). Learning styles and adaptive flexibility: testing experiential learning theory. *Management Learning, 33,* 5–33.

Mintzberg, H. (2004). *Managers Not MBAs: A Hard Look at the Soft Practice of Managing and Management Development.* New York: Berrett-Koehler Publishers.

Pfeffer, J., & Fong, C.T. (2002). The end of business schools? Less success than meets the eye. *Academy of Management Learning and Education, 1,* 78–95.

Porter, L., & McKibbin, L. (1988). *Management Education and Development: Drift or Thrust into the 21st Century?* New York: McGraw-Hill.

Tyson, L.D. (2005). On managers not MBAs. *Academy of Management Learning and Education, 4,* 235–236.

# 8 Kolb's Learning Styles and Approaches to Learning through the Use of Students' Critical Questions

*Patrícia Almeida, Helena Pedrosa de Jesus, and Mike Watts*

## INTRODUCTION

Is criticality a learning style? Being critical is of paramount importance in the world of higher education as, arguably, it is elsewhere. Is being critical a learned behavior, or are there general dispositions that lend some students a critical edge that others struggle to find?

In Portugal, according to the Framework Law on the Education System (Law no. 46/86, dated 14 October 1986, further amended by Laws no. 115/97 and no. 49/2005), the general aims of higher education are to emphasize the need for: (1) developing scientific and reflexive thought; (2) prompting a long-term search for cultural and professional development; and (3) enabling the concretization and integration of acquired knowledge into a strong intellectual structure. This is similar in many other countries where external evaluations of higher education have stressed the need for a greater degree of 'deep' critical learning as a way of avoiding simple procedural learning, and a need for conceptual (Beattie, Collins, & McInnes, 1997) and integrated learning (Kolb, 1984). This kind of learning involves being critical and, in the frame of our research, asking higher level questions. Cuccio-Schirripa and Steiner (2000) see the process of question generation and, in particular, the design and use of quality questions as exercises in the development of critical thinking skills:

> Questioning is one of the thinking processing skills which is structurally embedded in the thinking operations of critical thinking, creative thinking and problem solving. It consists of the smaller micro-thinking skills of recall, comprehension, application analysis, synthesis and evaluation . . . Questions guide knowledge construction in the formation and changing of the cognitive networks or schemata. (Cuccio-Shirripa & Steiner, 2000, p. 21)

We see critical thinking to imply a clear propensity to ask questions. In fact, in our view, the most significant indicator of critical thinking is the capacity to question, leading in turn to a deep approach to integrated learning. Therefore, in this chapter, we propose to explore the relationship (as indicators and consequences) between students' questions—in particular questions that demonstrate criticality—and their learning styles. More specifically, we intend to: (1) identify and characterize the types of questions students ask during their learning; (2) identify and characterize first-year chemistry students' learning styles and approaches to learning; (3) discuss the role of students' questions in the 'critical construction' of knowledge using Kolb's learning styles; and (4) describe teaching strategies used to match students' preferences.

## THEORETICAL FOUNDATIONS

### Student-Generated Questions

In recent years there has been an increasing emphasis on the important role that students' questions play in learning, as questions are an essential component of discursive activity, dialectical thinking (Chin & Osborne, 2008), and dialogic teaching (Wolfe & Alexander, 2008). Student-generated questions are an important element in the teaching and learning process and play a significant role in motivating meaningful learning. In fact, some studies show that the promotion of a true spirit of inquiry can improve the quality of teaching and, consequently, the quality of learning (Pedrosa de Jesus, Almeida, & Watts, 2007). Through students' questions, teachers can identify both 'nonstandard conceptions' as well as the main obstacles to the understanding of specific content, facilitating the design of classes that lead in the direction of students' needs and motivations (Teixeira-Dias, Pedrosa de Jesus, Neri de Souza, & Watts, 2005). We have argued elsewhere (Pedrosa de Jesus, Neri de Souza, Teixeira-Dias, & Watts, 2005) that asking questions is central to a learner's 'enculturation' into the patterns of language and thought, discussion, and criticism that are characteristic of an academic discipline, for example, chemistry. We have noted also that, on a more detailed and local level, question-asking is often the most effective way for learners to overcome, for instance, a gap in understanding, a particular impasse during problem solving, or to resolve difficult conceptual issues.

In spite of the educational significance of learners' questions, it is known that students generally are seen to ask few questions, and even fewer in the search of real—critical—knowledge. Student questioning is influenced by instructional models and lesson structures (Pizzini & Shepardson, 1991), by the social structure of the classroom, the students' role as participants, the controlling function of the teacher's own questions (Dillon, 1988), and the interest and innovation of the topics (Pedrosa de Jesus, Teixeira-Dias, & Watts, 2003). In an obvious sense, if the classroom culture inhibits questioning, few questions will be asked.

## Approaches to Criticality

In this chapter, we explore the nature of 'critical questions'. Our supposition is that, if we require university students to be critical thinkers, then one vehicle for achieving this is to enable them to ask critical questions. Some have argued that critical thinking is entirely composed of the asking of critical questions:

> The purpose of critical thinking is, therefore, to achieve understanding, evaluate viewpoints, and solve problems. Since all three areas involve the asking of questions, we can say that critical thinking is the questioning or inquiry we engage in when we seek to understand, evaluate, or resolve. (Maiorana, 1992, p. 22)

A survey of the literature in this vein would suggest that there exists a category of questions that, of themselves, are uniquely critical, that fully entail and serve to demonstrate criticality. Ruggerio (1996), for instance, generates the following list of critical questions:

> Is . . . good or bad?
> . . . correct or incorrect?
> . . . effective or ineffective?
> . . . relevant or irrelevant?
> . . . clear or unclear?
> . . . logical or illogical?
> . . . applicable or not applicable?
> . . . proven or not proven?
> . . . ethical or unethical?
> What are the advantages or disadvantages of . . . ?
> What are the pros or cons of . . . ?
> What is the best solution to the problem/conflict/issue . . . ?
> What should or should not happen . . . ?
> Do I agree or disagree . . . ?
> What is my opinion . . . ?

In our work, we have dispensed with such a separate category of 'critical questions' in favor of a designation of the actions and processes of 'critical questioning'. We are more interested in developing students who are 'critical questioners' than a simple category of question types that delineate critical questions. Our view is that 'being critical', asking critical questions, relates to three domains, which we describe as (1) context, (2) competency, and (3) realization. In this sense, we agree with Barnett (1997), who warns against the 'critical thinking industry', by which he means a mechanistic 'study skills' approach to being critical. Barnett describes his notion of 'critical being' as including thinking, self-reflection, and action:

> Critical persons are more than just critical thinkers. They are able criti-
> cally to engage with the world and with themselves as well as with
> knowledge. (Barnett, 1997, p. 1)

In this view, critical being is an approach of life, study, thinking, and criticality to which a university-educated person should aspire. In Barnett's criticality, he begins with skills for questioning, then progresses through an awareness of the standards of reasoning within disciplines. This leads on towards a wider ability to undertake critique by bringing new perspectives to bear. In his view, critical thinking—the simple deployment of a 'checklist' of cognitive skills by individuals—is inadequate. This is "thinking without a critical edge" (Barnett, 1997, p. 17).

## Questioning in a Critical Context

We understand 'context' as comprised of external factors, related to the external environment, that can affect or not affect the student's expression of a 'critical attitude'. We see situations and contexts in which it is appropriate and desirable to be critical, others where it is not. For example, it is possible to read a novel or watch a film simply for pleasure, where notions of criticality are low. The purpose may be undemanding, enjoyment, or escapism, with little intention to undertake any significant critique. In other instances, a university lecture, for example, on postcolonial literature, a 'fully critical mode' is essential. The important ingredient here is that the student is able to discern appropriate situations and contexts so that they can decide the appropriate points to apply their full critical faculties.

During learning, it is possible to identify some situations where students reveal a critical 'attitude' based on the kinds of questions they ask—or through their comments, responses, and arguments. Through our research studies we have evidence of the influence of context on students' criticality, for instance, during the development of chemistry mini-projects, in a course of topical lectures, and through a 'question box' used in chemistry and biology disciplines. One important aspect of context, then, can be the teaching approach and the subject content being taught, which can influence, positively or negatively, the student 'disposition' to be critical. Assessment methods, too, can influence students' criticality. In situations where question-asking is promoted and a positive environment is created, both through teaching or assessment, students appear to be more critical. In addition to the context, critical thinking has been defined as an integration of two dimensions: a set of cognitive skills and a disposition based on a willingness to apply those skills (Stupnisky, Renaud, Daniels, Haynes, & Perry, 2008). We assume that a 'critical questioning competency' should also entail those two dimensions.

Being critical, as the process of determining the authenticity, accuracy, or value of something, is characterized by the ability to question reasons and alternatives, perceive the total situation, and change one's view based on answers, solutions, and evidence. Critical questioning entails critical inquiry, so that critical questioners investigate problems, ask probing questions, pose new questions that challenge the status quo, discover new information that can be used appropriately, question authoritative and traditional beliefs, and challenge received dogmas and doctrines. Therefore:

> Critical questioners, critical learners, are curious, challenge authority, internalize, practice scientific and critical thinking and questioning. Critical questioners have the motivation, inclination to drive and involve themselves in meaningful critical thinking, while making decisions and/or solving problems. (Facione, Facione, & Giancarlo, 1996, p. 71)

One essential ingredient here is that a competent critical questioner is able to discern appropriate situations and contexts so that they can decide the appropriate points to apply their full critical faculties. To this extent, they have the capacity to 'switch on' an appropriate 'critical orientation' that drives their questioning within a particular context. Students adopting such a critical approach have the intention to understand, engage with, operate in, and value the subject, what Marton and Säljö (1976) call a 'deep approach'. These learners relate ideas and look for patterns and principles on the one hand and use evidence and examine the logic of the argument on the other hand.

We believe that students' capacity to be critical can be brought into being, developed, and honed. As we note earlier, we do not see that there is a single set of skills or critical questions that educators can engender in their students, nor that there are critical questions specific to particular disciplines, such as biology or chemistry. It is possible, in our view, to develop and to realize critical questioning both from the use of critical standards derived from within the discourses of a discipline and from standards developed in other subject areas too.

## Kolb's Learning Styles

Kolb's (1984) experiential learning theory is one of the most widely cited educational theories in higher education. It considers a cycle of concrete experience, reflective observation, abstract conceptualization, and active experimentation. These four learning modes are the basis for the definition of four different learning styles. However, here we are more concerned with David Kolb's less-known *Learning Theory of Growth and Development* (Kolb, 1984). He proposes a continuum with three major stages:

acquisition, specialization, and integration. This is a continuum of increasing complexity and relativism. Progress is made through the integration of dialectical adaptive modes among his four major quadrants or learning styles: divergence, assimilation, convergence, and accommodation. Growth involves increasing the affective, perceptual, symbolic, and behavioral complexity by achieving "higher level integration through dialectical conflicts" (Kolb, 1984, p. 134).

## METHODOLOGY

### Procedure

The 'Questions in Chemistry' project engaged 300 first-year chemistry students in science and engineering courses at the University of Aveiro, Portugal, over three academic years, and was developed in full collaboration between educational researchers and lecturers in the chemistry department. The work aimed at contributing to the development of pedagogical models that promote student-oriented approaches, stimulating students to be active and critical participants in their learning process, for teachers to act as promoters of innovative teaching strategies. Such work has been part of a research program designed to face the challenges associated with the implementation of the Bologna Process in Portugal and the development of the scholarship of teaching and learning within the university.

From the first day, students were told about the research project, teachers explained the aims of the project and that a researcher would be present in all their classes, charting their questions. Additional explanations of the project were provided at other strategic moments (for example, when the Learning Styles Inventory was administered and, later, when some students were invited to be interviewed).

### Participants

The sample for this specific study was composed of thirty undergraduate students (sixteen female, fourteen male; mean age 19 years) who were tackling foundation chemistry, although following different degree programs: environmental engineering, chemical engineering, teaching of physics and chemistry, biology, teaching of biology and geology, physics, chemistry and physical engineering. These students were selected on the basis of specific characteristics—their learning style according to Kolb's (1984) theory, their approaches to learning identified through interviews, the types and number of oral and written questions they raised, and their level of individual involvement observed during classes—and then analyzed in a deeper mode.

## Strategies to Foster Student-Generated Questions

Several teaching and learning strategies were designed and implemented, across the three academic years, to foster students to ask thought-provoking and critical oral and written questions. These strategies were also conceived to intentionally match students' individual learning styles as well as to mismatch those preferences at other times (Almeida, Pedrosa de Jesus, & Watts, 2008; Pedrosa de Jesus et al., 2007) in order to simultaneously motivate the learners and stretch their learning preferences. During the final semester of the study, new assessment processes compatible with the teaching strategies developed were also tested. The teaching and learning strategies have taken the following five forms (Almeida et al., 2008; Teixeira-Dias et al., 2005):

- 'Questions in Chemistry' lectures were lectures based on students' questions on a specific topic (for example, the ozone layer and conducting polymers).
- Conference lectures were lectures based on selected chemistry topics of wide scientific, technological, and social interest (for example, oscillating reactions and origin of the chemical elements).
- Seminar-tutorial sessions were based on the discussion of particular case studies related to the subject matter previously lectured on in the large classroom.
- Practical laboratory sessions were classes where students were confronted with a problem. Learners should design an experiment to solve that problem and carry out that experimental protocol.
- Mini-projects were projects designed to confront students with a simple research task, such as greenhouse effect and fireworks, and were carried out in the second semester of each academic year.

Other specific strategies, such as the exploitation of experimental devices and 'pen and paper' devices, were also implemented, as means of triggering students' questions.

## Data Gathering and Analysis

Observation is a valid and direct way of obtaining data from people. Gillham (2000, p. 46) argues that "it is not what they say they do. It is what they actually do". Throughout five semesters, from February 2002 to June 2004, all the chemistry classes (approximately 350 classes) were audio-recorded. Observation grids for every class were completed by a researcher, who was present at all classes. This way, oral questions were also collected. Video recording was also used in diverse contexts, for instance, during mini-projects sessions and exploitation of experimental devices. In this way, data were collected from a variety of sources including observation of all chemistry classes, instruments conceived to gather students' written questions, students' interviews, and the Portuguese version of the Learning Styles Inventory (Kolb, 1999).

## Instruments for Encouraging and Collecting Student-Generated Questions

Since asking questions requires conditions of trust (Watts, Alsop, Gould, & Walsh, 1997), learners need to build confidence to speculate and take risks. To create a secure environment that would encourage question-asking, the research team created two tools to try to eliminate the embarrassment that asking a question in class could cause. Students could deliver their questions in a written format through a software intranet system or question boxes.

### Software Intranet System

This system was available on limited access via a series of computers within the building dedicated to the teaching of first-year science and technology students, in the laboratories, tutorial rooms and the interconnecting corridors, giving relatively free access to chemistry students. The software allowed those students who had Internet facilities outside the university to work at a distance from the department and to access the system through use of an appropriate password.

### Question Boxes

A question box was placed in each laboratory and tutorial room. These were acrylic containers, very much like ballot boxes, with an outer compartment where a pad of Post-its was available for students' questions, which would be posted at any point in the session or the day.

## Learning Styles Inventory

The Learning Styles Inventory (Kolb, 1999) was adapted to a Portuguese context by Goulão (2001). This inventory was administered during the seminar-tutorial classes. The students were informed about the need to write their names in the inventory sheet, because its purpose was to relate their learning style with the questions they ask. They were given the opportunity to know the results from the inventory, because it was not anonymous. A session was designed to explain to students the characteristics of each learning style and its implications.

## Interviews

The thirty students selected for interview were chosen in consideration of the number and kinds of questions they raised and their particular attitudes in class. They also displayed distinct Kolb's learning styles characteristics. From the responses given, it was possible to confirm these students' learning styles, as well as to identify and characterize their learning approaches. All the interviews were semi-structured, audio-recorded and transcribed verbatim. Afterwards, content analysis was conducted.

## RESEARCH FINDINGS AND DISCUSSION

## Kolb's Learning Styles and Students' Questions

From the sample of thirty students, ten were mostly on the Acquisition phase, fifteen revealed to be in the Specialization phase, and only five were in the Integration phase. Questions associated with the Acquisition phase dealt mainly with relatively straightforward gaps in knowledge, where students were attempting to clear up matters of fact, confirm explanations, or clarify conceptual issues. Students may feel they have grasped an idea, or the structure of an argument, and are testing for reassurance that this is in fact the case. These are commonly closed questions, the answers to which will mainly rely upon memory processes. Examples of acquisition questions are:

> How does heavy water form?
> Is cianidric acid a weak or strong acid?
> What is the process that allows the two DNA chains to split apart?

Students asking Specialization questions tend to go beyond an initial search for information to establish relations and try to understand and interpret the surrounding 'disciplinary world'. These questions attempt to secure understandings, to expand knowledge into the neighboring terrain, and test constructs that are being shaped. Drawn from our project, some instances of these Specialization questions are:

> To make steam trains work, it is necessary to provide energy through heat, but it is also releasing heat. Is this an endothermic or an exothermic chemical reaction?
> Since one $O_2$ molecule can bind to each of four heme groups of haemoglobin, why is it that the second and following $O_2$ molecules are more easily bound than the first one?
> If the ink becomes colorless in the paper, why does this not happen in the beaker?

How can we quantify the acidity or the basicity of a solution, when the solvent is not water, or when in a gaseous medium?

Learners also revealed the ability to ask higher level Integration questions involving speculation or hypothesizing, anomaly detection. Students expressed skepticism or detected discrepant information or cognitive conflict, different application of principles learned, attempted to reconcile understanding, track in and around complex ideas and their consequences. An example of such questioning was:

If the variation of entropy of the universe is always higher than zero, that is, if we are going towards disorder, how do structures like planets, planetary systems, and galaxies form? Due to DNA complexity, at least apparently, it will have high entropy, going towards disorder? I wonder if it would make sense to design an $H_2/O_2$ fuel cell–based vehicle that would avoid carrying $H_2$ and $O_2$ in bottles by including an electrolytic cell, powered by solar panels, to decompose $H_2O$. Water has a high surface tension that allows, for instance, insects to rest on the water and not to sink. But, there is a huge Australian lizard which runs over the water and never drowns. I can't understand this because that lizard is really quite heavy. How is this possible? Water cannot sustain a mouse or a squirrel, and yet can sustain the Australian lizard?

Questions like these focused on explanations and causes, predictions, or on resolving discrepancies in knowledge. The learners seemed to challenge accepted reasoning and were more open, imaginative, and critical.

A panel of seven nonproject colleagues helped in the validation of this categorization of questions. A document with the characteristics of each kind of question and some examples of question types was given to each member of the panel. Then, according to the information given, each member classified ten new questions. The degree of concordance in judgment was 89%.

## Discussion of Findings

We suggest that students can—in general—ask each kind of question. So, although there is a clear hierarchy within the categories, this may apply to students as a broad tendency rather than a necessary limiting factor. Students showed the ability to raise higher level or deep questions, but a student asking Integration questions might also ask Acquisition and Specialization questions. There were some students who only asked Acquisition questions, but that may have been limited by the situation, the subject matter, the peer group pressure, the physical environment, and so on.

Students in Integrative mode raised questions that tended to reflect their curiosity, speculation, skepticism, critique. One of the major characteristics of these questions was the reorganization of concepts into novel patterns and to hypothesize new or different applications of principles learned. These were attempts to reconcile different understandings, resolve conflicts, test circumstances, and track in and around complex ideas and their consequences. They were pitched at a conceptually higher level, required an application or extension of taught ideas, and sprang from a deep interest of the students or arose from an effort to make sense of the world.

Moreover, some of these questions were asked critically, others not: it was all in the context. This was sometimes in the general context, where the lecturer urged the students to be critical, point out advantages, disadvantages, points for and against certain issues; where students' own disposition was critical, through tone, body language, use of terms and expressions. All in all, we found nothing in the many classrooms observed or interviews conducted to indicate any hostility, mischief, or personalization of any of the questions asked: the most critical of questions were 'on task' and appropriate to the context of a university lecture.

## CONCLUSIONS, IMPLICATIONS, AND RECOMMENDATIONS

We maintain that it is possible to create a learning environment that fosters students' critical questioning, and where the different characteristics of students' learning styles can be considered to the design of different teaching strategies.

While questions are certainly an indicator of students' learning, they also allow us to establish a link between Kolb's theory and approaches to critical questioning. We defined three categories of questions, according to Kolb's experiential learning theory: Acquisition questions, Specialization questions, and Integration questions. Each one of these categories is directly related to the acquisition, specialization, and integration phases defined and characterized by Kolb and colleagues. We conclude that students within each of these phases tend, predominantly, to ask questions that are congruent with that stage. Students in the acquisition phase ask mainly questions that are related to simple facts and concepts—acquisition questions. Students within the middle phase ask mainly specialization questions, those that go beyond the mere search for information. Students in the integration phase show the ability to ask higher level questions (Figure 8.1). However, at times, these students also asked acquisition and specialization questions, according to their needs and to the learning environment. These findings corroborate the assertions of Pedrosa de Jesus, Almeida, and Watts (2004).

In 2000, Chin and Brown established a relationship between students' questions and deep and surface approaches. Here we confirm the broad gist of this finding: students adopting a surface approach raised mainly surface questions, whose answer require only recall of information. Deep questions

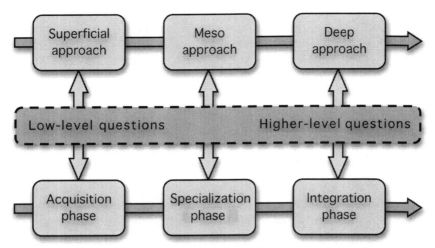

*Figure 8.1* Relationship between students' questions, approaches to learning, and Kolb's learning theory of growth and development.

showed a clear effort to use knowledge in an innovative way, and revealed reflection and critical thought.

In this way, the major contribution of our study is that it shows how students' questions represent a useful tool that allows us to establish a relationship between questioning, approaches to learning, and Kolb's theory, lying in different theoretical backgrounds (Kolb, 1984; Marton & Säljö, 1976). Nevertheless, both these theories have similar issues in common: that there is a continuum in learning development and students can 'move' along this continuum. They might remain at the base—acquisition phase or superficial approach—or move up until they reach a higher level of thinking, the integration phase, or deep approach. Between the base and the top of this continuum, there is a learning space where students have 'in-between' characteristics—the specialization phase or a 'meso' approach, as we call it (Pedrosa de Jesus, Almeida, Teixeira-Dias, & Watts, 2006)—as a mean of facilitating our explanation. It is important to emphasize that, as expected, the transition between stages does not always occur in a linear fashion. Frequently, repeated oscillations are required before a student moves from a lower level to an upper level.

## BIBLIOGRAPHY

Almeida, P., Pedrosa de Jesus, H., & Watts, M. (2008). Developing a mini-project: students' questions and learning styles. *Psychology of Education Review, 32,* 6–17.

Barnett, R. (1997). *Higher Education: A Critical Business.* London: Open University Press/SRHE.

Beattie, V., Collins, B., & McInnes, B. (1997). Deep and surface learning: a simple or simplistic dichotomy? *Accounting Education, 6,* 1–12.

Chin, C., & Brown, D.E. (2000). Learning in science: a comparison of deep and surface approaches. *Journal of Research in Science Teaching, 37,* 109–138.

Chin, C., & Osborne, J. (2008). Students' questions: a potential resource for teaching and learning science. *Studies in Science Education, 44,* 1–39.

Cuccio-Schirripa, S., & Steiner, H.E. (2000). Enhancement and analysis of science question level for middle school students. *Journal of Research in Science Teaching, 37,* 210–224.

Dillon, J.T. (1988). The remedial status of student questioning. *Journal of Curriculum Studies, 20,* 197–210.

Facione, P., Facione, N., & Giancarlo, C. (1996). The motivation to think in working and learning. In E. Jones (Ed.), *Preparing Competent College Students: Setting New and Higher Expectations for Student Learning* (pp. 67–79). San Francisco: Jossey-Bass.

Gillham, B. (2000). *Case Study Research Methods.* London: Continuum.

Goulão, M.F. (2001). *Ensino aberto à distância: cognição e afectividade* [*Open and distance education: cognition and affectivity*]. Unpublished PhD thesis, Lisbon, Open University.

Kolb, D.A. (1984). *Experiential Learning: Experience as a Source of Learning and Development.* Englewood Cliffs, NJ: Prentice Hall.

Kolb, D.A. (1999). *Learning Style Inventory, Version 3.* Boston: TRG Hay/McBer, Training Resources Group.

Law no. 46/86. D.R. No. 237, I Series of 14.10.86. Framework Law on the Education System. Assembly of the Portuguese Republic.

Law no. 49/2005. D. R. No. 166, I Series A of 30.8.05. Second amendment to the Basic Education System Act and first amendment to the Basic Higher Education Financing Act. Assembly of the Portuguese Republic.

Law No. 115/97. D.R. No. 109, I Series A of 19.9.97. Framework Law on the Education System. Assembly of the Portuguese Republic.

Maiorana, V.P. (1992). *Critical Thinking across the Curriculum: Building the Analytical Classroom.* Bloomington, IN: ERIC Clearinghouse on Reading and Communication Skills.

Marton, F., & Säljö, R. (1976). On qualitative differences in learning: I. Outcome and process. *British Journal of Educational Psychology, 46,* 4–11.

Pedrosa de Jesus, M.H., Almeida, P., Teixeira-Dias, J.J.C., & Watts, M. (2006). Students' questions: building a bridge between Kolb's learning styles and approaches to learning. *Education and Training, 48,* 97–111.

Pedrosa de Jesus, M.H., Almeida, P., & Watts, M. (2004). Questioning styles and students learning: four case studies. *Educational Psychology, 24,* 531–548.

Pedrosa de Jesus, M.H., Almeida, P., & Watts, M. (2007). Learners' questions meet modes of teaching: a study of cases. *Research Education, 78,* 1–20.

Pedrosa de Jesus, M.H., Neri de Souza, F., Teixeira-Dias, J.J.C., & Watts, M. (2005). Organising the chemistry of question-based learning: a case study. *Journal of Research in Science and Technology Education, 23,* 179–193.

Pedrosa de Jesus, M.H., Teixeira-Dias, J.J.C., & Watts, M. (2003). Questions of chemistry. *International Journal of Science Education, 25,* 1015–1034.

Pizzini, E., & Shepardson, D.P. (1991). Student questioning in the presence of the teacher during problem solving in science. *School and Mathematics, 91,* 348–352.

Ruggerio, V.R. (1996). *Becoming a Critical Thinker.* Boston: Houghton Mifflin.

Stupnisky, R.H., Renaud, R.D., Daniels, L.M., Haynes, T.L., & Perry, R.P. (2008). The interrelation of first-year college students' critical thinking disposition, perceived academic control, and academic achievement. *Research in Higher Education, 49,* 513–530.

Teixeira-Dias, J.J.C., Pedrosa de Jesus, H., Neri de Souza, F., & Watts, M. (2005). Teaching for quality learning in chemistry. *International Journal of Science Education, 27*, 1123–1137.

Watts, M., Alsop, S., Gould, G., & Walsh, A. (1997). Prompting teachers' constructive reflection: pupils' questions and critical incidents. *International Journal of Science Education, 19*, 1025–1037.

Wolfe, S., & Alexander, R.J. (2008). *Argumentation and Dialogic Teaching: Alternative Pedagogies for a Changing World*. London: Futurelab.

# 9 Relating Knowledge Structures to Learning Styles and University Teaching

*Ian M. Kinchin*

## INTRODUCTION

This chapter draws together work on knowledge structures, learning styles, and university teaching to show how interactions between these elements create serious implications for practice. This synthesis reports on the underlying unity that may be masked by the range of specialist languages employed within education, and uncovered by visualization using concept maps. It contends that certain approaches to teaching within the traditional lecture-based university course will inhibit students from adopting their preferred learning style, channeling students towards strategies that are rewarded even when meaningful learning has not occurred.

## KNOWLEDGE STRUCTURES

Knowledge structures can be represented using concept mapping as developed by Novak (Novak, 1998; Novak & Cañas, 2007). This is a graphical tool used to represent connections between ideas. Concepts are written in boxes and linked with arrows that carry explanatory labels. Concept mapping has been used effectively as a classroom tool to enhance learning in a variety of settings (Nesbit & Adesope, 2006). It has been shown to provide an arena for interpretation of teacher-student dialogue (Kinchin, 2003), and a vocabulary for the qualitative consideration of knowledge structures (Kinchin, Hay, & Adams, 2000), that have been taken as indicators of learning styles (Kinchin, 2000); see Figure 9.1. An important function of the map is to help make explicit the overall arrangement of concepts. This is particularly important for complex topics where students may display a fragmentary understanding and are frequently unable to integrate all the components to form a meaningful overview. Identifying key fragments of understanding, termed 'anchoring conceptions' by Clement, Zietsman, and Brown (1989), or 'threshold concepts' by Land, Meyer and Smith (2008), is vital as these form the foundations for future meaningful learning.

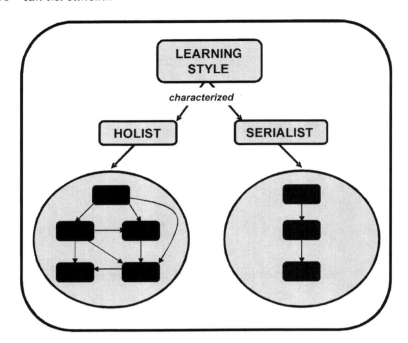

*Figure 9.1*    A comparison of holists and serialists in terms of the typical knowledge structures employed by extreme cases. Note: Adapted from Kinchin (2000).

Application of concept mapping discussed here presents some divergence with the philosophy that implicitly underpins much of the literature that has previously employed the tool. This philosophical tension is particularly evident in the field of science education, in which there exists an epistemological gap between the objectivist philosophy of science and the constructivist philosophy of concept mapping (Kinchin, 2001). There is a further divergence from traditional concept mapping studies by including qualitative description of maps to complement the quantification of characteristics. This echoes Novak and Gowin's (1984, p. 97) statement that "scoring was in many respects irrelevant" when looking for qualitative changes in understanding, and is further supported by Caine and Caine's (1994, p. 166), commenting that 'it is impossible to communicate the scope and depth of a student's abilities by means of a numerical grade'. To overcome the limitations of scoring protocols, a qualitative typology of concept maps was derived from observations of several thousand maps (Kinchin et al., 2000). The general properties of the three major concept map morphologies (Figure 9.2) can be summarized as:

- spokes: indicative of a student with a rudimentary knowledge of the field, and unable to make links between peripheral components. Spokes suggest a degree of learning readiness in that they can support further development without having to abandon existing understanding.

- chains: indicative of a rote learning approach and/or serialist learning style. Chains are elevated by traditional teaching approaches that focus on a single perspective and certainty; they dominate where teaching and learning concentrate on procedures and outcomes.
- networks: indicate a more holistic orientation to learning and a robust understanding of the discipline. They are often taken as indicators of deep/meaningful learning.

The application of concept mapping to the qualitative analysis of knowledge structures has allowed the visualization of the process of learning at university in novel ways that emphasize the organization of information (Hay, Kinchin, & Lygo-Baker, 2008). Concept mapping has been shown to be an elegant tool for the elicitation and representation of expertise (Hoffman & Lintern, 2006), allowing the surfacing and subsequent focus on key attributes of the quality of understanding (Copperman, Beeri, & Ben-Zvi, 2007).

## LINKING KNOWLEDGE STRUCTURES AND LEARNING STYLES

Concept mapping can be used to compensate when a learner exhibits a one-sided learning strategy (Huai, 1997), and may provide an indicator of a

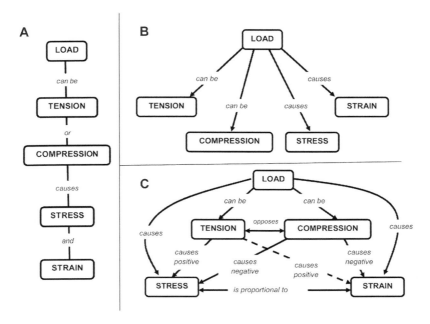

*Figure 9.2*   Examples of extreme chain (A), spoke (B), and net (C) concept map structures from an undergraduate engineering course. Note: Adapted from Kinchin and Alias (2005).

student's learning approach for a given context. Rayner and Riding (1997) have speculated that:

> The idea that "style awareness" may help reach the "hard to teach", and perhaps contribute to reducing failure generally by enhancing the learning process, is an elusive but tantalizing prospect which clearly merits further attention. (Rayner & Riding, 1997, p. 21)

Huai (1997) suggests that for 'holists', who have a 'global approach', concept mapping can help the learner to focus on critical details, whereas 'serialists' can be stimulated to take a wider perspective. Students who gain most from concept mapping may be those identified as 'visual-spatial learners', who excel when provided with visual representations. Such students reject rote memorization and have a need to see how the parts relate to the whole before they can make sense of isolated ideas. Whilst serialists may tend towards the production of chain-type maps and holists may tend towards the production of network-type maps (see Figure 9.1), the widespread production of linear concept maps has been linked to the ways in which students have received information during their lessons that promote linear knowledge structures (e.g., Cliburn, 1986). This linearity can be extremely pronounced within traditional university lectures. Whilst the lecture represents only one teaching scenario used in university education, it still forms the core of many undergraduate courses and so influences the development of knowledge structures.

## CONCEPT MAPPING AND TEACHING

Through direct observation of teaching, it is evident that knowledge structures exhibit different morphologies (e.g., spokes, chains, and networks) that serve different purposes in the acts of teaching and learning. Novice teachers can be helped to appreciate the significance of these structures by transforming their teaching plans into a range of different structures that depict the same content (Kinchin & Alias, 2005). Previously, where overall morphology of knowledge structures was not considered, the application of concept mapping reinforced the linear nature of teaching as material is sequenced for teaching (Martin, 1994). Once it is seen that structure complements content, teaching can then be considered in terms of a transformation cycle of knowledge structures as teachers extract elements from their own understanding to construct teaching materials. From these materials students then have to construct their own understanding of the topic (Kinchin, Cabot, & Hay, 2008a).

When classroom exchanges are considered in this way, it can be observed that teaching through summarizing content as bullet points represents *only* the linear chain of teaching. This does not grant the student access to the origins of the chain that remain hidden from view and leads students to adopt learning styles that emphasize rote memorization of content (Hay & Kinchin, 2007). The teacher needs to grant access to the underlying knowledge structure (or at least the appropriate elements of it) so that the student can relate the information to the context under consideration. This is particularly important when a course is being delivered by a series of lecturers who may share in an underlying understanding, but who are delivering lectures on their own specialisms within that field. The student may perceive this situation as a sequence of unrelated chains of information, each one isolated and discrete. Only if the lecturers use an underlying expert knowledge structure in an explicit fashion can students use it to structure their own emerging understanding.

## ACTIVATING PRIOR KNOWLEDGE

Prior knowledge is seen as an important factor in students' learning and is fundamental to their appreciation of new information presented within a course of instruction (Hailikari, Katajavouri, & Llindblom-Ylänne, 2008). West and Fensham (1974) comment that:

> Despite the obviousness of prior knowledge as a major factor in learning . . . and its wide acceptance intuitively by . . . teachers, they proceed to ignore it in so much of their regular practice. (West & Fensham, 1974, p. 62)

Ausubel (2000) recommends the use of introductory materials that support meaningful learning by activating relevant existing knowledge; this is often termed an 'advance organizer'.

The use of concept maps as advance organizers has been shown to contribute to meaningful learning (e.g., Willerman & Mac Harg, 1991). However, within the classroom it is possible that teachers may simply present their students with a concept map which may be viewed by the class as 'the right answer' to memorize. This is not seen as the point of a concept map—it is intended rather to reveal the personal perceptions of the map's author (Jonassen, Reeves, Hong, Harvey, & Peters, 1997). Memorization would be taking learning away from a constructivist standpoint and away from the active use of concept mapping towards a more passive reproduction of received information. This highlights the difference between using *concept maps* to summarize information and using *concept mapping* as a learning activity. This dichotomy is significant and indicative of different teaching philosophies: lessons that use teacher-produced maps are generally expository and product-centered, while those that feature a student concept mapping approach tend to be process-orientated, focusing on the students' construction of meaning (Cliburn, 1990).

## LINEARITY IN TEACHING

The widespread use of PowerPoint in university lectures can be exploited to provide a window into the mind of the university teacher, giving an explicit reference point for discussions on personal perspectives of teaching (Kinchin, Chadha, & Kokotailo, 2008b). The structure of the materials presented on slides along with the accompanying narrative supplied by the teacher often reveals a tendency towards the delivery of information arranged as linear structures. When teaching consists only of linear strings of information, the novice is forced into a surface approach to learning and ends up memorizing inert, decontextualized chunks of information. This is something that is recognized by students, but accepted as part of the 'examination game' (Kinchin & Cabot, 2007). In this way the novice is excluded from the expert's integrated knowledge base (Kinchin, 2008). To overcome this, lecturers need to allow access to their expert understanding of the subject helping the student to see how the string of information is related to a broader network of understanding. Only then can students start to develop their own emergent understanding towards expertise and become active participants in the discourse of the discipline. As described by Biggs:

> Teaching from lists is like sawing the branches off a tree, stacking them in a neat pile and saying, "There! See the tree? (Biggs, 2003, p. 76)

Stated so simply, it seems ludicrous that students are expected to construct complex, integrated understandings from materials that are presented to them as simplified linear threads, particularly when each thread is typically examined in isolation. However, the dominant knowledge structures observed to be presented in university lectures are the bulleted lists that are so characteristic of PowerPoint slides (Kinchin et al., 2008b). Such a delivery mode represents an economy of performance (i.e., it is quick and 'efficient') and supports the student strategy of collecting enough of the appropriate information to pass the exam. This situation supports a cycle of nonlearning where linear curriculum sequences are 'purified from networks of interdisciplinary connections' (Matusov, 2009), which is an approach to teaching that ignores the ecology of practice, does not support student participation (Northedge, 2003), and runs contrary to the view that "to learn is to participate in and contribute to the evolution of the communal practice" (Keiny, 2002, p. 208).

The linear presentation of materials denies the student access to disciplinary ways of thinking, hiding the lecturer's expertise and maintaining the separation of teaching and research (Kinchin & Hay, 2007), and thereby keeping the undergraduate as a 'perpetual novice' (*sensu* Lea, 2005). The thought processes that have led to the construction of linear teaching materials are often hidden, so the mental effort required to master the discipline has been done already for the student:

Just because the order is logical, it represents the survey of subject matter made by one who already understands it, not the path of progress followed by a mind that is learning. The former may describe a uniform straight-way course; the latter must be a series of tacks, zig-zag movements back and forth. (Dewey, 1910, p. 204)

Such observations on students' learning styles may only be reflecting the students' approaches to coping with materials in a nonlearning situation (*sensu* Kinchin, Lygo-Baker, & Hay, 2008c).

## PERSONAL TEACHING MODELS

When university academics are asked to construct concept maps to portray their personal models of teaching, the resulting structures exhibit a number of morphological types and include various teaching-related concepts: some concentrating upon the teacher's actions, some upon classroom strategies, and others with more of a focus on student learning. Two extreme models are depicted in Figure 9.3. The chain is indicative of strategic success (i.e., "It works for me") in which the participant selects what is considered essential information and selectively ignores the rest. Application of a chain

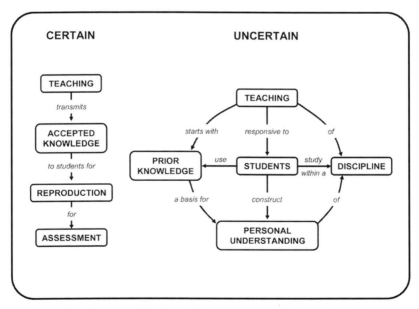

*Figure 9.3*   The linear model of teaching promotes a false certainty about the process, while the network structure accepts more uncertainty within the system—depicted as two exemplars drawn as indicative composites of typical components from a range of participants' responses.

model of teaching may indicate a survival strategy for a new university lecturer that is considered a 'safe system' to adopt (Canning, 2007).

The attractiveness of this model is easy to see: the boundaries are clear and the roles and responsibilities for student and teacher are easy to define. The goal is simply for the student to consume and reproduce accepted knowledge. The linear structure leaves no room for development through engagement with students, like that described by van Heerden (2005):

> I learned how to think like a chemist through nine years of education and three research positions. I thought about what that means though, only when I became a teacher. My discovery of how chemists think has evolved largely because of my interactions with students. I have come to believe that this discovery is absolutely critical for effective teaching; it has impacted upon my courses, my relationships with students, my pedagogical approaches, and my assessments of students' performances. (van Heerden, 2005, p. 95)

The network structure represents a model that is more likely to facilitate the teacher-student interactions described by van Heerden. It includes more sources of uncertainty (e.g., the variable nature of students' prior knowledge) that require teacher-student dialogue for a satisfactory resolution to be achieved. A move from 'accepted knowledge' (in the chain structure) to 'personal understanding' (in the network structure) requires a parallel shift in perspective from one that regards students as consumers of knowledge to one that regards students as producers of knowledge (e.g., Gamache, 2002).

## KNOWLEDGE STRUCTURES—A SOCIOLOGICAL PERSPECTIVE

There is an increasing recognition of the significance for student learning of the interactions between complementary knowledge structures in the development of expertise, creative thought, and problem-solving abilities (e.g., Hunter, Bedell-Avers, Hunsicker, Mumford, & Logon, 2008; Kinchin & Cabot, 2010; Kinchin et al., 2008a; Vance, Zell, & Groves, 2008). However, one of the most well-developed conceptual frameworks for the generic consideration of the variation in knowledge structures is that based on Bernstein's (2000) sociology of education.

Bernstein describes 'horizontal knowledge structures' (analogous to the chains described earlier) and 'hierarchical knowledge structures' (analogous to the networks described earlier). When elaborating upon horizontal knowledge, Bernstein (2000, p. 159) refers to a "segmental organization" in which "there is no necessary relations between what is learned in different segments" each of which is "directed towards a common competence". This resonates with the idea of 'chains of practice' that have been linked to the development of competence without understanding (Kinchin et al., 2008a). In contrast to horizontal structures, Bernstein (2000) sees hierarchical knowledge structures as attempting

> to create very general propositions and theories, which integrate knowledge at lower levels, and in this way shows underlying uniformities across an expanding range of apparently different phenomena. (Bernstein, 2000, p. 161)

This resonates with the view of integrated expert knowledge structures that are often hierarchical in structure (Bradley, Paul, & Seeman, 2006).

Further, this has been developed by Maton (2009) to consider how:

> curriculum structures play a role in creating conditions for students to experience cumulative learning, where their understandings integrate and subsume previous knowledge, or segmented learning, where new ideas or skills are accumulated alongside rather than build on past knowledge. (Maton, 2009, p. 44)

The segmented learning described by Maton equates to a surface approach that would result from the serial acquisition of chains, ultimately leading to cycles of nonlearning (Kinchin et al., 2008c). The cumulative learning that is described by Maton equates to the meaningful learning espoused by Novak (1998) that is typically represented by integrated networks. I contend that the linear teaching model represented in Figure 9.3 will promote segmented learning, whereas the networked teaching model will promote cumulative learning. Cumulative learning would be supported by advance organizers (as described earlier), whereas segmented learning would not as it does not build upon prior knowledge.

## THE STRUCTURE OF THE DISCIPLINE

We can also look beyond personal models of teaching to the structural representation of teaching as a discipline. Wignell (2007) described how weak boundaries work around a discipline (i.e., the more it overlaps with other disciplines). The more a discipline listens to other voices, the more dissenting voices there are within that discipline. In such instances, it is likely that the discipline will develop a knowledge structure which blends linear/segmented and hierarchical components. The field of education must develop weak boundaries as it needs to interact with other disciplines whether or not the other discipline has strong boundaries (e.g., physics) or weak boundaries (e.g., sociology). Therefore, in order to be able to relate to a variety of other disciplines, it may be important for teaching to accommodate both linear/segmented and networked/hierarchical models. Wignell

(2007, p. 203) goes on to describe the role of "dissenting voices" in directing a discipline towards a hierarchical or linear knowledge structure. Education has its share of 'dissenting voices' within the discipline—not least of which critique the value of the learning styles literature (e.g., Walsh, 2007). The discourse that surrounds such issues is, according to Wignell, likely to contribute to the shape of the discipline as a whole. For example, the formulaic application of learning styles research represents the segmented development of education in which there is a lack of unifying theory that allows disconnected acts to be put together in a way that fails to make the appropriate links. This then leads to dissatisfaction when the anticipated benefits of an innovation fail to materialize (e.g., Ritter, 2007), and elicits criticism of the level of scholarship evident within teaching (e.g., Sharp, Bowker, & Byrne, 2008)

## IN CONCLUSION

In order to find a way of managing the conflicting demands placed upon university teachers, it may be helpful to conceptualize the issue by thinking that the 'expert' teacher has to reconcile the tensions between the *chain of certainty* that is closely related to traditional assessment regimes and to the hegemony of the audit culture that prevails within universities, with the *network of uncertainty* that relates to the personal learning trajectories of students and the social values that are inherent in the disciplines (Figure 9.3). Understanding is then seen as the basis for the development of competence (Sandberg & Targama, 2007), and learning is the change in meaning structures and the relationship between them (Dall'Alba & Sandberg, 1996). This means that assessment of learning must refer to the students' ability to navigate between knowledge structures rather than reproduce a single knowledge structure. The latter might be seen as assessing nonlearning.

In Bernsteinian terms, the teaching of a discipline through a segmented discourse will lead to the development of a horizontal (linear) knowledge structure that is context-dependent. Teaching approaches need to support the student in breaking free from the confines of a narrow, segmented discourse and start to appreciate multiple perspectives. This can be supported by using a variety of teaching techniques that encourage student participation and address a range of learning style preferences exhibited within a cohort of students (e.g., Rogers, 2009). When Bernstein (2000, p. 171) illustrated his conceptual framework by considering his own discipline (sociology), he concluded that "the array of specialized languages which fragment the experience of the acquirer may shatter any sense of underlying unity". This conclusion may equally be applied to education. Fragmentation has also been used as a criticism of the learning styles literature where it has been interpreted as a lack of coherence in the field (e.g., Coffield, Moseley, Hall, & Ecclestone, 2004). Such a plurality may be reconceptualized as a strength (of both education in general and of learning styles in particular) as "diverse imaging shows the potential of the social" (Bernstein, 2000, p. 171). And surely, above all, teaching is a social activity. This knowledge structures perspective discussed here may offer a way forward in the development of a theoretical basis for the observation of teaching in higher education (e.g., Hatzipanagos & Lygo-Baker, 2006).

Styles research needs to acknowledge the teaching approaches to which individual students are (and have been) exposed—paying particular attention to the degree of linearity exhibited in the teaching materials used and in the underlying personal model of teaching that directs the teacher's approach in the classroom. If observed learning styles are a consequence of adaptation to the teaching that students have experienced, then it is possible that the perceived benefits of a classroom intervention may only be applicable to a student's approach to learning with a particular teacher. In short, learning styles research needs to be contextualized to have meaning and provide information on student learning characteristics that may be generalizable to other situations, and needs to be clear that learning style *preferences* are indicative of learning styles *as employed* by students in the classroom.

Students' learning styles may be obscured where the reflection has been undertaken by the teacher on the students' behalf. It may, therefore, be difficult to determine genuine learning styles in an environment that encourages nonlearning (Kinchin et al., 2008c). While the development of student strategies to cope with nonlearning may have short-term utility for the student, the moral purpose of teaching deserves to be supported by a pedagogic framework that allows teaching to develop in ways that reward the application of productive, personally rewarding learning styles.

## BIBLIOGRAPHY

Ausubel, D.P. (2000). *The Acquisition and Retention of Knowledge: A Cognitive View*. Dordrecht, Netherlands: Kluwer Academic Publishers.

Bernstein, B. (2000). *Pedagogy, Symbolic Control and Identity*. Oxford: Rowman & Littlefield Publishers.

Biggs, J. (2003). *Teaching for Quality Learning at University* (2nd ed.). Maidenhead: SRHE/OUP.

Bradley, J.H., Paul, R., & Seeman, E. (2006). Analysing the structure of expert knowledge. *Information and Management, 43,* 77–91.

Caine, R.N., & Caine, G. (1994). *Making Connections: Teaching and the Human Brain*. Menlo Park, CA: Addison-Wesley Publishing Company.

Canning, J. (2007). Pedagogy as a discipline: emergence, sustainability and professionalisation. *Teaching in Higher Education, 12,* 393–403.

Clement. J., Zietsman, A., & Brown D.E. (1989). Not all preconceptions are misconceptions: finding "anchoring conceptions" for grounding instruction on students' intuitions. *International Journal of Science Education, 11,* 554–565.

Cliburn, J.W. (1986). Using concept maps to sequence instructional materials. *Journal of College Science Teaching, 15*, 377–379.

Cliburn, J.W. (1990). Concept maps to promote meaningful learning. *Journal of College Science Teaching, 19*, 212–217.

Coffield, F.C., Moseley, D.V.M., Hall, E., & Ecclestone, K. (2004). *Should We Be Using Learning Styles? What Research Has to Say to Practice*. London: Learning and Skills Research Centre.

Copperman, E., Beeri, C., & Ben-Zvi, N. (2007). Visual modelling of learning processes. *Innovations in Education and Teaching International, 44*, 257–272.

Dall'Alba, G., & Sandberg, J. (1996). Educating for competence in professional practice. *Instructional Science, 24*, 411–437.

Dewey, J. (1910). *How We Think*. Boston: DC Heath & Co.

Gamache, P. (2002) University students as creators of personal knowledge: an alternative epistemological view. *Teaching in Higher Education, 7*, 277–294.

Hailikari, T., Katajavouri, N., & Llindblom-Ylänne, S. (2008). The relevance of prior knowledge in learning and instructional design. *American Journal of Pharmaceutical Education, 72*(5), Article 113, 1–8.

Hatzipanagos, S., & Lygo-Baker, S. (2006). Teaching observations: a meeting of minds? *International Journal of Teaching and Learning in Higher Education, 17*, 97–105.

Hay, D.B., & Kinchin, I.M. (2007). *Medical Students' Response to Variation in Expert Knowledge Structures: Rote Learning?* Paper presented at the 12th annual European Learning Styles Information Network (ELSIN) conference, 12–14 June, Dublin, Ireland.

Hay, D.B., Kinchin, I.M., & Lygo-Baker, S. (2008). Making learning visible: the role of concept mapping in higher education. *Studies in Higher Education, 33*, 295–311.

Hoffman, R.R., & Lintern, G. (2006). Eliciting and representing the knowledge of experts. In K.A. Ericsson, N. Charness, P.J. Feltovich, & R.R. Hoffman (Eds.), *The Cambridge Handbook of Expertise and Expert Performance* (pp. 203–222). Cambridge: Cambridge University Press.

Huai, H. (1997). Concept mapping in learning biology: theoretical review on cognitive and learning styles. *Journal of Interactive Learning Research, 8*(3/4), 325–340.

Hunter, S.T., Bedell-Avers, K.E., Hunsicker, C.M., Mumford, M.D., & Logon, G.S. (2008). Applying multiple knowledge structures in creative thought: effects on idea generation and problem-solving. *Creativity Research Journal, 20*, 137–154.

Jonassen, D.H., Reeves, T., Hong, N., Harvey, D., & Peters, K. (1997). Concept mapping as cognitive learning and assessment tools. *Journal of Interactive Learning Research, 8*(3/4), 289–308.

Keiny, S. (2002). *Ecological Thinking: A New Approach to Educational Change*. Lanham, MD: University of America Press.

Kinchin, I.M. (2000). *The Active Use of Concept Mapping to Promote Meaningful Learning in Biological Science*. Unpublished PhD thesis, University of Surrey, UK.

Kinchin, I.M. (2001). If concept mapping is so helpful to learning biology, why aren't we all doing it? *International Journal of Science Education, 23*, 1257–1269.

Kinchin, I.M. (2003) Effective teacher↔student dialogue: a model from biological education. *Journal of Biological Education, 37*, 110–113.

Kinchin, I.M. (2008). *Excluding the Novice: The Real Price of Reading Bullet Points in Lectures*. Paper presented at the annual Society for Research in Higher Education (SRHE) conference, 9–11 December, Liverpool, UK.

Kinchin, I.M., & Alias, M. (2005). Exploiting variations in concept map morphology as a lesson-planning tool for trainee teachers in Higher Education. *Journal of In-Service Education, 31*, 569–591.

Kinchin, I.M., & Cabot, L.B. (2007). Using concept mapping principles in PowerPoint. *European Journal of Dental Education, 11*, 194–199.

Kinchin, I.M., & Cabot, L.B. (2010). Reconsidering the dimensions of expertise: from linear stages towards dual processing. *London Review of Education, 8*, 153–166.

Kinchin, I.M., Cabot, L.B., & Hay, D.B. (2008a). Visualising expertise: towards an authentic pedagogy for higher education. *Teaching in Higher Education, 13*, 315–326.

Kinchin, I.M., Chadha, D., & Kokotailo, P. (2008b). Using PowerPoint as a lens to focus on linearity in teaching. *Journal of Further and Higher Education, 32*, 333–346.

Kinchin, I.M., & Hay, D.B. (2007). The myth of the research-led teacher. *Teachers and Teaching: Theory and Practice, 13*, 43–61.

Kinchin, I.M., Hay, D.B., & Adams, A. (2000). How a qualitative approach to concept map analysis can be used to aid learning by illustrating patterns of conceptual development. *Educational Research, 42*, 43–57.

Kinchin, I.M., Lygo-Baker, S., & Hay, D.B. (2008c). Universities as centres of non-learning. *Studies in Higher Education, 33*, 89–103.

Land, R., Meyer, J.H.F., & Smith, J. (2008). *Threshold Concepts within the Disciplines*. Rotterdam: SensePublishers.

Lea, M.R. (2005). Communities of practice in higher education: useful heuristic or educational model? In D. Barton & K. Tusting (Eds.), *Beyond Communities of Practice: Language, Power and Social Context* (pp. 180–197). Cambridge: Cambridge University Press.

Martin, D.J. (1994). Concept mapping as an aid to lesson planning: a longitudinal study. *Journal of Elementary Science Education, 6*, 11–30.

Maton, K. (2009). Cumulative and segmented learning: exploring the role of curriculum structures in knowledge building. *British Journal of Sociology of Education, 30*, 43–57.

Matusov, E. (2009). *Journey into Dialogic Pedagogy*. New York: Nova Science Publishers.

Nesbit, J.C., & Adesope, O.O. (2006). Learning with concept and knowledge maps: a meta-analysis. *Review of Educational Research, 76*, 413–448.

Northedge, A. (2003). Enabling participation in academic discourse. *Teaching in Higher Education, 8*, 168–180.

Novak, J.D. (1998). *Learning, Creating and Using Knowledge: Concept Maps as Facilitative Tools in Schools and Corporations*. Mahwah, NJ: Lawrence Erlbaum Associates.

Novak, J.D., & Cañas, A.J. (2007). Theoretical origins of concept maps, how to construct them and uses in education. *Reflecting Education, 3*, 29–42.

Novak, J.D., & Gowin, D.B. (1984). *Learning How to Learn*. Cambridge: Cambridge University Press.

Rayner, S., & Riding, R. (1997). Towards a categorisation of cognitive styles and learning styles. *Educational Psychology, 17*(1&2), 5–27.

Ritter, L. (2007). Unfulfilled promises: how inventories, instruments and institutions subvert discourses of diversity and promote commonality. *Teaching in Higher Education, 12*, 569–579.

Rogers, K.M.A. (2009). A preliminary investigation and analysis of student learning style preferences in further and higher education. *Journal of Further and Higher Education, 33*, 13–21.

Sandberg, J., & Targama, A. (2007). *Managing Understanding in Organizations*. London: Sage.

Sharp, J.G., Bowker, R., & Byrne, J. (2008). VAK or VAK-uous? Towards the trivialisation of learning and the death of scholarship. *Research Papers in Education, 23,* 293–314.

Vance, C., Zell, D., & Groves, K. (2008). Considering individual linear/nonlinear thinking style and innovative corporate culture. *International Journal of Organizational Analysis, 16,* 232–248.

van Heerden, A. (2005). Articulating the cognitive processes at the heart of chemistry. In T. Riordan & J. Roth (Eds.), *Disciplines as Frameworks for Student Learning* (pp. 95–120). Sterling, VA.: Stylus.

Walsh, K. (2007). Learning styles: do they really exist? *Medical Education, 41,* 618.

West, L.H.T., & Fensham, P.J. (1974). Prior knowledge and the learning of science: a review of Ausubel's theory and his process. *Studies in Science Education, 1,* 61–81.

Wignell, P. (2007). Vertical and horizontal discourse and the social sciences. In F. Christie & J.R. Martin (Eds.), *Language, Knowledge and Pedagogy: Functional Linguistic and Sociological Perspectives* (pp. 184–204). London: Continuum.

Willerman, M., & Mac Harg, R.A. (1991). The concept map as an advance organiser. *Journal of Research in Science Teaching, 28,* 705–711.

# 10 Illustrating a Complementary Paradigm for Styles Research

## From a Third-Person to a Second-Person Perspective

*Melodie Rosenfeld and Sherman Rosenfeld*

## INTRODUCTION

There is wide agreement that teachers should respect individual learning differences (ILDs). The 'one-size-fits-all' approach of traditional classrooms, which seemed to make sense during the Industrial Age, does not meet the needs of the Information Age. The US National Board for Professional Teaching Standards (NBPTS, 2009) claims that effective teachers

> believe all students can learn. . . . They recognize the individual differences that distinguish their students from one another and they take account for these differences in their practice. (NBPTS, 2009, online source)

Based on this line of reasoning, the educational research agenda should make individual learning differences, such as style preferences, a top priority. Currently, this has not been the case.

Interest in styles has waxed and waned over the past decades. For example, in the 1970s, there were promising hopes of exploiting Attribute-Treatment Interactions (ATI; Cronbach & Snow, 1977) and a plethora of learning styles instruments (e.g., Dunn, Dunn, & Price, 1979; Kolb, 1976; Torrance, 1980). The basic premise of ATI research—that there are specific educational 'treatments' that will differentially help people who have measurable 'attributes' (styles) to learn better—was not adequately supported by educational research (Jonassen & Grabowski, 1993). In addition, the learning styles field of research in the 1970s was disjointed, lacked strong theoretical foundation (Kozhevnikov, 2007), produced mixed research results (Jonassen & Grabowski, 1993), relied on inventories that lacked consistent reliability or validity (Coffield, Moseley, Hall, & Ecclestone, 2004), and had 'arbitrary distinctions and overlapping dimensions' (Kozhevnikov, 2007). Even more importantly, the styles field lacked a common conceptual framework and language for researchers (Sternberg, 2001).

Educational researchers seem to have responded to this situation in one of two ways: (1) many concluded that the field of styles research was not fruitful to pursue, so they abandoned it, and (2) some remained committed to styles research, so they redoubled their efforts, while using the same research paradigm. The first response is illustrated in a recent call for papers by the American Educational Research Association (AERA, 2008), the largest educational research organization. While it suggests over 200 topics, not one includes learning styles or the individual learning differences of students or teachers, even when one of the wider categories stated in the call is 'diversity of all kinds'. A similar response comes from the European Association of Research in Learning and Instruction (EARLI, 2009). Few of the 2,000 members from over forty countries engage in styles research.

The second response has been to continue to unify and improve conceptual understandings and constructs (e.g., Sadler-Smith, 2009). Zhang and Sternberg (2009) point to the considerable progress and renewed interest in styles research in the last few years, including increased dialogue among diverse researchers, empirical studies on the nature of intellectual styles, styles in online learning contexts, and new inventories for application in business settings. Nevertheless, these efforts have been largely located in the same traditional research paradigm. A recent analysis of styles research within the European Learning Styles Information Network (ELSIN) shows that close to 70% of the forty-five presentations in this research group utilized traditional, correlational research, in which research participants' voice and conscious involvement were not part of the study (Rosenfeld & Rosenfeld, 2008a).

In order to rekindle wider interest in styles, we suggest a third response: to conduct research based on a complementary paradigm, one that does give voice to learners about their own style preferences. We believe that this new paradigm—based on self-reflection and self-regulation (Boekaerts & Corno, 2005)—will complement the traditional paradigm and help to broaden and advance the field of styles research. Following we compare the traditional paradigm (a 'third-person' perspective) with the new paradigm (a 'second-person' perspective) and outline the theoretical framework of this complementary paradigm. Next, we present and analyze four studies which illustrate this new paradigm. We conclude with suggested directions for researchers and educators within the second-person paradigm.

## COMPARING THE TWO PARADIGMS

Over the last several decades, styles research has focused on a positivist research agenda that studies correlations between learners' styles scores and achievement. We call this approach a third-person perspective, since participants are related to from a distance, without directly involving their conscious awareness and self-reflection concerning their own styles preferences. The guiding assumption in these studies seems to be that participants should not be directly involved, since this approach is not sufficiently rigorous or objective. In addition, some researchers claim that learners' conscious awareness is often "inaccessible" to measurement (Wolz, 2003, p. 96). Thus, the third-person perspective does not focus on increased learner empowerment or self-regulation, which we believe to be the main goal of research-informed practice.

The second-person perspective can be distinguished from the third-person perspective in the following four areas (Table 10.1):

- Research goals: research within the second-person perspective attempts to understand the process and effects of learner change, and to use this understanding to empower individuals to be more effective learners and teachers;
- Research questions: the research questions focus on the effects that learners' increased sensitivity to styles preferences have on 'positive results' (Gusky, 1986), which include but are not limited to achievement;
- The role of styles inventories: styles inventories give learners meaningful terms, concepts, and scores to empower learners to understand their preferences and develop insights and effective practice concerning themselves and others. Learners are encouraged to question the scores they receive, rather than accept them at face value. Inventory scores then become a springboard for 'deep conversation' (Rainey & Kolb, 1995) rather than just a source of measurement;
- Research methodology: the complementary paradigm begins with qualitative research, in order to identify and better understand important phenomena and variables, which later can become the focus for quantitative research.

## THE THEORETICAL FRAMEWORK OF THE SECOND-PERSON PERSPECTIVE

The theoretical foundation of this complementary paradigm is social-cognitive theory, in which 'self-reflection' is a prominent feature (Bandura, 1986). Pajares (2002) describes this process as:

> Through self-reflection, people make sense of their experiences, explore their own cognitions and self-beliefs, engage in self-evaluation, and alter their thinking and behavior accordingly. (Pajares, 2002, p. 1)

Social-cognitive theory also focuses on 'self-regulation', in which the self-regulated learners have "emerged as metacognitively, motivationally, and behaviorally active participants in their own learning" (Zimmerman, 1990, p. 4). Social-cognitive theory also views research subjects as:

*Table 10.1*   Comparing Two Style Research Paradigms

|  | *Third-person perspective* | *Second-person perspective* |
|---|---|---|
| Research goals | Theory: To understand how styles (aptitudes) are matched to specific interventions (treatments). To improve conceptual understanding of style constructs.<br>Practice: To use this knowledge to maximize learning achievement, by matching learner styles to appropriate interventions. | Theory: To understand the process and effects of learner change as a result of increased sensitivity to style preferences.<br>Practice: To use this knowledge to increase learner or teacher effectiveness. |
| Examples of research questions | Correlation studies: What is the relationship between styles scores and learning achievement?<br><br>Intervention studies: What are the effects of a program that matches treatment to styles preferences? | Correlation studies: What is the relationship between learners' self-knowledge of their styles and "positive results" (including but not limited to achievement)?<br>Intervention studies: What are the effects of a program that develops learner sensitivity to styles?<br>Case studies: What characterizes learners with different style preferences in diverse learning contexts? |
| Role of style inventories | To provide reliable learning styles scores | To provide meaningful terms, concepts, and scores to empower learners |
| Methodology | Quantitative | Qualitative and quantitative |

self-organizing, proactive, self-reflecting and self-regulating rather than as reactive organisms shaped and shepherded by environmental forces or driven by concealed inner impulses. (Pajares, 2002, p. 1)

The second-person perspective is consistent with Sternberg's (2001) call for unifying styles research within the psychology of choice and decision making. Individuals often operate without an awareness of their own style preferences; in the complementary paradigm, the researcher helps individuals raise their degree of consciousness about styles (Sternberg & Zhang, 2001), thereby helping them become more effective learners or teachers.

## ILLUSTRATING THE SECOND-PERSON PERSPECTIVE

A series of four studies illustrates the second-person perspective (Rosenfeld & Rosenfeld, 2004, 2006, 2008b, 2008c). The main goal of the series was to investigate the development of teacher sensitivity to individual learning differences, namely styles preferences. Towards this end, the first author developed and mediated a long-term (56 hours), collaborative, constructivist professional development (PD) course, at a teachers' academic college in Israel, to help elementary and middle-school teachers increase their sensitivity to styles. Increased teacher sensitivity to styles indicates (1) increased conscious awareness and self-reflection about their own and others' styles preferences, (2) a developing repertoire to address diverse styles preferences in practice, and (3) the belief that failure can sometimes be attributed to a *mismatched* style preference rather than lack of ability

The PD was based on learning style theory (Honigsfeld & Schiering, 2004; Ojure, 1997) common in American studies of grade-school learners (e.g., Dunn et al., 1979; Johnston, 1998; McCarthy, 1980), where styles preferences are "differentially good fits to different [learning] environments" (Sternberg, 2001, p. 6), and can be disadvantaged in a mismatched learning context. Teachers learned about and discussed their own style preferences, based on their performance with five to seven style instruments, as mentioned following (see Appendix 10A for details.). During the PD, the teachers interviewed colleagues with extremely strong style preferences, discussed the implications of their own styles preferences on their learning and teaching, observed diverse learners, presented lessons matched to different styles, and shared their developing insights as learners and teachers.

After the PD, teachers submitted a final written project, in which they reflected on academic research articles about styles; compared styles constructs and models; designed a 4MAT learning unit (McCarthy, 1980); analyzed styles of other learners (family members, friends, students); recommended how to work with learners with diverse styles preferences; transformed school material to 'match' different styles; applied the Triarchic Abilities model (Sternberg, Ferrari, Clinkenbeard, & Grigorenko, 1996) to classroom assignments; and wrote critical incidents and insights documenting any changes they were undergoing (Rosenfeld & Rosenfeld, 2004). The four studies, outlined next, investigated to what extent the teachers changed as a result of the PD. The full studies are available online (Rosenfeld, 2008).

## Study 1: Understanding the Effects of the PD

*Background.* This pilot study (Rosenfeld & Rosenfeld, 2004) investigated teachers' changes due to the PD course. Teachers used five styles instruments (see Appendix 10A: Barsch, 1980; Johnston & Dainton, 1997; Kolb, 1976; Torrance, 1980; Witkin, Oltman, Raskin, & Karp, 1971).

*Research goal.* To understand the effects of the 56-hour PD course on the teachers.

*Research questions.* (1) What types of changes, if any, did the teachers undergo as a result of the PD? (2) What aspects of the PD facilitated teacher change? (3) What was the process of teacher change?

*Role of the styles inventories.* To provide meaningful terms, concepts, and scores to enable learners to understand themselves and colleagues.

*Methodology.* An analysis was conducted of teachers' (N = 14) sixty-two written, critical incidents, in which teachers described a real situation where they applied their knowledge of styles preferences to understand or improve a situation ('when I got it'). Other research tools included a pre/posttest, focus-group interviews, field notes, and a Likert-scale questionnaire in which teachers rated the usefulness of different parts of the PD.

*Evidence of a second-person perspective.* Data focused on teachers' reflections concerning (1) the results of their and colleagues' styles scores on the five instruments, (2) the PD course, and (3) the process of their own changing sensitivity to styles preferences.

*Findings.* Based on an analysis of the critical incidents, an empirical model of teacher change emerged (see Figure 10.1). When teachers increased sensitivity to styles preferences, they became more effective teachers; they improved their language, beliefs, and classroom practice, which led to 'positive results' with self and learners. Whereas we were encouraged with these findings, we wondered if they could be applied to a 'real-world' educational setting, which led to the second study.

## Study 2: Understanding Teacher Responses to Constructivist Learning Contexts

*Background.* This second intervention study was conducted in a middle school with science teachers (Rosenfeld & Rosenfeld, 2006). For eight years, the school had adopted Project-Based Learning (PBL) as its 'politically correct' constructivist learning context. Some teachers sabotaged PBL efforts, preferring to teach in a traditional, didactic mode. This 'dysfunctional' teaching staff felt they could not openly discuss pedagogical differences.

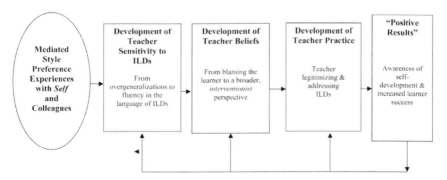

*Figure 10.1* Empirical model of developing teacher sensitivity to style preferences. Note. This model emerged from the data of Study 1. When teachers experienced style scores and preferences with colleagues, they improved their beliefs and practice, leading to "positive results" (Gusky, 1986), which included awareness of their own self-development and increased learner success. These results acted as a "feedback loop" to reinforce the other components in the model.

During the PD, the mediator worked with staff concerning styles preferences, hoping they could work together more effectively.

*Research goals.* (1) To investigate the effects of the PD concerning the teachers' increased sensitivity to styles preferences besides their own. (2) To understand any relationship between a teachers' styles preferences and preferred pedagogy.

*Research questions.* (1) How might a teacher's response to a constructivist (PBL) learning context be related to his or her own learning style preferences? (2) How might sensitizing teachers to their own and colleagues' styles preferences lead to positive changes in teachers and staff relations and help to sustain a constructivist learning context?

*Role of the styles inventories.* To provide meaningful terms, concepts, and scores to enable the staff to understand and legitimize themselves and colleagues with differing styles preferences.

*Methodology.* The science staff ($N$ = 11) participated in nine hours of PD divided into three three-hour workshops. Teachers discussed learning styles theory, experienced two style inventories (Johnston & Dainton, 1997; Kolb, 1976), and were interviewed during, after, and a year following the PD. The researchers designed and administered a questionnaire of preferences for a traditional or PBL learning context. Staff responses were analyzed according to their reported relations with other staff members and attitude to PBL.

*Evidence of a second-person perspective.* Data focused on teachers' reflections about their styles preferences and how these preferences affected their epistemological beliefs, pedagogical choices, and changing staff relations.

*Findings.* By listening to the teachers, we learned that this staff's dysfunction resulted partly from unconscious, unexamined style preferences and mismatched PBL pedagogy that teachers were required to enact. The mediator helped teachers identify and accept conflicting preferences with the help of styles concepts and scores. Interestingly, the science coordinator, who drove the school's PBL agenda, had an extremely strong style preference which was 'matched' to PBL. When she increased her sensitivity to styles preferences, she stopped stigmatizing her traditional staff, ultimately leading to healthier staff relations and the sustaining of PBL in the school. Study 2 reinforced the model of teacher change, derived from Study 1 (Figure 10.1), and raised the issue of teachers, like the science coordinator, with extremely strong style preferences. How might such strong preferences impact a teacher's language, beliefs, and practice? This question drove our third study.

## Study 3: Understanding Teachers with Extremely Strong Style Preferences

*Background.* This case study investigated three teachers (Rosenfeld & Rosenfeld, 2008c) who participated in the year-long (56-hour) PD course at the college. They were chosen because of their extremely strong styles preferences on seven styles instruments and were eager to share insights concerning their sensitivity to styles.

*Research goals.* (1) To understand the language, beliefs, and practice of teachers with extreme styles preferences. (2) To understand the implications of their strong styles preferences. (3) To use their increasing sensitivity to styles to empower these individuals to be more effective learners and teachers.

*Research questions.* (1) Who are these teachers as learners with extreme ILD preferences? (2) Before the PD course, what language, beliefs, and teaching practice are associated with these teachers? (3) After the PD course, what changes, if any, were there in the teachers' language, beliefs, and practice?

*Role of the styles inventories.* To provide meaningful terms, concepts, and scores to enable the teachers to understand and share about themselves with colleagues.

*Methodology.* The three teachers had extreme style preferences, based on their scores on five learning style inventories (Barsch, 1980; Felder & Silverman, 1988; Johnston & Dainton, 1997; Kolb, 1976; Torrance, 1980), one cognitive styles test (Witkin et al., 1971), and a simulation exercise based on the Triarchic Abilities Test (Sternberg, 1985). Two of the teachers had extremely strong and different learning style preferences and one teacher had extremely balanced scores (no style preferences at all) on the seven styles instruments. Data were collected from pre/posttest questions, written critical incidents, and multiple individual and focus group interviews during the year.

*Evidence of a second-person perspective.* The study included all of the teachers' styles scores but centered on the three teachers' own insights about the impact that their extremely strong styles preferences had on their language, beliefs, and practice.

*Findings.* The scores told us that these teachers had extreme preferences, but without the teachers' insights, we would not have understood the depth or the impact of their styles preferences on their learning and teaching. The data showed that these teachers with extremely strong style preferences (1) taught the way they preferred to learn, (2) overgeneralized and projected their own learning needs onto students, and (3) held initial pathognomonic (Jordan & Stanovich, 2001) beliefs about students who experienced learning difficulties and who had different style preferences than the teachers. By increasing their sensitivity to the legitimacy of styles other than their own, the three teachers reported more effective language, beliefs, and practice. The teacher with extremely balanced styles preferences continued to hold deficit beliefs about students even after the PD. The teachers acknowledged a direct connection between how they learn and teach. Their insights inform us about other learners who have extreme (or extremely balanced) style preferences. We wondered whether other teachers, with strong styles preferences, also held initial deficit beliefs about students. We also wondered to what extent the PD was effective on a large scale. This led to our fourth, quantitative study.

## Study 4: Evaluating the PD Intervention Quantitatively

*Background.* In the previous three qualitative studies when teachers increased sensitivity to styles preferences, they expressed more effective, 'interventionist' beliefs about learners experiencing difficulties: ("I can intervene to help") rather than 'pathognomonic' (blame-the-learner, deficit) beliefs (Jordan & Stanovich, 2001). The fourth study (Rosenfeld & Rosenfeld, 2008b) investigated these and other concepts quantitatively, with a large research sample.

*Research goals.* (1) To investigate the extent to which teachers developed effective 'interventionist' beliefs as a result of the PD. (2) To investigate the relationship between such beliefs and the teachers' own style preferences. (3) To measure the strength and distribution of teachers' styles and strength of preferences.

*Research questions.* (1) To what extent, if any, did the teachers increase their interventionist beliefs about students as a result of the PD course? (2) To what extent, if any, did the teachers' own styles preferences affect their interventionist beliefs before and after the PD course? (3) What was the distribution and strength of teachers' styles preferences?

*Methodology.* The study (1) measured teachers' ($N = 234$) strength of style preferences on five styles instruments (Barsch, 1980; Johnston & Dainton, 1977; Kolb, 1976; Torrance, 1980; Witkin et al., 1971), (2) developed scales to differentiate the strength of teachers' preferences on inventories, (3) developed tools for eliciting and measuring teacher beliefs about students, and (4) correlated teachers' strength of styles preferences with beliefs about students (interventionist versus pathognomonic).

*Role of style inventories.* To provide reliable scores which show the relative strength of teachers' style preferences.

*Evidence of a second-person perspective.* This was a correlational, quantitative study that focused on teachers' reflections on their own and colleagues' styles.

*Findings.* (1) The PD intervention significantly contributed to increasing teachers' effective (interventionist) beliefs about students. There was a significant ($p < 0.001$) increase in teachers' interventionist beliefs from the pretest (18%) (before the PD) to the posttest (49%) (after the PD). There was a significant decrease of teachers' pathognomonic beliefs ($p < 0.001$) from pretest to posttest. (2) Before the PD, some teachers' styles preferences were more 'at risk'; that is, these preferences are weakly correlated with effective (interventionist) beliefs about students. For example, none of the teachers who had extremely balanced scores ($N = 17$) held effective (interventionist) beliefs before the PD. Teachers with style preferences strongly matched to traditional school tasks were also more likely to hold pathognomonic ('blame-the-learner') beliefs about students who experienced difficulties. (3) Regarding distribution of style preferences, teachers matched to traditional school tasks (those with accommodator, left-hemisphere, sequential preferences) were significantly overrepresented in this large sample. Also, a high percentage of the teachers (about 60%) initially held pathognomonic beliefs about students, beliefs which have been shown to contribute to student learning failure (Jordan & Stanovich, 2001). After the PD, teachers significantly improved their beliefs about students (from pathognomonic to interventionist). The findings of this study support the claim that this type of PD should be included in teacher professional development.

## CONCLUSIONS

The second-person perspective, based on social-cognitive theory, defines learners as proactive, reflective, and active participants in their own learning. In the studies described earlier, research participants were not simply anonymous sources of styles scores. Instead, these research participants reflected on their styles and became sources of insights for both theory and practice. We suggest that the second-person perspective research paradigm is an example of 'use-inspired basic research' (Stokes, 1997), in which real-world problems catalyze basic research which then develops theoretical understanding. This approach is illustrated by the work of Louis Pasteur, whose scientific interest in applied problems (e.g., why wine and milk sour) led him to conduct basic research about science (i.e., the biology of microorganisms). The initial problems catalyzed basic research, which in turn was applied to solve further real-world problems. In the case of our studies, the real-world problem was that many educators have remained largely insensitive to styles differences, even after widespread calls for addressing these differences. Our response was to research the impact of a PD designed to increase teacher sensitivity to styles, which led us to uncover basic theoretical concepts that can then be applied to further real-world problems. Some of these problems, for example, in teacher development, are being addressed by other researchers as well (e.g., Evans & Waring, 2009).

Specifically, the second-person perspective in the described studies contributed to both theory and practice. With regard to theory, it helps to develop deeper understandings of: (1) the process and effects of teacher change, for individuals and teaching staffs, which occur as teachers increase sensitivity to styles; (2) the importance of cultivating effective (interventionist) teacher beliefs about students; (3) the conditions under which teachers with certain style preferences are mismatched to certain learning contexts (e.g., PBL); and (4) the importance of strength of style preference. In practical terms, the second-person perspective contributes to developing more informed interventions that: (1) develop and enact PD that sensitizes teachers to style preferences; (2) raise the issue of teacher beliefs about students; (3) help all teachers succeed in constructivist learning contexts (e.g., PBL); and (4) use the concept of strength of style preferences to help develop more effective learners, teachers, and learning contexts.

## SUGGESTIONS FOR FURTHER RESEARCH

We suggest that the following areas and questions might advance and broaden the field of styles research, using the second-person perspective:

### Understanding the Relationship Between Teachers' Sensitivity to Styles Preferences and Their Students' Success

When teachers increased their sensitivity to styles preferences, they reported positive effects on students (Studies 1 and 3). Further questions might include: when, how, and to what extent does increased teacher sensitivity to students' styles preferences make a difference in student achievement or other areas of success, such as increased cooperation, self-efficacy, learning motivation, and self-regulation?

### Increasing Learner Effectiveness with the second-Person Perspective

In the studies, teachers' sensitivity to styles was not done to them but with them. The same conscious process can benefit students, as reported in programs such as "Let Me Learn" (Johnston, 1998) for school-age learners. Further questions might include: how might students' conscious awareness of styles preferences optimize self-reflection, self-regulation, and effective learning choices they make?

### Understanding the Impact of Strength-of-Style Preference

Whereas some styles inventories determine the strength of a learner's preference (e.g., Johnston & Dainton, 1997; Kolb, 1976), few other studies have fleshed out the implications of such preferences among teachers or students. The second-person perspective gives voice to learners whose style preferences are the 'difference that makes a difference' in learning success, for example, those with extreme, strong preferences. A related concept is the flexibility of style preference (Kozhevnikov, 2007); perhaps increased teacher sensitivity to style preferences can encourage such learners to develop flexibility. Further questions might include: how does the strength of a style preference affect learning or teaching success in different learning contexts? How can we help teachers with no styles preferences ('extremely balanced') appreciate the difficulties of learners with less flexible, extreme style preferences?

## Determining When Styles Are Important to Address

The second-person perspective in Study 3 showed that teachers with extreme style preferences were disadvantaged when there was a strong mismatch between their styles and the task demands. Riding and Rayner (1998) have suggested that styles preferences are especially important to address when there is low student ability and high task complexity. We have suggested that younger learners with strong style preferences are especially disadvantaged in a mismatched learning situation (Rosenfeld & Rosenfeld, 2008a). Further questions might include: when do styles preferences make a significant difference? What is the role of variables that indicate that style preferences are especially important to address, such as: low learner ability, high task complexity, strong style preference, young age, and strong mismatch of the task to the learner's style?

## Sustaining Constructivist Learning Contexts

Study 2 revealed that teachers with styles matched to a traditional context were disadvantaged in a constructivist context (PBL). Other research has shown that some students with styles mismatched to traditional learning contexts flourish in PBL (Rosenfeld & Rosenfeld, 1999). Further questions might include: how can sensitizing teachers or students to styles preferences help them make a successful transition from traditional to constructivist learning contexts?

## Broadening the Target Groups for Styles Research

There are innumerable styles studies which use college-level students but a dearth of studies targeting younger populations (Rosenfeld & Rosenfeld, 2008a). We suggest applying the second-person perspective with younger learners as well as in other disciplines, such as business and management.

We believe that such research topics and questions based on the complementary second-person perspective can contribute to revitalizing the field of style research. By focusing on the conscious awareness and self-reflection of learners, this research paradigm holds promise for revealing important insights as well as for developing more effective learners and teachers in diverse educational contexts.

## BIBLIOGRAPHY

AERA—American Educational Research Association. (2008). Calls for proposals: Studies in diversity, section 2. Retrieved February 20, 2008, from http://www.aera.net/meetings/Default.aspx?menu_id=342&id=2944

Bandura, A. (1986). *Social Foundations of Thought and Action: A Social Cognitive Theory*. Englewood Cliffs, NJ: Prentice Hall.

Barsch, J. (1980). *Barsch Learning Styles Inventory*. Navato, CA: Academic Therapy Publishers.

Boekaerts, M., & Corno, L. (2005). Self-regulation in the classroom: a perspective on assessment and intervention. *Applied Psychology, 54*, 199–231.

Coffield, F., Moseley, D., Hall, E., & Ecclestone, K. (2004). *Should We Be Using Learning Styles? What Research Has to Say to Practice*. London: Learning and Skills Research Centre.

Cronbach, L.J., & Snow, R. E. (1977). *Aptitudes and Instructional Methods*. New York: Irvington Publishers.

Dunn R., Dunn K., & Price, G.E. (1979). *Learning Styles Inventory*. Lawrence, KS: Price Systems.

EARLI—European Association for Research in Learning and Instruction. (2009). Retrieved September 27, 2009, from http://celstec.org/content/earli-2009-conference-amsterdam

Evans, C., & Waring, M. (2009). The place of cognitive style in pedagogy: realizing its potential in practice. In L.F. Zhang & R.J. Sternberg (Eds.), *Perspectives on the Nature of Intellectual Styles* (pp. 169–208). New York: Springer.

Felder, R.M., & Silverman, L.K. (1988). *The Index of Learning Styles*. Retrieved October 15, 2009, from North Carolina State University site http://www.engr.ncsu.edu/learningstyles/ilsweb.html

Gusky, T.R. (1986). Staff development and the process of teacher change. *Educational Researcher, 15*, 5–12.

Honigsfeld, A., & Schiering, M. (2004). Diverse approaches to the diversity of learning styles in teacher education. *Educational Psychology, 24*, 487–508.

Johnston, C. (1998). *Let Me Learn*. Thousand Oaks, CA: Corwin Press.

Johnston, C., & Dainton, G. (1997). *Learning Combination Inventory (LCI) Users' Manual*. Glassboro, NJ: Rowan University.

Jonassen, D.H., & Grabowski, B.L. (1993). *Handbook of Individual Differences, Learning and Instruction*. Hillsdale, NJ: Lawrence Erlbaum Associates.

Jordan, A., & Stanovich, P. (2001). Patterns of teacher-student interaction in inclusive elementary classrooms and correlates with student self-concept. *International Journal of Disability, Development, and Education, 48*, 33–52.

Kolb, D.A. (1976). *The Learning Style Inventory (LSI) Technical Manual*. Boston: TRG Hay/McBer, Training Resources Group.

Kozhevnikov, M. (2007). Cognitive styles in the context of modern psychology: toward an integrated framework of cognitive style. *Psychological Bulletin, 133*, 464–481.

McCarthy, B. (1980). *4-MAT in Action*. Barrington, IL: Excel.

NBPTS—National Board for Professional Teaching Standards. (2009). *The Five Core Propositions*. Retrieved October 10, 2009, from http://www.nbpts.org/the_standards/the_five_core_proposition

Ojure, L.P. (1997). *An Investigation of the Relationship between Teachers' Participation in 4MAT Fundamentals Training and Teachers' Perception of Teacher Efficacy*. PhD dissertation, Blacksburg, Virginia Polytechnic Institute and State University. Retrieved January 10, 2010, from http://scholar.lib.vt.edu/theses/available/etd-6197-102045/unrestricted/Oj6241.pdf

Pajares, F. (2002). *Overview of Social Cognitive Theory and of Self-efficacy*. Retrieved January 13, 2010, from http://www.emory.edu/EDUCATION/mfp/eff.html

Rainey, M.A., & Kolb, D. (1995). Using experiential learning theory and learning styles in diversity education. In R. Sims & S. Sims (Eds.), *The Importance of Learning Styles* (pp. 129–146). Westport, CT: Greenwood Press.

Riding, R., & Rayner, S. (1998). *Cognitive Styles and Learning Strategies: Understanding Style Differences in Learning and Behavior*. London: David Fulton Publishers.

Rosenfeld, M. (2008). *Developing Teacher Sensitivity to Individual Learning Differences: Studies on Increasing Teacher Effectiveness*. PhD dissertation, University of Utrecht, The Netherlands. Retrieved from Utrecht University Igitur Archive   http://igitur-archive.library.uu.nl/dissertations/2008–1105–200421/UUindex.html

Rosenfeld, M., & Rosenfeld, S. (1999). *Understanding the "Surprises" in Project-Based Learning (PBL): An Exploration into the Learning Styles of Teachers and Their Students*. Paper presented at the European Association for Research in Learning and Instruction (EARLI), University of Göteborg, Sweden.

Rosenfeld, M., & Rosenfeld, S. (2004). Developing teacher sensitivity to individual learning differences. *Educational Psychology, 24*, 465–486.

Rosenfeld, M., & Rosenfeld, S. (2006). Understanding teacher responses to constructivist learning environments: challenges and resolutions. *Science Education, 90*, 385–399.

Rosenfeld, M., & Rosenfeld, S. (2008a). Illustrating a new paradigm: from a third-person to a second-person perspective. *Conference Proceedings of 13th Annual European Learning Styles Information Network (ELSIN) Conference: Styles and Cultural Differences* (pp. 115–128). Ghent, Belgium: Vlerick Leuven Gent Management School.

Rosenfeld, M., & Rosenfeld, S. (2008b). Developing effective teacher beliefs about students: do teachers' own individual learning differences (ILDs) make a difference? *Educational Psychology, 28*, 245–272.

Rosenfeld, M., & Rosenfeld, S. (2008c). Understanding teachers with extreme individual learning differences (ILDs): developing more effective teachers. *Teaching Education, 19*, 21–41.

Sadler-Smith, E. (2009). A duplex model of cognitive style. In L.F. Zhang & R.J. Sternberg (Eds.), *Perspectives on the Nature of Intellectual Styles* (pp. 3–28). New York: Springer.

Sternberg, R.J. (1985). *Beyond IQ: A Triarchic Theory of Human Intelligence*. New York: Cambridge University Press.

Sternberg, R.J. (2001). Epilogue: Another mysterious affair at styles. In R.J. Sternberg & L.F. Zhang (Eds.), *Perspectives on Thinking, Learning and Cognitive Styles* (pp. 249–252). Mahwah, NJ: Lawrence Erlbaum Associates.

Sternberg, R., Ferrari, M., Clinkenbeard, P., & Grigorenko, E. (1996). Identification, instruction, and assessment of gifted children: a construct validation of a triarchic model. *Gifted Child Quarterly, 40*, 129–137.

Sternberg, R.J., & Zhang, L.F. (Eds.) (2001). *Perspectives on Thinking, Learning and Cognitive Styles*. Mahwah, NJ: Lawrence Erlbaum Associates.

Stokes, D.E. (1997). *Pasteur's Quadrant: Basic Science and Technological Innovation*. Washington, DC: Brookings Institution Press.

Torrance, P. (1980). *Your Style of Learning and Thinking: Right, Left, or Whole Brain Dominance*. Athens: University of Georgia.

Witkin, H.A., Oltman, P.K., Raskin, E., & Karp, S.A. (1971). *Manual for the Embedded Figures Tests*. Palo Alto, CA: Consulting Psychologists Press.

Wolz, D.J. (2003). Implicit cognitive processes as aptitudes for learning. *Educational Psychologist, 38*, 95–104.

Zimmerman, B.J. (1990). Self-regulated learning and academic achievement: an overview. *Educational Psychologist, 25*, 3–17.

Zhang, L.F., & Sternberg, R. J. (Eds.) (2009). *Perspectives on the Nature of Intellectual Styles*. New York: Springer.

## APPENDIX 10A: SUMMARY OF THE STYLE CONCEPTS USED IN THE PROFESSIONAL DEVELOPMENT IN THE FOUR STUDIES

### *Learning Style Inventory* (LSI; Kolb, 1976)

| Four learning styles | Learner preferences |
|---|---|
| Diverger | Prefers feeling-watching (Concrete-Experience/ Reflective-Observation): Needs to personally connect to the topic in order to learn. Preferred question: **Why** learn the material? |
| Assimilator | Prefers thinking-watching (Abstract-Conceptualization/ Reflective-Observation): Needs to understand factual information in order to learn. Preferred question: **What** are the facts and theories? |
| Converger | Prefers thinking-doing (Abstract-Conceptualization/ Active-Experimentation): Needs to apply information in order to learn. Preferred question: **How** do the theories work? |
| Accommodator | Prefers feeling-doing (Concrete-Experience/ Active-Experimentation): Needs to self-discover information in order to learn. Preferred question: **What** if I did it this way? |

*Note.* Appropriate for older learners, from high school to adult

### *Learning Combination Inventory* (LCI; Johnston & Dainton, 1997)

| Learning style preferences | Explanation |
|---|---|
| Sequential processing style | Prefers clear order of cognitive tasks, reliance on teacher directions, neatness |
| Precise processing style | Prefers memorization of details, researched answers, taking tests |
| Technical processing style | Prefers construction of a product, reliance on technical reasoning, information from previous real-world experience |
| Confluent processing style | Prefers independence, nonconformance, and risk taking |

*Note:* Appropriate for learners of all ages, including first-graders.

## Left/Right Hemisphere Preferences Inventory
## (Torrance, 1980)

| Left-hemisphere characteristics | Right-hemisphere characteristics |
| --- | --- |
| sequential | associative |
| hierarchical | creative |
| logical | emotional |
| planned | spontaneous |
| objective | subjective |

*Notes:* Appropriate for learners from middle school to adult. 'Left/Right Hemisphere' is a *metaphor* for sequential versus associative preferences.

## Visual/Auditory/Kinesthetic Modalities Inventory
## (VAK; Barsch, 1980)

| Visual | Auditory | Kinesthetic |
| --- | --- | --- |
| * "show me" | * "tell me" | * "let me move" |
| * prefers watching to gain information | * prefers listening to gain information | * prefers moving to gain information |
| * prefers visual means (charts, graphs, pictures) to represent knowledge | * prefers verbal means (lecture, tape, talking aloud) to represent knowledge | * prefers physical means (walking, writing, constructing) to represent knowledge |

Note: Appropriate for learners from middle school to adult

## Group Embedded Figures Test
## (GEFT; Witkin et al., 1971)

| Field independent | Field dependent |
| --- | --- |
| * analytic | * global |
| * prefers small bits of information to understand | * prefers large picture to understand |
| * prefers working alone | * prefers working with others |

*Note:* Appropriate for adult learners only

## 4-MAT Model
## (McCarthy, 1980)

- Based on Kolb's LSI with Right/Left Hemisphere preferences.
- Appropriate for all grade levels.
- Provides a style-sensitive framework for designing lesson units.

## *Triarchic Abilities Model*
## (Sternberg, 1985)

| Analytic | Creative | Practical |
|---|---|---|
| Ability to analyze, evaluate, judge, and compare and contrast. Typically involve-din abstract problems. (critique, explain . . .) | Ability to generate new and unusual solutions. Typically involved in novelsituations. (invent, imagine,design . . .) | Ability to problem-solve using tacit-knowledge that has not been taught or ver-balized. Typicallyinvolved in everyday situations. (apply, demonstrate . . .) |

*Notes:* Appropriate for learners of all ages. Adapted to offer a wider range for assessment and project topics.

# 11 Teaching Secondary Teachers about Style
## Should We Do It?

*Elizabeth R. Peterson, Sarah S. Carne, and Sarah J. Freear*

## INTRODUCTION

The past few decades have seen a proliferation of research on learning styles and cognitive styles. An Internet search on Google for 'learning style' currently results in an astounding 91,900,000 hits and a search for 'cognitive style' results in 3,630,000 hits. Many of these sites contain learning style tests where you can "discover your learning style within two minutes" or be "one click away from Understanding Your Learning Style". These Web sites, along with a myriad of books and magazine articles, attempt to capitalize on the layperson's desire to make learning easier and to succeed in both education and the workplace. Such ambitions are not surprising given that success at school and in the workplace is known to have many lifelong benefits such as higher socioeconomic status, health, and well-being.

Similarly, teachers are often targets for style promoters. Snider and Roehl (2007) note that:

> the idea that teachers should match instructional method to a particular learning style is so pervasive that many educators and lay people alike consider it to be a fact. (Snider & Roehl, 2007, p. 881)

The popular media nurtures such ideas with Web sites aimed at teachers claiming: "your students will be more successful if you match your teaching style to their learning style" or "enhance educational success . . . by discovering how students learn best" (see also Dembo & Howard, 2007). In a domain where teachers are often held accountable for student performance (Woolery, 1996), it is easy to see why such claims are attractive. However, the evidence for such assertions about the value and benefits of style needs to be given careful consideration and this will be further discussed next.

At the same time as the media sings the praises of styles, within some governmental policies there is a seemingly parallel call for the 'personalization' of learning. In 2006, the 'UK Teaching and Learning in 2020 Review' argued that if schools are to improve the educational outcomes for all students they need to be working towards a vision of promoting personalized learning and teaching. Personalized learning was defined as:

> Taking a highly structured and responsive approach to each child's and young person's learning, in order that all are able to progress, achieve and participate. (Gilbert, 2006, p. 6)

While such definitions do not directly refer to style, the idea of making learning more individual is in line with the proposed applications and benefits of using style in the classroom.

Together, these issues provide a backdrop for this chapter on teaching teachers about individual differences in students' learning and cognitive styles. This chapter will define what we mean by the term 'style' before focusing on why they are argued to be important for educational success (academic and nonacademic) and the evidence for these claims. A study is then outlined which sets out to increase preservice secondary-school teachers' awareness of style research and to reflect on the relevance of styles to their teaching practice. We report what these preservice teachers saw as the advantages and disadvantage of styles and whether they thought learning about them was worthwhile and resulted in any personal change.

## SO WHAT ARE STYLES?

Numerous definitions of cognitive style and learning style have been proposed. Recently, attempts have been made to get style researchers to come to some form of consensus by voting on the definitions of these constructs (Armstrong, Peterson, & Rayner, submitted). The most preferred definitions indicate that styles are individual preferences that can affect a person's behavior. Where the definitions differ is in the extent to which each construct is seen as stable, hardwired, or whether they change with different learning tasks and environments. In this chapter, the generic term 'style' is adopted as we are concerned with whether teachers should be taught about styles in general, rather than on the subtleties of the underlying mechanisms, processes, or influences.

## WHY ARE STYLES ARGUED TO BE IMPORTANT FOR EDUCATIONAL SUCCESS?

A recent survey of ninety-four style researchers found that over 90% of them worked in the field because they wanted to improve students' learning processes and outcomes (Peterson, Rayner, & Armstrong, 2009), indicating a strong underlying belief that styles can make a difference to academic success.

## Academic Success

Numerous factors, including style, that are identified as influencing academic success in schools have been explored. Broadly, they can be grouped into internal attributes of the child (e.g., intelligence, study skills, prior experience, and academic self-efficacy) and external factors (e.g., school climate, classroom size, teacher-student relationships, parental support, and teacher feedback).

Style has been argued to be an internal individual differences factor that has often been overlooked in terms of its influence on academic success (Riding & Rayner, 1998). Textbooks on individual differences largely brush over style, instead focusing on how personality, intelligence, creativity, and mood influence our achievement. Despite this, many benefits of style knowledge within the education and applied sectors have been proposed (Kozhevnikov, 2007). The most common academic claims are that if teaching is matched to an individual's preferred style then academic success is improved[1] (Dunn, Griggs, Olson, Beasley, & Gorman, 1995; Lovelace, 2005) or that styles can be used to predict academic outcomes beyond intelligence (Sternberg & Zhang, 2001).

## Style Matching and Academic Success

Some style advocates argue that failing to account for students' styles is irresponsible for an educator. For example, Prashnig states that:

> It is every teacher's duty to create a learning environment and use methods of instruction which match their students' learning styles. (Prashnig, 2000a, p. 1)

Prashnig (2000b) even suggests students should consider changing schools if the teachers do not take their styles into account. There is, however, relatively little empirical research to justify Prashnig's and others' (see, for example, Carver, Howard, & Lane, 1999; Dunn et al., 1995; Lovelace, 2005) strong claims about the academic benefits of matching learning environments to individual styles.

Moreover, Hattie (2009) conducted a recent review of the influences on academic achievement by synthesizing over 800 meta-analyses involving 50,000 studies and over 200 million students. His results tell a useful story about which factors really do make a difference to student achievement and raise the question about where educators' time and effort should be directed. To compare the studies, Hattie calculated effect size to determine which educational interventions had the greatest impact on achievement. Identifying the level of effect size needed to show substantial gains in academic achievement is important. Hattie proposes that an effect size of 0.40 should be the benchmark for judging real change in student academic achievement because it is argued to be the average typical effect across all possible influences in education. Teaching alone is argued to have an average effect of between 0.20 and 0.40 and therefore interventions should be aiming to obtain gains greater than 0.40. Anything less could be attributed largely to teacher and developmental effects rather than the intervention.

Within Hattie's (2009) synthesis, his review of the styles literature involved an analysis of eight meta-analyses based on 411 studies, 1,218 effects, and 29, 911 people. He found the effect of matching a student's style of learning was $d = 0.41$, suggesting that learning styles are "somewhat" important for improving academic outcomes. However, Hattie notes that many style models featured in the meta-analytical reviews contain multiple learning attributes (e.g., study skill training and metacognitive awareness training) and it may be these features which lead to a rise in student achievement. Alternatively, it could be that students simply enjoy learning more when more effort is made to vary the learning environment and instruction, leading to more engaged students and subsequently higher levels of achievement.

Another problem with several of the style meta-analyses in Hattie's synthesis is that many were based on a review of correlational studies rather than on aptitude-treatment interactions. The mantra that 'correlation does not imply causation' is important here but also, is it that surprising that what a student learns correlates with their achievement (Hattie, 2009)? Interestingly, the meta-analyses which reviewed only studies which carefully match instruction type to students' styles showed minimal impact on achievement results. For example, Kavale and Forness (1987) in their meta-analysis of thirty-five studies of style interventions, which involved matching to modality preferences, found that there were no real benefits in teaching students according to their preferred modality with effect sizes of less than 0.20. These findings of Kavale and Forness (1987) stand in contrast to meta-analysis conducted by Rita Dunn and colleagues on the Dunn and Dunn model of learning,[2] which reported larger effect sizes. However, others have criticized Dunn's meta-analysis for being largely based on doctoral theses supervised by the test authors, and most used attitudinal rather than achievement outcomes and in some cases the calculations were wrong or misleading (Hattie, 2009; Kavale, Hirshoren, & Forness, 1998). These findings suggest that style matching is complex and may not lead to direct and substantial academic gain; however, there may be value in using style for nonacademic purposes.

## Style and Nonacademic Success

Educational success is increasingly being argued to be more than just academic success. A recent task force set up by the Organization for Economic Cooperation and Development (OECD), called the *Definition and Selection of Competencies* (DeSeCo) project (OECD, 2005), clearly acknowledged the importance of developing the socioemotional competencies that will lead to "successful lives" in a "well functioning society" (OECD, 2005, p. 4). Some style researchers argue that teaching about style can help develop social and emotional competencies and a greater understanding of the self and others as learners. For example, style has been argued to provide a mechanism through which teachers and students can learn to recognize and respect individual differences in their classrooms (e.g., Davidson, 1990; Evans & Waring, 2006; Morgan, 2009; Rosenfeld & Rosenfeld, 2008). Rosenfeld (2008) found that introducing teachers to styles during a professional development program enabled them to change from seeing the class to seeing individual learners (see also Chapter 10 in this volume). Similarly, Rosenfeld and Rosenfeld (2004, 2008) found that styles helped teachers reframe the way they interpreted their students' behavior, changing from talking about learning or motivational deficits to talking about learning differences. To our knowledge, using style to increase school students' tolerance of differences has not been conducted, but it is argued that the same principles used with teachers could be used to sensitize students to such differences in their peers.

By using style as a basis for dialogue about differences, some researchers have argued that it has the potential to improve teacher-student and peer relationships and increase understanding about how teams work (e.g., Chickering, 2000; Hunt & Beaty, 1995). One study found that when a teacher discussed style differences with a disruptive student and told the student that she admired her more creative style (which was different from the teacher's own more sequential style) the student's attitude to learning changed and she became an engaged member of the class (Rosenfeld & Rosenfeld, 2004). Researchers have also found that using style to help people understand differences in teams is beneficial. Hunt and Beaty (1995) found that students on a management course reported knowing about style differences helped the teams make sense of the differing perceptions of their fellow team members.

Starting a conversation between teachers and students about their own learning preferences has also been argued to be empowering (Fleming & Mills, 1992; Honigsfeld & Schiering, 2004). For example, tertiary students in Pheiffer, Andrew, Green, and Holley's (2003) study, when given feedback on their styles, commented on how their results enabled them to understand themselves and their learning needs and gave them ideas to improve their study technique. Indeed, Hall and Moseley's (2005) overview of thirteen leading models of style led them to argue that the most helpful aspect of style is that it can be used to encourage learner self-awareness and help them to focus on improving poor learning habits. In this way, style is argued to be a tool which can develop students' metacognitive skills and then their sense of self as a learner (see also Kolb & Kolb, 2009).

Indeed, inherent in many definitions of style, and embodied in many style inventories, is the control, planning, and monitoring of thinking and learning processes. Therefore, a potential benefit of style is to use it to explore and develop students' metacognitive awareness: their thinking about their thinking and learning.

In summary, while style cannot substantially improve academic outcomes, it seems it can be used to sensitize individuals to appreciate and respect learning differences in themselves and others. Relatively little is known about the process of developing teachers or students to become sensitive to learners' individual differences, especially in mainstream secondary education (Rosenfeld & Rosenfeld, 2004). Unlike the primary classroom, teaching in the secondary and tertiary sector typically follows more structured, traditional teaching and learning practices, and the need to get through the curriculum and be accountable for end-of-year exam performance often makes it difficult for teachers to explore these differences. Studies conducted have typically involved long and time-intensive professional development programs, for instance, the work by Rosenfeld and Rosenfeld (2004, 2008). The current study focused on preservice secondary teachers to explore whether they could be sensitized to individual differences after a brief introduction to style, encouraging them to explore the use of styles, and requiring them to write a short assignment on whether they thought styles were relevant to their practice.

## AN EMPIRICAL STUDY: INTRODUCING STYLE TO SECONDARY TEACHERS

As part of a secondary school training degree program, two hours of lectures were given introducing the students to the topic of cognitive styles and learning styles. The lectures briefly covered the development of research into style, including the appeal of style for education and tools to evaluate style research. The students were then introduced to some popular models, tests and style dimensions, and their strengths and weaknesses. The students were referred to a wider range of resources both endorsing and criticizing the style content. More information on the lectures is available from the first author.

Following the lecture and the second practicum where they were encouraged to use styles in their practice, the students were asked to write an essay on the relevance of styles to their teaching practice, why they would or would not use them, and whether learning about them had changed their views about style. They were told that they could be as complimentary or as antagonistic about style as they wanted, but they did need to justify their responses. Forty-four of the student teacher essays were analyzed and coded for common issues and themes. The results of this analysis are presented here.

## Appreciating Differences

The teacher trainees generally indicated that learning about style had changed the way they thought about student learning. Eighty percent of the teachers felt that they had gained knowledge about how to teach students with varying styles. More specifically, for some of these teachers (23%), it had provided a way of interpreting poor student performance without labeling or stereotyping them as 'unteachable' or 'slow'. As one teacher said, *"I did not realize learning styles affect teaching and learning effectiveness. I thought that those students who did not take notes in my class were lazy"*. Another commented that *"I am definitely more aware of the difference in the way each person learns and I have a greater tolerance of these differences."* Yet at the same time one teacher was wary of pampering the students and using style differences as an excuse for poor performance: *"While I am not advocating allowing the use of style as an excuse for misbehavior or not attempting learning tasks, I will be far more open to discussion with students about trying to match activities and tasks to style where appropriate in order to help us both achieve our learning goals."*

A quarter of the group commented that styles would be a useful way to start a dialogue with students about learning. For some this took the form of trying to work out what motivated their students. *"I will try and discuss with them to find some ways that they may be better motivated and interested to make learning really happen."* For others they thought it would benefit the students to know about their learning preferences *"I think it is important to have students understand how they best learn and what they can do to enhance their learning."*

Twenty-three percent of the teachers noted that the existence and application of styles within education is *"common sense"*. They commented that *"There is no reason that we only need to teach via direct instruction on the board and from the textbook"* and *"It is natural for students to be taught and learn by hearing, seeing, and writing and in one sense the VARK[3] model is just stating the obvious."*

Several teachers also appreciated the benefit of being aware of multiple style models. *"I have come to realize that, rather than convert to one model as the answer to the style debate, perhaps it is best practice to take a little of what you need from each."* Another teacher said, *"Using a greater variety of instructional methods should result in a greater chance of students securing the cues they each need for learning. Perhaps the most effective learning style would be a continuum of several different models, giving way to a holistic view of learning."*

Overall, learning about style differences seemed to give the teachers a wider appreciation of learning differences in the classroom. Whereas for some this was largely common sense, the majority felt that learning about style had led to positive changes in their perceptions of students and their practice.

## Questioning the Veracity of Styles as a Construct

Several teachers (11%) showed an awareness that many measures lacked evidence for reliability and validity and had been *"widely questioned"*. For some, this posed a barrier to engaging with the topic. *"If a critical review of 50 years work* [referring to the Coffield, Moseley, Hall, & Ecclestone (2004) report] *leads to a conclusion that further research is justified, how can we take any one model and implement it as teachers?"*

In addition, 30% struggled with the practicality of using many different styles in their teaching, noting, *"It is just unfeasible to deliver material to a class that is suitable for every possible learning style"*. Some teachers (7%) felt that students still need to learn in a traditional manner, for instance, for university: *"One has an obligation to those students who want to attend post-secondary education to prepare them for it. Universities continue to adopt old approaches to teaching and until they change it is important to teach students ways to cope in a learning environment that is not necessarily advantageous for them."*

Others acknowledged that accommodating all possible styles was difficult, but seemed to believe that by trying to adapt their teaching it may help improve some students' learning outcomes: *"Obviously it is not possible to offer all of these different styles every lesson but . . . using these different methods while teaching may enhance the learning of the different types of learners in the class."* A mathematics teacher highlighted the difficulty of using different learning styles in their subject which they saw as *"very rigid and logical in structure, so there will always tend to be bias towards the analytical end of the spectrum"*. Yet learning about styles also made this teacher *"wonder to what extent this [the negative attitude students often felt towards maths] is a direct result of their cognitive styles not being taken into account or them not being sufficiently engaged."*

These findings indicate that while teachers are aware of the psychometric weaknesses of some of the style questionnaires, and the difficulties associated with trying to cater for the many different styles in the classroom, an attempt to cater for a slightly wider range of styles was thought to help raise student engagement. These findings also suggest that teachers may benefit from further discussion on the extent that instruction can and should be fully individualized.

## Personal Change

Only two of the teachers stated directly that having learned about style they would not change their teaching approach. One felt she already used a variety of styles, but the other felt that time constraints prevented her from evaluating student styles needs and incorporating them into her already full teaching day. The majority of teachers (70%) directly indicated that they had changed or planned to change their teaching as result of learning about styles. By incorporating or considering style as part of their practice, they felt it would make them better teachers and help them *"create a learning environment that appeals and is successful to every student in the class."* In particular, the teachers felt they had gained ideas to make their lessons *"more interesting"* and *"less boring"*. One teacher commented that *"I found that the comprehension success rate increased two-fold when I used a variety of methods rather than using a lecturing and overhead style."* Or as another teacher said, *"Through a variety of techniques pupils are then more likely to: access easily the activities presented to them; be enthusiastic and committed to the subject they are studying; remain on task and focused during group or practical activities."* Overall, many of the teachers seemed to believe that *"Techniques such as these, combined with an ongoing reflection on diversity in learning styles will, I believe, make me a better teacher."*

Many (57%), having learned about different style models, commented on the type of learner that they thought they were. This insight not only enabled them to *"realize that I should not make assumptions, and classify other people's cognitive and learning styles as being the same as my own"* but also to look critically at their teaching style and appreciate that it may not be the best fit for all their students. As one teacher said, *"As teachers we need to be aware of our pupils' cognitive styles as well as our own to maximize on the impact we are having"*. Another commented that *"I used to force them to learn in the way I taught them with threatening disciplinal punishment. Although that made them comply, they did not really learn."*

Many teachers in the group appeared to think that having learned about style differences they had a responsibility to act on it: *"We need to allow our students to be exposed to as many opportunities to learn as possible"*. One said, *"It is a teacher's responsibility to understand the learning needs of our students. In teaching we need to utilize different approaches to motivate our students to learn with joy."* A couple took an even more accommodating approach and rather than just advocating the benefit of being aware of style differences and using a variety of instructional methods, they felt that it was their responsibility to match their teaching to the students' styles: *"Many students are eager to come to school and learn, the only thing inhibiting their learning process is the fact that we as teachers are not teaching to their preferred method."* Another said, *"As a teacher I have an obligation to teach the key issues or concepts of the curriculum in a number of ways so that all students have an equal chance of understanding the material."*

It is interesting to note that relatively few commented that style could be used to improve academic or achievement outcomes (16%) and only 5% believed using different learning styles helped students retain knowledge. In contrast, the majority of the comments indicated support for the more socioemotional benefits of style such as heightened awareness of individual differences or diversity in styles within themselves and amongst their students, greater insight into their own thinking and learning, and knowledge about how to teach or approach students with different learning needs. Therefore, while the teachers were not asked to directly comment on the academic or socioemotional benefits, the balance of spontaneous comments towards the socioemotional benefits is interesting and supports the findings of Hall and Moseley (2005) that a key benefit of style is that it can be used to develop a broader awareness of thinking and learning processes.

These findings suggest that learning about style resulted in some change in thinking and attitude for the majority of teachers, and in particular it seemed to broaden their appreciation of differences in themselves and their students. However, given that there is a lack of evidence to support matching teaching to students' learning style preferences, the fact that a few teachers were advocating matching is perhaps cause for some concern. Further discussion on the practicalities and evidence for and against this approach may therefore be needed when teaching student teachers about style.

## Study Limitations and Caveats

It is possible that the generally positive response to style was because the teachers were new to teaching, arguably more open to suggestions, and possibly idealistic. However, even if responses were overly optimistic, the fact that they found it beneficial to learn about styles and were given a mechanism to think about their own and their students' learning is in itself worthwhile. While it may be suggested that the teachers responded positively in an attempt to please their essay marker, they were expressly told that the markers were open to both positive and negative interpretations.

## CONCLUSION

This chapter set out to address the question of whether we should teach secondary teachers about style. We believe the answer is yes, but not because it is the hidden jewel for enhancing academic performance and success as some media claim, but more for the social and emotional benefits such as increased tolerance to diversity, a more positive language to talk about differences, ideas about how to vary instruction and increase student interest, and a way to encourage metacognitive awareness and a sense of self in themselves and their students. It appears that such benefits can be achieved by giving a relatively brief intervention which involves teaching teachers about style research and encouraging the use of and reflection on style in their practice.

Therefore, although Hattie's (2009) synthesis of style research suggests style is of marginal value for raising student achievement, we find ourselves agreeing with Rayner (2007) that rejecting style outright, because of marginal effect sizes for raising academic achievement, is throwing the proverbial baby out with the bathwater. Teachers in this study reported that learning about style helped them to consider ways of make the learning experience more student-centered, not necessarily through individualized instruction or matching teaching to students styles (although a couple proposed this), but more by stimulating them to consider differences in their own and their students' thinking and learning and helping teachers to respond more positively and constructively to diversity in their classrooms so they can engage more learners.

Our findings are broadly in keeping with previous researchers who have also tried to increase preservice teachers' sensitivity to the style field (e.g., Evans & Waring, 2006; Honigsfeld & Schiering, 2004; Rosenfeld, & Rosenfeld, 2004). Comparatively, our intervention was shorter, yet it still seemed to have a range of reported benefits. Longitudinal research could examine the extent to which these benefits are sustained and enacted throughout their teaching career. More research could also investigate whether students also perceive these benefits from learning about styles.

## NOTES

1. Some style advocates argue that we should teach students to be versatile in their learning styles rather than seek to match styles (e.g., Smith, 2001).
2. The Dunn and Dunn model largely looks at environmental learning preferences, such as preference for learning while eating, learning in a group or learning in a quiet place.
3. VARK is a model of style proposed by Fleming and Mills (1992) identifying four learning preferences: visual, auditory, read/write, and kinesthetic.

## BIBLIOGRAPHY

Armstrong, S.J., Peterson, E.R., & Rayner, S.G. (under review). Understanding and defining 'cognitive style' and 'learning style': a Delphi study. *Learning and Individual Differences.*

Carver, C.A., Howard, R.A., & Lane, W.D. (1999). Enhancing student learning through hypermedia courseware and incorporation of student learning styles. *IEEE Transactions on Education, 42,* 33–38.

Chickering, A.W. (2000). Creating community within individual courses. *New Directions for Higher Education, 109,* 23–32.

Coffield, F.C., Moseley, D.V.M., Hall, E., & Ecclestone, K. (2004). *Learning Styles and Pedagogy in Post-16 Learning: Findings of a Systematic and Critical Review of Learning Styles Models.* London: Learning and Skills Research Centre.

Davidson, G.V. (1990). Matching learning styles with teaching styles. *Performance and Instruction, 4,* 36–38.

Dembo, M.H., & Howard, K. (2007). Advice about the use of learning styles: a major myth in education. *Journal of College Reading and Learning, 37,* 101–109.

Dunn, R., Griggs, S.A., Olson, J., Beasley, M., & Gorman, B.S. (1995). A meta-analytic validation of the Dunn and Dunn model of learning-style preferences. *Journal of Educational Research, 88,* 353–362.

Evans, C., & Waring, M. (2006). Towards inclusive education: sensitising teacher individuals to how they learn. *Educational Psychology, 26,* 499–518.

Fleming, N.D., & Mills, C. (1992). Not another inventory, rather a catalyst for reflection. *To Improve the Academy, 11,* 137–149.

Gilbert, C. (2006). *Report on the Teaching and Learning in 2020 Review.* Nottingham, UK: Department for Education and Skills.

Hall, E., & Moseley, D. (2005). Is there a role for learning styles in personalised education and training? *International Journal of Lifelong Education, 24,* 243–255.

Hattie, J.A.C. (2009). *Visible Learning: A Synthesis of over 800 Meta-Analysis Relating to Achievement.* London: Routledge.

Honigsfeld, A., & Schiering, M. (2004). Diverse approaches to the diversity of learning styles in teacher education. *Educational Psychology, 24,* 487–508.

Hunt, P., & Beaty, L. (1995). The impact of knowledge about aspects of personal learning style on team effectiveness. In G. Gibbs (Ed.), *Improving Student Learning through Assessment and Evaluation.* Oxford: Oxford Centre for Staff Development.

Kavale, K.A., &. Forness, S.R. (1987). Substance over style: assessing the efficacy of modality testing and teaching. *Exceptional Children, 54,* 228–239.

Kavale, K.A., Hirshoren, A., & Forness, S.R. (1998). Meta-analytic validation of the Dunn and Dunn model of learning-style preferences. *Learning Disabilities Research and Practice, 13,* 75–80.

Kolb, A.Y., & Kolb, D.A. (2009). The learning way: meta-cognitive aspects of experiential learning. *Simulation and Gaming, 40,* 297–327.

Kozhevnikov, M. (2007). Cognitive style in the context of modern psychology: towards an integrated framework of cognitive style. *Psychological Bulletin, 133,* 464–481.

Lovelace, M.K. (2005). Meta-analysis of experimental research based on the Dunn and Dunn model. *The Journal of Educational Research, 98,* 176–183.

Morgan, H. (2009). What every teacher needs to know to teach native American students. *Multicultural Education, 16,* 10–12.

OECD. (2005). *The Definition and Selection of Key Competencies: Executive Summary.* Retrieved from www.oecd.org at February 3, 2010.

Peterson, E.R., Rayner, S.G., & Armstrong, S.J. (2009). Researching the psychology of cognitive style and learning style: is there really a future? *Learning and Individual Differences, 19,* 518–523.

Pheiffer, G., Andrew, D., Green, M., & Holley, D. (2003). *The Value and Use of Learning Styles: A Case Study.* Paper presented at European Learning Styles Information Network Conference, June 30th–July 3rd, Hull, England.

Prashnig, B. (2000a). Learning styles—here to stay. *Education Today, 2,* 30–31.

Prashnig, B. (2000b). Help, my teacher doesn't know my learning style. *Education Today, 3,* 13–14.

Rayner, S.G. (2007). A teaching elixir, learning chimera or just fool's gold? Do learning styles matter? *British Journal of Support for Learning, 22,* 24–31.

Riding, R.J. & Rayner, S. (1998). *Cognitive Styles and Learning Strategies: Understanding Style Differences in Learning and Behaviour.* London: David Fulton.

Rosenfeld, M. (2008). *Developing Teacher Sensitivity to Individual Learning Differences: Studies on Increasing Teacher Effectiveness.* PhD dissertation, University of Utrecht, The Netherlands.

Rosenfeld, M., & Rosenfeld, S. (2004). Developing teacher sensitivity to individual learning differences. *Educational Psychology, 24,* 465–486.

Rosenfeld, M., & Rosenfeld, S. (2008). Understanding teachers with extreme individual learning differences: developing more effective teachers. *Teacher Education, 19,* 21–41.

Smith, P.J. (2001). Technology student learning preferences and the design of flexible learning programs. *Instructional Science, 29,* 237–254.

Snider, V.E., & Roehl, R. (2007). Teachers' beliefs about pedagogy and related issues. *Psychology in the Schools, 44,* 873–886.

Sternberg, R.J., & Zhang, L.F. (Eds.) (2001). *Perspectives on Thinking, Learning, and Cognitive Styles.* London: Lawrence Erlbaum Associates.

Woolery, C. (1996). Holding teachers accountable for learning. *School Administrator.* Retrieved September 19, 2009, from http://findarticles.com/p/articles/mi_m0JSD/is_1_53/ai_77195557/?tag=content;col1

# 12 Patterns in Student Learning and Teacher Learning
## Similarities and Differences

*Jan D. Vermunt*

## INTRODUCTION

Fostering student learning often requires teachers learning about teaching and learning. Many contemporary educational innovations are aimed at improving the quality of student learning, for example, by taking individual differences between students into account, or by trying to enhance students' capacity to learn. While new models of teaching have been developed with that aim, it is mostly taken for granted that teachers also develop their expertise in the new teacher roles required by these models. Only more recently, processes of teacher learning are being studied in their own right.

This chapter is an attempt to reconcile not only style as a feature in learners and in teachers but also the concept of style as an interrelated construct resulting from the combination of personal and contextual influences. The latter is being attempted here from the starting point of the European tradition of learning approaches that has traditionally researched individual differences as 'how people can differ from one another in the population', using survey, statistical measurement, and factor analysis. In other words, a primary focus in the research leading to this discussion started with an interest in individuals while studying groups by seeking dimensions shared by all individuals but upon which individuals differ.

Further, recent research and developments on our model of student learning (framework on learning patterns; see Vermunt & Verloop, 1999; Vermunt & Vermetten, 2004) will be considered. One important extension of this model is to include phenomena of teacher learning. Therefore, recent research on describing and improving teacher learning will be dealt with as well, mostly in the context of educational innovation. The main issue that the chapter addresses is to what extent student learning and teacher learning can be conceptualized in the same terms or that different models are needed to account for both phenomena. The chapter consists of five sections: (1) patterns in student learning, (2) teaching to foster student learning and to enhance students' capacity to learn, (3) new teachers' roles and skills, (4) patterns in teacher learning, and (5) conclusions and prospects.

## PATTERNS IN STUDENT LEARNING

The first generation of models on patterns in student learning mostly incorporated two components: student motivation and cognitive learning strategies or approaches (e.g., Biggs, 1982; Entwistle & Ramsden, 1983). For example, in his 1982 model, Biggs discerned reproducing (surface), meaningful (deep) and organizing (achieving) strategies, and three parallel motives: instrumental (surface), intrinsic (deep), and achievement (achieving). 'Approach' and 'strategy' are concepts mostly used interchangeably, referring to a typical combination of more basic learning activities that students use to learn. A deep approach or strategy, for instance, refers to the combined use of learning activities like searching for relations in the subject matter, processing critically, and trying to structure different pieces of subject matter into a whole. A second generation of models on student learning added metacognitive components: knowledge and beliefs (the more static aspect of metacognition) and self-regulation of learning (the more dynamic, online aspect). In these models, student learning is conceptualized as involving cognitive processing strategies, metacognitive regulation strategies, learning motivation or orientation, and knowledge and beliefs about learning. Representations of this second generation of models are those of Pintrich and his collaborators (e.g., Pintrich, 2004) and our own work (e.g., Vermunt & Vermetten, 2004).

In our research on student learning, we started by interviewing university students varying in age, academic discipline, and type of university (open university and regular university) about the way they studied, their reasons and aims for studying, and their views about learning and teaching. These interviews were transcribed literally and analyzed in a phenomenographic way (Vermunt, 1996). Based on the results of these analyses, we developed a diagnostic instrument by selecting interview statements and transforming these into items of an inventory, supplemented by additional items. The items covered all four aforementioned components. In several development rounds the instrument, which was named the Inventory of Learning Styles (ILS), was constructed (Vermunt, 1998). Since its development, the ILS has been administered in various studies to thousands of students in a variety of countries, such as the Netherlands, Belgium, Finland, UK, Spain, Sweden, Norway, US, Argentine, Brazil, Indonesia, Sri Lanka, and China (see for an overview of ILS-related research and theory: Vermunt & Vermetten 2004).

Typically, these studies show four patterns in student learning characterized by strong relations between behavioral, knowledge/belief, and motivational components. In our earlier studies, we called these patterns 'learning styles'. These learning styles were conceived as a coherent repertoire of learning activities that students usually employ, their learning orientation, and their conception of learning, a whole that is characteristic of them at a certain period. Within this broader meaning learning style is thus a coordinating concept, in which the interrelations among cognitive, affective and regulative learning activities, conceptions of learning, and learning orientations are united. Learning style is *not* conceived of as an unchangeable personality attribute, but as the result of the temporal interplay between personal and contextual influences (Vermunt, 1996, 1998). Later on, because learning 'style' was often conceived by other people as something unchangeable, almost innate, an invariant attribute of students, deeply rooted in personality, we changed to use the more neutral term 'learning pattern' for the same phenomenon we previously described as a 'learning style' (e.g., Vermunt, 2005). In this chapter, I will use the term 'pattern' in the meaning as just described, both for students' learning as well as teachers' learning.

In many studies that used the ILS, four different learning patterns were identified. First, an *undirected* learning pattern was found, in which students hardly came to processing the subject matter, mainly because they had trouble with selecting what is more and less important within the huge amounts of study materials, showing lack of regulation in their studying, attaching much value to being stimulated by others (fellow students, teachers, study counselors) in their learning, and having an ambivalent learning orientation showing a lot of doubts about their study choice, own capacities, and the like. Second, a *reproduction-directed* way of learning was identified, in which students often used a stepwise processing strategy (combining learning activities like memorizing, rehearsing, detailed analyzing the subject matter), let their learning be regulated by external sources such as teachers and study materials, viewed learning mainly as the intake of knowledge from knowledgeable sources (such as books, teachers), and were certificate and self-test directed in their learning orientation. The third pattern which emerged was a *meaning-directed* way of learning, typified by the use of a deep processing strategy (relating, structuring, critical processing the study materials), self-regulation in learning (planning, monitoring, evaluating, reflecting, reading 'around' the prescribed materials), a learning conception in which learning was seen as an individual's construction of knowledge and one's own responsibility for learning was stressed, as well as personal interest in the subject matter as a learning orientation. And fourthly, an *application-directed* learning pattern was established, in which students used a concrete processing strategy (trying to concretize the subject matter, think of possible applications), involved both self and external regulation strategies, attached much importance to learning to use the knowledge they acquired, and were vocation oriented in their learning motivation. Overall, meaning-directed learning is mainly focused on relations *within* the subject matter of the studies; application-directed learning is focused most on relations *between* the subject matter and the world around.

These four distinctive learning patterns show up in a number of studies with different student populations in different countries all over the world. Whether one or the other way of learning is regarded as 'better' than another is a matter of perspective. In discussions with teachers and educational developers, meaning- and application-directed learning are, in general, viewed as more appropriate for studies in higher education than is undirected learning. Sometimes a distinction is made between university and higher vocational studies, in the sense that meaning-directed learning is viewed as most appropriate for university studies and application-directed learning as most appropriate for higher vocational studies. People often disagree on the value of reproduction-directed learning. Some see this as an important route to basic factual knowledge; others argue that this basic factual knowledge can as well, or even be better, acquired through meaning or application-directed learning (Vermunt, 2007).

One remark about undirected learning should be made here. Although different studies show very consistently that, in the long run, undirected learning is negatively related to study success, a (short) period of rather undirected learning may be a necessary phase for change and development in students' learning patterns to occur. A period of friction is therefore experienced in which they are dissatisfied with their old way of learning and experiment with new strategies. This is a period in which their conceptions of learning, study behavior, and learning orientation change at different rates, loosening the connections that normally exist between these learning components. It is also a period in which strong emotions are associated with leaving old learning patterns behind while new patterns have not yet been stabilized. Once students have left this undirected phase behind, a new way of learning may be established, again characterized by strong ties between their beliefs, motives, and behavior. For change and development to occur, a period of undirected learning thus may be utmost adaptive and even necessary. However, some students may stay stuck in this undirected way of learning and drop out.

Patterns in student learning have been found to be related to personal factors such as personality, epistemology, age, prior educational level and gender, and to contextual factors like subject area, type of university, perceived learning environment, and culture (for an overview of these relations, see Vermunt & Vermetten, 2004). An issue that has raised considerable interest is how stable these learning patterns are over time and contexts. Recent research indicates that how students learn today resembles how they learned yesterday, that student learning patterns are not deeply rooted in personality but can develop over time, and that actual ways of learning may vary across contexts to some degree. Research from Vermetten, Lodewijks, and Vermunt (1999) indicates that students show both stability and variability in their way of learning. Students may vary their learning strategies for different courses, but they are also consistent in their strategy use over different courses. Research from Vermunt and Minnaert (2003) shows that the stability of students' learning patterns over time is rather high, but not so high that they can or should be seen as unchangeable phenomena.

With regard to the relation between students' learning patterns and out-comes of learning, research indicates that, in general, meaning-oriented learning is related positively to academic performance. Undirected learning is related strongly and negatively to exam performance. Application-directed learning mostly shows no relation at all with exam results, and reproduction-directed learning shows no to a negative relation (Vermunt & Vermetten, 2004). More specifically, exam results are often positively related to students' use of relating and structuring and self-regulation strategies, and sometimes also to critical and analytical processing strategies. Exam results are consistently and negatively related to lack of regulation and ambivalence. Furthermore, subject specific relations show up, in which some ways of learning are beneficial in one subject area but not in another (Vermunt, 2005). Of course, what way of learning is 'rewarded' in exams heavily depends on the way teachers have constructed exams, frame exam questions, and score exam answers.

## TEACHING TO FOSTER STUDENT LEARNING AND TO ENHANCE STUDENTS' CAPACITY TO LEARN

If meaning- and application-directed learning are ways of learning that are most appropriate or valued for studying in higher education, the question arises how we can foster these ways of student learning in our teaching? And, moreover, how can we not only foster these mature ways of learning during our teaching but also make sure that students go on learning in this way when they are no longer in our classes but, for example, in working life? Or, in other words, how can we teach in such a way that students' capacity for lifelong learning is enhanced? The central theme of the 2007 European Learning Styles Information Network (ELSIN) conference in Dublin—'Exploring Style: Enhancing the Capacity to Learn'—was exactly putting this problem prominently on the agenda.

Theory and research on powerful learning environments may illuminate what we need here. In the literature (e.g., De Corte, Verschaffel, Entwistle, & Van Merriënboer, 2003), key features of powerful learning environments are mentioned as follows: (1) they prepare students for life-long, self-regulated, cooperative, and work-based learning; (2) they foster high-quality student learning; (3) the teaching methods change in response to students' increasing self-regulatory skills; and (4) the complexity of the problems dealt with increases gradually and systematically.

This means that, among other things, at the start of a curriculum, when students' capacity to self-regulate their learning is not yet very high, teachers may exert a rather strong control over their students' learning. In this way, teachers teaching and students' learning are in congruence with each other; they match (Vermunt & Verloop, 1999). To enhance students' capacity to self-regulate their learning further on in the curriculum, teachers should gradually and systematically withdraw their regulation of students' learning, at the same time training students in the skills they need to self-regulate their learning. Although this idea is widely accepted, actual educational practice often shows a different picture. In many educational institutions we see a constant regulation of student learning by the same teaching methods that are adopted by the institution throughout the years.

Most innovative teaching methods that are used nowadays share some common characteristics in the kind of learning they try to promote in students. Overall, these are student-centered teaching methods aimed at fostering active, meaning-directed, application-directed, self-regulated, and cooperative student learning. Main teaching-learning methods used on a large scale nowadays to achieve this include assignment-based teaching, problem-based learning, project-centered learning, competency-based teaching, dual learning, and autodidactic learning (for a more elaborate discussion of these teaching-learning methods, see Vermunt, 2007). All these teaching-learning methods foster active student learning based on problems, cases, or assignments, but they increase in the degree of self-regulation they demand from students and in the magnitude and complexity of the problems on which students work. When they are applied progressively throughout a curriculum, students are challenged to develop their capacity to learn.

## NEW TEACHERS' ROLES AND SKILLS

The roles teachers are expected to fulfill in these teaching-learning methods may vary considerably. In more traditional teaching, teachers should mainly be able to explain the subject matter well, to regulate their students' learning, and to motivate students to learn. In assignment-based teaching, skills like designing assignments, giving feedback, coaching, and getting and maintaining students at work are important. In problem-based learning the teacher is expected to fulfill roles like tutor, skills trainer and assessor, problem designer, and block coordinator. Project-centered learning assumes that a teacher can supervise project groups, coach the cooperation within groups, and deal with 'free rider' behavior of students. In competency-based teaching, teachers fulfill roles such as study career counselor, competency assessor, or professional growth counselor. Dual trajectories call for teachers to switch between roles such as being a mentor, portfolio coach, authentic assessment designer, or being able to clarify and steer students' concerns. In all these student-centered teaching-learning methods, teachers must be able to fulfill roles like diagnostician, challenger, model, activator, monitor, reflector, and evaluator of students' learning processes (Vermunt, 2007; Vermunt & Verloop, 1999).

For many teachers these are new roles for which they need new skills that they have not yet mastered. Too often, when introducing new teaching methods, there is a huge need for teacher learning which is heavily underestimated. Many times educational innovations have failed because they did not recognize the need for teacher learning or pedagogic development. New models for teaching students may be developed, fostering active, meaning-directed, application-directed, self-regulated, and cooperative student learning, but if these methods are too difficult for teachers to use, when, for example, they are based on a different conception of teaching and learning than teachers hold, when the principles on which they are based are not understood by teachers, or when teachers do not have the skills to realize the way of teaching in practice, they will not be implemented properly in classroom practices.

## PATTERNS IN TEACHER LEARNING

Educational innovation succeeds or fails with the teachers that shape it. When an educational institution decides to implement changes in approaches to teaching, teachers have to adapt their way of teaching. This assumes that they learn new things themselves, along the lines of the Shulman and Shulman (2004) model of teacher learning: they must develop another perspective on teaching and learning, need to be willing to learn new skills and play different roles, understand the purpose and application of the innovation, develop skills to realize new teaching in practice, reflect on their experiments with the new teaching to learn from them, and form part of a community of teachers who all share in learning new things.

Many studies have been conducted on student learning. However, studies on teacher learning are rare. For this reason a few years ago, we started a series of studies on teacher learning, with the aim of increasing our understanding of how teachers learn and what kind of learning activities they employ in doing so (e.g., Bakkenes, Vermunt, & Wubbels, in press). One of the central questions in these studies was how experienced teachers learn in, for, and from their professional practice. In an interrelated research project, ninety-four secondary teachers were followed in their learning experiences during one year. The research project took place in the context of the introduction of active and self-regulated learning in the classroom. Teachers were interviewed, observed in their classrooms, administered questionnaires about their beliefs and motives, and six times during the research year they e-mailed a digital log about a learning experience they had had in the previous six weeks. Several articles about the project have been published recently in the scientific research literature (e.g., Bakkenes et al., in press; Hoekstra, Beijaard, Brekelmans, & Korthagen, 2007; Meirink, Meijer, Verloop, & Bergen, 2009; Zwart, Wubbels, Bolhuis, & Bergen, 2008).

## Teachers' Learning Activities

The learning experiences from the digital logs were content-analyzed in terms of learning activities that the teachers employed to learn something. The analyses resulted in the identification of various categories of such learning activities, which are described following.

### Experimenting within the Boundaries of One's Theory of Practice

Some things in class do not go well; teachers are dissatisfied about these things. They think of another way of working and try it out in a class. When it goes well, better than before, they continue using that way of teaching and expand it to other classes and/or lessons. When it does not go well, they stop using it. These kinds of experiments were found a lot in the logs. A teacher of chemistry phrased such a learning experience as follows:

> My aim was that in a block hour of 100 minutes 10 short determinations could be done. These determinations were collected in a scheme so the data could be compared. Furthermore, I wanted to test these experiments with the students to learn from them for future practicals in our school. . . . I learned a lot from this lesson. First, the number of experiments was too high. It is possible, but not for a first time. . . . I felt and feel very satisfied about the fact that I have learned a lot for a next time. All in all a very helpful lesson.

### Experimenting with Extension of One's Theory of Practice

This type of experimenting is done on a deeper level than the previous learning activity. Here, teachers also make use of new knowledge or ideas gained from others and integrate these into their own theory of practice. For example, one teacher wrote in his log:

> Bill from the institute for further education introduced the concept of 'visible learning', in which both the teacher and the student are highly active in the lesson. . . . In a short enumeration of possible ways of working in visible learning, Bill mentioned the 'in-between conversation'. . . . In the two weeks after this meeting I practiced these in-between conversations in four lessons. It went like a bomb. . . . In short, an easy, relaxed but highly effective activity.

### Developing One's Theory of Practice

Teachers think about why things happen as they do in the class, try to find explanations. They take ideas of others into consideration, such as books or lectures about new teaching and learning methods, active and meaning-directed learning, etc. They try out new things, not so much small things, for just one lesson, but they try to develop their own teaching over a longer period of time. One teacher reported such a learning experience as follows:

> *Recently we came to talk about intrinsic and extrinsic motivation. The previous period I have experienced rather heavily that students just do what they want to do and often that is just a tiny little bit. I hate this and have the tendency to write off these students. . . . Recently, I had a discussion with a colleague which brought me to the following learning issue: 'At school in the lessons there MUST be surplus value for the student. Students should be able to gain something from the other students or the teacher'. . . . I am going to put this knowledge central in the redesign of my teaching the next months. School may not develop into a kind of elevated homework institute.*

### Learning by Observing Others

Teachers watch each other in the classroom and draw conclusions from those observations. A nice example is the following statement:

> *I went observing the class of Mary, a colleague, and then I had a learning experience. Obviously not everybody is able to just build active and self-regulated learning methods into one's lessons. In my view the teaching activities we had thought of were not so difficult to use, I do it regularly. . . . However, her lesson went messy and noisy and Mary evaluated on hindsight that she had absolutely not succeeded in building active and self-regulated learning into her lesson. For me the learning moment is that a colleague has so much trouble to switch over to this way of working. I had not realized that previously. For me it was an eye-opener that evidently this does not go just naturally.*

### Thinking about Experiences

Things happen that touch teachers in some way and they start thinking about it, trying to infer more general principles from these experiences. These generalizations then become a new piece of personal theory of practice. One teacher phrased it as follows:

> *A while ago the following happened to me. One of my students told her neighbor that she might still drop my subject area, on which I reconfirmed that in a kind of casual way. During the next break she started crying: I had looked so seriously making that remark that the remark also got across seriously. . . . This again makes it clear to me how careful I should be with my words, also with grown-up students; words are sometimes weighted on a gold scale. I think it is important to stay alert on this, because also active and self-regulated learning*

*will only succeed when there is a good relation and trust bond between teacher and student.*

## Avoiding Learning

It sometimes happened that teachers in fact disagreed with the pedagogy of active and self-regulated learning, but participated anyway in trying out teaching-learning methods aimed at fostering this way of learning, often under pressure from the school leadership. However, these teachers primarily wanted to see these experiments fail. When that happened, they were confirmed in their own existing ideas and saw that as 'learning'. Thus, their experiments were aimed at confirming their own existing theory of practice. For example, a teacher wrote:

> *This year I have experimented in class 4 with the deadline for the reading file, by having the students make a year plan for themselves. On June 6 everyone should have handed in three book reports. The instructions for this I have given them in October last year. Until now, May 26, I have only received about 15 of the 180 book reports! . . . I have learned a lot again:*
> *—Students cannot plan, anyway not over a longer period of time.*
> *—I should unlearn to keep believing in the good willingness of students.*
> *—I should think more of myself.*
> *—Active and self-regulated learning is a misleading slogan.*

## Experiencing Friction

Feelings of confusion, helplessness, nondirectedness, being lost prevail with a number of teachers. They get confused because the pedagogy of active and self-regulated learning does not connect to their own beliefs and practices, their own personal theory of practice. They feel they do not know any more what is good teaching, or what is bad teaching. The old way of teaching obviously does not suffice any more but the new way of teaching they are not (yet) able to practice. Moreover, they do not know well what or how to learn about this new way of teaching. Striking is the following testimony:

> *My general feeling now is one of confusion and powerlessness. When my students have to work independently, most of the time I am not satisfied. So I fall back again on more didactic teaching. Because I feel at home that way, that is the way I was educated. At the same time I ask myself whether that is really so bad. . . . Nobody of my colleagues knew these kinds of problems. With them it all went easily and well and these things did not happen. . . . Anyway, I was pretty*

*disappointed in my colleagues and have not got any further. I have to go back to teacher education, start all over again!*

## Towards Teachers' Learning Patterns

Further analyses revealed the beginnings of *patterns* in the learning activities of these teachers (Vermunt, Bakkenes, Brekelmans, & Wubbels, 2008), in the sense of combinations of activities relating to their conceptions of learning and teaching and to their orientations towards learning about the innovation (see the preceding definition of a 'pattern'). Most teachers in their learning were sharply focused upon improving their *immediate performance* in class: they wanted to be able to use what they had learned quickly in their teaching. Another group of teachers was (also) *meaning-directed* in their learning: this group wanted to know why things in class work as they work, looked for reasons behind it, worked at extension of their theory of practice, often involved knowledge and 'theory' from outside, and often worked for a longer period of time on a certain theme. A third group, substantial in size, could be characterized as *undirected* in their learning. These teachers struggled with the educational innovation, often did not know well how they could *teach* in another way, and did not know as well how they could *learn* about teaching in another way.

## CONCLUSIONS AND PROSPECTS

## Conclusions about Student and Teacher Learning Patterns

The main issue that this chapter addressed was to what extent student learning and teacher learning can be conceptualized in the same terms or that different models are needed for both phenomena. How teachers learn was the subject of a large research project discussed here and in scientific articles referred to in the reference list. Teachers' learning activities turned out to be mutually associated in three underlying learning patterns: (1) an *immediate performance-oriented* pattern, mainly aimed at improving one's immediate performance in the classroom; (2) a *meaning-oriented* pattern, aimed at understanding underlying principles and extending one's theory of practice; and (3) a *undirected* pattern, characterized by experiencing problems with (learning about) the educational innovation, sometimes combined with avoiding learning (see also Oosterheert & Vermunt [2001] for research on student teachers' learning).

Comparing and contrasting the results of the research on student learning and teacher learning, it can be concluded that in both student learning and teacher learning *meaning-oriented* learning and *undirected* learning play a major role. These dimensions are important aspects of models conceptualizing both student and teacher learning, although the way these phenomena manifest themselves in concrete appearance differs for both populations. For example, meaning orientation in student learning manifests itself as the search for understanding relations between different parts of the study texts and between different courses, and trying to structure one's ideas and thoughts into a personal understanding of the literature. However, teachers do not learn predominantly by studying books. Meaning orientation in teacher learning is manifested more by a search for understanding relations between different classroom experiences they have had, and between new ideas and their own experiences, and by trying to structure one's reflections into a personal theory of practice. *Application-directed* learning, identified as an important dimension in student learning especially among older and advanced students, resembles the way of learning among teachers directed towards *immediate performance* improvement in the classroom. *Reproduction-directed* learning, a major dimension in student learning, did not have an equivalent in teacher learning. It seems that this type of learning is typical for students' learning as long as they are within education boundaries, but after they leave the school it is no longer considered a useful way of learning.

Teachers respond to educational change with different patterns of learning. From the viewpoint of adopting innovative teaching methods, some of these patterns turned out to be more favorable. A meaning-oriented pattern, for example, proved to be a way of learning that offers a good opportunity for teachers to build an integrated knowledge base or theory of practice for their teaching, when innovation and change are more the rule than the exception. In the coming decade educational institutions will continue renewing their teaching, on larger and smaller scale. In these new forms of learning and teaching, teachers get other roles than in traditional teaching, meaning that teachers should learn to fulfill these new roles. Finding out which pedagogical approaches are most suited to achieve this objective, and further developing these approaches, is therefore an important task for the years to come.

Teacher learning therefore turns out to be a prerequisite for fostering student learning and thereby enhancing students' capacity to learn. Educational innovations have often ignored the need for teacher learning. Recent research on teacher learning shows that this was a major omission (e.g., Lieberman & Pointer-Mace, 2008). Teachers are the most important agents in bringing about educational change and development. Therefore, the most important prerequisite to foster students' capacity to learn is making sure that teachers get the opportunity and time to learn about new pedagogies, for example, to take individual differences in learning into account. In view of the results of the studies discussed here, fostering teacher learning means giving teachers ample opportunities to: experiment with new ways of teaching within and with an extension of their theory of practice; develop their theory of practice; learn by observing others; think about their experiences; and use the frictions that inevitably will occur in a constructive way, such that they do not feel tempted to avoid learning about new pedagogical approaches.

The fact that student learning and teacher learning are partly parallel phenomena gives the opportunity to teach teachers about taking student learning patterns into account by taking their own patterns in learning into account. In this way teacher professional learning may be a model for what the teachers can do later on with their own students. The fact that reproduction-directed learning is a way of learning that obviously loses its value after the school years should warn us not to stimulate this way of learning in students, when we want to prepare our students for lifelong professional learning.

## Prospects for Future Research on Student and Teacher Learning Patterns

I conclude with listing five directions into which research on learning patterns should develop in future years in my view. First, further research on patterns in teacher learning should be conducted. Since the study of teacher learning processes has just begun, much more research is needed to provide further evidence on the nature of teacher learning patterns, the beginnings of which were outlined in this chapter. This research should include both the nature and development of teacher learning patterns, as well as pedagogies to foster teacher learning. Moreover, diagnostic instruments for teacher learning should be developed, because there are, to my knowledge, no reliable and valid large-scale instruments to assess teacher learning patterns as described earlier yet.

Second, research on the interaction and interplay between the student and teacher learning patterns should be fostered. In this chapter, research evidence on patterns in student learning and teacher learning, gathered in different studies, was compared and contrasted. One step further would be to gather research evidence on student learning patterns, and teaching and learning patterns of *teachers of those students* in the same study. Questions to be answered in this type of research are: how do teachers with a certain teaching 'style' or pattern interact with students with different and similar learning patterns? How does that interaction affect students' learning processes and outcomes differentially? How do teachers learn from studying these differential students' learning processes and outcomes themselves to deepen their understanding of student learning and to expand their teaching repertoire? Finally, how do teachers learn from studying the interplay between their own learning and teaching to deepen their understanding of themselves as teachers?

Third, the pedagogy of learning patterns should be further developed. What does it mean when we advocate that education should take into account individual differences between students and teachers in their learning patterns? Should we adapt instruction in such a way that it suits preferences in learning patterns optimally (e.g., give application-oriented assignments to application-oriented students), or should we try to develop the 'weaker' sides of a learner (and, for example, give meaning-oriented assignments to application-oriented students)? Should we group teachers, in a professional development program, according to similarity in their learning patterns, or, on the contrary, according to differences? In my view, there is an urgent need for sound research and theory development in the field of pedagogies of learning patterns, both about student learning and teacher learning.

Fourth, principles to promote more favorable learning patterns in real settings, for both students and teachers, should be designed and studied. Future research should be directed at the way in which promotion of more favorable ways of learning can be realized concretely in different types of learning environments, for students, teachers, and students and teachers together.

Finally, a third generation of learning pattern models should be developed, one that incorporates affective, social/collaborative, subject specific, and environmental components. Further ahead, when research on neuroscience and learning has yielded new insights, a fourth generation may also include biological components in a developing model of learning pattern.

## BIBLIOGRAPHY

Bakkenes, I., Vermunt, J.D., & Wubbels, T. (in press). Teacher learning in the context of educational innovation: learning activities and learning outcomes of experienced teachers. *Learning and Instruction*.

Biggs, J.B. (1982). Student motivation and study strategies in university and C.A.E. populations. *Higher Education Research and Development, 1*, 33–55.

De Corte, E., Verschaffel, L., Entwistle, N., & Van Merriënboer, J. (Eds.) (2003). *Powerful Learning Environments: Unraveling Basic Components and Dimensions*. Oxford: Pergamon.

Entwistle, N.J., & Ramsden, P. (1983). *Understanding Student Learning*. London: Croom Helm.

Hoekstra, A., Beijaard, D., Brekelmans, M., & Korthagen, F. (2007). Experienced teachers' informal learning from classroom teaching. *Teachers and Teaching: Theory and Practice, 13*, 191–208.

Lieberman, A., & Pointer-Mace, D.H. (2008). Teacher learning: the key to educational reform. *Journal of Teacher Education, 59*, 226–234.

Meirink, J.A., Meijer, P.C., Verloop, N., & Bergen, Th.C.M. (2009). How do teachers learn in the workplace? An examination of teacher learning activities. *European Journal of Teacher Education, 32*, 209–224.

Oosterheert, I.E., & Vermunt, J.D. (2001). Individual differences in learning to teach: relating cognition, regulation and affect. *Learning and Instruction, 11*, 133–156.

Pintrich, P.R. (2004). A conceptual framework for assessing motivation and self-regulated learning in college students. *Educational Psychology Review, 16*, 385–407.

Shulman, L.S., & Shulman, J.H. (2004). How and what teachers learn: a shifting perspective. *Journal of Curriculum Studies, 36*, 257–271.

Vermetten, Y.J., Lodewijks, H.G., & Vermunt, J.D. (1999). Consistency and variability of learning strategies in different university courses. *Higher Education, 37*, 1–21.

Vermunt, J.D. (1996). Metacognitive, cognitive and affective aspects of learning styles and strategies: a phenomenographic analysis. *Higher Education, 31*, 25–50.

Vermunt, J.D. (1998). The regulation of constructive learning processes. *British Journal of Educational Psychology, 68*, 149–171.

Vermunt, J.D. (2005). Relations between student learning patterns and personal and contextual factors and academic performance. *Higher Education, 49*, 205–234.

Vermunt, J.D. (2007). The power of teaching-learning environments to influence student learning. *British Journal of Educational Psychology Monograph Series, II, 4*, 73–90.

Vermunt, J.D., Bakkenes, I., Brekelmans, M., & Wubbels, T. (2008). *Teachers' Approaches to Learning and Outcomes of Learning in the Context of Educational Innovation*. Paper presented at the EARLI SIG 14 Learning and Professional Development Conference, August, Jyväskylä, Finland.

Vermunt, J., & Minnaert, A. (2003). Dissonance in student learning patterns: when to revise theory? *Studies in Higher Education, 28*, 49–61.

Vermunt, J.D., & Verloop, N. (1999). Congruence and friction between learning and teaching. *Learning and Instruction, 9*, 257–280.

Vermunt, J.D., & Vermetten, Y.J. (2004). Patterns in student learning: relationships between learning strategies, conceptions of learning, and learning orientations. *Educational Psychology Review, 16*, 359–384.

Zwart, R.C., Wubbels, Th., Bolhuis, S., & Bergen, Th.C.M., (2008). Teacher learning through reciprocal peer coaching: an analysis of activity sequences. *Teaching and Teacher Education, 24*, 982–1002.

# 13 Enhancing Feedback Practice
## A Personal Learning Styles Pedagogy Approach

*Carol Evans and Michael Waring*

## INTRODUCTION

This chapter identifies how understandings of personal learning style(s) (Evans & Waring, 2009; Rayner, 2000) can be used to inform the nature of feedback within an integrated curriculum design. The last decade has seen an abundance of research in relation to assessment practices in education (Nicol, 2008; Swaffield, 2008), including extensive work carried out around the application of formative assessment and feedback on learner performance (Black & Wiliam, 1998). However, notable within this mass of research is the limited attention paid to how an understanding of personal learning style(s) can enhance our understanding of effective feedback practices. Even less attention has been paid to the potential relationship between the nature of feedback and cognitive style as it impacts on the self-regulatory practices of those who are preparing to teach, that is, student teachers (STs). Little is understood about the technologies of feedback within initial teacher education (Higgins, Hartley, & Skelton, 2002; Lizzio & Wilson, 2008; Mutch, 2003; Orrell, 2006). In other words, there is a lack of tacit as well as explicit knowledge and understanding of those mechanisms (processes and strategies) by which feedback is generated, offered, and engaged with by STs in initial teacher education (ITE). By exploring with STs their individual understandings of feedback, awareness of their own learning can be enhanced as they learn to teach (Evans & Waring, 2006; Nielsen, 2008). By making such knowledge and understanding explicit to STs, it provides opportunities for them to think about how they cater for individual learning differences (ILDs) through their design and delivery of assessment and feedback practices within their own teaching environments. Fundamentally such participant research can help to inform and improve higher education (HEI) practice by improving the nature of and mechanisms by which feedback is offered to STs. In summary, this chapter will make an explicit link between theory and practice by exploring the metacognitive potential of an understanding of cognitive styles as part of a Personal Learning Styles Pedagogy (PLSP) and how this can inform the development and enhancement of feedback within ITE. Recommendations will be made in relation to informing the nature of feedback practices.

It should be noted that within this context, cognitive styles are perceived as higher order heuristics that affect how individuals respond to events and ideas they experience (Rayner, 2000). They are seen as consistent differences in the ways in which individuals organize and process information (Messick, 1984). A PLSP explicitly addresses how, in practice, one can use an understanding of cognitive styles in association with other aspects of an individual's approach to learning.

## FEEDBACK: COULD DO BETTER?

This chapter concentrates on one dimension of assessment, namely feedback. Feedback can be conceptualized as "information provided by an agent (e.g., teacher, peer, book, parent, self, experience) regarding aspects of one's performance or understanding" (Hattie & Timperley, 2007, p. 81). Sustained dissatisfaction with the quality of assessment, including feedback, has been reported widely within the UK, US, and Australasian contexts (Angelo, 1996; Boud & Falchikov, 2007; Fearn, 2009; Hattie & Timperley, 2007; HEFCE, 2007; Orrell, 2006; Rae & Cochrane, 2008). Despite pockets of innovation and excellence, assessment practices in higher education are seen to be relatively weak and even broken (Race, 2002). This is the result of a number of factors, such as a lack of constructive alignment (Biggs, 1999) between curricula learning outcomes, learning and teaching methods, and assessment (Rust, O'Donovan, & Price, 2005). In addition, inadequacies in feedback involving ambiguity and opacity; negativity; lateness and lack of clarity of assessment criteria contribute to the problem (Hounsell, 2003). Bicen (2009) argues that feedback is the lynchpin for learning and validation. However, she, along with many others, also makes the point that most learners fail to understand or are unable to interpret feedback correctly because of the disparity between learner and tutor perceptions of such feedback (Burke, 2009; Carless, 2006; Gibbs & Simpson, 2004; Hattie & Timperley, 2007; Weaver, 2006). This being the case, the impact of feedback either in terms of guidance or motivation is often at best limited (Crisp, 2007; Duncan, 2007). To overcome this 'blind spot' in relation to strategies for learners to make effective use of feedback, Burke (2009) argues for more explicit attention to be paid to how learners actually use and perceive feedback.

Such attention has to take account of the needs and interpretations of an increasingly diverse student population, accompanied by larger group sizes and less tutor contact time (Bloxham & West, 2004; Rust et al., 2005). We also need to be more cognizant of the ways in which the nature of feedback may impact differentially on students with varied learning profiles, as well as the way in which cognitive style(s) mediates the accessibility of feedback and interacts with other individual differences (Gibbs & Simpson, 2004). If assessment is to be equitable, all students need to receive feedback which is appropriate to their learning needs (Knight & Yorke, 2003). However, from a self-regulatory perspective, STs must be educated in how to engage with any feedback they are given to make the best use of it.

It is asserted that feedback is an essential principle for efficient learning (Boud & Falchicov, 2007; Higgins et al., 2002). There are a number of studies that identify key principles of effective assessment feedback (Handley, Price, & Millar, 2008; Nicol, 2008). For feedback to be effective, it needs to: (1) be timely (Bloxham, 2008; Ellery, 2008; Rae & Cochrane, 2008); (2) be appropriate to the purpose of the assessment task and level of student understanding (Gibbs & Simpson, 2004); (3) be provided in conjunction with the learner having sufficient knowledge of how to be able to use feedback effectively (Hattie & Timperley, 2007); (4) be accessible to the learner (Weaver, 2006); (5) involve an equitable dialogue between student and tutor to clarify meanings, expectations, misconceptions, and future actions (Rust et al., 2005); (6) identify actions including strategies to enable the student to improve (Boud, 2000; Burke, 2009); (7) focus on performance (Gibbs & Simpson, 2004); (8) be able to feed forward (Duncan, 2007; Higgins, Hartley, & Skelton, 2001); and (9) inform the process of learning and focus on a self-regulation level (Hattie & Timperley, 2007; Higgins et al., 2002). We also know that feedback is enhanced when it is given by peers (Bicen, 2009; Davies, 2006; Kim, 2009; Liu & Carless, 2006; Rust et al., 2005) and that this is contingent on learners being specifically taught how to peer- and self-assess (Boud, 2000; Higgins et al., 2002; Kim, 2009). However, in spite of knowing this, the potential of feedback to enhance learning and understanding is not being realized. This is especially so in terms of the promotion of the learner's self-regulatory practices (Hattie & Timperley, 2007) and the effective application of formative assessment (Black, Harrison, Lee, Marshall, & Wiliam, 2003; Hounsell, 2003; Yorke, 2003). An understanding of cognitive styles research may assist those giving and receiving feedback by allowing them to consider alternative approaches and in so doing enable greater access to feedback.

## EMPLOYING A PERSONAL LEARNING STYLES PEDAGOGY TO INFORM FEEDBACK PRACTICES

Any model of feedback must take account of the way STs make sense of and use feedback information (Juwah et al., 2004). When adopting a PLSP, the focus is on self-regulation, with learners being challenged to experiment with a variety of approaches to learning rather than perpetuating established and engrained learning behaviors. Of course, such behaviors may not be the most appropriate to address the demands of specific tasks. As part of the PLSP, learners are encouraged to critically examine the ways in which they go about learning. This approach therefore focuses on five key interrelated areas (for a fuller outline, see Evans & Waring, 2009): (1) exploration of teacher beliefs/modeling and support in relation to learning and creating opportunities to model ideas in practice; (2) careful selection and application of models so as to suit the needs of specific learners; (3) creating optimal conditions for learning; (4) student voice by having full involvement of learners in the process of learning; and (5) design of learning environments. We argue that a focus on cognitive styles as part of a PLSP is highly relevant within the context of individual learning differences (ILDs) and the enhancement of feedback practices for STs. It provides an individual focus on both cognitive and affective aspects of learning, enabling STs to begin to question why and how they go about learning. In so doing it assists in the development of the ST's self-regulation skills and practices.

A personal learning style (PLS) is one which includes a range of cognitive and learning styles and involves the disposition to adopt specific strategies within a learning context (Evans & Waring, 2009, p. 170). An individual's habitual or typical way of perceiving, remembering, thinking, and problem solving is their cognitive style (Messick, 1984). A learning style is a broader construct which is seen to be more responsive to particular situational and task demands. A PLS involves physiological and affective behaviors, as well as cognitive ones. It is associated with preferences with regard to working environments, learning processes, and approaches to study. It is built on the premise that an individual has access to a range of styles, some of which are more stable than others (Curry, 1983; Riding & Cheema, 1991; Rayner, 2000; Zhang & Sternberg, 2005).

Our notion of a PLS builds on both the work of Curry and Rayner by exploring in practical settings the ways in which specific style constructs impact on learning to inform pedagogy. The clear distinction between core (cognitive styles) and frame constructs (learning preferences) is purposefully less well defined in our model compared to that of Curry or Rayner. This highlights the increasing awareness of the operation of cognitive style constructs at different hierarchical levels, with some having more impact on learning behaviors than others (Kozhevnikov, 2007). In our approach, we acknowledge the multidimensional nature of cognitive styles, as well as the pejorative nature of them in that in certain situations and for certain tasks some styles are more useful and/or perceived more highly. Our focus is on identifying with STs, the most appropriate styles and strategies they can use to maximize learning outcomes for themselves and others.

Within this chapter we have chosen to concentrate on examining the role of the intuition and analysis dimensions of cognitive style in relation to STs' perceptions of feedback. This decision was made based on evidence from previous research findings related to the role of analysis and intuition in mediating access to learning (Evans & Waring, 2008a, 2008b). The focus on one empirical study in this chapter is significant in that it not only explicitly explores the relationship between the Cognitive Style Index (CSI) and student perceptions of feedback, but at the time of writing there were no other published studies exploring this.

The instrument used to measure the intuition and analysis dimensions of cognitive style was the modified version of Allinson and Hayes's (1996) Cognitive Style Index (Hodgkinson & Sadler-Smith, 2003). It was chosen on the basis of its high reliability and validity (Coffield, Moseley, Hall, & Ecclestone, 2004). This measure was also selected because this version of the CSI suggests that individuals have the capacity to use both analytic and intuitive thought supporting the multidimensional nature of style underpinned by Epstein's (1994, 2004) Cognitive Experiential Self-Theory (CEST). When working with STs, using a PLSP approach, it is important to demonstrate how analysis and intuition can be used effectively in teaching situations. An understanding of dual process theory (Epstein, Pacini, Denes-Raj, & Heier, 1996; Shiloh, Salton, & Sharabi, 2002) has much to offer in this respect by enabling individuals to consider their learning behaviors. All individuals have the capacity to process information using both systems—rational (analytic) and experiential (intuitive)—with behavior being influenced jointly by the two systems along a continuum reflecting their relative importance. Therefore, how individuals use these systems together may have a very important impact on individual decision making and ability to give and take on board feedback (Shiloh et al., 2002).

## METHODOLOGY

A concurrent mixed method design was employed in the research reported here (Tashakkori & Teddlie, 2003). The project involved a multistrand design in which both qualitative and quantitative data were collected and analyzed independently. The reported findings reflect the results of both sets of data analysis. The study involved 140 STs from two universities, with 83% participating in all aspects of the study: fifty-nine STs studying for a Master's PGCE in physical education at University X (group A); thirty-four STs studying for a Master's in teaching (group B); and twenty-three STs studying for a Master's PGCE in mathematics at University Y (group C). The age range of the STs was 21 to 49 years (mean age = 21). In groups A and C, all STs were UK students studying for a one year postgraduate certificate in teaching. Group B comprised international STs from a range of countries (Canada, US, India, Pakistan, and Tajikistan) studying two concurrent MA programs within the UK.

Acknowledging the complex rather than unitary nature of style (Hodgkinson & Sadler-Smith, 2003), all STs completed the Cognitive Style Index (CSI) of Allinson and Hayes (1996) in its modified form. In this context, analysis relates to reflectivity, rational, sequential, and logical thinking; intuition relates to impulsivity, creativity, and thinking on one's feet. The CSI is a robust, reliable, and valid measure of cognitive style (Coffield et al., 2004) and is quick and straightforward to administer. The quantitative data generated from the CSI was analyzed using Statistical Package for the Social Sciences (SPSS) (mean, median, standard deviation, frequency distributions of CSI scores) in order to identify style patterns and groupings within the data.

All STs completed a questionnaire inviting their views on the nature and value of different types of feedback that they had received on their academic and professional work. Building on the research of Hattie and Timperley (2007), the questionnaire sought to elicit ST perceptions of the value of different forms of feedback (about task; about processing of the task; about-self-regulation; and about the self as a person), as well as to rank order their preferences in relation to questions considering sources, form, timing, and nature of feedback. Furthermore, open-ended questions explored ST perceptions of the value of different sources of feedback, the format and timing of feedback, along with a consideration of the role STs played in proactively seeking out feedback. The quantitative data yielded from the questionnaire were analyzed using SPSS (pearson correlations, one way between groups ANOVA). Inductive content analysis procedures involving the systematic comparison of the data were employed on the qualitative data (Krippendorff, 2004).

## FINDINGS

### Analysis and Intuition Style Dimensions

The mean analysis score was 27.2 ($SD$ = 6.9; $N$ = 116) and the mean intuition score was 21.7 ($SD$ = 6.6; $N$ = 116). There was no statistically significant difference in the scores of the three groups, enabling the collapse of the data into one set for analysis. Having analyzed the distribution of scores and using the two dimensions of the CSI, the STs' scores were divided into four cognitive style groups on the basis of median scores (analysis median score = 28; intuition median score = 22): Style 1 = high analysis and low intuition ($n$ = 33); Style 2 = high analysis and high intuition ($n$ = 25); Style 3 = low analysis and low intuition ($n$ = 17); and Style 4 = low analysis and high intuition ($n$ = 33).

Within this study, as in previous ones (Evans & Waring, 2006, 2007, 2008a, 2008b), those STs in the Style 3 group (low analysis/low intuition) received lower grades in their teaching, raising the question as to whether Style 3 represents an impoverished style. Shiloh and colleagues (2002) have also identified that complementary styles (high rational/high intuitive [Style 2 in this study]) and low rational/low intuitive styles (Style 3 in this study) may be more affected by the way in which information is presented in making a decision and, consequently, this has implications for the design of feedback to STs.

## Variations in Student Perceptions of Feedback: Consensus and Difference

Taking into account the sample size, style differences were discernible in a number of areas supporting previous findings (Evans & Waring, 2006, 2007, 2008a, 2008b). In relation to feedback preferences, the STs highlighted the importance of the following in influencing their performance: face-to-face contact with their tutor; the timelines of feedback; their own proactivity in seeking out feedback; the importance of clarity in assessment criteria; feedback focused on the process of learning rather than self-regulation; and the importance of positive feedback given at the personal level. The statistically significant differences ascertained using one way between groups ANOVA and Tukey HSD tests are shown in Table 13.1.

STs valued most highly face-to-face feedback from their tutor as the principal mode of feedback, something also identified by Rae and Cochrane (2008). Style 1 STs valued face-to-face feedback more than Style 3 STs, supporting previous findings (Evans & Waring, 2007, 2008a, 2008b). Style 1 STs' greater proactivity in seeking out feedback compared to Style 2 STs was statistically significant. However, 85% of all STs claimed to actively seek out feedback:

> *I actively seek out feedback on my work immediately after, so that the information is fresh in my mind and I can link it to the performance.* (Style 1 ST)
> *I want feedback when achieving lower marks than expected and wanting to improve for next time.* (Style 2 ST)
> *I want extra feedback when I have not achieved the level of work I aimed for. If I have achieved the level I expected I am less likely to seek feedback, but will take on board any comments made.* (Style 3 ST)
> *On placement I actively sought out feedback to improve my teaching because I feel I benefit a lot from talking to current teachers and getting ways to improve my lessons.* (Style 4 ST)

Apart from Style 3, all STs identified the importance of receiving feedback as soon as possible after submission of their work. The justification for this revolved around the currency of their thoughts on completion of the assessed piece of work and their perceived ability to retain and act upon those thoughts in the short term. STs of all styles did not wish to seek out feedback if they thought they had done well in the assessment, or if they deemed the quality of the work that they had submitted to be poor:

> *I do not seek further feedback if I get a grade I think reflects the effort put into the piece of work.* (Style 4 ST)
> *I don't seek feedback when I am aware I have achieved my target.* (Style 1 ST)

*Table 13.1*  Cognitive Style and Feedback Preferences (One Way between Groups ANOVA)

| N = 108 | F | p | Partial eta squared | Tukey HSD | Style 1HA/LI Mean (SD) | Style 2HA/HI Mean (SD) | Style 3LA/LI Mean (SD) | Style 4LA/HI Mean (SD) |
|---|---|---|---|---|---|---|---|---|
| Q3. Face-to-face feedback | 2.98 | 0.039 | 0.08 | 1 and 3 | 1.06 (0.35) | 1.28 (0.46) | 1.41 (0.51) | 1.16 (0.45) |
| Q8. Seeking out feedback | 4.75 | 0.004 | 0.12 | 1 and 2 | 0.91 (0.29) | 0.44 (0.77) | 1.24 (0.56) | 1.15 (0.51) |
| Q9. Giving of feedback to my peers | 2.88 | 0.040 | 0.08 | | 10.18 (5.5) | 10.00 (4.40) | 10.18 (6.0) | 6.76 (5.90) |
| Q14. Clarity of assessment criteria | 3.13 | 0.029 | 0.08 | 1 and 2 | 1.15 (0.51) | 1.72 (0.93) | 1.35 (0.70) | 1.51 (0.76) |

Note. HA/LI = high analysis/low intuition; HA/HI = high analysis/high intuition; LA/LI = low analysis/low intuition; LA/HI = low analysis/high intuition.

*I do not seek out feedback if I feel that my work is not of high enough caliber and I know that I did not do a good job.* (Style 2 ST)

*If I have passed work—don't need to know how to improve as I will not do it again.* (Style 3 ST)

STs with high levels of analysis were more in favor of feedback focusing on specific content areas ($r = -0.193$, $p < 0.05$; $N = 108$). Those with higher intuition scores were more likely to value video feedback on their teaching more highly ($r = -487$; $p < 0.01$; $N = 108$). Although statistically significant, the strength of the relationship in both cases was relatively low.

Working alone and self-reliance were preferred by 70% of STs in comparison to collaborative peer working. The majority of STs did not see the value of giving feedback to their peers as an important way of learning when compared to receiving feedback from their tutor. However, male and female Style 4 STs did value such an approach more highly than other styles, something also identified by Evans and Waring (2008b).

Whereas Styles 1 and 4 were the only STs to acknowledge the importance of the way in which the feedback was phrased, the predominant factor affecting all STs, in terms of their ability to take on board feedback, was the degree of credibility and expertise that they perceived the person making the assessment to have:

*When someone gives feedback that is not really qualified to do it, it is hard to reflect upon it and respect their view.* (Style 2 ST)

*Who is giving me the feedback? If it is someone I don't respect, I'm not going to fully listen.* (Style 3 ST)

*Depends who is providing the feedback. I need to respect the person providing the feedback and value their opinion.* (Style 1 ST)

*When taking on board feedback, I like to feel that they are in a more knowledgeable position than me and have something to offer.* (Style 4 ST)

Style 2 STs were more likely to self-attribute in relation to their ability and disposition in being able to assimilate feedback. Style 1 STs were most likely to attribute a lack of time as a consequence of their poor time management to explain their level of attainment.

Important features highlighted by Rae and Cochrane (2008) are the need for assessment to be clearly presented from the outset and for the learners to receive instruction on how to make the best use of the feedback they receive. Clarity of assessment criteria was rated as very important by 88% of STs. Within this, it was perceived to be least important to Style 2 STs.

The importance of affect in this study cannot be underestimated. Positive feedback from the tutor (PFT) and personal feedback (PF) were ranked first and third, respectively, when STs were asked to place in rank order a number of statements relating to what they felt was most important in enabling them to make progress. PFT was most important to Styles 2 and 4 females and least important to Style 3 males. However, differences between the style groups were not statistically significant.

In relation to the specific nature and form of feedback, differences were more evident at the course and gender levels rather than at the cognitive styles level. However, further research is required in this area to verify such findings.

## PRACTICAL IMPLICATIONS

It is argued here and elsewhere (Evans & Waring, 2009) that adopting a PLSP requires the incorporation of a number of fundamental approaches to instruction that are required to improve assessment feedback practice within HEIs. Aligned with the work of Nicol (2008), these fundamental approaches focus on three interrelated areas: (1) ensuring clarity regarding assessment demands; (2) ensuring student involvement in the process; and (3) encouraging self-regulation within learners.

## Assessment Design and Clarity

We know that cognitive style impacts on an ST's ability to engage positively with different types of assessment practice (Evans & Waring, 2009; Vickerman, 2009). Clarification of assessment criteria was very important to the majority of STs within the study. When information about assessment is posted incrementally rather than at the outset of the course, it is known that this can be disadvantageous to STs with a more holistic perspective (Evans, 2004). Riding (2002) identifies the importance of providing such information from the outset in order to provide STs of particular styles with a choice in how they go about completing tasks. For example, analytic STs may be easily overloaded by the provision of detailed information at the beginning of a course and need to be systematically taken through this (Evans, 2004). This would involve ensuring that all information about assessment and associated feedback is explicit and accessible through the provision of clear outlines of all assessment requirements and feedback protocols at the beginning of a course. In so doing, this should provide STs with a route map through the various elements of their assessment (Rust et al., 2005), thus allowing for the direct involvement of STs in assessment design—including, quite crucially, in feedback.

End loading of most or all assessment should be discouraged. To enable feedback to be utilized in subsequent assignments, so as to facilitate feed forward (Carless, 2006), staggered and progressive assessments should be encouraged. In addition, because much of an ST's time is spent in a school-based environment away from the university, the conceptions of assessment by school-based mentors need to be considered and their thinking aligned with a desired set of conceptions associated with the assessment innovations (Brown, 2004).

## Ensuring Student Involvement in the Process

The central involvement of the ST in assessment design and in the generating of assessment criteria with their peers and tutors in the assessment of their own and each other's work in ITE is important. Examples include: collaborative discussion, justification and agreement over the criteria to be used to assess, as well as the associated weighting of them; peer assessment of each other in the classroom; presentations and written assignments involving the giving of feedback to peers, along with constructive feedback they receive from their peers (i.e., back feedback; Kim, 2009) and tutors. One must be mindful that, even though STs may have particular preferences, it is essential that they are offered a holistic learning experience incorporating many forms of feedback in a way that is accessible rather than alienating. Therefore, even though STs may express certain preferences in receiving feedback, alternative forms of feedback should not be excluded. Training in self and peer feedback should, therefore, be an essential element of ITE course designs.

The importance of STs' levels of engagement, prior knowledge, and epistemological beliefs, in addition to their cognitive styles, needs careful consideration (Handley et al., 2008). For highly analytic STs, peer working may be more problematic and course tutors need to be sensitive to such issues in the design and development of collaborative learning opportunities, along with any decisions as to the weighting of group assessed work. Careful consideration needs to be given to examining what feedback can most effectively be given to a group, and what needs to be given at an individual level. STs need to be allowed to develop the skills to make the most of tutorial opportunities, as well as being guided in their use of resources (Burke, 2009). The need for such focused support for a learner is also highlighted by Prosser and Webb (1994).

STs need to be systematically helped to reflect on, and change, their understanding of the nature of the task in the context in which the task is undertaken. STs should be encouraged in one-to-one feedback to consider alternative approaches to the giving and receiving of feedback; this is contingent on such approaches being modeled explicitly with STs in the teaching in both university-based and school-based settings. In this way, STs should be encouraged to summarize their own work to different audiences of their peers, acting on the feedback they receive to consolidate their own ideas in order to refine their versions of the assessments. Importantly, they should also be encouraged to utilize such techniques with their own students.

## Encouraging Self-Regulation within Learners

As part of encouraging self-regulation within learners, STs need to explore their own learning beliefs and patterns of working. Thus, dialogue between the tutor and themselves should get them to consider their own and others' interpretations of feedback, and identify for them what is most effective and what is obfuscatory. This is vital to 'disambiguating feedback' (Draper, 2009) and needs to involve reciprocal learning strategies on behalf of the tutor and ST. The importance of such dialogue around notions of effective feedback cannot be underestimated. A very powerful and successful tool to facilitate such dialogue is the use of analysis software on video footage taken of teaching episodes (conducted by the ST and by others) in a university- and school-based context (Carillo-de-la-Pena, Casereas, Martinez, Ortet, & Perez, 2009).

The ability to self-assess is crucial as part of self-regulation, that is, if STs are to be able to act on feedback more effectively and become effective lifelong learners (Boud & Falchikov, 2007; Sadler, 2005; Taras, 2003). A focus on the process of learning and understanding of one's own cognitive approaches may help to facilitate more accurate and reliable self-assessment. Consequently, sufficient time needs to be allocated to acquiring knowledge and understanding of assessment processes and to enhancing dialogue around how STs make use of feedback (Rust et al., 2005). The consideration of self-regulation strategies with STs by explicitly modeling alternative ways of doing and by identifying a range of strategies to overcome learning barriers, including the use of reinforcement strategies to embed the use of new or alternative approaches through doing and through reflection, are critically important.

The role of feedback on learners' motivational beliefs and self-esteem is an area that requires further research attention (Hattie & Timperley, 2007; Juwal et al., 2004; Nicol, 2008). The importance of the 'personal relational' dimension to feedback has been highlighted in this study and elsewhere (Handley et al., 2008). In relation to ITE programs, careful consideration needs to be given to the amount and nature of school-based mentor training that focuses on the giving and receiving of feedback. Such training needs to be progressive and developmental and sensitize mentors to the needs of STs, along with reinforcing in practical ways the principles of effective feedback. Allied to this, STs also need training in how to make the most of all feedback situations associated with their learning to teach.

## FUTURE DIRECTIONS FOR RESEARCH

The cognitive style dimensions (analysis and intuition) did have an impact on ST perceptions of effective feedback. Limited evidence was found regarding the differential impact of these style dimensions on preferences regarding the format of feedback. However, more research is required involving larger samples to clarify this. How these dimensions of cognitive style interact with other cognitive styles (e.g., intuitive-experiential and analytical-rational; object-visual, spatial-visual, and verbal; leveling-sharpening; impulsivity-reflectivity), in addition to other individual difference factors such as gender, culture, age, and previous learning experiences, is also an area requiring further exploration.

In attending to self-regulation, along with dialogue to increase our understanding of what constitutes effective feedback practice, it can be argued that to ignore cognitive style constructs is to be negligent, as their inclusion can add richness to our understanding of why STs can or cannot engage with feedback. In addition, such an approach offers a valuable insight into how STs process feedback.

Within this chapter we have highlighted that certain style combinations as part of a personal learning style may represent more negatively oriented learning profiles for those STs training to be a teacher. More work is required to examine the predictive nature of style across different contexts. As part of this, it will be especially important to explore whether a styles profile demonstrating low analysis and intuition leads to poorer teaching performance. From a learning perspective, if these profiles can be identified from the outset, ITE can be tailored more readily to attend to ST needs.

The importance of aligning feedback to the specific needs of individual STs has been identified along with the importance of developing ST self-regulation skills. Promotion of self-regulation demands that the tutor and mentor assist STs to consider learning possibilities for themselves through targeted support that is not wholly dictated. The question for ITE providers is: how are they structuring and assisting STs in developing the essential skills of autonomy, self-control, self-direction, and self-discipline? One answer to this would be to adopt a PLSP.

## BIBLIOGRAPHY

Allinson, C.W., & Hayes, J. (1996). The Cognitive Style Index: a measure of intuition-analysis for organizational research. *Journal of Management Studies, 33,* 119–135.

Angelo, T. (1996). Transforming assessment: high standards for higher learning. *AAHE Bulletin, 48,* 3–4.

Bicen, P. (2009). Group-based assessment as a dynamic approach to marketing education. *Journal of Marketing Education, 31,* 96–108.

Biggs, J. (1999). *Teaching for Quality Learning at University.* Buckingham, UK: SRHE and Open University Press.

Black, P., Harrison, C., Lee, C., Marshall, B., & Wiliam, D. (2003). *Assessment for Learning: Putting It into Practice.* Maidenhead, UK: Open University Press.

Black, P., & Wiliam, D. (1998). Assessment and classroom learning. *Assessment in Education, 5,* 7–75.

Bloxham, S. (2008). *Guide to Assessment,* ESCalate, HEA. Retrieved July 20, 2009, from http://escalate.ac.uk/4148

Bloxham, S., & West, A. (2004). Understanding the rules of the game: marking peer assessment as a medium for developing students' conceptions of assessment. *Assessment and Evaluation on Higher Education, 29,* 721–733.

Boud, D. (2000). Sustainable assessment: rethinking assessment for the learning society. *Studies in Continuing Education, 22,* 151–167.

Boud, D., & Falchikov, N. (Eds.) (2007). *Rethinking Assessment in Higher Education. Learning for the longer term.* Oxon, UK: Routledge.

Brown, G.T.L. (2004). Teachers' conceptions of assessment: implications for policy and professional development. *Assessment in Education, 11,* 301–318.

Burke, D. (2009). Strategies for using feedback students bring to higher education. *Assessment and Evaluation in Higher Education, 34,* 41–50.

Carillo-de-la-Pena, M.T., Casereas, X., Martinez, A., Ortet, G., & Perez, J. (2009). Formative assessment and academic achievement in pre-graduate students of health sciences. *Advances in Health Science Education, 14,* 61–67.

Carless, D. (2006). Differing perceptions in the feedback process. *Studies in Higher Education, 31,* 219–233.

Coffield, F., Moseley, D., Hall, E., & Ecclestone, K. (2004). *Learning Styles and Pedagogy in Post-16 Learning: A Systematic and Critical Review.* London: Learning and Skills Research Centre.

Crisp, B.R. (2007). Is it worth the effort? How feedback influences students' subsequent submission of assessable work. *Assessment and Evaluation in Higher Education, 32,* 571–581.

Curry, L. (1983). An organisation of learning styles theory and constructs. In L. Curry (Ed.), *Leaning Style in Continuing Education.* Halifax, Canada: Dalhousie University (ERIC Document Reproduction Service Number ED 235 185).

Davies, P. (2006): Peer assessment: judging the quality of students' work by comments rather than marks. *Innovations in Education and Teaching International, 43,* 69–82.

Draper, S.W. (2009). What are learners actually regulating when given feedback? *British Journal of Educational Technology, 40,* 306–315.

Duncan, N. (2007). 'Feed-forward': improving students' use of tutor comments. *Assessment and Evaluation in Higher Education, 32,* 271–283.

Ellery, K. (2008). Assessment for learning: a case study using feedback effectively in an essay-style test. *Assessment and Evaluation in Higher Education, 33,* 421–429.

Epstein, S. (1994). Integration of the cognitive and the psychodynamic unconscious. *American Psychologist, 49,* 709–724.

Epstein, S. (2004). *Intuition from the Perspective of Cognitive-Experiential Self-Theory.* 5th Heidelberg Meeting on Judgment and Decision Processes 'Intuition in Judgment and Decision Making', University of Heidelberg, February 19–22.

Epstein, S., Pacini, R., Denes-Raj, V., & Heier, H. (1996). Individual differences in intuitive-experiential and analytical-rational thinking styles. *Journal of Personality and Social Psychology, 71,* 390–405.

Evans, C. (2004). Exploring the relationship between cognitive style and teaching. *Educational Psychology, 24,* 509–531.

Evans, C., & Waring, M. (2006). Towards inclusive teacher education: sensitising individuals to how they learn. *Educational Psychology, 6,* 499–518.

Evans, C., & Waring, M. (2007). Using the CSI in educational settings. In L.M. Lassen, L. Bostrum, & H.H. Henrik Knoop (Eds), *Laering og laeringsstile om unikke og faelles veje I paedagogikken* [*Learning and Learning Styles: About Unique and Common Ways in Pedagogy*] (pp. 103–122). Virum, Denmark: Dansk Psykologisk Forlag.

Evans, C., & Waring, M. (2008a). Trainee teachers' cognitive styles and notions of differentiation. *Education and Training, 50,* 140–154.

Evans, C., & Waring, M. (2008b). *How Can an Understanding of Cognitive Style Enable Trainee Teachers to Have a Better Understanding of Differentiation in the Classroom?* Asia Pacific Educational Research Association Conference, Educational Innovation and Quality in Education: Policy and pedagogical engagement across contexts, 26–28 November, Singapore.

Evans, C., & Waring, M. (2009). The place of cognitive style in pedagogy: realising potential in practice. In L.F. Zhang & R.J. Sternberg (Eds.), *Perspectives on the Nature of Intellectual Styles* (pp. 169–208). New York: Springer.

Fearn, H. (2009). Small places win big smiles as overall satisfaction falls. *Times Higher Education, 1*, 909: 10.

Gibbs, G., & Simpson, C. (2004). Conditions under which assessment supports students' learning. *Learning and Teaching in Higher Education, 1*, 3–31.

Handley. K., Price, M., & Millar, J. (2008). *Engaging students with assessment feedback*. Oxford Brookes University. Retrieved February 18, 2010, from https://mw.brookes.ac.uk/download/attachments/28536/FDTL_Feedback-ProjectReportApril2009.pdf?version=1

Hattie, J., & Timperley, H. (2007). The power of feedback. *Review of Educational Research, 77*, 81–112.

Higgins, R., Hartley, P., & Skelton, A. (2001). Getting the message across: the problem of communicating assessment feedback. *Teaching in Higher Education, 6*, 269–274.

Higgins, R., Hartley, P., & Skelton, A. (2002). The conscientious consumer: reconsidering the role of assessment feedback in student learning. *Studies in Higher Education, 27*, 53–64.

Higher Education Funding Council for England (HEFCE) (2007). *National Student Survey*. Retrieved June 10, 2009, from http://www.hefce.ac.uk/learning/nss/data/2007

Hodgkinson, G.P., & Sadler-Smith, E. (2003). Complex or unitary: a critique and empirical reassessment of the Cognitive Style Index. *Journal of Occupational and Organisational Psychology, 76*, 243–268.

Hounsell, D. (2003). Student feedback, learning and development. In M. Slowey & D. Watson (Eds.), *Higher Education and the Lifecourse* (pp. 67–78). Milton Keynes, UK: Open University Press.

Juwah, C., Macfarlane-Dick, M., Matthew, B., Nicol, D., Ross, D., & Smith, B. (2004). *Enhancing Student Learning through Effective Formative Feedback*. York, UK: The Higher Education Academy Generic Centre.

Kim, M. (2009). The impact of an elaborated assessee's role in peer assessment. *Assessment and Evaluation in Higher Education, 34*, 105–114.

Knight, P., & Yorke, M. (2003). *Assessment, Learning and Employability*. Maidenhead, UK: SRHE/Open University Press.

Kozhevnikov, M. (2007). Cognitive styles in the framework of modern psychology: toward an integrated framework of cognitive style. *Psychological Bulletin, 133*, 464–481.

Krippendorff, K. (2004). *Content Analysis: An introduction to Its Methodology* (2nd ed.). Thousand Oaks, CA: Sage Publications.

Liu, N.-F., & Carless, D. (2006). Peer feedback: the learning element of peer assessment. *Teaching in Higher Education, 11*, 279–290.

Lizzio, A., & Wilson, K. (2008). Feedback on assessment: students' perceptions of quality and effectiveness. *Assessment and Evaluation in Higher Education, 33*, 263–275.

Messick, S. (1984). The nature of cognitive styles: problems and promise in educational practice. *Educational Psychologist, 19*, 59–74.

Mutch, A. (2003). Exploring the practice of feedback to students. *Active Learning in Higher Education, 4*, 24–38.

Nicol, D. (2008). *Transforming Assessment and Feedback: Enhancing Integration and Empowerment in the First Year*. Glasgow, Scotland: Quality Assurance Agency.

Nielsen, T. (2008). Implementation of learning styles at the teacher level. *Education and Training, 50*, 167–182.

Orrell, J. (2006). Feedback on learning achievement: rhetoric and reality. *Teaching in Higher Education, 11*, 441–456.

Prosser, M., & Webb, C. (1994). Relating the process of undergraduate essay writing to the finished product. *Studies in Higher Education, 19*, 25–38.

Race, P. (2002). *Why Fix Assessment? A Discussion Paper*. Staff and Departmental Development Unit, Leeds University. Retrieved June 10, 2009, from http://www.leeds.ac.uk/sddu/online/fix_assess.html

Rae, A.M., & Cochrane, D.K. (2008). Listening to students: how to make written assessment feedback useful. *Active Learning in Higher Education, 9*, 217–230.

Rayner, S. (2000). Reconstructing style differences in thinking and learning: profiling learning performance. In R.J. Riding & S. Rayner (Eds.), *International Perspectives on Individual Differences* (pp. 115–180). Stamford, CT: Ablex.

Riding, R. (2002). *School Learning and Cognitive Style*. London: David Fulton.

Riding, R.J., & Cheema, I. (1991). Cognitive styles—an overview and integration. *Educational Psychology, 11*(3&4), 193–214.

Rust, C., O'Donovan, B., & Price, M. (2005). A social constructivist assessment process model: how the research literature shows us this could be best practice. *Assessment and Evaluation in Higher Education, 30*, 231–240.

Sadler, D.R. (2005). Interpretations of criteria-based assessment and grading in higher education. *Assessment and Evaluation in Higher Education, 30*, 75–194.

Shiloh, S., Salton, E., & Sharabi, D. (2002). Individual differences in rational and intuitive styles as predictors of heuristic responses and framing effects. *Personality and Individual Differences, 32*, 415–429.

Swaffield, S. (Ed.) (2008). *Unlocking Assessment: Understanding for Reflection and Application*. London: Routledge.

Taras, M. (2003). To feedback or not to feedback in student self-assessment. *Assessment and Evaluation in Higher Education, 28*, 549–565.

Tashakkori, A., & Teddlie, C. (Eds.) (2003). *Handbook of Mixed Methods in Social and Behavioural Research*. Thousand Oaks, CA: Sage.

Vickerman, P. (2009). Student perspectives on formative peer assessment: an attempt to deepen learning? *Assessment and Evaluation in Higher Education, 34*, 221–230.

Weaver, M.R. (2006). Do students value feedback? Student perceptions of tutors' written responses. *Assessment and Evaluation in Higher Education, 31*, 379–394.

Yorke, M. (2003). Formative assessment in higher education: moves towards theory and the enhancement of pedagogic practice. *Higher Education, 45*, 477–501.

Zhang, L.F., & Sternberg, R.J. (2005). A threefold model of intellectual styles. *Educational Psychology Review, 17*, 1–53.

# Part III

# Personal Diversity

Style Differences in Lifelong
Learning and Workplace Contexts

# 14 Learning Styles and Personal Pedagogy in the Virtual Worlds of Learning

*Glenn Hardaker, Annie Jeffery, and A'ishah A. Sabki*

## INTRODUCTION

University education in virtual worlds is only just beginning to offer a realistic alternative to face-to-face teaching through the recent widespread access to broadband on 'desktop' and mobile devices. As we move towards the adoption of more 'participative technologies', we need to recognize the complexity of an increasing need for teachers to have personalized knowledge of the groups they are working with and the technologies they are using (Knapp & Glenn, 1996). Informed by key research in the field, this chapter provides a pragmatic perspective on the application of learning style and personal pedagogy to what is called 'Second Life' (Johnson, Levine, Smith, & Stone, 2010; Kingsley & Wankel, 2009). The chapter also specifically defines cognitive styles and explores the importance of context sensitivity. We then explain the importance of context to Second Life by characterizing learning styles in relation to traits or states. The focus of the chapter then moves into the challenging area of providing a conceptualization of learning styles in virtual worlds by embracing the essence of a Personal Learning Styles Pedagogy (PLSP; Evans & Waring, 2009) that for the purpose of this research is shaped, in part, by a culturally responsive teaching perspective (Gay, 2000). The chapter then shifts to exploring our case research in Second Life (2008–2009), which has enabled the conceptual architectural drawings for future buildings in Second Life. The chapter concludes by identifying some key issues for learning styles and personal pedagogy in moving forward in virtual worlds.

Virtual worlds, such as 'Second Life', 'Open Sim', and 'World of Warcraft', provide opportunities to support learning styles and personal pedagogy with adaptive content and the use of flexible online classrooms (Aldrich, 2005). Learning environments in Second Life often take the form of amphitheaters or traditional teaching spaces that adopt a traditional instructional pedagogical approach that supports a 'one-to-many' style. Insights into the potential for personalized learning are provided by this case research into virtual world's courses on New Hope Island and EdTech Island in Second Life. For instance, the learner is able to communicate using traditional sight, sound, and touch but also through showing texture, form, sight, and sound (Johnson et al., 2010). Sound is an essential component of creating an immersive gaming experience (Aldrich, 2005). As Johnson and colleagues (2010) explain, this is reflected in the way virtual worlds facilitate rich expression through the use of communication tools for personalized learning.

## DEFINING LEARNING STYLE AND CONTEXT SENSITIVITY

It is claimed that learning is a cognitive process that is intrinsic to the learner in both formal and informal settings (Courtney, 1989). People differ in several ways not only in outward appearances such as skin color, height, or gender but also inwardly in relation to cognitive style. The concept of 'style' itself is quite commonplace in our everyday language. For the purpose of this research, cognitive styles will be considered as a construct (concept, idea) in the same way as personality and intelligence, for example. Various frameworks have been suggested in an attempt to demystify the relationship between different style concepts, such as cognitive style and learning style. Curry (1983) provides a widely accepted framework through her proposed heuristic 'style onion' in which learning constructs are organized into three levels that overlay a central personality dimension. The inner layer of this style onion is made up of the cognitive personality elements that are perceived as higher order constructs (Messick, 1984), such as cognitive style; the middle layer is comprised of the 'information processing style', typically the learning style that is seen as a much broader construct than cognitive styles; and the outer layer consists of learning preferences for understanding people's learning experiences.

From the research of Curry it is suggested that constructs located in the center are more stable and more trait-like, while nearer the surface, the more amenable a construct is to external influence and reflected by instability (Rayner & Peterson, 2009). According to Riding and Rayner (1998), cognitive style is the usual way in which a particular person assesses, perceives, and remembers, whereas learning style is used to highlight the effect of cognition within a learning context. Therefore, a personal learning style (PLS) is summarized (Evans & Cools, 2009) as including a range of cognitive and learning styles and strategies. Evans and Cools go on to explain that personal learning styles is seen to be context specific and socialized. Here we can see the importance of a learner's cultural context and what in earlier research was alluded to as being external influences.

The move from behaviorist to cognitive psychology over the last fifty years or so has seen changes in our perception of how behavior and cognition are linked. It is suggested, however, that the way we function as people is dictated by three elements or factors: sociocultural, psychological, and physiological (Greene, 1995). A cultural outlook on cognition requires an understanding of how culture influences and shapes cognition and the world around us (Greene, 1995). The research conducted by Curry (1987) and later by Riding and Cheema (1991), reflected in the heuristic of their 'onion model' and cognitive control models, respectively, found that learning preferences explicitly address the learning context as an important factor in determining learning behavior.

Evans and Cools (2009) extend early research by defining personal learning styles (PLS) with a greater focus on cultural sensitivity. Our case research in Second Life adopts the view that learning styles is context specific and socialized and needs personalized teaching methods. This is seen to be necessary because the process of learning is shaped by the learning context of increasingly diverse student groups and in turn this is influenced by their cultural socialization (Gay, 2000). The challenging issue for learning styles research that explores issues of cultural sensitivity is dealing with the complexities of the trait-or-state nature of style in relation to understanding construct stability (Evans & Graff, 2008). Ramírez and Castañeda (1974) capture the essence of our viewpoint on how learning is situated in a cultural context through the child's eye:

> The sociocultural system of the child's home and community is influential in producing culturally unique preferred modes of relating to others . . . as well as a preferred mode of thinking, perceiving, remembering, and problem solving. (Ramírez & Castañeda, 1974, p. 32)

Sadler-Smith (2001) also made this point when identifying how a principal objection to notions of learning styles tools is their limited consideration to the social context within which learning takes place. Therefore, a key challenge in understanding personalized learning styles (PLS) in virtual worlds is in dealing with the complexities of rapid changes in environments. This raises issue about the ability to adapt to learning situations that accept that learning styles, and in particular the outer layer, is context sensitive and socialized.

## CHARACTERIZING LEARNING STYLES AND CULTURE

Characterizing learning styles as the cognitive and psychological behaviors exhibited by learners provides a moderately good indication of how people actually perceive information (Keefe, 1979). Nonetheless, we need to consider how culture affects and influences the way we see the world as this very same culture will have a significant bearing upon how and what we learn (Nieto, 2000). Culture as a modern anthropological concept, and as treated in this chapter, refers to the entire integrated pattern of human behavior that governs everything about us and molds our instinctive actions and natural inclinations. Grasha (1990) and Terpstra and David (1985) see culture in this way as affecting the preferences of learners especially within the context of student interaction, cognition, and knowledge acquisition. The culture in which a person is immersed is unlikely to be the same culture that they experience within virtual worlds, and for many this is viewed to lead to inconsistencies in the acquisition of knowledge. Kolb and Fry (1974) also found that culture and cultural ideals were part of the socialization in which everyone is engaged and as a consequence their research suggested that education and more precisely learning styles were influenced by culture. This arguably is why some cultures fair better than others within education. To sum up, the notion of a connection between learning styles and culture is important to this research in viewing culture as instrumental in shaping personal pedagogy and the virtual classroom. Contemporary pedagogical styles in education are currently changing to those which encourage the active participation of students, and learning styles research needs to reflect this through a greater focus on the social and cultural context (Gay, 2000).

A personal learning styles (PLS) approach that includes a range of cognitive and learning styles and strategies (preferences) embraces the importance of culture (Evans & Cools, 2009). An individual's learning preferences are of significant importance in understanding the function of learning styles. Reichmann and Grasha (1974) identified three learning preferences: (1) dependent learners, who prefer a highly structured environment whereby they are set tasks and are assessed by teachers; (2) collaborative learners, who are most comfortable when in a group environment; they lean towards discussion led solutions and collaborative projects; and (3) independent learners, who like to have some bearing or influence over the content and structure of the information that is disseminated to them.

The interpretation of learning preference (dependent learner, collaborative learner, independent learner) identified by Reichmann and Grasha (1974) is supported by more recent research of Sadler-Smith, Allinson, and Hayes (2000). With the framing of teaching using new technologies, autonomous methods (independent learners) may include types of learning that are not contingent upon an educator being present and may include virtual world's learning. This is in contrast to dependent methods that rely upon the educator as being instrumental in facilitating the learning process and this typically includes traditional classroom lectures through to virtual world's classrooms. While collaborative methods used by learners continues to include real-world group discussions and role play, we are increasingly seeing a shift of such methods being undertaken in virtual worlds such as Second Life.

These preferences and strategies to learning need to be considered in the cultural context in which they take place as well as in connection to outside elements involved in this learning process, for instance, teachers or technology (Fry, Ketteridge, & Marshall, 2003). It is clear that the 'virtual generation' (Proserpio & Gioia, 2007) have moved 'virtual worlds education' into high levels of personalization, in which cultures are shifting and generating fast showing similarities in movement and growth to how spiders spin silk. The implications for learning styles in relation to this research have the potential for understanding some of these complexities of personal learning styles adoption in virtual worlds and exploring some of the issues of state-or-trait nature of styles.

## PERSONAL LEARNING STYLES PEDAGOGY IN VIRTUAL WORLDS

Personal Learning Styles Pedagogy (PLSP) has an emphasis on individual differences in learning and an understanding of how different teaching approaches may impact on learners in different ways (Evans & Waring, 2009). PLSP provides clarity and focus to technology-led research such as personalized learning environments (PLEs) that are based on sensitivity to learners' needs. A personal pedagogy perspective also extends opportunity for research in the area of forms of a pedagogy that is focused on equality, understanding, and cultural pluralism offered by scholars such as Delpit (1995), Bennett (1999), and Gay (2000). Their research demonstrated the need for investment or commitment to learning about people's differences and of particular note is the research on culturally responsive teaching styles (Gay, 2000) that demonstrates the importance of style in shaping the engagement and learning experience.

Riding and Rayner (1998) found that personalized pedagogies adopting styles–led differentiation techniques will result in authentic teaching connected to individual differences. Personal Learning Styles Pedagogy seeks to provide a leveling opportunity for diverse learners by providing personalized teaching techniques and styles. Gay (2000) found embodiment of culturally responsive pedagogy enables empathy with ethnicity, socio-economic factors, gender, age, religion, and other related aspects of the learner's background. A Personal Learning Styles Pedagogy that starts from research into cultural psychology and culturally responsive practices (Gay, 2000) supports the move from a "pedagogy of poverty" to a "pedagogy of plenty" (Tomlinson, 2005, p. 20). This perspective naturally supports the increasingly referenced individual learning differences (ILDs) when referring to cognitive and learning styles constructs (Rosenfeld & Rosenfeld, 2004) and patterns of learning (Vermunt, 2007).

Issues of pedagogy of poverty and plenty are highlighted in relation to the fundamental question about the state-or-trait nature of style (Evans & Waring, 2009) and indicates an increasing need to understand the flexibility within the concept of state. This is in contrast to the behaviorist perspective, which primarily focuses on observable behavior and is the main theoretical perspective currently driving many educational developments in e-learning applications (Watson, Ahmed, & Hardaker, 2007). Virtual worlds, such as Second Life, reflect greater diversity in pedagogical approaches but with a common vision for personalized learning.

With the emergence of Web 2.0, we have seen a shift toward social networking and the opening of opportunities for more diversity in pedagogical design. Virtual worlds were integral to the growth of social networking in immersive environments (Dawley, 2009). The belief that genuine education comes from experience does not mean that all experiences are equally educative. Some experiences are educative and some are diseducative (Dewey, 1938). An experience may engender a careless attitude to others based on style and the cultural sensitivity towards the learning experience. This can clearly lead to moderating future activities and at its worse lead to diseducation in a virtual world. As a consequence, e-pedagogy in immersive virtual worlds needs to be personalized in supporting a culture of modification that is context sensitive. The state-or-trait nature of style has particular relevance due to the modifiable nature of virtual worlds. Evans and Waring (2006), in a study looking at styles of learning and cognition, found that certain situations and for certain people, cognitive styles are modifiable. Swain and Pearson (2001) argue that there are considerable differences in levels of access and experience of virtual worlds in the context of a person's behavioral, psychological, and cultural context.

There is, however, a need for greater understanding of style flexibility (Armstrong, 2002) in facilitating personal learning in virtual worlds. Now we provide insight into how virtual worlds seem to demonstrate styles flexibility. This raises issues about the ability to adapt to learning situations that accept that learning styles, and in particular the outer layer of Curry's onion model, is context sensitive and socialized.

## A CASE FOR LEARNING STYLES AND PERSONAL PEDAGOGY IN SECOND LIFE

A number of universities are exploring e-pedagogy and personalized learning in Second Life and these developments provide opportunities for exploring learning styles and the ability to adapt to learning situations. The learning styles and personal pedagogy–related research reported in this chapter was conducted between 2008 and 2009 in virtual worlds courses on New Hope Island and EdTech Island in Second Life. Both islands were commisisoned as immersive environments and include a focus on sensory tools for teaching. Various courses were researched that considered personal learning styles into the pedagogy design process. For example, the course "Social Network Learning in Virtual Worlds" teaching activities (Boise State University, US) considered how an exploration of personal learning and learning preferences might aid social presence and interaction within virtual worlds. The research adopted a performance ethnography approach (Denzin, 2003) and Stegner (1990) eloquently describe the rationale of this as a type of case research:

> I seek a writing form that is part memoir, part essay, part autoethnography . . . I write from scenes of memory, re-arranging, suppressing, even inventing scenes, forgoing claims to exact truth or factual accuracy, search instead for emotional truth, for deep meaning.(Stegner, 1990, pp. 4–5)

Such an approach is less certain than more established interpretive enquiry methods (Denzin, 2003), but at the same time is natural to the virtual worlds enquiry context. This is because the researcher's performances involve co-participation in an interpretive process. Using the aforementioned approach, a tactic involving theatre analogy scripts can be utilized in the context of virtual worlds and pedagogic research. The idea of edited experiences from group experiences was part of this same approach. We also engaged with the research design ideas of Lincoln (1995) on 'authentic adequacy', in that the research was intended to: (1) reflect the researcher's personality in words and visual expression; (2) be able to address core issues of the learning styles and personal pedagogy; (3) engage with those who are 'challenging' existing educational provision to reach and provide a voice; (4) that the researchers explore their interpretation of the situation, during, before, and after the research to consider critical subjectivity; and (5) a research design rooted in formal teaching and virtual worlds teaching to generate 'facilitated openness' between researchers, educators, and learners by enabling reciprocity. In this way, the research of virtual worlds learning and teaching realized a conceptualized potential in the 'performance ethnography' context of civic, participatory, and collaborative initiative.

Students were involved from the US, Canada, UK, Oman, Poland, Australia, Italy, Brazil, and Macao. Students were from a wide range of education-related professions, including teachers, managers, technologists, and administrators. The case research presented in this chapter is therefore based on experiences of a small number of Second Life university classroom initiatives focused on personal e-pedagogy with learning styles being instrumental in the curriculum design process. The research led to the design of conceptual architectural drawings that, in part, have been implemented and in part leave challenges for the future.

The case for personalized and adaptive virtual world university classrooms explore constructs of learning styles in the context of personal pedagogy. These constructs are rooted in some core sensory applications applied in the adaptable virtual world's classroom that integrate the design and application of educational resources with the classroom environment. These worlds are 'core', 'asynchronous', and 'synchronous' sensory applications that support the university educational experience and include:

- Literature Trees: e-books, research journals, sectoral reports, and note cards;

- Sound Pods: soundscapes, sound clips, streamed audio, archives, news feeds, spoken word, music, and Internet radio;
- Visual Walls: Flickr, YouTube, newsfeeds, broadcasts, Second Life snapshots, object collections, and image libraries;
- Subject Forums: social networking, blogs, wiki, Web pages, RSS, Twitter, Facebook, and e-mail;
- Blogs, Wikis and Collaborative Tools: social networking, blogs, wiki, Web pages, RSS, Twitter, Facebook, e-mail, and tagging.

The Second Life classroom in our case research presents a central gathering space with interconnecting pathways that facilitate the building of adaptable and personalized learning communities underpinned by a learning styles design perspective (see Figure 14.3). This approach supports recent research into personal learning that is both context sensitive and socialized (Evans & Waring, 2009). The formation of communities of practice is a well-known essential element for constructivist pedagogy and the formation of a social presence online (Aragon, 2003; Wenger, 1999). The case research is shaped by actual university classrooms in Second Life and Figure 14.1 provides a visual representation of a university class in Second Life that was part of this research. The central gathering space is a learner activity space for exploring individuality and cultural context.

The architectural drawings (Figures 14.2, 14.3, and 14.4) provide a useful illustrative insight into how learners enter through the flexible

*Figure 14.1*   Central gathering space.

learning classroom gateway into a large space for orientation by educators. The communal and immersive experience is enhanced by the opportunity to discuss and compare notes on the sounds visitors encounter. For example, an immersive experience is encouraged by using ambient noises such as bird calls, rain, and time-sensitive soundscapes. The orientation space allows for the profiling of learning styles and providing personalized resources and customized classrooms based on a styles perspective with an emphasis on the cultural context. Angela Elkordy explained some of this:

> The creator shapes the experience to reflect his/her own context-referenced reality. In the sim, the mixed content enhanced my Second Life experience because they added depth to the immersive experience by using more of the 'senses' or 'intelligences' . . . content permitted and necessitated almost a different kind of perception than one might use in real life, such as in the sound garden, or the galaxy sim.
>
> Student—Angela Elkordy (2009)

From the orientation, space learners may travel to the Literature Tree. The Literature Tree is centered on supporting learning styles with a focus on learning preferences for working with perceptual content. For example, texture, multimedia (photos and videos), case notes, textural, auditory narratives, and text documents.

> I am a teacher educator in emerging technology. I often show pictures of Second Life simulations such as the Sound Garden where students can learn and hear the sights and sound of the jungle; the Art Box where an art teacher can introduce artworks while actually walking into the painting; or a language teacher can actually teach a traditional cultural dance in the Pumkinweirdo simulation; and how an astronomy instructor can stand on the Milky Way swirling while lecturing the facts of our galaxy?
>
> Teacher—Denise Knowles (Los Medanos College, Pittsburg, California, US)

The libraries enable learners and teachers to select resources based on an awareness of their learning style enabled by a personal pedagogy approach. The Second Life case illustrates immersive classroom environments that adopted a constructivist pedagogy that provides learners with opportunities to scaffold their personal learning experience. The teachers on New Hope Island and EdTech Island had a library of interactive content that was embedded in the virtual worlds in sensory applications. For example, the embedded library of content includes: Sound Gardens, Galaxy Simulation Art Box, High Speed Streamed video (see Figure 14.2).

In the words of Christopher Frey:

EdTech Soundgarden Swing    New Hope Ducks and Hummingbirds    New Hope Kingfisher Sits by the Frog pond

*Figure 14.2*   Sound gardens and soundscapes.

> The gardens at New Hope and EdTech Island are designed as "sound-scape" or Sound Gardens. The Sound Garden experience opens Second Lifers to the possibilities of using complex audio to create a highly immerse environments.
>
> Student—Christopher Frey (2009)

This is seen as extending what is currently possible in a traditional classroom environment by using virtual world's tools for personalization and adaptation. Learners will have choices that can be negotiated in class that meet the needs of learning preferences from autonomous to collaborative learning. The learning constructs of personalized learning styles in Second Life are highly susceptible to external influence and ongoing instability. For example, in Second Life, learners may be using multiple identities that have emerged from virtual worlds even though registered with a recognized international university. This phenomenon appears to reflect the thinking of Rayner and Peterson (2009), in which they describe the surface construct as being susceptible to external influence moves to an unprecedented level with multiple identities of many learners.

Personal learning is supported on New Hope Island and EdTech Island by learners having the opportunity to choose a path to a Shared Pod (learning space). Each Shared Pod is centered around personalized perceptual tools and is intended to host a small learning community. During the initial stages, learners would typically choose a path based on a shared interest and reflecting their personal learning preference. The group of learners could design their activity and then select resources from their store. The journey to the pod is intended to investigate the formation of culturally responsive learner community through negotiated learning. As Angela stated:

> It's a strange thing to describe ... the lack of the traditional "prior knowledge and experience" makes this issue, usually something to contend with in traditional instructional settings, null and void. You

feel your learning experience is being shaped because you don't have preconceived notions of the situation.

Angela Elkordy (2009)

On New Hope Island and EdTech Island, the teacher could go with the learner along corridors, into rooms, and different locations that prompts responses and enables the shaping of personalized learning in a cultural context that is socialized. The journey may include avatars walking and flying to different locations, and this type of functionality provides the ability to build far more empathy with the context of the learners (see Figure 14.3). Here, a teacher explains how Shared Pods and supporting resources provide an early insight into how virtual worlds are supporting personal pedagogy.

> Our sonic environments shape our experiences and our interactions, something that is recognized within the games industry. Soundscapes place the listener at the centre of the environment, the sense of place expands outwards from the person. The earpoint is always the focus of the design, which centres the experience. Looking can divide the field of vision into manageable pieces, and hearing can bring the work together. These sonic environments feature highly in creating presence, immersion and ways to engage with the multisensory environment.
>
> Annie Jeffery—New Hope Island Teacher

A post-pod learning space such as the Sound Garden on New Hope Island enables learners to regroup after Shared Pod learning activities. This supports a socialized and context sensitive learning environment.

## Second Life Scenario: Exploring Learning Styles and Personalized Learning in Virtual Worlds

Here we bring together our research into one scenario for illustrative purposes in providing more insight into our research findings, and in part, the future potential of Second Life, which is illustrated in the architectural drawing used as a method of visualizing our research.

Liyana's arrival at the University Island was unfamiliar to her even though she has been a resident on New Hope Island in Second Life for many years. The location was unconventional by being high in the mountains that is only accessible through flying to the central gathering space and by following the sign postings in the sky that provide intuitive navigation to the desired destination. On arrival, the welcome was managed via a central gathering space (see Figure 14.3: locations 2 and 3). This gathering space platform allows the teacher to use learning styles tests to establish

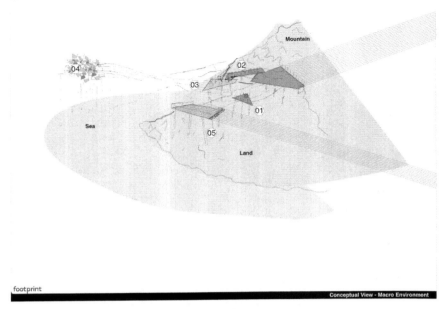

*Figure 14.3*   Conceptual view—macro environment.

Liyana's profile on arrival, along with other learners, and this is visualized on the Visual Wall illustrating the learning style of Liyana.

The avatar, Liyana, decides to look for resources at the Sensory Store and Literature Tree, where she knows she will find support for her personal learning style for working with perceptual content (see Figure 14.4: Sensory Store 01, Literature Tree). She walks up to the 'search tree' in the Sound Garden (Sensory Store 02—Sounds Pods) and types the word 'immigration'. The tree search conducts a search of the libraries of learning content based on Liyana's learning styles profile, and the tree returns a list of all the immigration-related audio files in the 'Sound Garden' and these subject specific resources are context sensitive to her learning style. Liyana's student peers also gather to download their resources along with the teacher Fatimah. When they have downloaded their resources, they follow the appropriate sign postings and enter the personalized 'Sound Pods'. The personalized resource collections are attached to the avatar's memory store. Liyana and her peer learners then 'teleport' back to the central gathering space with interconnecting pathways that leads to the university classroom Shared Pods (see Figure 14.5).

The central gathering space with interconnecting pathways takes Liyana to her Shared Pod (see Figure 14.5) via a series of glass tubes or pathways which crisscross the landscape. As Liyana enters the pathways that lead to the Shared Pods (New Hope Island, Sound Garden), she notices that she

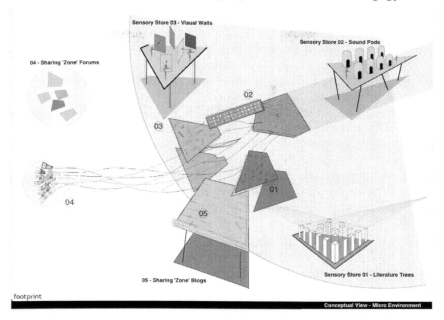

*Figure 14.4* Conceptual view—micro environment.

is encouraged to make contact with other learners through visual contact and proximity in places (proximity triggers sensory responses). The overall personal pedagogy design that creates the 'flow' experience (Hoffman, Novak, & Duhachek, 2002) takes into account the learning styles of the learners in the Shared Pods with specific support for learning preferences in the context of autonomous through the collaborative learning. Joe, another learner, enters the Shared Pod (see Figure 14.5) via a glass tube from below, which enables entry via teleport (avatars can walk, elevate, fly, or teleport in Second Life) or by means of elevation. Platforms at the entrance enable pod entrants to interconnect before they enter the Shared Pod learning space (New Hope Island, Sound Garden), perhaps sharing experiences of the journey and discussion of the Literature Tree resources, ensuring compatibility base on subject knowledge and learning preferences.

The entry platform has the potential to serve as a post-experience space for learner interaction and reflections. Once all the registered learners reach their Shared Pod, along with the teacher Fatimah, they begin to use the personalized resources (sonic sounds, Simulation Art Box, broadband video streaming) that are both context sensitive and socialized. The learners' preferences to select or favor one technique or combination of techniques over another in their acquisition of knowledge are supported by the research of Sadler-Smith and colleagues (2000). This provides Liyana, Joe, and other learners with continuity of experience that is achieved by culturally responsive teaching that engages with learning styles preferences. The educational 'experience' is enriched by a mix of content from both mainstream traditional sources in combination with personalized resource. For example, university classroom Shared Pods can support collaborative learning by sending and displaying content from texting, audio conferencing, or simply e-mail. In contrast, autonomous learning may be supported by streamed video and online journals. Liyana and Joe, along with their student peers, interchange between asynchronous communications (immersive educational resources) and synchronous communications with the teacher, and these are supported by the Visual Wall through small autonomous and collaborative projects of the learner community.

The virtual classrooms provide opportunities in our present times to support personal learning styles and the way students choose to interface with their learning environment using what is being called sensory technologies (Johnson et al., 2010). This provides new opportunities for exploring Personal Learning Styles Pedagogy that supports the outer layer of the 'onion model' (Curry, 1983) that is more context sensitive and socialized (Rayner & Peterson, 2009).

## CONCLUDING COMMENTS: STYLES AND PERSONALIZATION IN VIRTUAL WORLDS

As virtual worlds become part of mainstream society, we can see the move towards simple augmented reality. Advances in mobile devices are enabling

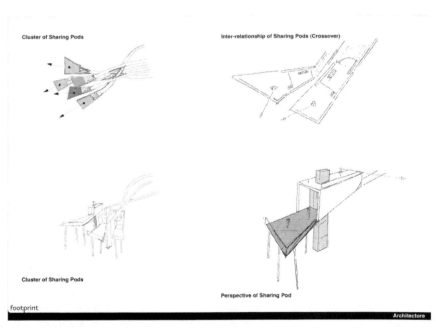

*Figure 14.5*   Architecture: personalized and adaptable virtual worlds classrooms.

learners to combine the real world with virtual information and now this is as near to hand as any other application on a laptop or smart phone (Johnson et al., 2010). Being able to move between real world and virtual worlds illustrates the increasing complexity of knowing the learner. A key challenge in virtual worlds is how to maintain continuity of experience with the challenges of unprecedented freedom of movement in virtual worlds. Or that the external and physical side of activity cannot be separated from the internal side of activity; from freedom of thought, desire and purpose (Dewey, 1938).

Our case research explores university education in virtual worlds and the potential for a styles-based 'lens'. This is coupled with a 'PLSP' perspective that is, in part, influenced by culturally responsive teaching methods in the classroom. Evidence suggests that student learning is greatly improved if technologies, such as Second Life, incorporate or relate to student experiences (Sianjina, 2000; Wlodkowski & Ginsberg, 1995).

Diversity in virtual worlds is challenging mainstream teaching methods in universities and creates an increasing need for teaching methods that can support more intuitively the complexities of learner diversity. The PLSP approach, as a pedagogy underpinned by culturally responsive teaching, seems well placed to deal with the complexities of diversity and associated learner preferences in virtual worlds. We need to develop a greater understanding of the fundamental nature of the PLSP in virtual worlds. For instance: what is the range of influencing factors to style? Or what are the implications of virtual world experiences on style? And are there cultural differences in style in virtual worlds? Answers to these central considerations and questions would then support personal learning, and the related concept of freedom of intelligence (Dewey, 1938), as an enabler in adapting to context-sensitive learning situations.

## ACKNOWLEDGMENTS

Jon Hallett, Footprint Designs, UK.
Angela Elkordy, Eastern Michigan University, US.
Christopher Frey, Academy of Tucson High School, US.
Denise Knowles, Los Medanos College, Pittsburg, US.

## BIBLIOGRAPHY

Aldrich, C. (2005). *Learning by Doing.* San Francisco: Pfeiffer.
Aragon, S.R. (2003). Creating social presence in online environments. *New Directions for Adult and Continuing Education, 100,* 57–68.
Armstrong, S.J. (2002). Effects of cognitive style on quality of research supervision. In A. Francis, S.J. Armstrong, M. Graff, J. Hill, S. Rayner, E. Sadler-Smith, et al. (Eds.), *Proceedings of the 7th Annual Conference of the European Learning Styles Information Network* (pp. 13–24). Ghent, Belgium: Gent University.

Bennett, C. (1999). *Comprehensive Multicultural Education: Theory and Practice* (4th ed.). Boston: Allyn & Bacon.

Courtney, S. (1989). Defining adult and continuing education. In S.B. Merriam & P.M. Cunningham (Eds.), *Handbook of Adult and Continuing Education* (pp. 37–50). San Francisco: Jossey-Bass.

Curry, L. (1983). *An Organization of Learning Styles Theory and Constructs.* Paper presented at the Annual Meeting of the American Educational Research Association, Montreal, Canada (ERIC No. ED 235 185).

Curry, L. (1987). *Integrating Concepts of Cognitive Learning Styles: A Review with Attention to Psychometric Standards.* Ottawa: Canadian College of Health Services Executives.

Dawley, L., (2009). *Social network knowledge construction: emerging virtual world pedagogy.* Retrieved from http://edtech.boisestate.edu/ldawley/SNKC_pdf.pdf

Delpit, L. (1995). *Other People's Children: Cultural Conflict in the Classroom.* New York: The New Press.

Denzin, N.K. (2003). Searching for yellow stone. *Symbolic Interaction*, 26, 181–193.

Dewey, J. (1938). *Experience and Education.* New York: Collier Books.

Dolog, P., Henze, N., & Nejdl, W. (2004). *Personalization in distributed e-learning environments. Proceedings of the 13th international World Wide Web Conference* (pp. 170–179), May 17–22, New York.

Evans, C., & Cools, E. (2009). The use and understanding of style differences to enhance learning. *Reflecting Education*, 5, 1–18.

Evans, C., & Graff, M. (2008). Exploring style: enhancing the capacity to learn? *Education and Training*, 50, 93–102.

Evans, C., & Waring, M. (2006). Towards inclusive teacher education: sensitizing individuals to how they learn. *Educational Psychology*, 6, 499–518.

Evans, C., & Waring, M. (2009). The place of cognitive style in pedagogy: realising potential in practice. In L.F. Zhang & R.J. Sternberg (Eds.), *Perspectives on the Nature of Intellectual Styles* (pp. 169–208). New York: Springer.

Fry, H., Ketteridge, S., & Marshall, S. (2003). *A Handbook for Teaching and Learning in Higher Education: Enhancing Academic Practice.* London: Kogan Page.

Gay, G. (2000). *Culturally Responsive Teaching Theory, Research, and Practice.* New York: Teachers College Press.

Grasha, A. (1990). Using traditional versus naturalistic approaches to assessing learning styles in college teaching. *Journal on Excellence in College Teaching*, 1, 23–38.

Greene, J.O. (1995). An action-assembly perspective on verbal and nonverbal message production: a dancer's message unveiled. In D.E. Hewes (Ed.), *The Cognitive Bases of Interpersonal Communication* (pp. 51–85). Hillsdale, NJ: Lawrence Erlbaum Associates.

Hoffman, D.L., Novak, T.P., & Duhacheck, A. (2002). The influence of goal-directed and experiential activities on online flow experiences. *Journal of Consumer Psychology*, 13, 161–170.

Johnson, L., Levine, A., Smith, R., & Stone, S. (2010). *The 2010 Horizon Report.* Austin, TX: The New Media Consortium.

Keefe, J. (1979). Learning style: an overview. In NASSP's (Eds.), *Student Learning Styles: Diagnosing and Prescribing Programs* (pp. 55–61). Reston, VA: National Association of Secondary School Principals.

Kingsley, J., & Wankel, C. (2009). In J. Kingsley & C. Wankel (Eds.), *Higher Education in Virtual Worlds: Teaching and Learning in Second Life* (pp. 1–10). Bingley, UK: Emerald Group Publishing Limited.

Kolb, D.A., & Fry, R.E. (1974). *Toward an Applied Theory of Experiential Learning.* Cambridge, MA: MIT Alfred P. Sloan School of Management.

Knapp, L.R., & Glenn, A.D. (1996). *Restructuring Schools with Technology.* Boston: Allyn & Bacon.

Lincoln, Y.S. (1995). Emerging criteria for quality in qualitative and interpretive inquiry. *Qualitative Inquiry,* 1, 275–189.

Messick, S. (1984). The nature of cognitive styles: problems and promises in educational practice. *Educational Psychologist,* 19, 59–74.

Nieto, S. (2000). *Affirming Diversity: The Sociopolitical Context of Multicultural Education.* New York: Longman.

Proserpio, L., & Gioia, D.A. (2007). Teaching the virtual generation. *Academy of Management Learning and Education,* 6, 193–212.

Ramírez, M., & Castañeda, A. (1974). *Cultural Democracy, Bicognitive development and Education.* New York: Academic Press.

Rayner, S., & Peterson, E.R. (2009). Reaffirming style as an individual difference: toward a global paradigm or knowledge diaspora? In L.F. Zhang & R.J. Sternberg (Eds.), *Perspectives on the Nature of Intellectual Styles* (pp. 107–134). New York: Springer.

Reichman, S., & Grasha, A. (1974). A rational approach to developing and assessing the construct validity of a student learning scale instrument. *Journal of Psychology,* 87, 213–223.

Riding, R., & Cheema, I. (1991). Cognitive styles—an overview and integration. *Educational Psychology,* 11, 193–215.

Riding, R.J., & Rayner, S. (1998). *Cognitive Styles and Learning Strategies: Understanding Style Differences in Learning and Behaviour.* London: David Fulton.

Rosenfeld, M., & Rosenfeld, S. (2004). Developing teacher sensitivity to individual learning differences. *Educational Psychology,* 24, 465–487.

Sadler-Smith, E. (2001). A reply to Reynolds's critique of learning styles. *Management Learning,* 32, 291–304.

Sadler-Smith, E., Allinson, C.W., & Hayes, J. (2000). Learning preferences and cognitive style: some implications for Continuing Professional Development. *Management Learning,* 31, 239–256.

Sianjina, R.R. (2000). Educational technology and the diverse classroom. *Kappa Delta Pi Record,* 37, 26–29.

Stegner, W. (1990). *Collected Stories of Wallace Stegner.* New York: Penguin.

Swain, C., & Pearson, T. (2001). Bridging the digital divide: a building block for teachers. *Learning and Leading with Technology,* 28, 10–13.

Terpstra, V., & David, K. (1985). *The Cultural Environments of International Business.* Dallas: South-Western.

Tomlinson, C.A. (2005). *Differentiated Instruction as a Way to Achieve Equity and Excellence in Today's Schools. Building Inclusive Schools, a Search for Solutions.* Conference Report (pp. 19–21). Canadian Teachers' Federation Conference, Ottawa, Ontario, Canada, November 17–19.

Vermunt, J.D. (2007), *Student Learning and Teacher Learning.* Keynote address at the 12th Annual European Learning Styles Information Network (ELSIN) conference: Trinity College, Dublin, Ireland, June 12–14.

Watson, J., Ahmed, P.K., & Hardaker, G. (2007). Creating Domain Independent Adaptive e-Learning Systems using the Sharable Content Object Reference Model. *Campus-Wide Information Systems,* 24, 45–71.

Wenger, E. (1999). Communities of practice: the key to a knowledge strategy. *Knowledge Directions,* 1, 48–63.

Wlodkowski, R.J., & Ginsberg, M.B. (1995). *Diversity and Motivation: Culturally Responsive Teaching.* San Francisco: Jossey-Bass.

# 15 Cultures of Learning
## Cultures of Style

*Zarina M. Charlesworth*

## INTRODUCTION

The face of higher education worldwide is becoming increasingly multicultural. This is largely due to the continued growth in the number of internationally mobile students, which has increased by 59% between 2000 and 2007, going from 1.9 to 3.0 million (OECD, 2009), an average annual increase of 7%, and it is not showing signs of slowing down. The result of this 'indelible influence' (Nguyen, Terlouw, & Pilot, 2006) is not limited to an increasingly diverse student body but also has wide-reaching implications for teaching and learning. With respect to learning styles, it is no longer sufficient to look at the style dimension in isolation; rather, it is imperative to consider its relationship with the social and cultural contexts in education. In doing so, educators will have a solid basis upon which to embrace this change and look for ways of how best to deal with increasing diversity experienced in the classroom.

Arguably one cannot cover learning and culture in a few short pages; however, this chapter will put learning into context, provide a definition of styles, as well as one of culture and its influence on learning, followed by some recent empirical research. Finally, we will look at how this translates into practice and how it supports the call for a paradigm shift not only in how we see learning styles but also in how we conduct style research in the future.

## LEARNING IN CONTEXT

The mind-body duality, common to Western psychological thought, is not appropriate when looking at learning across diverse cultures. Indeed, not only anthropologists and sociologists but theorists in other fields as well are coming to see that:

> learning cannot be separated from the contexts in which it occurs, and to re-conceptualize cognition and learning as activities that occur through social interaction. (Lattuca, 2002, p. 711)

Researchers who have focused on the importance of the social and contextual influences on learning (Lattuca, 2002; Lave, 1997; Lave & Wenger, 1991; Rogoff, 1990) see learning as essentially a social and cultural activity in contrast to previously popular behavioral and cognitive models that place learning at the individual level of activity. Within this framework, putting formal learning into context calls for looking at schools as a social context. Schools in turn can be seen as cultural microcosms reflecting the society in which they are embedded (Burnett, 1970; Packer & Goicoechea, 2000) and where cultural norms and practices impact upon learning practices (Greeno, 1997; Nulty & Barrett, 1996) and so interact with students' learning styles and conceptions of what learning is (Purdie, Hattie, & Douglas, 1996). Lingbiao and Watkins (2001) speak of 'pedagogical flow' in terms of characteristic teaching practices found in one country that are linked to social-cultural practices.

Expectations and familiarity with country-specific pedagogical practices are brought by internationally mobile students with them as they enter what is sometimes a completely new world of education. These cultural experiences of learning and teaching are not easily shrugged off. Students, however, constantly work towards conceptual consonance (Lindblom-Ylänne, 2004), which implies actively seeking coherence between a student's conceptions of learning and approaches to study and the study practices necessary for success. Prior school experience will have influenced the manner in which they go about learning and their preferred learning styles, which might no longer be appropriate in their new setting. It is this context, that of the internationally mobile student in the 21st-century higher education classroom, that we are concerned with here.

## LEARNING STYLES

One specific aspect of learning, and the focus of the research presented following, is that of learning styles. Despite its limitations and the criticism of some of its theoretical foundations (Coffield, Moseley, Hall, & Ecclestone, 2004; Sternberg & Grigorenko, 2001), the notion of learning style provides practitioners and researchers with a base upon which to work with the individual needs of learners and to adapt course delivery and pedagogical material (Chevrier, Fortin, LeBlanc, & Théberge, 2000). Although any predictive or diagnostic value remains largely to be proven, the use of learning styles instruments as a tool for self-development and to raise awareness is now well accepted (Garner, 2000; Presland, 1994; Sadler-Smith, 1997). Educators faced with increasing diversity in the classroom can draw on styles research to increase their level of understanding and awareness in relation to this.

The styles discipline is, however, fraught with multiple definitions (Rieben, 2000; Zhang, 2002) making it a 'fuzzy knowledge domain', often unclear even to those researching styles. Many definitions touch on one or more dimensions of learning style but few provide a clear theoretical construct. To clarify for the reader the position taken here is that the term 'learning style' refers

> to an individual set of differences that include not only stated personal preference for instruction or an association with a particular form of learning activity but also individual differences found in intellectual or personal psychology. (Riding & Rayner, 1998, p. 51)

Research in the area of learning styles tends to be quite ethnocentric, often focusing on single countries or nationalities. If we are to move forwards, however, with styles research in a multicultural setting, then the way in which we conceptualize styles needs to change. The inclusion of a cultural perspective is one way in which this change or shift can be brought about in the contemporary paradigm.


## CULTURE

As previously stated, it is beyond the scope of this chapter to examine the concept of culture in full; however, it is important to provide the reader with a working definition. One way of looking at culture is to see it as an ever-evolving collective and individual phenomenon impacted upon by external traditions and mediated by the individual (Perregaux, 1994; Segall, Dasen, Berry, & Poortinga, 1999; Triandis, 1972). *Impacted upon* and *mediated by* suggest that the individual is both shaped by and a shaper of culture. This perspective

> emphasizes that human beings are not passive recipients of cultural forces and that they themselves create the context in which their behavior is shaped. (Segall et al., 1999, p. 2)

It is well suited for research on individuals that find themselves in a new context such as internationally mobile students. Additionally, culture can be seen as the set of values and significations and behaviors acquired, shared, and applied by members of a group who have a shared affiliation (Camilleri, 1986; Perregaux, 1994). This aspect of culture combined with the previous allows us to take the influence of both the old and new groups into account. One further definition of culture that is pertinent here is that of *subjective culture* as put forth by Triandis (1972), and which is the way in which a cultural group perceives the man-made component of its environment. In other words

> the perception of rules and the group's norms, roles, and values are aspects of subjective culture. (Triandis, 1972, p. 4)

The reference to rules, norms, and roles is of interest here as it ties culture together with formal learning. Finally, Segall and colleagues (1999) clearly express the point at which culture and learning intersect as:

> Human behavior can best be understood as the product of learning, particularly learning that results from experiences with other people or with ideas, institutions, or other products of the behavior of other people. In short, we are largely what we are because of culturally based learning. (Segall et al., 1999, p. 5)

Based on the forgoing, it follows that learning shapes behavior that is conditioned by culture in turn. Although one must be careful not generalize or to stereotype societies,

> the basic notion that behaviors shared by members of a society tend to be compatible with the society's values is reasonable. (Segall et al., 1999, p. 37)

These behaviors also include ones related to learning and study. It is important to avoid, however, the rather narrow-sighted view that nationality equals culture and this especially so in today's world where an increasing number of students have more than one nationality. This issue, rarely addressed in research, is discussed later in this chapter.

Pulling together the preceding perspectives allows us to see culture as an ever-evolving collective and individual phenomenon impacted upon by external traditions and mediated by the individual. More specifically in terms of learning, one may also be looking at cultures of learning (Harkness & Keefer, 2000; Li, 2003; Salili, 1996; Tharp, 1994). This leads us to the question of whether or not culture and learning styles share a reciprocal influence as aspects of a learning culture.

## THE INFLUENCE OF CULTURE ON LEARNING STYLES

Within the context of higher education and in light of the increasingly multicultural higher education classroom, we need to consider the extent to which culture might influence how students go about their learning. Reuchlin (1991) suggests that each individual when faced with a learning task might have more than one way of going about it and the selection of one or another method can be linked to a difference between individuals. Camilleri (1986) not only supports this view, but also expands it by adding that these differences may further be conditioned by one's culture. Thus, in addition to individual differences, a cultural component can be expected to have a further influence on people's choice of the way in which they go about their learning and in turn their preferred learning style.

Turning to the literature concerning the relationship between culture and learning styles, we find it is rather noncommittal. A major difficulty is that the culture-related learning styles literature suffers from a lack of coherence in the measures used as well as in the theoretical base upon which it relies. At the risk of conflating style research by comparing results from studies based on models that measure different concepts, it is nonetheless worth making an overview of what published research has to say. Research that has used either the Kolb (1984) or Honey and Mumford (1986) models provides data in support of the idea of a cultural influence on learning style preferences (Auyeng & Sands, 1996; Barron & Arcodia, 2002; Jaju, Kwak, & Zinkhan, 2002; Wong, Pine, & Tsang, 2000). This data must, however, be interpreted with caution. In some instances, detailed information about the sample is lacking and most studies do not address the concept of culture, leaving one to suppose that nationality was a substitute.

Research using other models also largely supports the idea that there is a cultural component to one's preferred learning style (Kember & Gow, 1991; Ramburuth & McCormick, 2001; Smith & Smith, 1999). The research presented next provides further support for the influence of culture on learning styles.

## THE CASE OF INTERNATIONAL HIGHER EDUCATION: METHODOLOGY

The following sections draw on earlier work done (Charlesworth, 2007, 2008a, 2008b, 2009) with undergraduate management degree students of diverse nationalities. The initial research focused on learning styles and was based on the definition put forth by Honey and Mumford (1986). Style differences were identified as four levels of preference for learning: activist, reflector, theorist, and pragmatist. The activist being rather impulsive and prone to using trial and error; the reflector taking time for synthesis and the search for meaning; the theorist more analytical and at home with logical argument; and the pragmatist the problem solver with a strength in practical application.

The framework for the research comprised not only learning styles but also culture, which in turn had implications for the research design. Where quantitative methods were appropriate for measuring the learning style preferences of the samples studied, the sociocultural aspect called for rather more qualitative methods. The result was a research design that relied on a mixing of methods calling for the use of both quantitative and qualitative approaches. This convergence of methods can be seen as a 21st-century moderate post-positivist response to positivist and constructivist paradigms of the 19th and 20th centuries (Dasen & Mishra, 2000) and is particularly well suited to do research with multicultural populations. Styles research might also benefit from more mixed methods studies rather than taking the more traditional quantitative, psychometric approach.

Relying on a quantitative study alone would not have allowed for the triangulation of data. Quantitative data only tell half the story in the best of situations. As we are dealing with multicultural students, the room for misinterpretation is great and chances are that the story told would be far from complete. On the other hand, quantitative data is relatively easier to collect and does give a benchmark which when combined with qualitative findings allows for a level of interpretation not otherwise attainable. A number of authors (Crahay, 2006; De Ketele & Maroy, 2006; Tashakkori & Teddlie, 1998) suggest that the same vocabulary should be used in respect to the criteria used for the evaluation of both quantitative and qualitative research. The research presented next was evaluated using the following three criteria: pertinence, validity, and reliability.

## THE CASE OF INTERNATIONAL HIGHER EDUCATION: FINDINGS

The initial sample comprised students of fifty-seven different nationalities and in various semesters of higher education, aged 20 to 26 years old ($N$ = 615). The data were collected over a three-year period. A subsample of French, Indonesian, and Chinese students ($n$ = 212) was analyzed in depth in addition to being subject to qualitative analysis. Student numbers dictated the choice of the aforementioned nationalities. Although nationality was taken as basis for selection, all the students in the subsample were classified as homogeneous (having grown up and been schooled in their home country) or heterogeneous (having grown up in their home country or abroad but been schooled in international schools) to control for differences in response within the subsample.

The instrument used for the quantitative research was an adaptation of the Honey and Mumford Learning Styles Questionnaire (Lashley, 2002). The qualitative research included semistructured interviews with twenty-four of the subsample participants, as well as a series of participant-run focus groups held during specially scheduled workshops.

In order to better illustrate the relationship between learning styles and culture, the findings presented refer only to the subsample results. Data were analyzed both cross-sectionally and longitudinally for the different semesters of study. Statistically significant differences in learning style preferences between the subgroup populations were shown in the first semester of study only. The data suggest that learning style preferences evolve over the period of higher education and in the case of the populations sampled, the change evidenced showed a certain convergence in the level of style preference among the students by their sixth semester of study. The results for the subsample for only their first semester of study are shown in Figure 15.1.

The data support the idea that there are different learning style preferences between students of Eastern versus Western origin, which is largely what would have been expected based on what the literature suggests with

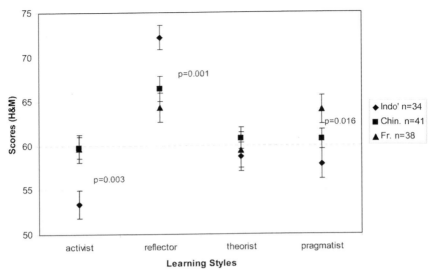

*Figure 15.1*   Learning style preferences of semester 1 subsample ($n = 113$).
Note. Error bars equal one standard error both ways.

the Eastern sample having a somewhat lower preference for the activist style and somewhat higher preference for the reflector style. The extent to which the Indonesian sample sets itself apart from the Chinese was not predicted, nor was the similarity between the Chinese and the French samples to have been expected. Interestingly, the French sample showed a considerably higher preference for the pragmatist style than did their peers.

The differences between the two Southeast Asian populations are of interest as they highlight the fact that one must be careful when speaking of the 'Asian' student as there may indeed be a number of 'Asian' students just as one would expect to find a number of 'European' students. Although there may be instances in which one would choose to speak of students in terms of East and West, as we will see following, it is important to realize that there may be multiple cultures of learning in the East just as there certainly are in the West.

Selected findings from the focus groups held as part of the qualitative data collection will allow for a better understanding of the results presented earlier. These findings are presented only for the expanded cultural groups to include Southeast Asian ($n = 53$ participants), European ($n = 54$ participants), and international ($n = 55$ participants). The reason for this is twofold. In the first instance, it was not possible to hold focus groups for all the nationalities present in the sample. In the second, there seems to be in fact an East-West divide in the findings with the Indonesian and Chinese students being very similar in their views and with the French together with other European students also agreeing.

In the focus groups the students both wrote about and discussed three questions related to learning: (1) what is learning? (2) what are the best strategies for academic learning? and (3) what are the criteria necessary for success in academic learning? Interestingly, there was little difference in the students' responses on the first and second question. The third question, however, shows considerable divergence in the manner in which the participants saw learning. Figure 15.2 shows the frequency in percentage with which reference was made to coded descriptors within the culturally clustered focus groups. The Southeast Asian students overwhelmingly believe in the power of reflection, passion, hard work, and work-play balance, to name some, things that are all completely under their control. The European and international students, on the other hand, feel that good teachers, interesting courses, and a good environment—things beyond their control—are all very important criteria for academic success. Interestingly, none of the Southeast Asian groups referred to these same criteria.

In summary, we have qualitative support for a more reflective Asian learner who places a lot of emphasis on the importance of their input in their learning versus a somewhat more active European learner who might enjoy a faster-paced learning experience and who expects both the educator and the institute in which they are studying to contribute largely to their success.

To a certain extent, the results presented earlier might seem to fit with a still all-too-common Western misconception about the Asian student. For example, in the West a 'passive' learner is someone who does not engage and might be qualified as unmotivated and uninterested, whereas in the East a 'passive' learner is someone who is listening, taking things in, and showing respect (Biggs, 1996; Kember & Gow, 1991). Problems occur when this attitude is displayed by an Eastern student in a Western classroom and not correctly interpreted by the educator. What we are seeing are indeed differences in how students might prefer to go about their learning; however, replacing the idea of 'passive' with 'reflective' suddenly puts a different light on what the student is actually doing. Adding to this the qualitative findings, we now see the reflective Asian student as one who is focused, disciplined, and hardworking and for whom the onus for learning rests with themselves and not the teacher.

This only provides a partial explanation of the results related to why Asian students may be showing a higher preference for the reflector style than their French peers do. The data, however, also suggest that the Chinese students have quite a high preference for an active style of learning and certainly a lot higher than did the Indonesian students. According to Tan (2007), different cultural groups within the Asian diaspora might be more face-conscious than others. In the classroom this suggests that learners for whom face gain is important will tend to ask questions and take a more active role, whereas those for whom face loss is more important will

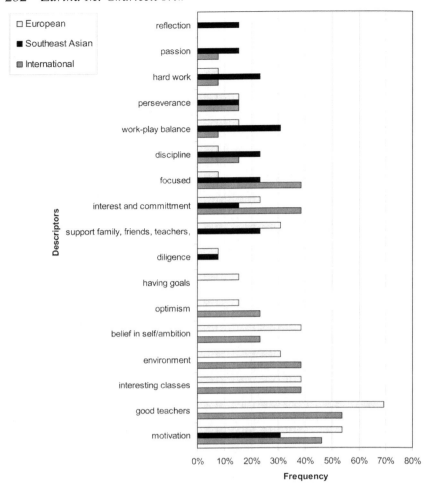

*Figure 15.2*   Criteria necessary for success in academic learning. Note: Adapted from Charlesworth (2009).

exhibit more self-effacing behavior in order to avoid shame and embarrassment (Hwang, Ang, & Francesco, 2002; Tan, 2007). This may be sufficient to explain these differences in classroom behavior. Nonetheless, when it comes to describing the criteria necessary for success, both the Indonesian and Chinese students agree.

The findings with respect to the French students still need further analysis. Here we have a larger number of students with a preference for an active style as well as, to a lesser extent, a pragmatist style and for whom the onus for their learning is to a certain extent on external factors. It is possible that these students, as they are just entering higher education, have yet to take responsibility for their studies.

## PRACTICAL IMPLICATIONS

Turning now to the applied context of these findings, it seems clear that in today's increasingly multicultural higher education classrooms educators who understand the differences in their students' learning styles and in their approaches to learning are in a position to offer them a better learning experience.

The results presented earlier support the idea that students will bring expectations conditioned by their culture and previous school experience with them as they enter higher education. This emphasizes the need to facilitate both the individual's understanding of their own style preferences (Sadler-Smith & Smith, 2004) as well as of their new instructional environment and, along with that, perhaps new expectations. It is worth noting that all of the research presented here took place at the outset of the students' higher education experience. Barron (2002) reminds us of the specific nature of the foreign students' needs and requirements with suggestions, which go past providing help to deal with standard culture shock and homesickness issues and are for host universities to

> recognize the different learning approaches and methods that many international students bring with them. (Barron, 2002, p. 40)

What is important is that any efforts made go past the traditional learning skills programs and provide students with guidelines concerning the types of behavior, from class involvement to evidence of critical thinking that is expected of them.

In the business sector, practitioners involved in on-the-job and management training need also to take culture and its influences on one's practice seriously. It is suggested that on-the-job training, particularly appreciated by the activist learners, be supplemented with handouts and theory for the more reflective and theorist learners. Alternatively, leadership and training courses at a more senior level, and possibly having a more theoretical base, need broadening, with case studies or actual issues, in order to address those individuals with more activist styles.

## IMPLICATIONS FOR STYLE RESEARCH

To date, styles research has rarely taken culture into the equation. The research presented here supports the idea that culture does, however, influence learning styles. This provides us with a compelling argument for the need for a paradigm change in how we look at learning styles. Integrating a cultural perspective in styles research will take the increasing internationalization of education into account and allow styles research to better understand and explain the diversity of the 21st-century higher education classroom as well as the workplace.

## BIBLIOGRAPHY

Auyeng, P., & Sands, J. (1996). A cross-cultural study of the learning style of accounting students. *Accounting and Finance, 36*, 261–270.

Barron, P. (2002). Issues surrounding Asian students hospitality management in Australia: a literature review regarding the paradox of the Asian learner. *Journal of Teaching in Travel and Tourism, 2*, 23–45.

Barron, P., & Arcodia, C. (2002). Linking learning style preferences and ethnicity: international students studying hospitality and tourism management in Australia. *Journal of Hospitality, Leisure, Sport and Tourism Education, 1*, 15–27.

Biggs, J.B. (1996). Western misperceptions of the Confucian-heritage learning culture. In D.A. Watkins & J.B. Biggs (Eds.), *The Chinese Learner: Cultural, Psychological and Contextual Influences* (pp. 45–67). Hong Kong: Comparative Education Research Centre.

Burnett, J.H. (1970). Culture of the school: a construct for research and explanation in education. *Council on Anthropology and Education Newsletter, 1*, 4–13.

Camilleri, C. (1986). *Cultural Anthropology and Education*. Paris: UNESCO/ Kogan Page.

Charlesworth, Z.M. (2007). *Learning Styles in International Higher Education: The Influence of Culture*. Doctoral dissertation, University of Geneva, Switzerland.

Charlesworth, Z.M. (2008a). Learning styles across cultures: suggestions for educators. *Education and Training, 50*, 115–127.

Charlesworth, Z.M. (2008b). Meeting the challenge of the international hospitality classroom. *Hospitality Revue, 4*, 47–51.

Charlesworth, Z.M. (2009). Cultures of learning: the missing variable. *Reflecting Education, 5*, 52–65.

Chevrier, J., Fortin, G., LeBlanc, R., & Théberge, M. (2000). La construction du style d'apprentissage [The construction of learning style]. *Education et Francophonie*. Retrieved January 22, 2003, from http://www.acelf.ca/c/revue/ revuehtml/28–1/07-chevrier.html

Coffield, F., Moseley, D., Hall, E., & Ecclestone, K. (2004). *Should We Be Using Learning Styles? What Research Has to Say to Practice*. London: Learning and Skills Research Centre.

Crahay, M. (2006). Qualitatif–quantitatif: des enjeux méthodologiques convergents? [Qualitative–quantitative: the challenge of converging methodologies]. In L. Paquay, M. Crahay, & J.-M. De Ketele (Eds.), *L'analyse qualitative en éducation: des pratiques de recherche aux critères de qualité* (pp. 31–52). Bruxelles: De Boeck.

Dasen, P.R, & Mishra, R.C. (2000). Cross-cultural views on human development in the third millennium. *International Journal of Behavioural Development, 24*, 428–434.

De Ketele, J.-M., & Maroy, C. (2006). Quels critères de qualité pour les recherches en education [Quality criteria for research in education]. In L. Paquay, M. Crahay, & J.-M. De Ketele (Eds.), *L'analyse qualitative en éducation: des pratiques de recherche aux critères de qualité* (pp. 219–249). Bruxelles: De Boeck.

Garner, I. (2000). Problems and inconsistencies with Kolb's and Honey's learning styles. *Educational Psychology, 20*, 341–348.

Greeno, J.G. (1997). On claims that answer the wrong questions. *Educational Researcher, January/February*, 5–17.

Harkness, S., & Keefer, C.H. (2000). Contributions of cross-cultural psychology to research and interventions in education and health. *Journal of Cross-Cultural Psychology, 31*, 92–109.

Honey, P., & Mumford, A. (1986). *The Manual of Learning Styles: Revised Version*. Maidenhead, UK: Peter Honey.

Hwang, A., Ang, S., & Francesco, A.M. (2002). The silent Chinese: the influence of face and kiasuism on student feedback-seeking behaviors. *Journal of Management Education, 26*, 70–98.

Jaju, A., Kwak, H., & Zinkhan, G.M. (2002). Learning styles of undergraduate business students: a cross-cultural comparison between the US, India, and Korea. *Marketing Education Review, 12*, 49–60.

Kember, D., & Gow, L. (1991). A challenge to the anecdotal stereotype of the Asian student. *Studies in Higher Education, 16*, 117–128.

Kolb, D.A. (1984). *Experiential Learning: Experience as a Source of Learning and Development*. New York: Prentice Hall.

Lashley, C. (2002). Learning styles and hospitality management education. *The Hospitality Review, April*, 56–60.

Lattuca, L.R. (2002). Learning interdisciplinarity: sociocultural perspectives on academic work. *The Journal of Higher Education, 73*, 711–739.

Lave, J. (1997). The culture of acquisition and the practice of understanding. In D. Kirshner & J.A. Whitson (Eds.), *Situated Cognition: Social, Semiotic, and Psychological Perspectives* (pp. 17–35). Mahwah, NJ: Lawrence Erlbaum Associates.

Lave, J., & Wenger, E. (1991). *Situated Learning: Legitimate Peripheral Participation*. New York: Cambridge University Press.

Li, J. (2003). U.S. and Chinese cultural beliefs about learning. *Journal of Educational Psychology, 95*, 258–267.

Lindblom-Ylänne, S. (2004). Raising students' awareness of their approaches to study. *Innovations in Education and Teaching International, 41*, 405–421.

Lingbiao, G., & Watkins, D.A. (2001). Identifying and assessing the conceptions of teaching of secondary school physics teachers in China. *British Journal of Educational Psychology, 71*, 443–469.

Nguyen, P.M., Terlouw, C., & Pilot, A. (2006). Culturally appropriate pedagogy: the case of group learning in a Confucian heritage culture context. *Intercultural Education, 17*, 1–19.

Nulty, D.D., & Barrett, A. (1996). Transitions in students' learning styles. *Studies in Higher Education, 21*, 333–346.

OECD (2009). *Education at a Glance*. OECD Publishing: Paris.

Packer, M.J., & Goicoechea, J. (2000). Sociocultural and constructivist theories of learning: ontology, not just epistemology. *Educational Psychologist, 35*, 227–241.

Perregaux, C. (1994). *Odyssea*. Neuchâtel: Commission Romande des Moyens d'Enseignement et d'Apprentissage (COROME).

Presland, J. (1994). Learning styles and continuous professional development. *Educational Psychology in Practice, 10*, 179–184.

Purdie, N., Hattie, J., & Douglas, G. (1996). Student conceptions of learning and their use of self-regulated learning strategies. *Journal of Educational Psychology, 88*, 87–100.

Ramburuth, P., & McCormick, J. (2001). Learning diversity in higher education: a comparative study of Asian international and Australian students. *Higher Education, 42*, 333–350.

Reuchlin, M. (1991). *Les différences individuelles à l'école* [*Individual differences at school*]. Paris: Presses Universitaires de France.

Riding, R., & Rayner, S. (1998). *Cognitive Styles and Learning Strategies*. London: David Fulton.

Rieben, L. (2000). A quelles conditions la notion de style d'apprentissage peut-elle devenir heuristique pour le champ de l'éducation? [Under what conditions might learning style be a heuristic for the field of education?]. *Education et Francophonie*. Retrieved January 22, 2003, from http://www.acelf.ca/revue/XXVIII/articles/08-rieben.html

Rogoff, B. (1990). *Apprenticeship in Thinking: Cognitive Development in Social Context*. New York: Oxford University Press.

Sadler-Smith, E. (1997). 'Learning style': frameworks and instruments. *Educational Psychology, 17*, 51–64.

Sadler-Smith, E., & Smith, P. (2004). Strategies for accommodating individual's styles and preferences in flexible learning programmes. *British Journal of Educational Technology, 34*, 395–412.

Salili, F. (1996). Accepting personal responsibility for learning. In D.A. Watkins & J.B. Biggs (Eds.), *The Chinese Learner: Cultural, Psychological and Contextual Influences* (pp. 85–105). Hong Kong: Comparative Education Research Centre.

Segall, M.H, Dasen, P.R., Berry, J.W., & Poortinga, Y.P. (1999). *Human Behavior in Global Perspective: An Introduction to Cross-Cultural Psychology* (2nd ed.). Needham Heights, MA: Allyn & Bacon.

Smith, P.J, & Smith, S.N. (1999). Differences between Chinese and Australian students: some implications for distance educators. *Distance Education, 20*, 64–75.

Sternberg, R.J., & Grigorenko, E.L. (2001). A capsule history of theory and research on styles. In R.J. Sternberg & L.F. Zhang (Eds.), *Perspectives on Thinking, Learning, and Cognitive Styles* (pp. 1–21). Mahwah, NJ: Lawrence Erlbaum Associates.

Tan, P.L. (2007). *Learning Styles and Cultural Values among adult Learners: A Cross-Cultural Investigation*. Paper presented at the 12th Annual European Learning Styles Information Network (ELSIN) Conference, June 12–15, Trinity College, Dublin, Ireland.

Tashakkori, A., & Teddlie, C. (1998). *Mixed Methodology: Combining Qualitative and Quantitative Approaches*. Thousand Oaks, CA: Sage.

Tharp, R.G. (1994). Intergroup differences among Native Americans in socialization and child cognition: an ethnographic analysis. In P.M. Greenfield & R.R. Cocking (Eds.), *Cross-Cultural Roots of Minority Child Development* (pp. 87–105). Hillsdale, NJ: Lawrence Erlbaum Associates.

Triandis, H.C. (1972). *The Analysis of Subjective Culture*. New York: Wiley.

Wong, K.K.F., Pine, R.J., & Tsang, N. (2000). Learning style preferences and implications for training programs in the hospitality and tourism industry. *Journal of Hospitality and Tourism Education, 12*, 32–40.

Zhang, L.F. (2002). Thinking styles and modes of thinking: implications for education and research. *The Journal of Psychology, 136*, 245–261.

# 16 Personalizing Web Environments on Cognitive Style

## The Effect on Users' Performance

*Nikos Tsianos, Panagiotis Germanakos, Zacharias Lekkas, and Costas Mourlas*

## INTRODUCTION

Finding and presenting information on the World Wide Web (WWW) has been a challenging and urgent problem almost from the beginning of the proliferation of Web sites (Pitkow & Kehoe, 1996). The vast number of Web sites makes it hard, or indeed impossible, to find the appropriate site (Lawrence, Giles, & Bollacker, 1999). Similarly, the growing size and complexity of Web sites makes it very difficult to locate information within specific Web pages. The problem of finding and presenting information in a site has become an important area of research, with several solutions currently being pursued.

This research has also provided a good basis for the developing notion of personalization and for the advent of adaptive hypermedia systems (Brusilovsky & Nejdl, 2004; Eklund & Sinclair, 2000) that take into account users' individual characteristics, aiming to provide tailor-suited information. Therefore, Web adaptation and personalization techniques and paradigms are employed in order to alleviate such problems by presenting information based on the needs and preferences of users, by dynamically adapting the user's view according to the task at hand. In parallel, Web-based educational applications have also proliferated throughout the extensive development of the Internet, along with a significant research interest on this channel of instruction. Individual differences in e-learning constitute an interdisciplinary research area, and most approaches derive from the fields of computer science and/or psychology, as a result of combined efforts to improve the effectiveness of Web-based education.

The integration of human factors or traits in Web-based education is therefore in the scope of many researchers. In accordance with the aim of this chapter, which focuses on individual differences in information processing and personalization, we consider how this research is being carried out in two distinct ways: (a) computer scientists have developed systems that usually adapt on users' learning or cognitive styles (Carver, Howard, & Lane 1999; Gilbert & Han, 2002; Papanikolaou, Grigoriadou, Kornilakis, &

Magoulas, 2003) or respond to their current affective state (Picard, 1997), whereas (b) researchers mainly from the field of psychology have examined the role of different cognitive traits in computer-mediated learning (Bilda & Gero, 2007; De Stefano & Lefevre, 2007; Federico, 2000; Graff, 2003, 2005; Parkinson & Redmond, 2002; Workman, 2004). It is evident that the constructs of learning and cognitive styles have proven to be quite popular in this area. Moreover, there have been efforts to build more complex models of human factors that may be proven useful in e-learning applications (Germanakos, Tsianos, Lekkas, Mourlas, & Samaras, 2008; Lin, Kinshuk, & Patel, 2003).

On the basis of the aforementioned research directions in e-learning, we are in the process of developing and evaluating both a theoretical model of information processing in the Web (Germanakos et al., 2008) and a corresponding adaptive hypermedia system that implements our theoretical approach and assumptions (Germanakos, et al., 2007). Our experimental model is comprised of three dimensions: cognitive style, cognitive processing efficiency, and emotional processing. The first dimension is unitary, whereas cognitive processing efficiency is comprised of (a) working memory span (WMS) (Baddeley, 1992) and (b) speed and control of information processing (Demetriou, Efklides, & Platsidou, 1993). The emotional aspect of the model focuses on different aspects of anxiety (Cassady, 2004; Cassady & Johnson, 2002; Spielberger, 1983) and self-regulation. This model is under an ongoing procedure of empirical evaluation through a number of consecutive experiments.

In this chapter, we present experimental results that are related to the construct of style and the effect of personalization on this specific construct. The underlying theory and psychometric tools are the same in both settings (educational and commercial), whereas the method that was applied in order to provide personalized environments is described separately for each experiment.

## THEORETICAL BACKGROUND

Cognitive style has been defined by Messick (1976) as consistent individual differences in preferred ways of organizing and processing information and experience, a construct that is different from learning style (Sadler-Smith, 2001). Cognitive styles represent an individual's typical or habitual mode of problem solving, thinking, perceiving, or remembering, and

> are considered to be trait-like, relatively stable characteristics of individuals, whereas learning strategies are more state-driven techniques that are used to cope with changing situations and tasks. (McKay, Fischler, & Dunn, 2003, p. 1).

The use of cognitive style has also been supported by Sternberg (1997, p. 158) as "a construct that can be placed at the interface between cognition and personality". According to Curry's (1983) three-layered onion model, cognitive style theories fall into the innermost layer of 'cognitive personality style', which is the most stable and relatively permanent; the factor of stability is quite important in user profiling considerations, which will be discussed later. While remaining aware of an impressive number of cognitive and learning style theories (Cassidy, 2004; Rayner & Riding, 1997), we have used the concept of cognitive rather than learning style for a number of reasons:

- Cognitive style is not restricted to the context of strictly educational settings, because the focus is on information processing in general. This seems to be better aligned with the generic structure of the Web, where learning can be widely differentiated from traditional classroom environments and strategies.
- Learning style is "a construct that by definition is not stable—it was grounded in process and therefore susceptible to rapid change" (Rayner, 2001, p. 2174).
- Most learning style theories, such as Kolb and Kolb's (2005) Learning Style Inventory (LSI), Honey and Mumford's (1986) Learning Style Questionnaire (LSQ), or Dunn and Dunn's (1989) Learning Style Inventory (LSI), have a social dimension in the proposed typologies; some types are more socially oriented in learning than others. However, Web-based education is often an individual process, usually asynchronous. Therefore, because we are also interested in building a generic model of information processing in the Web, this family of typologies includes parameters that are not found in Web-based environments.

More specifically, the Cognitive Style Analysis (CSA) theory has been used for quite relevant reasons. The CSA is actually derived from a factor analytic approach integrating previous cognitive style theories, summarizing a number of different yet highly correlated constructs into two distinct independent dimensions (Riding & Cheema, 1991). This covers a wide array of the former cognition-based style typologies, without going into unnecessary theoretical detail for the needs of Web education depth.

Most importantly, the two independent scales of the CSA (verbal/imager and wholist/analyst) correspond ideally to the structure of Web environments. A personalized environment that is supported by an automated mechanism can be altered mainly at the levels of content selection and hypermedia structure; the content is essentially either visual or verbal (or auditory), whereas the manipulation of links can lead to a more analytic and segmented structure, or to a more holistic and cohesive environment. These are actually the differences in the preferences of learners that belong to each dimension of the CSA scales (Sadler-Smith & Riding, 1999).

Subsequently, the mapping of personalized educational material on learners' preferences (or profiles) can take an actual form of well-defined rules and it does not rely on heavily hypothesizing or is susceptible to designers' subjective reasoning (e.g., what is considered to fit better, an accommodator or an assimilator, according to Kolb's theory?). An interesting empirical set of data lending support to this position and with reference to the physiological basis of cognitive style and the use of the CSA as a psychometric tool of classification is the reported correlation with hemispherical preference and electroencephalography (EEG) measurements of cognitive style (Glass & Riding, 1999; McKay et al., 2003). This seems to strengthen the relationship between cognitive style and physical/biologically-based modes of information processing. Further, the CSA has been also applied in other multimedia applications with significant results (Ghinea & Chen, 2003). Finally, the test has been developed electronically, removing the need to construct an electronic version of a psychometric tool.

At this point we must clarify that we are not unaware of reports that question the reliability of the CSA (Peterson, Deary, & Austin, 2003; Rezaei & Katz, 2004). The assessment of style is still an issue, and definitely practical reasons such as the ones described earlier should not become the sole criterion of adopting a theory. However, judging from our results that will be presented later, research-wise the CSA has been shown to support its underlying theoretical basis, at least within the boundaries of a Web-based environment.

Conclusively, our rationale behind using the construct of cognitive style as a personalization factor in adaptive hypermedia is to provide environments that are matched to individuals' information-processing preferences in order to increase their levels of comprehension and performance. Consequently, our research hypothesis is that those who receive information in the supposedly ideal condition of matched cognitive style will assimilate Web information in a more efficient way.

## METHOD

### E-Learning Experiment

The e-learning experiment, a between-participants design, was set up involving a memory test in order to assess the differences in performance between learners who were taught in a personalized, matched-to-their-preferences way, and those who were taught in a way that was not consistent to their cognitive preferences. Those that were classified as intermediates (no cognitive style preference) received a nonpersonalized balanced environment. Essentially, the three conditions (matched, mismatched, and 'intermediate' way of teaching) were expected to provide statistically significantly different results only if the factors involved are indeed important for Web-based learning.

All 138 participants were students from the Universities of Cyprus; approximately 30% were male and 70% were female, and their age varied from 17 to 22 with a mean age of 19. Participation in the experiment was voluntary, although most students were willing to take the course as an additional help on a difficult academic subject that is part of their academic curriculum.

The e-learning environment was an e-based introductory course on algorithms. The specific subject was chosen mainly because students at the social sciences departments, where the experiment took place, had absolutely no experience of programming and computer science and traditionally perform poorly. By controlling the factor of experience in that way, we divided our sample in two groups: almost half of the participants were provided with information matched to their cognitive preferences, whereas the other half were taught in a mismatched way. We expected that users in the matched condition would outperform those in the mismatched condition. The two groups were divided randomly, in the sense that each user that logged into the system was placed in the opposite to the previous user condition.

In order to evaluate the effect of matched and mismatched conditions, participants took an online memory test on the subject they were taught (algorithms). This exam was taken as soon as the e-learning procedure ended, in order to control for long-term memory decay effects. The dependent variable that was used to assess the effect of adaptation to users' preferences was participants' score at the memory test.

Learners accessed the environment through a Web browser, using personal computers located at the laboratories of both universities. Participants took the online CSA test before participating at the online course, along with a visual working memory span (VWMS) test (Demetriou, Christou, Spanoudis, & Platsidou, 2002) in order to explore possible interactions that would be of interest in our wider research framework. The profiling procedure lasted for about 20 minutes; after that, users were encouraged to take a 5- to 10-minute break. The course lasted approximately 40 minutes, and the memory test about 15 minutes.

## Personalization Rules for the Educational Environment

According to each learner's style preference, different aspects of the learning environment were personalized in order to provide matched environments. In sum, the mapping rules were the following, in relation to each specific preference:

- Imager: Images, diagrams, and schemes are used, when possible, for the representation of information. Specifically, instead of lengthy verbal descriptions, a schematic approach has been adopted as an equally important mean of instruction. Text is also used, but is reduced by approximately 40% in comparison to verbal learners.
- Verbal: The prominent representation of information is textual, and images are used when required, accompanying and not replacing texts.
- Analyst: In the analytic condition, learners are free to navigate through the educational environment. They are not guided externally, although they may choose to follow a linear suggested path. They also have access to a separate index of concepts in order to follow an analytic path in accessing information and forming knowledge. The information is extensively interconnected because hypertext is used to a greater extent, and users can access at the same time different parts of the educational content.
- Wholist: In the wholist condition, learners navigate through the environment in an externally guided way, which provides prefixed linkage and descriptions of the sequentially interconnected information. The organization of the distinct parts of the course is strict and outlined in a clear way. Users have access to previously acquired information, but they do not have access to links that lead to information of chapters not visited. Additional guiding information is constantly given.
- Intermediate: Intermediate users are provided with an environment which combines characteristics of all dimensions of cognitive style, in order to maintain a balance; moreover, they serve as a control group in our experiments.

## Commercial Web Site Experiment

In this experiment, a within-participants methodology was applied, seeking out to explore if the personalized condition serves users better at finding information more accurately and fast. A pilot study that involved a between-participants design demonstrated inconsistent effects, suggesting that a within-subjects approach would yield more robust results.

The number of participants was eighty-nine; they all were students from the Universities of Cyprus and Athens and their age varied from 18 to 21, with a mean age of 19. They accessed the Web-based hypertext environments using personal computers located at the laboratories of both universities, divided in groups of approximately twelve participants. Each session lasted about 40 minutes. Almost 20 minutes were required for the user-profiling process (CSA test and VWMS test); the remaining time was devoted to navigating in both hypertext environments, which were presented sequentially (as soon as they were done with the first environment, the second one was presented). Participation in this experiment was voluntary, although within the context of a course on adaptive HCI systems.

The hypertext content was about a series of laptop computers: general description, technical specifications, and additional information were available for each model. Based on an initial analysis of a number of commercial Web sites, we considered that the original (raw) version of the laptop manufacturer's Web site, which we chose to experiment with, was designed without any considerations towards cognitive style preferences and was quite balanced.

In each condition, users were asked to fulfill three tasks. They actually had to find the necessary information to answer three sequential multiple-choice questions that were given to them while navigating. All six questions (three per condition) were about determining which laptop excelled with respect to the prerequisites that were set by each question. There was certainly only one correct answer that was possible to be found relatively easy, in the sense that users were not required to have hardware-related knowledge or understanding.

As soon as users finished answering all questions in both conditions, they were presented with a comparative satisfaction questionnaire; users were asked to choose which hypertext environment was better (on a 5-point scale, where 1 means a strong preference for environment A and 5 for environment B), regarding usability and user friendliness factors.

The dependent variables that were considered as indicators of differences between the two hypertext environments were: (1) task accuracy (number of correct answers), (2) task completion time, and (3) user satisfaction.

At this point a few clarifications about the methodology are necessary:

- Users did not know which the personalized condition was, nor were they encouraged to use any additional features.
- To avoid training effects, half of the users received the raw condition first (considered as environment A), whilst the other half started the procedure with the personalized (again considered as environment A).
- To avoid a possible effect of differences in difficulty of each set of three questions, they were alternated in both environments. Due to a design error, the division was not in half, but fifty-three participants received the first combination and thirty-six the alternated. However, there was not observed any effect; all questions were proven of equal difficulty.
- The within-participants design, finally, allowed the control of unmeasured individual differences (variables) amongst users.

## Personalization Rules for the Commercial Environment

The way that the commercial environment was altered according to users' style preferences is illustrated in Figure 16.1. In general, the same approach with the case of the e-learning experiment was followed, albeit rather simpler, along with a few context-dependent modifications.

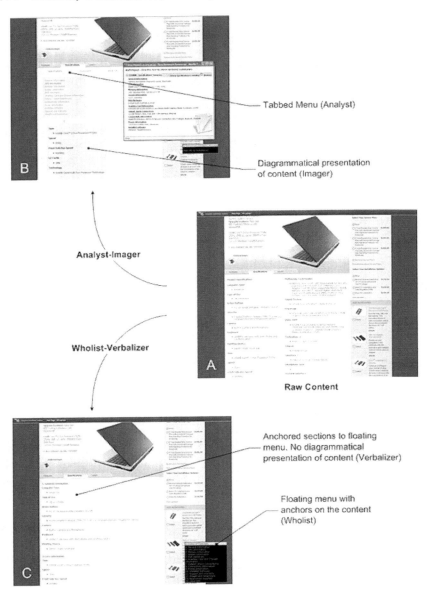

*Figure 16.1*　Commercial environment adaptation.

## RESULTS

### E-Learning Experiment

As expected, the mean score of those that received environments matched to their cognitive style is higher than the mean score achieved by those that learned within the mismatched condition (see Table 16.1). Because the variance of participants' scores was homogeneous (Levene's statistic = 0.20, $p = 0.980$), one-way analysis of variance was performed on the data. The difference in score between the three groups (matched, mismatched, and intermediates) is statistically significant ($F(2,137) = 3.48, p < 0.05$).

Post hoc analysis has shown that the difference is significant only between groups in the matched and the mismatched condition (8.74 percentage points in the memory test), whilst intermediates do not differ from any of the other two categories (see Table 16.2).

As depicted in the theoretical framework section, intermediate users have no specific cognitive style preference. Consequently, they received a nonpersonalized (although balanced) environment; this may explain the fact that their mean score does not differ significantly from those that learned in the matched condition, because any environment could be proven as matched for them. Still, the fact that their score also does not differ from the mismatched condition participants could perhaps be attributed to some other variable that may be of significant importance in performance, as long as there are not cognitive style preferences to be satisfied.

We should note that a closer inspection of a table of means for all categories of learners placed in both axes of cognitive style (imager/intermediate/verbalizer and wholist/intermediate/analyst) shows that the differences in

*Table 16.1*   Descriptives of Differences in Mean Score (%) of Matched and Mismatched Condition

|  | N | M | SD | Minimum | Maximum |
|---|---|---|---|---|---|
| Matched | 53 | 66.53 | 18.901 | 13 | 100 |
| Mismatched | 61 | 57.79 | 18.149 | 9 | 93 |
| Intermediate | 24 | 58.58 | 18.429 | 22 | 93 |
| Total | 138 | 61.28 | 18.821 | 9 | 100 |

*Table 16.2*   Post Hoc Analysis (Tukey HSD) of Differences in Mean Scores (%)

| (I) Matched Environment | (J) Matched Environment | Mean Difference (I-J) | Std. Error | Sig. |
|---|---|---|---|---|
| Matched | Mismatched | 8.741(*) | 3.472 | 0.034 |
|  | Intermediate | 7.945 | 4.549 | 0.192 |
| Mismatched | Matched | –8.741(*) | 3.472 | 0.034 |
|  | Intermediate | –0.796 | 4.455 | 0.983 |
| Intermediate | Matched | –7.945 | 4.549 | 0.192 |
|  | Mismatched | 0.796 | 4.455 | 0.983 |

*Note:*\* The mean difference is significant at the 0.05 level.

score are often very high between the two conditions, with the exception of the verbalizer-wholist learners, who do not seem to benefit from the personalization of the Web content. This can be explained by the fact that the specific cognitive style preference is considered to be complementary (Riding & Wigley, 1997) and more adaptive to mismatched situations.

Although learners' VWMS was not a factor of personalization in this experiment, this measurement was also available. This independent variable had no effect of its own, nor interaction with each experimental condition (matched/ mismatched/intermediate environment) on participants' scores. Also, in the mismatched and intermediate condition, VWMS is insignificant.

However, in the matched condition VWMS becomes significant, because a 3 × 3 ANOVA has shown interaction between WMS and the wholist/analytic dimension on participants' scores ($F(4,52) = 3.516$, $p < 0.05$). According to theory, analysts are in further need of working memory span in order to use their analytic mode of processing; thus, analysts with low working memory span should perform worse—which is the case with this experiment. Besides that, wholists also benefit from high levels of VWMS (although not from medium levels), whilst intermediates demonstrate a rather reverse behavior (see Table 16.3). This latter finding is somehow puzzling, and it should be further experimentally investigated.

The results of this experiment may support the notion that applying a cognitive style theory in the context of the Web could be proven useful for learners, or at least that mismatching the Web environment to their preferences may hamper their performance. The mean difference of approximately 9% is not striking, of course, but taking under consideration the little variance of participants' scores, it could be supported that organizing

*Table 16.3* Estimated Marginal Means of Wholist/Analyst Dimension Interaction with Visual Working Memory Span (VWMS) Test (% score)

| W/A Dimension | VWMS | Mean |
| --- | --- | --- |
| Analyst | Low | 63.000 |
| | Medium | 100.000 |
| | High | 87.000 |
| Intermediate | Low | 85.500 |
| | Medium | 66.400 |
| | High | 74.833 |
| Wholist | Low | 56.917 |
| | Medium | 55.357 |
| | High | 76.400 |

information in the Web space according to learners' preferences can provide added value to an e-learning application.

## Commercial Web site

The most robust and interesting finding was the fact that users in the personalized condition were more accurate in providing the correct answer for each task. The same user in the raw condition had a mean of one correct answer, whereas in the personalized condition the mean rose to 1.9.

Because the distribution was not normal and the paired samples $t$-test assumptions were not met, Wilcoxon Signed Ranks Test was performed, showing that this difference is statistically significant at zero level of confidence ($Z = -4.76$, $p < 0.001$). This is probably a very encouraging finding, implying that personalization on the basis of these factors (cognitive style and VWMS) benefits users within an e-commerce environment, as long as there are some cognitive functions involved (such as information seeking).

Equally interesting is the fact that users in the personalized condition were significantly faster at task completion. The mean aggregated time of answering all three questions was 541 seconds in the raw condition, and 412 in the personalized. A paired samples $t$ test was performed ($t(88)$ = 4.67, $p < 0.001$) demonstrating significance at zero level of confidence. Again, this second dependent variable (time) shows that the personalized hypertext environment is more efficient.

Concerning the satisfaction questionnaire, thirty-one users leaned towards the personalized environment, thirty-eight had no preference, whereas twenty preferred the raw version. This descriptive statistic is merely indicative of whether participants would consciously observe any positive or negative effects of the personalized condition. A considerable percentage leaned towards that condition (or at least users did not seem somehow annoyed by such a restructuring), but overall it cannot be supported that they were fully aware of their increase in performance, as shown by the abovementioned findings.

In sum, the specific experiment in a rather clear way shows that users performed better within the personalized environment, and these findings are statistically very robust. It could be argued, of course, that there is no way to be fully aware if information processing was more efficient at a deeper level, or users simply found the personalized condition more to their (perhaps unconscious) liking, thus devoting more conscious cognitive effort. Nevertheless, such an increase in performance, which is consistent with the findings of the previously conducted experiment in the field of e-learning, provides support for the further development and application of our theoretical model in different Web-based hypertext/hypermedia environments.

## DISCUSSION

The basic objective of this research was to evaluate whether the construct of cognitive style can constitute a meaningful personalization factor in both fields of e-learning and commercial Web sites. Through the empirical evaluation that was described earlier, it was demonstrated that users' information retention was more accurate and efficient, both in terms of providing correct answers to the online exam and the task questions, and in task completion time in the second experiment.

According to these findings, it may be supported that personalization incorporating the assessment of cognitive style differences reveals a significant effect on users' performance, with corresponding implications for designers of both educational and commercial adaptive Web sites. As stated in the introductory section, the purpose of employing personalization techniques is to assist users in locating and processing Web information more efficiently, according to their needs and preferences. Correspondingly, the construct of cognitive style seems to reflect certain information processing characteristics in a way that is compatible to the structure and form of e-learning and commercial Web sites.

Further, educators and designers of Web sites should consider employing profiling and personalization techniques based on the construct of style, considering that it has been demonstrated that there is a viable method of designing Web environments based on the implications of a style theory. Moreover, there are probably even more possibilities and implementations for researchers and designers to focus upon in experimental research.

Additionally, even though style remains an issue of controversy in the field of education, perhaps our research shows that this specific construct is more suitable for the Web in relation to traditional settings, such as classrooms, because Web interactions can be more individualistic, with less intervening factors and real-life settings considerations (such as social parameters). However, the profiling procedure could be rather time consuming for the case of commercial Web sites, especially in the absence of a universally accepted and validated style theory that could be applied in numerous contexts, with interchangeable user profiles. In this case, perhaps it would be more feasible for designers to take into account the diversity of individuals' preferences, and to provide them with a number of alternative structures and modes of presentation.

Nevertheless, it is required to further experiment with various types of commercial Web sites in order to establish a rigid connection between human factors and information processing in Web-based hypermedia environments, no matter how representative our case study might have been. The same applies on the case of e-learning, because the role of style could as well be differentiated in relation to the academic subject. Thus, our future work will be focused on improving and extending the methodology of our experiments in both domains, along with the inclusion of cognitive factors such as working memory, and the integration of biometric sensors for real-time monitoring of emotional arousal.

## BIBLIOGRAPHY

Baddeley, A. (1992). Working memory. *Science, 255,* 556–559.

Bilda, Z., & Gero, J.S. (2007). The impact of working memory limitations on the design process during conceptualization. *Design Studies, 28,* 343–367.

Brusilovsky, P., & Nejdl, W. (2004). *Adaptive Hypermedia and Adaptive Web.* Hampshire, UK: CSC Press LLC.

Carver, C.A., Jr., Howard, R.A., & Lane, W.D. (1999). Enhancing student learning through hypermedia courseware and incorporation of student learning styles. *IEEE Transactions on Education, 42,* 33–38.

Cassady, J.C. (2004). The influence of cognitive test anxiety across the learning–testing cycle. *Learning and Instruction, 14,* 569–592.

Cassady, J.C., & Johnson, R.E. (2002). Cognitive test anxiety and academic performance. *Contemporary Educational Psychology, 27,* 270–295.

Cassidy, S. (2004). Learning styles: an overview of theories, models, and measures. *Educational Psychology, 24,* 419–444.

Curry, L. (1983). *An Organization of Learning Styles Theory and Constructs.* Paper presented at the Annual Meeting of the American Educational Research Association, Montreal, Quebec, April 11–15.

Demetriou, A., Christou, C., Spanoudis, G., & Platsidou, M. (2002). The development of mental processing: efficiency, working memory, and thinking. *Monographs of the Society for Research in Child Development, 67,* 1–155.

Demetriou, A., Efklides, A., & Platsidou, M. (1993). *The Architecture and Dynamics of Developing Mind: Experiential Structuralism as a Frame for Unifying Cognitive Development Theories.* Chicago: University of Chicago Press.

De Stefano, D., & Lefevre, J. (2007). Cognitive load in hypertext reading: a review. *Computers in Human Behavior, 23,* 1616–1641.

Dunn, R., & Dunn, K. (1989). *Learning Style Inventory.* Lawrence, KS: Price Systems.

Eklund, J., & Sinclair, K. (2000). An empirical appraisal of the effectiveness of adaptive interfaces of instructional systems. *Educational Technology and Society, 3,* 165–177.

Federico, P. (2000). Learning styles and student attitudes toward various aspects of network-based instruction. *Computers in Human Behavior, 16,* 359–379.

Germanakos, P., Tsianos, N., Lekkas, Z., Mourlas, C., Belk, M., & Samaras, G. (2007). *An Adaptive Web System for Integrating Human Factors in Personalization of Web Content.* Demonstration in the Proceedings of the 11th International Conference on User Modeling (UM), Corfu, Greece, June 25–29.

Germanakos, P., Tsianos, N., Lekkas, Z., Mourlas, C., & Samaras, G. (2008). Capturing essential intrinsic user behaviour values for the design of comprehensive Web-based personalized environments. *Computers in Human Behavior, 24,* 1434–1451.

Ghinea, G., & Chen, S.Y. (2003). The impact of cognitive styles on perceptual distributed multimedia quality. *British Journal of Educational Technology, 34,* 393–406.

Gilbert, J.E., & Han, C.Y. (2002). Arthur: a personalized instructional system. *Journal of Computing in Higher Education, 14,* 113–129.

Glass, A., & Riding, R.J. (1999). EEG differences and cognitive style. *Biological Psychology, 51,* 23–41.

Graff, M.G. (2003). Learning from Web-based instructional systems and cognitive style. *British Journal of Educational Technology, 34*, 407–418.

Graff, M.G. (2005). Differences in concept mapping, hypertext architecture, and the analyst–intuition dimension of cognitive style. *Educational Psychology, 25*, 409–422.

Honey, P., & Mumford, A. (1986). *A Manual of Learning Styles.* Maidenhead, UK: Peter Honey.

Kolb, A.Y., & Kolb, D.A. (2005). *The Kolb Learning Style Inventory—Version 3.1 2005 Technical Specifications.* Boston: Haygroup Experience Based Learning Systems.

Lawrence, S., Giles, C.L., & Bollacker, K. (1999). Digital libraries and autonomous citation indexing. *IEEE Computer, 32*, 67–71.

Lin, T., K., & Patel, A. (2003). Cognitive trait model for persistent student modelling. In D. Lassner & C. McNaught (Eds.), *EdMedia 2003 Conference Proceedings* (pp. 629–632). Norfolk, VA.

McKay, M.T., Fischler, I., & Dunn, B.R. (2003). Cognitive style and recall of text: an EEG analysis. *Learning and Individual Differences, 14*, 1–21.

Messick, S. (1976). *Individuality in Learning.* San Francisco: Jossey-Bass.

Papanikolaou, K.A., Grigoriadou, M., Kornilakis, H., & Magoulas, G.D. (2003). Personalizing the interaction in a Web-based educational hypermedia system: the case of INSPIRE. *User-Modelling and User-Adapted Interaction, 13*, 213–267.

Parkinson, A., & Redmond, J.A. (2002). *Do Cognitive Styles Affect Learning Performance in Different Computer Media?* Proceedings of the 7th Annual Conference on Innovation and Technology in Computer Science Education (pp. 39–43). Aarhus, Denmark, June 24–28.

Peterson, E.R., Deary, I.J., & Austin, E.J. (2003). The reliability of Riding's Cognitive Style Analysis test. *Personality and Individual Differences, 34*, 881–891.

Picard, R.W. (1997). *Affective Computing.* Cambridge, MA: MIT Press.

Pitkow, J.E., & Kehoe, C.M. (1996). Emerging trends in WWW user population. *Communications of the ACM , 39*, 106–108.

Rayner, S. (2001). Cognitive styles and learning styles. In N.J. Smelser & P.B. Baltes (Eds.), *International Encyclopedia of Social & Behavioral Sciences* (pp. 2171–2175). Cambridge, UK: Elsevier Science Ltd.

Rayner, S., & Riding, R. (1997). Towards a categorisation of cognitive styles and learning styles. *Educational Psychology, 17*(1&2), 5–27.

Rezaei, A.R., & Katz, R. (2004). Evaluation of the reliability and validity of the cognitive styles analysis. *Personality and Individual Differences, 36*, 1317–1327.

Riding, R.J., & Cheema, I. (1991). Cognitive styles—an overview and integration. *Educational Psychology, 11*(3&4), 193–215.

Riding, R.J., & Wigley, S. (1997). The relationship between cognitive style and personality in further education students. *Personality and Individual Differences, 23*, 379–389.

Sadler-Smith, E. (2001). The relationship between learning style and cognitive style. *Personality and Individual Differences, 30*, 609–616.

Sadler-Smith, E., & Riding, R.J. (1999). Cognitive style and instructional preferences. *Instructional Science, 27*, 355–371.

Spielberger, C.D. (1983). *Manual for the State-Trait Anxiety Inventory (STAI).* Palo Alto, CA: Consulting Psychologists Press.

Sternberg, R.J. (1997). *Thinking Styles.* New York: Cambridge University Press.

Workman, M. (2004). Performance and perceived effectiveness in computer-based and computer-aided education: do cognitive styles make a difference? *Computers in Human Behavior, 20*, 517–534.

# 17 Improving Business Education for the 21st Century
## The Role of Cognitive Styles

*Kristin Backhaus*

## INTRODUCTION

Business educators face the challenge of preparing a diverse population of students to meet the demands of a rapidly changing business environment. In fact, business schools are often criticized for failing to adequately prepare students and, in times of economic difficulty, are even blamed for sending ill-prepared students into the business world (Bennis & O'Toole, 2005). On a day-to-day basis, business educators, like all other teachers, struggle to find ways to reach students, enable them to succeed, and to improve learning outcomes. In this chapter, I propose a framework for applying cognitive styles research to a set of four specific issues facing business educators. Following the advice of Sternberg, Grigorenko, and Zhang (2008), this approach seeks to connect theory and empirical research to the practice of education. Moreover, the chapter demonstrates one way that the style paradigm can be used to inform teaching and learning.

## COGNITIVE STYLE: A BRIEF REVIEW

Cognitive style is defined as a consistent individual difference in gathering and processing information (Messick, 1984). Cognitive style is considered to be automatic and deeply pervasive (Rayner & Riding, 1997). According to Sternberg and colleagues (2008), style sits at the interface between cognition and personality and as a result affects both the learner's approach to learning and the outcomes of their experience.

Although researchers generally believe that cognitive style has an impact on learning outcomes, there is no single, agreed-on style theory on which to base a discussion of pedagogy (Mortimore, 2009). Leading style researchers echo the call for development of consensus in style theory, and more rigorous empirical and practical research about style (Rayner, 2008). In the absence of a uniting theory, this chapter focuses on one broad style dimension that runs within a number of different cognitive style theories, the analytic/holistic dimension. This dimension is chosen for use here based on

Miller's (1987) suggestion that all cognitive style frameworks are subordinate to this one broad dimension. The analytic/holist dimension is subsumed within the cognition-centered theories, and is related specifically to the way in which people organize information (Rayner, 2000). On the analytic end of the bipolar continuum, processing is described as structured, sequential, and detail oriented (Allinson & Hayes, 1996). The holistic end of the continuum is described as divergent, global thinking with an emphasis on big picture rather than detail-level thinking (Allinson & Hayes, 1996; Miller, 1987). Sadler-Smith (1999a) identifies three 'lead theories' within the analytic/holist category: Kirton's (2003) adaptor/innovator dimension, Riding and Cheema's (1991) holist/analytical dimension, and Allinson and Hayes's (1996) intuitive/analyst dimension.

Before continuing, it is important to raise and discuss the debate among style researchers about the use of bipolar, unidimensional style conceptions. Unidimensional models like the analytic/holistic continuum have sometimes been used to oversimplify learners' approaches to processing information, pigeonholing learners into groups that may or may not reflect their ability to use other styles (Evans & Sadler-Smith, 2006). However, the unidimensional model has received empirical support (Hayes, Allinson, Hudson, & Keasey, 2003) and has a rich array of research findings that have meaningful implications for business education (Allinson, Armstrong, & Hayes, 2001; Armstrong, 2000; Coffield, Moseley, Hall, & Ecclestone, 2004; Sadler-Smith, 1999a). Further, style researchers who have developed and validated unidimensional models emphasize that they are measuring learners' preferred styles, and that it is both possible and necessary for individuals to use their less preferred style when the situation demands it (Hayes et al., 2003; Kirton, 2003).

## BALANCING STYLES

The purpose of the chapter is to connect style theory to practice by applying the analytic/holist dimension to specific business education issues. I argue that effective instructional delivery of business education depends on balancing 'analytic' and 'holist' styles in the learning environment. Overemphasis on either end of the continuum results in an imbalance that leaves students unprepared to utilize both forms of processing effectively. It is important to outline the underlying assumptions of the discussion. First, the style framework used here assumes that styles are preferred ways of processing information, but students can learn to use their less preferred style more effectively (Allinson & Hayes, 1996). Second, this discussion uses as a basis the finding that there is a relationship between teachers' cognitive styles and their teaching styles (Evans, 2004; Evans, Harkins, & Young, 2008), such that analytics and holists tend to use different methods that correspond with their own ways of processing information. This preference for a specific teaching style may reinforce adherence to a single way of processing information, rather than valuing different styles. Third, the chapter suggests that the use of teaching methods that balance analytic/holistic styles can assist students in improving their learning outcomes (Evans et al., 2008). Fourth, and very importantly, the suggestions are propositions about the ways in which style research can be applied to a particular learning environment. Empirical data exist to support the recommendations, but there is no implication of a causal relationship between the business education issues we explore and the failure to use a balanced analytic-holistic teaching approach. Instead, the discussion presents ideas that can be adopted and potentially tested empirically to see if overall learning outcomes in these areas can be improved.

## EMPHASIS ON ANALYTIC PROCESSING

It has long been argued that business education tends to focus on the development of rational decision-making skills at the expense of the development of intuition (Burke & Sadler-Smith, 2006; Mintzberg, 1994). Sadler-Smith explores the need for better training for intuition in a number of studies and two recently published books (Sadler-Smith, 2008, 2009; Sadler-Smith & Burke, 2009; Sadler-Smith & Shefy, 2004, 2007). He argues that the norm of rationality, a vital tool for managerial decision making, has been the main focus of business school curriculum. However, both linear and nonlinear decision-making tools are necessary for effectiveness in a rapidly changing environment (Vance, Groves, Yongsun, & Kindler, 2007). Miller and Ireland (2005) suggest that intuitive decision making involves novel approaches, and individuals require training and practice to develop the ability to invoke such approaches.

In a related sense, there also have been calls to improve the ability of business students to create innovative and practical solutions to business challenges (Davenport, Prusak, & Wilson, 2003). Business schools bear the responsibility of preparing leaders to be innovative, but have been criticized for failing to foster an innovative spirit among their graduates (Doria, Rozanski, & Cohen, 2003; Mintzberg & Gosling, 2002). It can be argued that both of these issues reflect a reliance on analytical processing, and a corresponding lack of emphasis on, and development of, holistic thinking processes. Empirical research has shown that the business school environment favors analytic thinking to the extent that more analytic students tend to have higher grade point averages (Backhaus & Liff, 2007; Skinner & Drake, 2003) and perform better on business projects (Armstrong, 2000). It could be argued that pedagogical practices and evaluation methods encourage and favor analytic processes. There are a variety of instructional practices that can be adopted to balance skill development and prevent bias in assessment or evaluation. In the following section, I outline the ways in which the use of case studies, journaling, mind mapping, and alternative evaluation methods can be used.

## Case Studies

The case study teaching method is a useful way to develop critical thinking and decision-making skills among business students (Corey, 1996). The analysis of real-life business situations offers both analytic and holistic students the opportunity to work to their strengths. Case analysis requires both detail level thinking and broad thematic comprehension (Klebba & Hamilton, 2007). Further, case studies are recognized as an excellent tool for development of higher levels of tolerance for ambiguity (Banning, 2003). Case studies allow students to think on a practical basis, both within and outside the paradigm, benefitting both types of thinkers. While analytic students may excel at analyzing all of the specific details of the case, intuitive students may be stronger at developing new or innovative ways of solving problems (Kirton, 2003). In the case debriefing, instructors can call upon the strengths of both types of thinkers to create breadth and depth of analysis. Instructors can use the case to illustrate the use of intuition in decision making and to show how both global and detail level analysis are needed to develop useful recommendations for a company.

## Journaling

Sadler-Smith and Burke (2009) suggest the use of journaling for developing greater awareness of intuitive processes. Citing Taggart (1997), they describe a process in which students describe in detail their intuitions, creative thoughts that had not yet been evaluated by their rational minds. The process is useful as a means of helping students who prefer analytic processing to recognize situations in which they use holistic processing. It is also useful in validating thought processes of holistic as well as analytic thinkers.

## Mind Mapping

Mind mapping, a process of visually representing connections between ideas (Buzan, 1991), can help develop greater cognitive flexibility. Sadler-Smith and Burke (2009, p. 250) refer to "cognitive mapping" in their work on developing intuition among managers, stating that it can "open up intuitive processes." Mind mapping can be an effective way for those who do not learn sequentially to visualize the relationships among concepts. It allows for reflection and deeper levels of interpretation of ideas. It holds appeal for visual learners, and also allows for a creative spin on ideas. While it is a task that is more likely to correspond with intuitive learners' preferences, it is a good stretch activity for analytics. Sharing maps among different types of learners can help them benefit from the other ways of thinking. Oregon Health and Science University, for instance, utilized the mind mapping technique to improve scientific reasoning and innovation in health care education (Lamont, 2009).

## Alternative Evaluation Methods

Each of the preceding instructional methods is designed to encourage the use of holistic processing methods as an analog to analytic methods that are already popularly used to teach the business school curriculum. But it is also important to develop grading methods that value and encourage both types of processing. Research demonstrates that teachers' cognitive styles affect their teaching methodology (Evans & Waring, 2008), so it is important for them to make efforts to be flexible in delivery and assessment. Rubrics are an effective way to assess student work thoroughly and objectively, especially when developed in tandem with other instructors (Goodrich-Andrade, 2005). The rubric can be developed so that it recognizes both detail-level and global-level thinking. The exercise of rubric development can also have the effect of sensitizing instructors to their own cognitive style, perhaps allowing them to stretch outside of their preferred style when necessary. For example, Fraser and colleagues (2005) describe the use of a rubric for assessing business writing. Through a collaborative process, business faculty developed a writing rubric that incorporated both analytic and holistic elements, providing a comprehensive view of student achievement in the business program.

## IMPROVEMENT OF ANALYTIC PROCESSING

Balancing delivery of the business curriculum is not simply a case of introducing more opportunities for holistic style processing. The value of analytic processing also needs to be supported. Pfeffer and Fong (2004) report that business graduates tend to show weaknesses in their ability to apply analytical skills to improvement of business operations. Further, experts worry that students lack sufficient understanding of basic business processes to enable them to be adaptable on the job (Augier & March, 2007). The following set of instructional techniques is designed to help students improve their use of analytic processing and develop the flexibility to work more comfortably outside their preferred style. These techniques include shifting styles and the use of collaborative processes.

## Shifting Styles

As I have indicated, business education is predominantly analytic in its approach, but it does not always yield strong analytic thinking among its graduates. Imagine the case of students who prefer a holistic style. Courses are generally structured in a linear, sequential, teacher-focused style, but they tend to prefer more informal, divergent learning environments (Evans & Waring, 2006). Faced with a mismatched learning environment, students may need assistance to perform effectively. Teachers can provide structured notes, slides, and detailed lists of important concepts to assist them in remembering details. Students can be directed to use textbook Web sites that provide detailed information that students might have overlooked in their own preparation (Backhaus & Liff, 2007). Even students who prefer analytic processing can benefit from individual assistance and notes to improve their understanding of detailed information.

Going beyond this, students can be encouraged to process information more effectively by shifting style. Encouraging crossover of analytic and holist style behaviors can be done by first helping students to recognize their own preferences, and second, helping them develop strategies for using their less preferred style. The greater the students' level of metacognition, or awareness of the way they think and what they know, the more aware they will be of how to best accomplish a cognitive task (Ramocki, 2007). Student awareness can be increased first by exposing them to a cognitive style measure. This could be followed with a discussion of how their preferred ways of thinking are conducive to certain types of projects, and an acknowledgment of where they tend to run into difficulties. Having conducted a brief lesson on cognitive styles, instructors can then use the techniques discussed here to help both types of students understand the material. During in-class review of concepts, pairing analytics with holists will help students see the information from a different perspective. The pace and interactivity will suit the learning needs of holists while helping them focus on the detail level, and analytics will appreciate the opportunity to rehearse detail-level knowledge and see how it fits at a global level.

## Collaboration

A number of the recommendations made so far have mentioned collaboration as a component of the activity. Collaboration is particularly important in addressing skill development among students with diverse cognitive styles. First, it provides further exposure to different ways of thinking, as discussed earlier. Second, it involves managing the differences created by different cognitive styles (Kirton, 2003). Kirton (2003) describes this phenomenon in his work on group function. He suggests that before a work group can engage in solving the problem that they have come together to solve, they must first solve the problem of how to work together. Awareness of cognitive style differences and their impact on the ways in which people think and solve problems reduces intragroup conflict.

In the design of collaborative exercises, instructors may wish to consider group composition. Group composition is the configuration of attributes of members of a team (Bell, 2007). Personality dimensions, as an example of team member attributes, have been demonstrated to predict differences in team performance (Bell, 2007). Cognitive style has also been shown to relate to team performance outcomes (Liu, Magjuka, & Lee, 2008). Liu and colleagues (2008) found that groups composed of a mixture of different styles outperformed those with homogeneous styles. Conversely, other findings suggest that heterogeneity leads to difficulty in group process and increased team conflict (Tyran & Gibson, 2008). In a study of Armstrong and Priola (2001), homogeneous holist teams were found to engage in more behaviors aimed at maintaining group harmony and more task-oriented behaviors than homogeneous analytic teams. Other research found that teams characterized as 'adaptive' (similar to analytic) on the Kirton Adaption-Innovation scale were more concerned with advancing a project, whereas teams characterized as more 'innovative' (holist) worked more independently with looser time schedules (Buffinton, Jablokow, & Martin, 2002).

With that in mind, assuming that heterogeneous teams will experience more initial conflict, but presumably better long-term outcomes than homogeneous teams, instructors may wish to compose teams made up of various cognitive styles. Students will fare best if given basic group process training before engaging in their work together. Instructors also might choose to form homogeneous teams as an opportunity to compare and contrast the strengths of analytic teams versus holist teams. At the completion of a group exercise, the instructor may debrief, asking each group to describe their process, then comparing and contrasting the different approaches of each type of team. Again, this provides students with a greater meta-awareness of style and its contribution to problem solving.

## WHERE WE GO FROM HERE

### Online Learning

Style research has provided a good foundation for development of recommendations for ways to improve education, particularly in the area of business education. However, as business education delivery models begin to change, there is more for us to learn. Online delivery, hybrid courses, and increased use of technology in business school (Arbaugh et al., 2009) create new learning conditions, and we are not certain of the differential effect of these conditions on students. Some studies have been conducted examining relationships between cognitive style and Internet- or computer-based instruction, but so far, no conclusive evidence has emerged regarding the impact of style on learning. For example, Liu and colleagues (2008) found that cognitive style was not a useful indicator of student online learning performance. On the other hand, Manochehri and Young (2006) found that certain cognitive styles were significantly related to increased knowledge when comparing Web-based to instructor-led formats. In an examination of the usefulness of podcasts for instruction, Hodges, Stackpole-Hodges, and Cox (2008) found a relationship between cognitive style and learner success. Heaton-Shrestha, Gipps, Edirisingha, and Linsey (2007) found that, while cognitive style was not predictive of academic success using a virtual learning environment, it did shape the way students used the technology. The mixed outcomes make it difficult to draw conclusions about specific pedagogical methods.

Two studies have resulted in some practical implications. It appears that analytics benefit from delivery of online content that is structured and sequential (Sadler-Smith & Smith, 2004), while holists tend to get lost in the sequence of steps because they can not yet see the big picture (Choi, Lee, & Jung, 2008). Until more research is conducted, it is difficult to draw conclusions about ways to adapt or direct learning conditions to meet the needs of all learners. Further research should be conducted examining virtual learning environments and Web-based learning and their relationship to cognitive style.

## Simulations

Business simulations are widely used, especially in strategic management or business policy 'capstone' courses (Mitchell, 2004). The Internet has made implementation of business simulations simple and affordable, thus increasing their use even further (Arias-Aranda, 2007). In an effort to bring greater relevance to business education, instructors are more frequently using business simulations in class. Research has shown positive learning outcomes for strategic management simulations, with students gaining a better understanding of decision making and its effects on business outcomes (Anderson, 2005). Again, there has been little research on business simulations and cognitive style. In a study with a small sample, Backhaus (2009) found no relationship between cognitive style and individual performance on a business simulation. Style researchers should explore the ways in which students' cognitive style impacts their use of and performance in business simulations. It would be particularly interesting to explore ways in which their methods of decision making differ based on their cognitive styles.

## CONCLUSION

Frequent criticism of business education centers on its failure to provide a balanced education that emphasizes both analytical decision making and intuition. Contemporary demands are reinvigorating the discussion about ways of thinking, and those demands suggest that we reconsider how we provide both undergraduate and MBA education. First, a greater level of metacognitive awareness among both faculty and students will help us to foster greater appreciation of a diversity of cognitive styles. There are strengths in all styles, and as such they must be nurtured and drawn out. Second, scrutiny of business education should lead to intensified efforts to study the impact of cognitive styles on various pedagogical methods. This will involve a few elements. A more cohesive framework for cognitive style that melds the best and most rigorous elements of style theory must be developed. With that strengthened framework, educators and business practitioners can test the assumptions that we have compiled about how best to educate people to compete in a rapidly changing business environment. Much more research needs to be conducted into newer educational technologies and their effects on learners. For example, how do virtual learning environments impact different types of learners? What about learning material in digital format? Are learners equally equipped to benefit from podcasts, video clips, PowerPoint presentations, videoconferences?

Further, to what extent are business educators prepared to teach diverse learners? Does their academic training prepare them to deal with diversity, or are they programmed to teach and learn in one particular way, based on the traditions of their own disciplines? Finally, do we equally value different learning styles? Are there built-in biases toward certain types of learners simply because they tend to fit within the parameters we have already set forth? Can we prepare for future business challenges under the present system? Organized and intensified attention to cognitive styles is one path that we can follow to expand our knowledge of business learners and business education for the future.

## BIBLIOGRAPHY

Allinson, C.W., Armstrong, S.J., & Hayes, J. (2001). The effects of cognitive style on leader-member exchange: a study of manager-subordinate dyads. *Journal of Occupational and Organizational Psychology, 74*, 201–220.

Allinson, C.W., & Hayes, J. (1996). The Cognitive Style Index: a measure of intuition-analysis for organizational research. *Journal of Management Studies, 33*, 119–135.

Anderson, J.R. (2005). The relationship between student perceptions of team dynamics and simulation game outcomes: an individual-level analysis. *Journal of Education for Business, 81*, 85–90.

Arbaugh, J.B., Godfrey, M.R., Johnson, M., Leisen Pollack, B., Niendorf, B., & Wresch, W. (2009). Research in online and blended learning in the business disciplines: key findings and possible future directions. *The Internet and Higher Education, 12*, 71–87.

Arias-Aranda, D. (2007). Simulating reality for teaching strategic management. *Innovations in Education and Teaching International, 44*, 273–286.

Armstrong, S.J. (2000). The influence of individual cognitive style on performance in management education. *Educational Psychology, 20*, 323–339.

Armstrong, S.J., & Priola, V. (2001). Individual differences in cognitive style and their effects on task and social orientations of self-managed work teams. *Small Group Research, 32*, 283–312.

Augier, M., & March, J.G. (2007). The pursuit of relevance in management education. *California Management Review, 49*, 129–146.

Backhaus, K. (2009). *KAI Style and Team and Individual Performance on a Business Simulation.* Paper presented at the 14th European Learning Styles Information Network (ELSIN) conference, June 17–19, Bulle-en-Gruyère, Switzerland.

Backhaus, K., & Liff, J.P. (2007). Cognitive styles and approaches to studying in management education. *Journal of Management Education, 31*, 445–466.

Banning, K.C. (2003). The effect of the case method on tolerance for ambiguity. *Journal of Management Education, 27*, 556–567.

Bell, S.T. (2007). Deep-level composition variables as predictors of team performance: a meta-analysis. *Journal of Applied Psychology, 92*, 595–615.

Bennis, W.G., & O'Toole, J. (2005). How business schools lost their way. *Harvard Business Review, 83*, 151–152.

Buffinton, K., Jablokow, K., & Martin, K. (2002). Project team dynamics and cognitive style. *Engineering Management Journal, 14*, 25–30.

Burke, L., & Sadler-Smith, E. (2006). Instructor intuition in the educational setting. *Academy of Management Learning and Education, 5*, 169–181.

Buzan, T. (1991). *The Mind Map Book.* New York: Penguin.

Choi, I., Lee, S.J., & Jung, J.W. (2008). Designing multimedia case-based instruction accommodating students' diverse learning styles. *Journal of Educational Multimedia and Hypermedia, 17*, 5–25.

Coffield, F., Moseley, D., Hall, E., & Ecclestone, K. (2004). *Should We Be Using Learning Styles? What Research Has to Say to Practice.* London: Learning and Skills Research Centre.

Corey, R.E. (1996). *The Use of Cases in Management Education.* Boston: Harvard Business School Publishing.

Davenport, T.H., Prusak, L., & Wilson, H.J. (2003). *What's the Big Idea?* Boston: Harvard Business School Press.

Doria, J., Rozanski, H., & Cohen, E. (2003). What business needs from business schools. *Strategy and Business, 32*, 39–45.

Evans, C. (2004). Exploring the relationship between cognitive style and teaching style. *Educational Psychology, 24*, 509–530.

Evans, C., Harkins, M.J., &Young, J. (2008). Exploring teacher styles and cognitive styles: evidence from school teachers in Canada. *North American Journal of Psychology, 10*, 567–582.

Evans, C., & Sadler-Smith, E. (2006). Learning styles in education and training: problems, politicization and potential. *Education and Training, 48(2/3)*, 77–83.

Evans, C., & Waring, M. (2006). Towards inclusive teacher education: sensitising individuals to how they learn. *Educational Psychology, 26*, 499–518.

Evans, C., & Waring, M. (2008). Trainee teachers' cognitive styles and notions of differentiation. *Education and Training, 50*, 140–154.

Fraser, L. Harich, K., Norby, J., Brzovic, K., Rizkallah, T., & Loewy, D. (2005). Diagnostic and value-added assessment of business writing. *Business Communication Quarterly, 68*, 290–305.

Goodrich-Andrade, H. (2005). Teaching with rubrics. *College Teaching, 53*, 27–30.

Hayes, J., Allinson, C.W., Hudson, R.S., & Keasey K. (2003). Further reflections on the nature of intuition-analysis and the construct validity of the Cognitive Style Index. *Journal of Occupational and Organizational Psychology, 76*, 269–278.

Heaton-Shrestha, C., Gipps, C., Edirisingha, P., & Linsey T. (2007). Learning and e-learning in HE: the relationship between student learning style and VLE use. *Research Papers in Education, 22*, 443–464.

Hodges, C.B., Stackpole-Hodges, C.L., & Cox, K.M. (2008). Self-efficacy, self-regulation, and cognitive style as predictors of achievement with podcast instruction. *Journal of Educational Computing Research, 38*, 139–153.

Kirton, M.J. (2003). *Adaption-Innovation in the Context of Diversity and Change.* New York: Routledge.

Klebba, J.M., & Hamilton, J.G. (2007). Structured case analysis: developing critical thinking skills in a marketing case course. *Journal of Marketing Education, 29*, 132–137.

Lamont, J. (2009). Managing critical knowledge in higher education. *KM World, 18*, 20–25.

Liu, X., Magjuka, R.J., & Lee, S. (2008). The effects of cognitive thinking styles, trust, conflict management on online students' learning and virtual team performance. *British Journal of Educational Technology, 39*, 829–846.

Manochehri, N., & Young. J.I. (2006). The impact of student learning styles with Web-based learning or instructor-based learning on student knowledge and satisfaction. *Quarterly Review of Distance Education, 7*, 313–316.

Messick, S. (1984). The nature of cognitive styles: problems and promise in educational practice. *Educational Psychologist, 19*, 59–74.

Miller, A. (1987). Cognitive styles: an integrated model. *Educational Psychology, 7*, 251–268.

Miller, C.C., & Ireland, R.D. (2005). Intuition in strategic decision making: friend or foe in the fast-paced 21st century? *Academy of Management Executive, 19*, 19–30.

Mintzberg, H. (1994). The fall and rise of strategic planning. *Harvard Business Review, 72*, 107–114.

Mintzberg, H., & Gosling, J. (2002). Educating managers beyond borders. *Academy of Management Learning and Education, 1*, 64–76.

Mitchell, R.C. (2004). Combining cases and computer simulations in strategic management courses. *Journal of Education for Business, 79*, 198–204.

Mortimore, T. (2009). *From Style Theory to Practical Teaching-Developing Strategies and Exploring Their Impact.* Paper presented at the 14th European Learning Styles Information Network (ELSIN) conference, June 17–19, Bullen-en-Gruyère, Switzerland.

Pfeffer, J., & Fong, C.T. (2004). The business school 'business': some lessons from the US experience. *Journal of Management Studies, 41*, 1501–1520.

Ramocki, S.P. (2007). Metacognition and transfer: keys to improving marketing education. *Journal of Marketing Education, 29*, 18–24.

Rayner, S.G. (2000). Reconstructing style differences in thinking and learning: profiling learning performance. In R.J. Riding & S.G. Rayner (Eds.), *International Perspectives on Individual Differences* (pp. 115–180). Stamford, CT: Ablex.

Rayner, S.G. (2008). *Are You Researching in Style? What about Epistemology, Paradigm Shifts and the RIG?* Paper presented at the 13th Annual Conference of the European Learning Styles Information Network (ELSIN). Gent: Vlerick Leuven Gent Management School.

Rayner, S., & Riding, R. (1997). Towards a categorization of cognitive styles and learning styles. *Educational Psychology, 17*, 5–29.

Riding, R.J., & Cheema, I. (1991). Cognitive styles—an overview and integration. *Educational Psychology, 11*, 193–215.

Sadler-Smith, E. (1999a). Intuition-Analysis style and approaches to studying. *Educational Studies, 25*, 159–173.

Sadler-Smith, E. (1999b). Intuition-analysis cognitive style and learning preferences of business and management students: a UK exploratory study. *Journal of Managerial Psychology, 14,* 26–38.

Sadler-Smith, E. (2008). *Inside Intuition.* Abingdon, UK: Routledge.

Sadler-Smith, E. (2009). *The Intuitive Mind.* New York: Wiley.

Sadler-Smith, E., & Burke, L.A. (2009). Fostering intuition in management education: activities and resources. *Journal of Management Education, 33,* 239–262.

Sadler-Smith, E., & Shefy, E. (2004). The intuitive executive: understanding and applying "gut feel" in decision making. *Academy of Management Executive, 18,* 76–91.

Sadler-Smith, E., & Shefy, E. (2007). Developing intuitive awareness in management education. *Academy of Management Learning and Education, 6,* 186–205.

Sadler-Smith, E., & Smith, P. (2004). Strategies for accommodating individual's styles and preferences in flexible learning programmes. *British Journal of Educational Technology, 35,* 395–412.

Skinner, N.F., & Drake, J.M. (2003). Behavioral implications of adaption-innovation: III: Adaption-innovation, achievement motivation, and academic performance. *Social Behavior and Personality: An International Journal, 31,* 101–105.

Sternberg, R.J., Grigorenko, E.L., & Zhang, L.F. (2008). Styles of learning and thinking matter in instruction and assessment. *Perspectives on Psychological Science, 3,* 486–506.

Taggart, W. (1997). Discovering and understanding intuition. *Exceptional Human Experience: Studies of the Unitive, Spontaneous, Imaginal, 15,* 174–188.

Tyran, K.L., & Gibson, C.B. (2008). Is what you see, what you get? The relationship among surface- and deep-level heterogeneity characteristics, group efficacy, and team reputation. *Group and Organization Management, 33,* 46–76.

Vance, C.M., Groves, K.S., Yongsun, P., & Kindler, H. (2007). Understanding and measuring linear-nonlinear thinking style for enhanced management education and professional practice. *Academy of Management Learning and Education, 6,* 167–185.

# 18 Learning-Styles-Based Differentiating Instruction for At-Risk Students

## Rationale, Research Documentation, Assessment Tools, and Alternative Approaches

*Rita Dunn and Andrea Honigsfeld*

## INTRODUCTION

This chapter offers an overview of learning-styles-based differentiating instruction for at-risk students. First, the authors place the Dunn and Dunn model of learning styles in the larger context of style research and acknowledge and respond to the scholarly criticism that has been evoked by the model. Based on the Dunn and Dunn model, the authors identify eight considerable challenges educators face and offer a rationale for using learning-style-responsive instruction in kindergarten–12th grade (K–12) schools by synthesizing seminal research conducted with the model. After three research-based learning-style assessment tools are introduced, several school-based alternative approaches to working with at-risk students are outlined. The authors conclude that many at-risk students might not need special education services if their diverse learning needs were accommodated.

## CRITICAL PERSPECTIVES ON LEARNING STYLES

Among many others, Zhang and Sternberg (2005) recognized that style researchers and practitioners have been continuously faced with three critical issues. To date, debates continue (1) whether style should be viewed as value-laden or value-free, (2) whether styles are perceived as relatively permanent, stable characteristics (also referred to as traits) or more flexible, modifiable states, and (3) finally, whether the various theoretical models of style are different constructs each identifying unique features or similar constructs merely bearing different labels. In addition, learning style has been a subject of several critical reviews that question the core construct of style (Stahl, 2004), the validity of the many instruments that have been developed to measure it (Coffield, Moseley, Hall, & Ecclestone, 2004), the research methodologies (Curry, 1990), or the relevance of using learning style methodology in practice (Willingham, 2005). More specifically, some have criticized the statistical procedures in the two meta-analyses conducted on the Dunn and Dunn model (Kavale, Hirshoren, & Forness, 1998; Kavale & LeFever, 2007). As an overall recommendation, Coffield and colleagues (2004) suggested that

> the research field of learning styles needs independent, critical, longitudinal and large-scale studies with experimental and control groups to test the claims for pedagogy made by the test developers. (Coffield et al., 2004, p. 144)

Despite the critical reviews, or perhaps in face of them, extensive research continues to emerge focusing on (1) "conceptual integration of previous work on styles as well as proposals of new styles" (Zhang & Sternberg, 2005, p. 4) and (2) "empirical research aimed at investigating the relationships among the different style labels" (Zhang & Sternberg, 2005, p. 4). Since the early inception of the Dunn and Dunn model in 1978, a pragmatic and practitioner-oriented emphasis has been central to the model's creators and researchers both associated with (see Dunn & Griggs, 2007) and independent of St. John's University (see, for example, Boström & Lassen, 2006; Given, 2002; Kutay, 2008; Orden, 2004; Thies, 1999–2000). The unique contribution of the Dunns is reflected in the comprehensive and integrative nature of the model and its assessment tools. Recently, those conducting research specifically with the Dunn and Dunn model have focused on developing a suite of assessment instruments and related instructional approaches that help translate learning style theory into practical pedagogy (Burke & Dunn, 1998; Dunn, Rundle, & Burke, 2007; Missere & Dunn, 2008; Rundle & Dunn, 1995–2006). The following section undergirds the importance of continuing this line of research and pedagogical practice.

## EIGHT CHALLENGES EDUCATORS FACE IN THE US

The United States' No Child Left Behind (NCLB) legislation mandated increased achievement among officially classified at-risk students and sought to measure academic gains through standardized test scores without developing and implementing pedagogy that would support such change.

1. The first challenge many educators have encountered historically is to improve student achievement with data-driven decisions emerging from test scores, dropout rates, attendance numbers, opinion surveys, gap analyses, demographic statistics, and performance growth. Such data, although often readily available in the US educational context, cannot be effectively used to identify the *causes* of academic failures;

additionally, they certainly cannot suggest how to manage educational diversity and improve instruction for all learners. Such data only document what is wrong—not *why,* and certainly not *how to replace what is wrong with what would be better.*

2. The second challenge is that educators are frequently trained and retrained to try emerging educational programs, new teaching materials, and instructional resources that come along without first methodically researching for whom it is and for whom it is *not* effective. Many administrators admire new ideas and accept without questioning commercial promoters' statements concerning the value of the merchandise they sell.

3. The third challenge is that teachers and administrators in many schools and school districts adopt new programs on face value. It is only after implementation that the professionals realize that the innovation works no better than the previously discarded program—but often with different students.

4. The fourth challenge is that teachers often are required to implement more than one new program at a time. Adopting a new instructional approach with fidelity requires (a) conscious monitoring to determine for whom it is effective and for whom it is not, (b) the skills for examining its effects objectively, and (c) data-driven analyses and publications to develop public awareness about its impact.

5. These lead to the fifth challenge. In the US, most teachers receive limited training in evaluating program effectiveness or even in determining the effects of the instruction they deliver. In addition, when more than one instructional approach is explored or implemented simultaneously, no one actually knows which contributed to either achievement gains or losses—or for whom, mostly because group rather than individual progress is what most researchers focus on.

6. The sixth challenge is that commercial vendors and consultants use the word 'research' differently from the way educational researchers do. When researchers examine the effects of a program on subgroups of students, such as English language learners' (ELLs) or at-risk students' achievement and/or attitudes or behaviors, valuable knowledge is developed concerning whether a particular approach is worthy of adoption for poor achievers or not.

7. A seventh challenge is that many researchers insist on an experimental/control design, believing that it alone provides objective data. That perception is inaccurate when seeking to increase *individuals'* achievement. When involved in school-based studies, a counterbalanced, repeated-measures design is a stronger plan for identifying which method is best for Poorly-Achieving-Patrick as opposed to Highly-Achieving-Henrietta or Adequately-Achieving-but-Apathetic-Alex. Because we know that individuals learn differently from members of their own family as well as from their classmates, seeking

*group* improvement is neither as efficient nor as promising as identifying which methods tend to help at-risk students reverse their failing school performance, and enhance their achievement on all assessments including standardized tests.

8. An eighth challenge is not recognizing that individuals labeled as 'at-risk' do not necessarily learn in the same way or with the same instructional strategies. Individual needs within this group vary by age, gender, motivation, perceptual strengths, and cognitive processing to a potentially greater degree; thus the most at-risk students may benefit more greatly from an awareness of their style differences and the provision of learning-style-responsive activities.

There is no single strategy that improves achievement for all—or even most—learners and, therefore, there is no best way to teach everyone—or even most required core subjects. Educators who continue to advocate any single approach to teaching reveal limited understanding of decades of research on learning styles. There are many effective instructional strategies, but teachers need to experiment with those that seem to be responsive to how each learner begins to concentrate on, process, absorb, internalize, and retain new and difficult academic information. Then they need to discern which produces the most short-term gains versus long-term retention, and the best attitudes among at-risk students.

## WHY DIFFERENTIATING THROUGH LEARNING STYLES IS RECOMMENDED FOR INSTRUCTIONAL IMPROVEMENT

Dunn and Dunn and their colleagues engaged in four decades of doctoral research at St. John's University, New York, exploring which methods impacted most on poorly performing versus well performing learners. See *Synthesis of the Dunn and Dunn Learning-Style Model Research: Who, What, When, Where, and So What?* (Dunn & Griggs, 2007) for more on the following: Through ongoing experiments at elementary through higher education levels in many disciplines, researchers identified what appeared to be most effective with auditory versus visual/print versus visual/picture versus tactual versus kinesthetic learners. Through repeated studies, they found that some students absorb and retain what someone is saying better when they interact verbally—either with the speaker, someone nearby, or by talking to themselves. They learned who remembers best independently, in a pair or a small group, or with either an authoritative or collegial adult. They learned who needs quiet and who needs sound while concentrating, and who is distracted by either or both, who needs bright light and who becomes hyperactive in the very same amount of illumination. They found who learns best passively and who requires active engagement—and how much; who thinks sequentially and who thinks globally—and how to teach to both types of processors simultaneously. They learned about students who need, and those who defy, imposed structure. They also learned who tends to do what teachers ask, who will not, and how to work with many nonconformists who function poorly in conventional schools.

In addition, they experimented with seven different ways of teaching an identical curriculum, with whom each strategy worked well and with whom it did not (e.g., Ansalone & Ming, 2006; Braio, Dunn, Beasley, Quinn, & Buchanan, 1997; Tully, Dunn, & Hlawaty, 2006). These diverse strategies are explained later in this chapter to guide interested readers toward reducing the number of at-risk students by differentiating instruction for all (Dunn & Dunn, 2008; Dunn & Honigsfeld, 2009).

## A PROPOSAL FOR THE USE OF LEARNING STYLE DIAGNOSTIC TOOLS

We propose that all school-aged students—especially those at risk for academic failure—should be assessed for their learning styles when they first enter school and then reassessed periodically, preferably every two or three years. Using learning style assessments, raising awareness about diverse learning needs, and implementing learning-style-responsive instructional strategies with those most at risk are likely to prevent (1) numerous unnecessary referrals, (2) misdiagnosing students who do not actually have learning disabilities, or (3) misidentifying the needs that struggling youth have when they merely learn *differently* from many other children.

To substantiate our recommendation, first we will examine the broader educational and legal context for administering diagnostic assessments for at-risk students. Then, we will explore several learning style assessments available for students in grades 2 to high school and conclude with the benefits of drawing on the findings gained from these tools.

### Response to Failure: A Failed Response

In 2001, a Commission on Excellence in Special Education was established in the US to strengthen schooling for students with disabilities. After holding more than a dozen public hearings and meetings across the US, the commission analyzed feedback received from administrators, education officials, parents, the public, and teachers. The responses were summarized in a report entitled *A New Era: Revitalizing Special Education for Children and Their Families* (U.S. Department of Education Office of Special Education and Rehabilitative Services, 2002). In the executive summary of that report, nine findings were highlighted, one of which stated that the current system uses an antiquated model that waits for a child to fail, instead of a model based on prevention and intervention. It chastised that "too little emphasis is put on prevention, early and accurate identification of learning, and behavior problems" (Summary of Findings, para. 2). Aligned with those findings, one of the commission's three major recommendations was to create a "model of prevention, not a model of failure" (Summary of Major Recommendations, para. 5).

## Creating a Culture of Success

The commission is not the only group of educators and researchers who argue that instead of waiting for a child to fail, failure must be prevented. Proponents of learning-styles-based differentiated instruction have advocated creating a culture of successful learners by identifying and responding to students' learning styles as early as first grade (Burke & Shea Doolan, 2006; Dunn & Blake, 2008; Dunn & DeBello, 1999; Dunn & Griggs, 2007; Milgram, Dunn, & Price, 1993).

In an effort to improve special education, in 2004 Public Law (PL) 108–446, also known as the reauthorization of IDEA (Individuals with Disabilities Education Act), was signed. In response to previous criticisms, regulations for evaluations and assessments of potentially academically at-risk students were identified as follows:

> The local educational agency shall use a variety of assessment tools and strategies to gather relevant functional, developmental, and learning skills, including information provided by the parent that might assist in determining whether the child has a disability. It required that the content of the child's individualized education program (IEP) include prescriptions related to enabling the child to be involved in, and evidence progress in the general education curriculum, or, for preschool children, to participate in appropriate activities. It stipulated that no single measure or assessment be the sole criterion for determining whether a child has a disability or for determining an appropriate educational program for the child. It also required the use of technically sound, research-based instruments that assess the relative contribution of cognitive and behavioral factors, in addition to physical or developmental factors. (Public Law (PL) 108–446, 2004, pp. 58–59)

However, no specific guidelines are offered within the framework of PL 108–446. Instead, each state or local education agency is given discretionary rights concerning the type of diagnostic tools or assessments to use. Correct interpretation of the law encourages districts to establish Child Study Teams (CSTs) or Instructional Support Teams (ISTs), which offer teachers a framework to hold regular pre-referral meetings to discuss individual student progress and to consider multiple interventions or assessment tools that are research-based, relevant to the needs of the learner in question, and helpful toward that individual making positive academic progress.

---

*Lakeland Central School District: learning styles in their response to intervention program*

As reported by Lois Favre, Assistant Superintendent, in adopting and developing a Response to Intervention Program as required by NCLB, the Lakeland Central School District (www.lakelandschools.org) has used the Dunn and Dunn model, its strategies, and the student reports to build a strong base of differentiated strategies. They use the self-reported student profiles as a guide to interventions that work for students (strengthening Tier 1 instruction for all students). In recent years, they have seen a reduction in their classification rate and, more important, they have seen students receive remediation quickly, and be returned to their general education program. Remediation is no longer a life sentence! Many strategies are tried before a student is classified. The use of data to inform next steps in the instructional program begins with the individual profile and continues as teachers plan lessons using the group profile to assist in how to differentiate their lessons to meet the needs of students.

---

## IDENTIFYING LEARNING STYLES: INSTRUMENTS, INTERPRETATIONS, BASES FOR DIFFERENTIATION

Before we consider kindergarten–12th grade (K–12) learners as being at risk and assigning them to special education classes, it is imperative that teachers and parents make a concerted effort to identify accurately how students learn, using thoroughly researched, valid, and reliable assessments. In fact, administering such assessments would benefit all children whether they are at risk of failure, struggling, on grade level, or excelling in school, for knowledge of how they prefer to study and master challenging content, as this makes cognitive processing less stressful and more enjoyable. Therefore, utilizing learning style assessments may serve as a tool for (1) identifying and managing learning differences as presented in a diverse classroom, (2) developing inclusive educational practices, and (3) preventing overreferrals of at-risk students for special education services.

Parents and educators intuitively know that each child learns differently from the next. Some of those differences are observable either during in-school instructional time or at home while doing homework. More often than not, though, learning-style characteristics either are not apparent or may be misinterpreted. For example, what are some of the reasons for students' lack of concentration or misbehavior in school? Why do some constantly fidget or frequently move or get out of their seats? Are students disinterested in the material or are they tactual learners who need to manipulate objects while learning? Do many healthy children need frequent mobility? Does sitting passively in hard chairs for any length of time diminish concentration? Are some global processors unable to focus on fact after fact without understanding the entire concept—which often is the last item discussed in the lesson? How do conventional school requirements affect many youth personally? Do many previously failing students become scholars or professionally successful *after* formal schooling?

Certain learning-style assessments accurately answer these questions about children who do not function maximally during school hours. Teams of doctoral core faculty and graduate students at St. John's University, collaborating with Professors Rita and Kenneth Dunn, accepted the challenge of designing and periodically redesigning appropriate, reliable, and valid instruments based on more than thirty-five years of research on learning styles (Dunn & Griggs, 2007). Each assessment described following has been developed and widely tested for a particular age group. Each has been field tested internationally to establish its validity and reliability.

## What is Common among All These Learning Style Instruments?

### Dimensions of Assessment

Each of the instruments based on the Dunn and Dunn model assesses students' individual strengths in the following areas: (1) instructional environment: sound, light, temperature, and seating design; (2) emotional variables: motivation, single- or multi-task persistence, conformity (responsibility), and need for internal or external structure; (3) sociological variables: learning alone, with a partner, in a small group or team, with peers, with an authoritative or collegial adult, and/or in any combination of these; (4) physiological variables: auditory, visual, visual/print, visual/picture, tactual, and/or kinesthetic perceptual preferences; food or liquid intake, chronobiological energy levels, and mobility needs; and (5) indications of global versus analytic processing preferences and impulsive versus reflective inclinations.

### Benefits to Students

Each Web-based interactive assessment invites learners to identify how they prefer to learn as they begin reading an engaging story. The multiple-choice questions embedded in the story line and illustrated graphically allow both analytic and global processors to work well with each appropriate instrument. By taking the assessment and then receiving an itemized report, students have an increased opportunity to develop metacognitive awareness of their own learning strengths. They receive detailed feedback on every dimension of their learning style profile, including recommendations for how to capitalize on their strengths and study skills to cope in varied instructional settings. Critical to this exchange is providing guidance to students and their caretakers on how such information may be most effectively used.

### Information for Educators

Teachers and administrators have access to three types of outcome reports. The first two also are available to each student: a computerized graphic representation of each student's preferred learning style, called the *One Page Student Report* and the *Full Report*, which is a multi-page narrative explanation and study guide based on each individual student's strengths. Combining information from the individual reports and group profiles, teachers can obtain recommendations concerning how to: (1) redesign the classroom environment to match students' environmental needs; (2) use the best time of day for each student to be most productive; (3) respond to perceptual and processing style differences; (4) group students for instruction based on various dimensions of learning preferences; and (5) identify students who need learning-style-based accommodations (such as informal seating, snacks, or periodic mobility) while learning to enhance the effectiveness of how they learn.

## What is Unique About Each Assessment?

### Elementary Learning Style Assessment (ELSA)

ELSA (Dunn et al., 2007) is designed for children ages 7 to 9. ELSA includes three stories, each followed by a series of questions that assess students' individual learning styles. Before they begin, users are prompted to choose a story either about pirates or the circus. Humor, illustrations, and exciting happenings make the instrument interesting to youngsters who are made aware that there are no *right* or *wrong* answers to the questions posed, only their preferences, thus reducing stress and increasing spontaneous and more accurate responses.

### Learning Style: The Clue to You! (LS: CY!)

LS: CY! (Burke & Dunn, 1998) is appropriate for ages 9 to 13. Similar to ELSA, the assessment of learning style occurs through a global format. Students read a detective story as they answer questions about their own learning inclinations.

### Learning in Vogue: Elements of Style: (LIVES)

LIVES (Missere & Dunn, 2008) is designed for ages 14 to 18. An opening poem invites students to consider styles that are fashionable. Stories, humor, and illustrations help high-school students determine their personal learning style strengths.

## Implications for At-Risk Students

Since each instrument identifies individuals' learning patterns—a term synonymous with their learning *strengths*—the emphasis is shifted from deficiencies (what students do not have or are not able to do) to preferences and strengths. This shift is viewed by many educators as integral and instrumental in creating a culture of prevention and success in the schools rather than a culture of failure (Brand, Dunn, & Greb, 2002; Dunn, Honigsfeld, & Shea Doolan, 2009; Favre, 2007; Mitchell, 2000).

## HOW TO APPLY LEARNING STYLES THEORY TO EDUCATIONAL PRACTICE: DIFFERENTIATING INSTRUCTION BASED ON LEARNING STYLE STRENGTHS

One of the prevailing criticisms of the Dunn and Dunn model is that most research and practical, school-based implementations are carried out by St. John's doctoral graduates (over 160 of them personally mentored by Dr. Rita Dunn). To counter this criticism, a case study of St. George's School in Wanganui, New Zealand, under the leadership of Charlotte Humphrey, is included to demonstrate learning styles implementation in New Zealand.

---

### Learning in style Down Under: St George's School, Wanganui, NZ

Teachers at St George's School in Wanganui, New Zealand recognize and agree that learning style approaches can make all the difference to the self-esteem and attainment of students at risk of underachievement. The same is true, in fact, for high-achievers and for others who fall somewhere between the two extremes on the scholastic continuum.

What's special then about St George's? St George's has maintained a proud commitment to learning styles education since the early 1990s. All staff at St George's complete the Building Excellence survey and undertake yearly professional development based on the Dunn and Dunn learning style model. St George's students enjoy regular opportunities to assess and/or review their learning styles using age-appropriate, online interactive inventories. Their parents

*continued*

*continued*

and caregivers are an integral part of the process and, having received their children's individual learning style reports, are invited to attend a hands-on learning styles evening early in the school year.

As a result, there exists in the school a strong culture of respect for individual difference, and students whose learning strengths and preferences differ from their teachers' or their classmates' are unlikely to become dislocated or isolated. Instead, they are encouraged to make responsible decisions and choices about where and how they might best approach new and difficult tasks, meet their objectives, and experience success.

A few specific and successful strategies used to enhance the performance of at-risk learners include:

- team learning activities for introducing new or challenging information and ideas in inquiry lessons;
- a Circle of Knowledge to summarize learning at the end of a unit or after a shared experience (Students can 'pass' when unsure but are not penalized and will benefit from listening to other children's responses.);
- reading activity cards to provide a range of options for children who need choices and variety;
- a taped line (or a long mat) to safely accommodate mobile readers who like to walk up and down with their books;
- Velcro task cards (which stick to the carpet or the wall) so tactile and kinesthetic students can bend and stretch as they look for connections between texts;
- spelling 'sliders' for matching various patterns within words (e.g., fixed initial blends slide past alternative endings);
- vocabulary jigsaws (which are cut through the letters rather than between them) to help students build an internal image of a word and improve sight reading;
- color-coded, self-correcting, lift-the-flaps materials (e.g., a tactile grid for making sense of the periodic table in science) made and explained by older or more confident students;
- scale models (for example, animal enclosures) to motivate hands-on learners to explore dimensions and ratios in math;
- alphabet floor mats (with word classes, capital letters and hyphens) for spelling and word study;
- wrap-arounds for matching corresponding sentences;
- out-of-school visits to trigger episodic memory/memory of location.

As demonstrated in the case study, Charlotte Humphrey at St. George's in Wanganui, New Zealand, identifies key steps for her staff to promote a shared understanding of learning styles and help students acquire practical ways to use their learning styles when learning new and difficult information:

- staff receives professional development to enable them to become familiar with the theory and practical implementation of the elements of the Dunn and Dunn Learning Styles Model;
- students' learning styles are assessed regularly and their individual learning strengths identified;
- parents are informed about learning styles and about their children's learning style preferences through workshops, school visits, and newsletters;
- staff provides for a range of learning style preferences (in particular global/analytic, A/V/T/K) when planning units of study;
- the classroom environment caters for a variety of different learning styles;
- over time, students learn to use their learning strengths without prompting.

In addition to this vignette, Table 18.1 summarizes key, research-based, well-documented instructional approaches that respond effectively to a variety of learning styles.

## CONCLUSION: HOW WILL EDUCATORS COPE WHEN THERE ARE NO MORE AT-RISK LEARNERS?

Assessing students' learning styles must be the first instrument used by any team or any other concerned educator to reveal students' existing strengths rather than their weaknesses. At-risk students need an opportunity to recognize their strengths and so must all educators who work with them. To make schooling successful, students need to express their instructional preferences verbally and advocate for strategies responsive to their personal learning needs. Above all, educators need to consider learning styles before hastily referring children and misdiagnosing them with disabilities instead of recognizing and celebrating their individual differences.

## BIBLIOGRAPHY

Ansalone, G., & Ming, C. (2006). Programming students for academic success: the PLS—an alternative to traditional tracking. *Educational Research Quarterly, 29*, 3–10.

*Table 18.1* Summary of Learning-Style-Responsive Instructional Strategies

| *Learning-style instructional resources* | *Descriptions* | *What type of learners do they work for?* |
| --- | --- | --- |
| Tactual and Kinesthetic Resources and Activities | • Pic-a-holes<br>• Task cards<br>• Learning circles<br>• Electroboards<br>• Wall games<br>• Floor games | Those who:<br>• have tactual and kinesthetic perceptual preferences<br>• may also have visual perceptual preferences<br>• are motivated, persistent, responsible<br>• need structure |
| Programmed Learning Sequences (PLSs) | • Illustrated, interactive story book on target subject<br>• Learning occurs in small increments<br>• Periodical reinforcements through game-like tactual resources<br>• Audio support allows students to follow along | Those who:<br>• are motivated<br>• need structure<br>• are persistent and/or responsible<br>• work well alone or in a pair<br>• have visual/tactual preferences |
| Contract Activity Packages (CAPs) | • Objectives<br>• Activity alternatives<br>• Reporting alternatives<br>• Alternative resources<br>• Small-group techniques<br>• Objectives-based assessment | Appropriate for two types of learners:<br>• motivated, auditory, and visual, task-persistent learners<br>• auditory and/or visual learners who may be non-conforming and challenging to reach |

Boström, L., & Lassen, L.M. (2006). Unraveling learning, learning styles, learning strategies and metacognition. *Education and Training, 48,* 178–189.

Braio, A., Dunn, R., Beasley, T.M., Quinn, P., & Buchanan, K. (1997). Incremental implementation of learning style strategies among urban low achievers. *Journal of Educational Research, 91,* 15–25.

Brand, S., Dunn, R., & Greb, F. (2002). Learning styles of students with attention deficit hyperactivity disorder: who are they and how can we teach them? *The Clearing House, 75,* 268–273.

Burke, K., & Dunn, R. (1998). *Learning Styles: The Clue to You* (LS: CY). Retrieved March 11, 2009, from http://www.learningstyles.net

Burke, K., & Shea Doolan, L. (2006). What professors need to know about their students' learning styles: how can educators help to produce the best learners? In R. Sims & S. Sims (Eds.), *Learning Styles and Learning: A Key to Meeting the Accountability Demands in Education* (pp. 163–174). Hauppauge, NY: Nova Science Publishers.

Coffield, F., Moseley, D., Hall, E., & Ecclestone, K. (2004). *Learning Styles and Pedagogy in Post-16 Learning: A Systematic and Critical Review.* London: Learning and Skills Research Centre.

Curry, L. (1990). One critique of the research on learning styles. *Educational Leadership, 48,* 50–56.

Dunn, K.J., & Dunn, R. (2008). Teaching to at–risk students' learning styles: solutions based on international research. *Insights on Learning Disabilities: From Prevailing Theories to Validated Practices, 5,* 89–101.

Dunn, R., & Blake, B.E. (Eds.) (2008). *Teaching Every Child to Read: Innovative and Practical Strategies for K–8 Educators and Caretakers.* Lanham, MD: Rowman & Littlefield.

Dunn, R., & DeBello, T.C. (Eds.) (1999). *Improved Test Scores, Attitudes, and Behaviors in America's Schools: Supervisors' Success Stories.* Westport, CT: Bergin & Garvey.

Dunn, R., & Dunn, K. (1978). *Teaching Students through Their Individual Learning Styles: A Practical Approach.* Reston, VA: Prentice Hall.

Dunn, R., & Griggs, S.A. (2007). *Synthesis of the Dunn and Dunn Learning-Style Model Research: Who, What, When, Where, and So What?* Jamaica, NY: St. John's University.

Dunn, R., & Honigsfeld, A. (2009). *Differentiating Instruction for At-Risk Students: What to Do and How to Do It.* Lanham, MD: Rowman & Littlefield.

Dunn, R., Honigsfeld, A., & Shea Doolan, L. (2009). Impact of learning-style instructional strategies on students' achievement and attitudes: perceptions of educators in diverse institutions. *The Clearing House, 82,* 135–140.

Dunn, R., Rundle, S., & Burke, K. (2007). *Elementary Learning Styles Assessment* (ELSA). Retrieved March 11, 2009, from http://www.learningstyles.net

Favre, L.R. (2007). Analysis of the transformation of a low socioeconomic status African American, New Orleans elementary facility into a Demonstration Learning Style School of Excellence. *Journal of Urban Education: Focus on Enrichment, 4,* 79–90.

Given, K.B. (2002). *Teaching to the Brain's Natural Learning Systems.* Alexandria, VA: ASCD.

Kavale, K.A., Hirshoren A., & Forness, S.R. (1998). Meta-analytic validation of the Dunn and Dunn model of learning-style preferences: a critique of what was Dunn. *Learning Disabilities Research and Practice, 13,* 75–80.

Kavale, K.A., & LeFever, G.B. (2007). Dunn and Dunn model of learning-style preferences: critique of Lovelace meta-analysis. *The Journal of Educational Research, 101,* 94–97.

Kutay, H. (2008). *Learning Styles and Culture.* Saarbrücken, Germany: VDM Verlag.

Milgram, R.M., Dunn, R., & Price, G.E. (Eds.) (1993). *Teaching and Counseling Gifted and Talented Adolescents: An International Learning Style Perspective.* Westport, CT: Praeger.

Missere, N., & Dunn, R. (2008). *Learning in Vogue: Elements of Style (LIVES).* Retrieved March 11, 2009, from http://www.learningstyles.net

Mitchell, D. (2000). Using learning styles to help learning disabled students meet the new standards: to each his own. *IMPACT on Instructional Improvement, 29,* 37–42.

Orden, M.V. (2004). Perceptual strengths and hemispheric preferences of SMU's education students and faculty, school year 2003–2004: a correlational study. *Saint Mary's University Research Journal, 6,* 1–54.

Public Law 108–446–DEC. 3, 2004. Retrieved July 1, 2008, from http://www.copyright.gov/legislation/pl108–446.pdf

Rundle, S., & Dunn, R. (1995–2006). *Building Excellence Survey.* Retrieved March 11, 2009, from http://www.learningstyles.net

Stahl, S.A. (2004). Different strokes for different folks? A critique of learning styles. In L. Abbeduto (Ed.), *Taking Sides: Clashing on Controversial Issues in Educational Psychology* (3rd ed.; pp. 98–107). Gilford, CT: McGraw-Hill/Dushkin.

Thies, A.P. (1999–2000). The neuropsychology of learning styles. *National Forum of Applied Educational Research Journal, 13,* 50–62.

Tully, D., Dunn, R., & Hlawaty, H. (2006). Effects of programmed learning sequences on the mathematics test scores of Bermudian middle-school students. *Research in Middle-Level Education Online, 30,* 1–11.

U.S. Department of Education Office of Special Education and Rehabilitative Services. (2002). *A New Era: Revitalizing Special Education for Children and Their Families (Summary of Findings,* para. 2). (*Summary of Major Recommendations,* para. 5). Retrieved from http://www2.ed.gov/inits/commissionsboards/whspecialeducation/reports/images/Pres_Rep.pdf at March 11, 2008.

Willingham, D.T. (2005). Do visual, auditory, and kinesthetic learners need visual, auditory, and kinesthetic instruction? *American Educator, 29,* 31–35.

Zhang, L.F., & Sternberg, R.J. (2005). A threefold model of intellectual styles. *Educational Psychology Review, 17,* 1–53.

# 19 Putting Style Theory into Practice in the UK Secondary School
## Inclusive Classrooms for Vulnerable Learners

*Tilly Mortimore*

## INTRODUCTION: STYLE THEORY, INCLUSION, AND THE CHALLENGE OF THE SECONDARY SCHOOL

This chapter will show how understanding the concept of style, as defined following, can help professionals to include every learner in their classroom. It will explore the challenges that secondary schooling can pose for vulnerable learners, and suggest practical ways to utilize research into style theory so that students can understand their preferences and take control of their learning.

Attitudes to diversity and individual differences in education are changing radically. Theory, for example, has moved on from a 'medical' model that presented disability as rooted in personal, biological, or cognitive impairments and emphasized personal tragedy, expert diagnosis, and specialized, separate facilities. Activists claim this 'medical model' promotes dominance and reduces choice, encouraging discrimination, oppression, and exclusion from society (Barton, 1996). An emergent 'social' model switched focus from the disability, relieving the individual of the 'problem', thereby suggesting that it is the physical and conceptual barriers which oppress disabled people.

Internationally, this 'social' model is changing the ways educationalists work. Provision designed by 'experts', which label and segregate individuals, is being reframed. Mainstream teachers are charged with identifying and removing barriers set up in our classrooms and systems. A strong international agenda aims to exchange social exclusion, linked with disability, for social justice and equally shared resources. In the UK and the US, disability legislation applied to education (Special Educational Needs and Disabilities Act [SENDA], 2001; The Individuals with Disabilities Education Improvement Act [IDEIA], 2004) gives all students the right to be educated together.

Inclusion therefore refers to learners in ordinary schools, following the same curriculum at the same time, in the same classroom, fully accepted by everybody, in ways that make the student feel no different from other students. It is not simply a matter of locating children in a mainstream school and expecting them to change and adapt to school life. This radical concept is not an easy option. Creating suitable learning support for the whole student population demands changes across curriculum, delivery, and systems. Inclusion creates controversy among parents, policymakers, teachers, and learners (Cigman, 2007). Nind, Rix, Sheehy, and Simmons (2005) emphasize the need to move beyond a model centered upon the 'special' student's need for diagnosis and individualized programs towards dismantling barriers, adapting instructional goals, arrangements, lesson formats, materials, delivery style, and classroom environment. Booth and Ainscow (2002) stress the need for an inclusive culture, which welcomes everyone, where staff, students, and carers collaborate with each other and where differences are acknowledged and respected. However, many mainstream classroom teachers feel ill-equipped for vulnerable learners. How might style theory offer them support?

People travel life's road at different speeds. They face different challenges along the way; any student can be dealing temporarily with personal or environmental risks—adolescence, gender, ethnicity, discrimination, poor skills, English as an additional language, low income, poor housing, ill health, unemployment, family breakdown. Classrooms are full of vulnerable learners. It is clear, however, that "some individuals and some groups disproportionately, are forced along a tougher, less direct path, from which it becomes hard to rejoin the main road" (Equalities Review, 2007, p. 10). Some display specific learning differences, such as (SpLD)/dyslexia, Asperger's syndrome, speech, language, and communication difficulties, attention deficit (hyperactivity) disorder (AD(H)D), dyspraxia. Others bring difficult home lives with them into school. Some children simply find a classroom environment hard to take, particularly when stress and individual learning differences combine to cause social and emotional disturbances or mental health issues.

Examinations and league tables in secondary school increase the pressure. This is a particular feature in the UK, where the current generation of students has been described as the most assessed and tested cohort in 100 years. Transition, especially to and from secondary school, is a risky time. Vulnerable survivors of primary school, whose learning identity has already been affected by classroom failures, hit the start of adolescence just as they transfer to a larger, alien environment where they must cope with new people, routines, and rules. They may have moved from a single classroom with one teacher to separate areas and many teachers. Curriculum delivery frequently changes from experience-based multisensory modes to more verbal and auditory modes (Galton & Willcocks, 1983). A verbally presented curriculum, demanding sustained periods of attention and listening skills alongside logical, verbal responses, frequently causes difficulties for vulnerable learners (Mortimore, 2008). Behavior frequently becomes harder for educators to handle as learners reach adolescence. The 'sixty-four dollar' question is: can style theory help to make inclusive classrooms easier to manage?

## THE IMPACT OF STYLE THEORY UPON
## TEACHING AND LEARNING

This chapter adopts the following definition of style. Cognitive style is defined as an individual's habitual or preferred way of processing information. Learning style is the application of that preferred cognitive style to a learning situation (Riding & Rayner, 1998). The focus here is therefore upon exploring the more flexible learning style preferences rather than examining the deeper cognitive levels within Curry's (1983) onion metaphor.

Coffield, Moseley, Hall, and Ecclestone's (2004) critique of the theoretical and methodological foundations of the whole style field severely challenged researchers and practitioners. They suggested that adopting style theory promotes the attachment of detrimental or oversimplistic style labels of the visual/auditory/kinesthetic type to learners and lends credence to 'neuromyths' such as right-brain/left-brain thinking (Goswami, 2004). This perspective switches attention from inclusive pedagogy and learning contexts to a medical 'within-the-person' deficit model that takes insufficient account of the range of factors surrounding the learner. However, despite limited empirical evidence, experience (e.g., Mortimore, 2008; Reid, 2005) demonstrates that the adoption of learning style theory in UK educational policy has contributed positively to pedagogy in secondary school classrooms, where external pressures and public assessments threaten their capacity to meet the needs of individual learners.

The style approach focused attention upon individuals and their diverse needs, developing educationalists' understanding of learning and promoted pedagogic strategies. It opened teachers' eyes to the unseen barriers throughout secondary school institutions, where auditory-verbal modes of teaching still predominated. It brought multimodal, if not multisensory, ways of teaching into mainstream secondary and post-16 contexts for all learners. This has resulted in more flexible practice, acknowledgment of diversity, and a realization of the importance of metacognitive processes. Style theory links effectively with personalized learning or 'better-fit pedagogy' as explored by Claxton (2002) and Deakin Crick (2006). Finally, and crucially, it has provided a language system for dialogues about learning processes.

Existing, if limited, research (Dunn & Dunn, 2008; Mortimore, 2008) indicates these outcomes have enriched students' learning experience. A styles-based perspective, managed appropriately and flexibly, avoiding labeling or making rigid links between style and strategies, seems to provide a chance for vulnerable students to consider how they learn. It offers respect for their ways of dealing with learning tasks, alongside the chance to rebuild confidence and relationships with teachers. Experienced practitioners combine adjustments to classroom context and attitudes with helping individuals take control of their learning (Mortimore, 2008; Reid, 2005). How we learn is complex. Therefore the aim is not to 'diagnose' but to understand and use style to transform passive learners. Exploring how students approach learning tasks allows them to take control, to go beyond simple information processing and retrieval, to apply logic and practice higher order strategies (Wallace, 2002). Flavell (1987) called this 'planfulness' and researchers agree that students who develop a repertoire of the type of strategies, described later, will be the most successful learners (Ridsdale, 2004). This involves metacognition, or recognizing their own thinking processes, understanding the nature of learning and then exercising choice and strategic thinking.

## STYLE AND THE LEARNER: USING BETTER-FIT PEDAGOGY TO DEVELOP INDEPENDENT LEARNERS

At this point, three crucial elements converge:

1. To tailor pedagogy to the individual, students and their teachers need ways of understanding their own study preferences. These may be underpinned by individual cognitive structures.
2. Teachers and students then need to develop explicit metacognitive strategies that will allow the students to take control of their learning and become independent strategic learners.
3. Teachers also need ways of adjusting their pedagogy and classroom environments to suit these preferences. Learners need self-knowledge to be able to select what suits them best.

These three elements could be said to reflect the conceptual structure of Curry's (1983) onion model. There is an interplay of style processes starting with one, the individual learning performance, and unfolding, through strategy development, into diversifying the learning context and/or community to allow learners and teachers to construct a successful learning environment together.

Style theory overviews (e.g., Coffield et al., 2004; Riding & Rayner, 1998) reveal varied options, assessment instruments, and research controversies. These do not answer the important question: how can practitioners select an appropriate measure, method, and approach? Firstly, applying style to practical classroom work involves different criteria from those applied in research studies. As argued earlier, practitioners are not concerned with 'diagnosing' style and labeling individuals. They should take a pragmatic, flexible approach designed to develop strategic thinking and provide a broad range of teaching and learning modes that will challenge and support all learners. Hence, the selection of any style paradigm or instrument should reflect explicit learning aims.

Three approaches are presented here as alternative examples of a pragmatic approach: (1) Riding's cognitive style model (1991); (2) the style mapping profile, which is intended to identify learners' spontaneous preferences for processing information from their environment; and (3) Dunn and Dunn's (1993) learning style model.

Riding and Cheema (1991) suggested that many different existing styles models can be combined into two principal cognitive style groups. Riding (1991) devised a two-dimensional model encompassing these constructs and provided a simple and accessible way of analyzing style. These dimensions were termed the wholistic/analytic and verbalizer/imager style continua (Riding, 1991). The wholistic/analytic continuum indicates an individual's preference for processing information in wholes or parts. The verbalizer-imager continuum indicates individual preferences for representing information as words or as mental images. Everyone's style preference falls somewhere along each continuum. These two dimensions are independent of each other and each style is equally effective. The validity of these continua has been questioned, but learners find them understandable and easy to relate to their preferences. They also lead nicely to suggestions for practical support. Riding devised a computer-based assessment tool, the Cognitive Styles Analysis (1991), which researchers now aim to improve (Peterson, Deary, & Austin, 2003).

The style mapping profile provides a clear picture of the student's learning preferences across a range of experiences. The aim is to increase style awareness rather than to label. This should enable both teacher and learner to be strategic and develop style flexibility beyond the 'comfort zone'. Specific preferences affect the mastery of challenging or new material. Proficient learners will be less disadvantaged by a mismatch; however, mismatching can hinder more vulnerable students

The Dunn and Dunn (1993) learning styles model assesses five domains that influence learning: reflective, emotional, sociological, physical, and psychological factors:

- reflective factors: environmental factors (e.g., noise or silence, place of study, light and temperature, time of day); internal factors (e.g., tendencies to reflect, explore, record, and analyze performance);
- emotional factors: motivation, responsibility, persistence, and personal goals;
- sociological factors: preferred social groupings or relationships. Dunn and Dunn highlight the role of emotions in swaying vulnerable learners;
- physiological factors: need for mobility or tactile experiences; physical influence of surroundings;
- psychological factors: cognitive needs (e.g., preferring a particular presentation mode or wholistic versus analytic approach).

To explore these domains, and offer the opportunity for discussion rather than labeling, it is possible to use observational checklists

(Mortimore, 2008), questionnaires such as the Pupil's Assessment of Learning Styles (PALS, Given & Reid, 1999; Reid, 2005), the Learning Styles Inventory (Burke & Dunn, 1998), or the computer administered Studyscan (Zdzienski, 1997).

The learner's personality and thinking skills interact with classroom climate, pedagogical assumptions, learning styles, and cultural factors. The world of the classroom involves the interplay of individual and environmental factors. Here children will need an explicit scaffold to develop awareness and control of their personal models of learning and to create links between both personal and group aspects of learning. Style constructs must illustrate how learners process information and how they are affected by environmental conditions. Failure can lead to a rigid approach to learning, often linked with low confidence and a reluctance to take risks.

## PRACTICAL APPROACHES: ESTABLISHING FRAMEWORKS FOR LEARNING

To help students explore their preferences and develop strategic, flexible ways of learning, these two interlinked approaches can be combined:

- a style-mapping approach based on their understanding of preferences in learning processes or cognitive style; and
- explicit development of metacognitive strategies.

Metacognitive strategies emerge from a style focus but will need to be scaffolded by explicit teaching and practice (Reid, 2005). Likewise, the development of a metacognitive approach will encourage an understanding of preferences.

### Utilizing Preferred Learning Modes or Cognitive Style

Learning can be seen as consisting of three interlocking stages (Reid, 2005): (1) getting the information in—access via modes of presentation; (2) working on the information—process, storage, and revision; and (3) getting the information out—modes of expression. Each phase makes different demands upon learners. These can be reduced by responding to individual preferences. Simplify task demands, alter the ways in which information is presented, offer help with organizing responses, and broaden what is acceptable, particularly for assessment. Consider what demands are made by particular curriculum subjects at each phase and then identify the most flexible ways of dealing with each demand. For example, the 'easy' task of making a note of instructions for a science experiment includes listening, understanding, sequencing, organizing, remembering, copying, writing, spelling, losing the place in the text on the whiteboard, finding it again, and so on, usually simultaneously. Weak literacy, deficits in language, memory, attention, or automaticity will mean that learners struggle with something teachers consider simple. They may not be poor scientists but they are being set up to fail.

Regardless of style construct preferred, the following three principles should be observed. First, metacognitive approaches to learning and self-knowledge must be specifically taught and supported or scaffolded. Many vulnerable learners will never have stepped back to observe how they learn or established positive dialogues with teachers. They will be accustomed to negative exchanges. Supportive partnerships between experts and novices provide language for discussing learning. Secondly, use strengths to compensate for weaknesses. Many vulnerable learners have been exposed as failures by both teachers' overreliance upon the auditory/verbal medium and the complex combination of cognitive skills involved in seemingly simple demands. Analyze the demands of set tasks and ensure that presentation modes are sufficiently varied to match everybody's strengths. Thirdly, offer a choice of methods and presentation. Use their strengths, but let learners have opportunities to experiment and select suitable strategies. Here are some ways to utilize preferences:

### Stage One: Accessing Information

How do students prefer to obtain information? Reading or listening, watching or doing? Vary the presentation modes. Some people absorb information better when reinforced with images, as in a video. Others find learning through carrying out a procedure—trial and error—is more successful. Some learn through the auditory or verbal channel alone; others listen and make notes or mind maps, while their friends prefer to read silently. Some process information sequentially and respond to lists and logical order. Others prefer a big picture or concept map of a topic. Research suggests that vulnerable learners respond to multisensory strategies (Ott, 2007). This indicates a clear need for multimodal delivery.

Flexibility, showing that many ways to achieve a goal are acceptable, is key. Are students sourcing information independently provided with multimedia sources? Or is success dependent on navigating print in a textbook? Are Web sites adjusted, with ICT programs making them accessible to poor readers? Are students expected to take notes? If so, have they tried different forms of note taking, and been helped to choose the medium/shape that suits their style preference?

### Stage Two: Processing Information

Once information is located, it needs to be transformed—an important planning stage that students frequently skip. For tasks to be converted into a suitable format for their preference, students must be forced to pause, reflect, and select a strategy. Students must ask themselves: What is the task? Is it problem solving? Is it compare and contrast? Is it using information as evidence to answer a question? Do I understand the wording of the instructions?

### Stage Three: Modes of Expression

This builds on stages one and two. Frequently, it is a piece of written work. Vulnerable students will find a blank page intimidating and will need a previously established framework. They also need to be aware of genre conventions. Strategies for scaffolding will be provided later. However, any written text may only be a shadow of what vulnerable learners know. Is it always essential to demand a written piece? Knowledge of style preference must also challenge conventional modes of assessing understanding. Would another way of demonstrating knowledge be more appropriate? What about poster presentations, taped pieces, chaired discussions, drama workshops, or a video plus commentary? Using group presentations with contributions tailored to individual preferences can demonstrate truly personalized learning.

## FROM STYLE THEORY TO PRACTICE

This section shows how applying two theoretical frameworks, one focused upon style preference, the other upon developing strategic thinking and metacognition, can support practice in the classroom at each phase.

## Style Preference—The Cognitive Toolkit

Riding and Rayner (1998) suggest that learners use the cognitive toolkit related to their position on the two continua—wholist/analytic and imager/verbalizer. A wholistic preference predisposes learners to make connections and creative links; deal easily with structure; use mind maps and plans; and need a 'big picture' of the lesson's aims at the outset. Wholistic difficulties tend to manifest in lost detail, minimal evidence to back ideas, and weak use of logical steps. Analytic learners tend to be good on detail; have a strong sense of order, and step-by-step logic. They prefer lists and sequences but they struggle to make connections, to plan the whole of a coherent project, or to keep a sense of proportion within a piece of writing.

Vulnerable learners must be rescued from the intimidating blank page and helped to use strategies such as writing frames as a springboard to be discarded once confidence is established (see Table 19.1). Wray's cross-curricular ideas (www.warwick.ac.uk/staff/D.J.Wray) reveal the schema

*Table 19.1*   Templates for Planning and Storing Information

| Templates for wholistic preferences | Templates for analytic preferences |
| --- | --- |
| Brainstorms (random or structured) | Grids |
| Frames | Lists |
| Mind or concept maps | Boxes (one keyword per box) |
| | Time lines |
| | Chains |
| | SPSO |

underpinning different types of writing. When researching, learners should be encouraged to select simple templates to store information.

SPSO (Situation, Problem, Solution, Outcome, see Table 19.2) refers to a sequential approach where the writer starts with a situation, adds a problem, finds a solution, and describes the outcome (Mason, 1990). This may be the final outcome or it may produce another problem which will take the writer down the chain again until the final outcome is eventually reached. It can be used across the curriculum, from science experiments to creative writing (Mortimore, 2008).

Referring to the example in Table 19.2, we know that the marriage generates further chains of problems which end in tragedy! SPSO can help students to understand this information, generating a schema upon which to hang detail. The following process prepares for writing.

The planning structure and template choice of a wholistic frame or analytic chain, customized for the relevant genre, should be established at the organizing stage. Mind-mapping software is also useful. Students should practice converting information from one form of structure to another to help develop style flexibility, but also to demonstrate how, for example, SPSO can be used as a note-taking device to extract key facts for revision.

## Further Cognitive Tools: Mind's Eye or Mind's Ear?

Students may also prefer a predominantly visual or verbal approach, combining and interchanging in response to context. Strengths and weaknesses

*Table 19.2*   SPSO in Practice

| Using SPSO to Analyze Shakespeare's Romeo and Juliet | |
| --- | --- |
| Situation | Romeo has fallen in love with Juliet |
| Problem | Their two families loathe each other |
| Solution | The lovers marry secretly |
| Outcome | Everyone is pleased and they live happily ever after |

**brainstorm** ⟹ **writing frame (plan)** ⟹ **text**

*Figure 19.1* The three stages of writing.

are associated with each preference and affect each phase of learning. At phase one, more visual learners may find following verbal information difficult without visual reinforcement. Strong verbalizers may find purely graphic presentations difficult to absorb or interpret. It is sometimes the case that literacy and memory difficulties associated with dyslexia, or the visual processing strengths associated with autism, may make learners respond better to visual media. The predominantly verbal secondary school classroom favors auditory/oral learning over a multisensory, experienced-based approach. This challenges those students who need a multimodal approach, particularly those with ADHD-type differences who need the stimulus of physical movement (Dunn & Dunn, 1993). Teachers must be prepared to introduce visual and practical strategies and to encourage every learner to create and use pictures in the mind's eye for accessing and processing information. A starting point would be utilizing video, TV, cartoons, comic strips, maps, diagrams, or drama work.

At phase two, students can use PowerPoint to develop visual concept maps (search the Internet for examples), visualization practice, drawing, cartooning. All students can develop skills in visualizing and creating pictures in the mind's eye by focusing on an object and imagining around size, color, place, time, smell, touch, and sensation. This generates vocabulary for those whose preference for the visual is fueled by difficulties with language. These preferences can also extend to ways of learning spelling or revising for exams where mind maps can be used in a range of ways.

To show what they have learnt, at phase three students can play the role of the reporter (the digestive system through the eye of the apple pip), can augment written work with diagrams or drawings, present their information visually through posters, include a kinesthetic element through drama presentations, or make and demonstrate models. Assessment can be undertaken through workshops which group students in ways that promote individuals' strengths, rather than penalizing weaknesses, and encourage cooperation. A style approach demands creative thinking about assessment strategies at all levels.

## Using the Mind's Ear: Verbal Strategies and Support

Difficulties with speech and language processing play a role in differences such as SpLD, ADHD, and dyspraxia and often manifest themselves in areas beyond the curriculum such as behavior difficulties, where students become frustrated by their inability to express themselves verbally (Tommerdahl, 2009). However, strong verbalizers will rely upon verbal communication and will prefer to consolidate learning through discussion, dialogue, role-play, self-talk, or presentations. They may enjoy presenting findings orally or creating 'radio programs', particularly if they have difficulties with written language. Try pairing strongly verbal learners with visualizers to allow them to support each other and develop flexibility. All the learners in a group will benefit from the provision of vocabulary and text for structuring phrases.

## Developing Strategic Thinking and Metacognition in Classroom Learning

Metacognition can be developed in group activities. The Effective Lifelong Learning Inventory (ELLI) enables students to measure and develop their strength in seven crucial dimensions. Deakin Crick (2006) demonstrates the application of learning dimensions to class project work. ELLI helps children to acquire curriculum knowledge while deepening understanding of supporting each other's learning. Learners are not categorized and each individual moves towards the positive end of the dimension. The ELLI inventory is available online and provides a graphic representation of the learner's profile. Each dimension has a positive and negative pole (Deakin Crick, 2006, pp. 9–10). These comprise:

1. Changing and learning versus static and stuck: changing and growing as a learner;
2. Critical curiosity versus passivity: asking questions, going below the surface of things and coming to independent conclusions;
3. Meaning making versus data accumulation: making learning personally meaningful by connecting new with previous knowledge;
4. Creativity versus being rule bound: risk taking, playfulness, lateral thinking, and using imagination and intuition in learning;
5. Learning relationships versus isolation and dependence: learning collaboratively and independently;
6. Strategic awareness versus being robotic: actively managing learning processes, strategies, and feelings; and
7. Resilience versus fragility and dependence: persisting in the face of confusion, not knowing, and failure.

Expressing dimensions of learning in these accessible terms helps learners to become strategic. These dimensions have strong resonance with learning and memory theory and other style constructs, such as strategic, surface, and deep learning or reproduction-directed versus meaning-directed learning (Vermunt, 1992). They have been applied across age groups (using animal metaphors to clarify the dimensions), helping students to consider how they learn, which learning situations tap different dimensions, and which dimensions might need strengthening.

Using this combination of practical application of style preference and development of metacognitive knowledge can link an individual's psychological cognitive structure and learning behavior to the social setting of the classroom in a way that allows individual understanding to develop group levels of strategic awareness.

## ADAPTING PEDAGOGY AND CLASSROOMS TO FACILITATE ACCESS—INCLUSIVE PRACTICES

It is a teacher's responsibility to engage and include diverse learners. Educators must monitor their approaches, reduce their use of analytic verbal styles of delivery, and diversify strategies, activities, and materials. This is crucial in areas such as mathematics, where most learners experience anxiety (Chinn & Ashcroft, 2006), where a mismatch of style may be truly destructive and multisensory methods and kinesthetic activities must underpin the development of abstract concepts (Clausen-May, 2005). However, alongside pedagogy, the classroom environment, whether physical or emotional, can create barriers. Style has a role to play in: whole group work and peer support; managing the team around the learner; and designing and resourcing the classroom.

Discussion of Dunn and Dunn's (2008) model with students highlights the role played by the classroom environment in creating success. Varying social structures for study (individual, group, panels, workshops, peer evaluation, and support), responding to students' feedback about the experience, and allowing them manageable freedom of choice help develop relationships across the classroom team. Ensuring that everyone—learners, teaching assistants, support staff, permanent and temporary teachers— understands how working with style may develop strategic resilient learners ensures shared aims and approaches. ELLI can be effective here.

The physical environment can be transformed (see Given & Reid, 1999). Simple alterations make a room more welcoming in terms of sound, light, and temperature; introducing carpeting or plants. Rearrange seating, move shelving to alter working areas, or separate students with different needs. The key is to offer flexibility in structure, furniture, grouping, access to and type of resources, and to reflect regularly on how alterations might affect the learners in your care.

## CONCLUSION

In spite of contemporary disputes over the validity of style research, models of style, and relevance to learning and teaching in the school system, experience testifies to the success of establishing a metacognitive mind-set for learners and teachers adopting a flexibility of approach. To meet the challenge of diversity in education and the workplace, educators need to be aware of the individual ways in which learning can take place and how children can be helped to understand, honor, utilize, and develop their own preferences and the preferences of others in the learning community. The cognitive strategies and environmental adjustments suggested do not involve difficult or costly changes but can have a significant impact upon the relationships between educators and their charges and help to make the resulting learning environments truly inclusive.

## BIBLIOGRAPHY

Barton, L. (Ed.) (1996). *Disability and Society: Emerging Issues and Insights.* Harlow, UK: Addison Wesley Longman.

Booth, T., & Ainscow, M. (2002). *Index for Inclusion: Developing Learning and Participation in Schools.* Bristol, UK: Centre for Studies in Inclusive Education (CSIE).

Burke, K., & Dunn, R. (1998). *Learning Styles: The Clue to You* (LS: CY). Retrieved March 7, 2010, from http://www.learningstyles.net

Chinn, S.J., & Ashcroft, R. (2006). *Mathematics for Dyslexics: Including Dyscalculia* (3rd ed.). London: Wiley.

Cigman, R. (2007). *Included or Excluded. The Challenge of the Mainstream for Some SEN Children.* London: Routledge.

Clausen-May, T. (2005). *Teaching Maths to Pupils with Different Learning Styles.* London: Paul Chapman.

Claxton, G. (2002). *Building Learning Power: Helping Young People Become Better Learners.* Bristol, UK: TLO.

Coffield, F., Moseley, D., Hall, E., & Ecclestone, K. (2004). *Should We Be Using Learning Styles? What Research Has to Say to Practice.* London: Learning and Skills Research Centre.

Curry, L. (1983). *An Organization of Learning Styles Theory and Constructs.* Paper presented at the Annual Meeting of the American Educational Research Association, Montreal, Canada (ERIC No. ED 235 185).

Deakin Crick, R. (2006). *Learning Power in Practice: A Guide for Teachers*: London: Paul Chapman.

Dunn, K.J., & Dunn, R. (2008). Teaching to at-risk students' learning styles: solution based on international research. *Insights on Learning Disabilities: From Prevailing Theories to Validated Practices, 5,* 89–101.

Dunn, R., & Dunn, K. (1993). *Teaching Secondary School Students through Their Individual Learning Styles.* Boston: Allyn & Bacon.

Equalities Review. (2007). Retrieved March 7, 2010, from http://www.equalityhumanrights.com/search-results/index.html?q=disability

Flavell, J.H. (1987). Speculations about the nature and development of metacognition. In F. Weinert & R. Kluwe (Eds.), *Metacognition, Motivation and Understanding* (pp. 21–29). London: Lawrence Erlbaum Associates.

Galton, M., & Willcocks, J. (1983). *Moving from the Primary Classroom.* London: Routledge.

Given, B., & Reid, G. (1999). *Learning Styles: A Guide for Teachers and Parents.* Lancashire, UK: Red Rose Publications.

Goswami, U. (2004). Neuroscience, science and special education. *British Journal of Special Education, 31*, 175–183.

Mason, M. (1990). *Illuminating English. Book 3: Writing for Learning.* Wigan, UK: Training Research Agency Consultancy Enterprises.

Mortimore, T. (2008). *Dyslexia and Learning Style* (2nd ed.). Chichester, UK: Wiley.

Nind, M., Rix, J., Sheehy, K., & Simmons, K. (2005). Models and practice in inclusive curricula. In M. Nind, J. Rix, K. Sheehy, & K. Simmons (Eds.), *Curriculum and Pedagogy in Inclusive Education: Values into Practice* (pp. 1–9). London: Routledge.

Ott, P. (2007). *Teaching Children with Dyslexia. A Practical Guide.* London: Routledge.

Peterson, E.R., Deary, I.J., & Austin, E.J. (2003). The reliability of Riding's Cognitive Styles Analysis Test. *Personality and Individual Differences, 34*, 881–891.

Reid, G. (2005). *Learning Style and Inclusion.* London: PCP.

Riding, R.J. (1991). *Cognitive Styles Analysis.* Birmingham, UK: Learning and Teaching.

Riding, R.J., & Cheema, I. (1991). Cognitive styles—an overview and integration. *Educational Psychology, 11*, 193–215.

Riding, R.J., & Rayner, S. (1998). *Cognitive Styles and Learning Strategies.* London: David Fulton.

Ridsdale, J. (2004). Dyslexia and self-esteem. In M. Turner & J. Rack (Eds.), *The Study of Dyslexia* (pp. 249–281). New York: Kluwer.

Special Educational Needs and Disability Act. (2001). Retrieved March 7, 2010, from http://www.opsi.gov.uk/acts/acts2001/ukpga_20010010_en_1

The Individuals with Disabilities Education Improvement Act. (2004). Retrieved March 7, 2010, from http://www.in.gov/ipas/2411.htm

Tommerdahl, J. (2009). What teachers of students with SEBD need to know about speech and language difficulties. *Emotional and Behavioural Difficulties, 14*, 19–31.

Vermunt, J.D.H.M. (1992). *Learning Styles and Guidance of Learning Processes in Higher Education.* Amsterdam: Lisse, Swets and Zeitlinger.

Wallace, B. (2002). *Teaching Thinking Skills in the Primary Years.* London: David Fulton.

Wray, D. (s.d.). Retrieved March 7, 2010, from http://www.warwick.ac.uk/staff/D.J.Wray/index.html

Zdzienski, D. (1997) *Studyscan.* Limerick: ISL.

Part IV

# Summing Up

The Journey Continues . . .

# 20 Researching Style
## More of the Same
## or Moving Forward?

*Eva Cools and Stephen Rayner*

## INTRODUCTION

In summing up the research in this book, it is clearly demonstrated that styles are studied across diverse research domains and from different conceptual, theoretical, and methodological points of view (see also Appendix 1A). Indeed, more than ten years ago, Riding (2000) wrote in the concluding chapter of a similar book to this one that a strategic approach to advance the style field involves four critical issues: (1) reduce the large number of style labels to some fundamental cognitive style dimensions; (2) develop simple, valid, and direct cognitive style measures suitable for worldwide use; (3) clearly situate cognitive style in the context of other individual differences and develop a model on how the various constructs interact in affecting behavior; and (4) establish clear relationships between cognitive style measures and objectively observable behavior to find relevant applications of cognitive styles in practice. Over the past decade, his plea has been followed by similar calls from others (e.g., Cools, 2009a; Curry, 2006; Kozhevnikov, 2007; Rayner, 2006; Sadler-Smith, 2009a, 2009b).

In 2006, Lynn Curry gave a keynote address at the European Learning Styles Information Network (ELSIN) conference in Oslo, with the telling title *Enabling Life Long Learning at Work and at School: What Should We Do If We Meant It?* She invited style scholars to focus on three major paths: (1) theory: conceptual clarification in the bewildering array of conceptualizations of the style concept; (2) measurement: clear demonstration and accumulation of the validity and reliability of measures; and (3) relevance: continuous attention to the relevance of the field for practice. At the same conference, Rayner (2006) also emphasized the need to (1) generate a consensual theory of style differences that demonstrates construct validity, and at the same time (2) seek an integration of theoretical and applied research methodologies to produce functional theory and practically relevant findings. It is clear from these recent calls that the style field needs to continue working on the scientific rigor of its theory and measurement as well as its relevance to increase its value as a field of study within the individual differences psychology (Armstrong & Rayner, 2002; Cools, 2009a; Evans,

Cools, & Charlesworth, 2010; Rayner & Peterson, 2009); otherwise it may become sidelined by mainstream scientific researchers and left to the indulgences of practitioners (see also Moskvina & Kozhevnikov, Chapter 2). The question is: are we there yet? Do we see signs of a paradigm shift? Or, to use the words of Lynn Curry: what should we do if we meant it?

To address this question we will look at the field of styles from three perspectives: theory, measurement, and application (see Figure 20.1). Importantly, the choice for a figure with three intersecting circles is not a coincidence. Although we discuss the theoretical, methodological, and applied perspective consecutively in this chapter, ideally these three aspects are dealt with in combination, implying that the 'holy grail' of a paradigm shift is located within the cross section of the three aspects. From a more realistic perspective, Appendix 1A clearly showed that the chapters presented in this book each dealt with one or two of these aspects.

## THEORETICAL AND CONCEPTUAL EVOLUTIONS

We are not the first, and certainly will not be the last, to call for further theoretical and conceptual development of the style field, although we are also optimistic about the evolution that has recently taken place in this

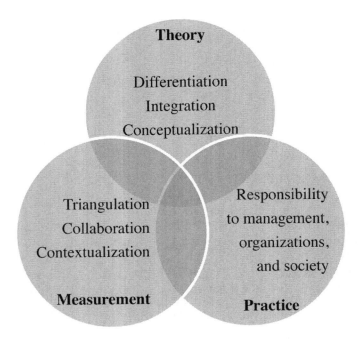

*Figure 20.1*  Moving the style field forward.

regard. As rightly observed by Moskvina and Kozhevnikov (Chapter 2), there is an urgent need for reintegration of style research into the domain of mainstream psychology. There is also the need, as identified by other researchers (e.g., Rayner & Peterson, 2009; Zhang & Sternberg, 2009a), for style research aimed at affirming the structure and function of style differences in an individual's psychology.

The last decade has seen a renewed interest in style and progress has been made to increase the justification of style as a field of study (see also Chapter 1). It is beyond the scope of this concluding chapter to go into detail in all current theoretical and conceptual evolutions in the style field, but we particularly want to emphasize and call for further work in examining the *integration* (i.e., reconciliation, unification), *differentiation* (i.e., distinction), and *conceptualization* of style as a phenomenon. Unifying initiatives such as the three-stage Delphi study on how people who work in the style field define the concept of cognitive style and learning styles and how they perceive the future of their field (Armstrong, Peterson, & Rayer, in press; Peterson, Rayner, & Armstrong, 2009) and the integrative overview of the field that has been presented at the latest Academy of Management conference in Chicago—entitled *Thinking Styles in Managerial Learning, Cognition and Behavior: An Integrative Overview* (Sadler-Smith & Armstrong, 2009)—demonstrate that the field of styles is moving towards a higher level of maturity. Similarly, conceptual models such as Zhang and Sternberg's (2005) types of thinking styles and Sadler-Smith's (2009b) duplex model represent recent efforts to develop integrated cognitive style models, fitting into the unifying trend identified by Moskvina and Kozhevnikov (Chapter 2). In addition, building further on previous attempts of theoretical development (i.e., Curry's [1983] onion model, Sternberg's [1997] theory of mental self-government, and Riding and Rayner's [1998] theory of cognitive styles and learning strategies), Rayner and Peterson (2009) recently presented an interesting four-layered model of an individual's learning performance, which aims to bring different individual characteristics and contextual elements together in an integrative model of learning performance. Further empirical testing of these models and other related models are necessary to show how they can be used in applied settings. Furthermore, replication of past research on the one hand and comprehensive reviews of research evidence from existing style models on the other hand (such as the one of Zhang and Fan on the theory of mental self-government, Chapter 4) also contribute to justification and reaffirmation of the field, because research and reviews such as these clearly continue to demonstrate how style differences impact upon and matter in diverse contexts.

Further, more research needs to be conducted on the relationships between different style-related concepts (e.g., cognitive style, learning styles, approaches to learning) on the one hand and on the link between styles and other individual differences, such as ability, personality and affect, on the other hand. Empirical testing of Curry's (1983) widely cited onion model or the model of individual learning performance of Rayner and Peterson (2009), or neurophysiological studies on the brain functioning of people with different cognitive styles will contribute to this work. This way, we want to stimulate further clarification in the field with regard to the three controversial and still unresolved issues as identified by Zhang and Fan (Chapter 4): styles as traits versus states (stability versus malleability), styles as value-laden versus value-free, and styles as different constructs versus similar constructs with different labels. Finally, there are structural issues related to the defining of style as a construct that continue to challenge researchers—reflected in the splitting trend of recent style research identified by Moskina and Kozhevnikov (Chapter 2). The direction of this research might result in new insights into finer-grained differences between people with similar cognitive styles in relation to how mobile or fixed are their preferences. Similarly, studies on the relationship between learning style and learning flexibility, such as the one of Sharma and Kolb (Chapter 5) and Boyatzis and Mainemelis (Chapter 7), move forward in exploring the same area but from a different style perspective utilizing a different model of learning.

## METHODOLOGICAL AND MEASUREMENT EVOLUTIONS

According to Creswell (2003), the research approaches a scholar can choose from have multiplied over the last two decades, leading to a vast array of potential research methods, data collection procedures, and data analysis techniques. The question remains whether this diversity is already represented in how methodology and measurement are applied in the style field to empirically investigate style differences and their effect. Different style scholars called for increasing the number of qualitative and mixed-method approaches (Priola, Smith, & Armstrong, 2004; see also Roodenburg & Roodenburg, Chapter 3; Rosenfeld & Rosenfeld, Chapter 10) as well as the use of multisource approaches (Berr, Church, & Waclawski, 2000), of longitudinal designs (see Vanthournout, Donche, Gijbels, & Van Petegem, Chapter 6), and of emerging insights from social cognitive neuroscience and related fields (Lieberman, 2007; Sadler-Smith, 2009b). The underlying justification behind these calls towards more diversity in methodology and measurement lies in increasing the rigor as well as the relevance of style research.

## What Picture Do We Get From the Style Field at this Moment?

A recent systematic study of the methodological practices of the field of cognitive styles gives a partial picture (Cools, 2009b; Cools, Armstrong, & Sadler-Smith, 2010).[1] Based on a carefully designed selection process (see Armstrong & Cools, 2009), a methodological review study was conducted on 102 style-related articles within the field of business and management, representing 175 different empirical studies. These studies were content-analyzed using a coding scheme that has been developed in alignment with methodological studies in other fields, such as entrepreneurship, management, work and organizational psychology, and negotiation (e.g., Aguinis, Pierce, Bosco, & Muslin, 2009; Austin, Scherbaum, & Mahlman, 2002; Buelens, Van De Woestyne, Mestdagh, & Bouckenooghe, 2008; Ketchen, Boyd, & Bergh, 2008; Scandura & Williams, 2000). Coding dimensions included the theoretical framework, the research design, measurement, and data analytic approach.

Three striking conclusions can be drawn from this content analysis. First, the field of cognitive style research mainly uses quantitative (95%), cross-sectional (99%), and single-source (97%) designs. Secondly, it heavily relies on self-reports (60%), sample surveys (77%), and student samples (50%). Third, research on cognitive styles can be mainly localized in the UK and the US, based on the affiliation of the first authors and the nationality of the samples. Interestingly, with regard to the first two observations, similar findings (mainly quantitative and cross-sectional research designs, and mainly use of students samples) have been reported in recent analyses of the 2007 (Rosenfeld & Rosenfeld, 2008) and 2009 (Evans et al., 2010) proceedings of the European Learning Styles Information Network conference. While these results might both indicate a potential vulnerability to threats posed by internal and external validity issues, the study of Cools (2009b) also found a rather strong emphasis on construct validity in the cognitive style field in comparison with other domains, exemplified, for instance, in the fairly high attention for reliability (i.e., reports of reliability estimates in 68% of the studies), and exploratory (36%) and confirmatory (34%) factor analyses. In this sense, the chapter of Roodenburg and Roodenburg (Chapter 3) is an important contribution to further establish the construct validity of style research by using psychometrics appropriately.

## Where Do We Want to Go from Here?

Based on the results of this methodological review (Cools et al., 2010) as well as a consistent argument presented by different contributors of this book, we wish to encourage researchers to work on three key aspects of methodology: triangulation, collaboration, and contextualization. We argue that each and all three in combination reflect our contention that as researchers we urgently need to further enhance the rigor of the field and to close the relevance gap.

### Triangulation

To strengthen the findings of empirical style research, it will be important to strive for *triangulation* (i.e., cross verification, cross examination) with regard to (1) the research design and (2) data collection. A shift towards more diverse *research designs* (i.e., qualitative, mixed-method, and longitudinal designs), in addition to the overrepresentation of cross-sectional and quantitative designs, provides style scholars with the unique opportunity to strengthen their conclusions and gain deeper insights into the implications of style differences. Vanthournout and colleagues (Chapter 6) also make a plea for using longitudinal designs to empirically study the potential stability versus changeability of students' approaches to learning, as there is currently still a lack of these types of inquiries. Bringing in a time dimension in style research will also lead to a higher level of contextualization (see following) as it makes it possible to also obtain a better grasp on the influencing factors, which will contribute to more specific, applicable, timely, and relevant findings for people in practice (Cools, 2009a). Rosenfeld and Rosenfeld (Chapter 10) clearly show the advantages of using what they call a second-person perspective in addition to the widely used third-person perspective in their research on teachers' sensitivity to style differences. Other authors have also used mixed-method research designs with positive effects, for example, in the studies reported by Almeida, Pedrosa de Jesus, and Watts (Chapter 8), Peterson, Carne, and Freear (Chapter 11), Evans and Waring (Chapter 13), and Charlesworth (Chapter 15).

With regard to *data collection*, self-reports are still the most widely used approach of collecting style data, although different ways of measuring cognitive styles exist (e.g., laboratory-based tests, perceptual tasks, physiological assessments, computer-based instruments; see also Moskvina & Kozhevnikov, Chapter 2). Potential progression toward research beyond this hegemony of self-reporting includes increasing the use of other-source data, behavioral observations, brain imaging techniques, or other neurological/neurophysiological methods. The advantage of adding these other sources to the data and knowledge creation is that they do not start from how people perceive themselves, but from how others perceive them or from their actual behavior or brain reaction when engaged in a task or activity. In this sense, a more 'objective' measure can be added to the subjective perception of self-report measures, although other reports and behavioral observations of course will always include an aspect of interpretation.

*Collaboration*

The last couple of years have seen an increase in the internal dialogue between researchers and academics in the style field (Zhang & Sternberg, 2009a). There is also a noticeable increase in the number of international collaborations reported in the field (Evans et al., 2010). In this sense, networks of scholars such as ELSIN are invaluable communities of knowledge creators, who can contribute to building a strong unified community of practice (Evans et al., 2010). To further increase the relevance of the style field to people in practice, we believe still higher levels of collaboration are important in the future. Zhang and Sternberg (2009b, p. 297) also acknowledge that "cross-disciplinary and international collaborations would play a pivotal role in further stimulating the field of intellectual styles to become more widely accepted". We see this *collaboration* possible in two complementary ways.

First, there is a lack of collaboration *between academics and practitioners*, exemplified, for instance, in the conclusion that about 92% of the studies in Cools's (2009b) methodological review were conducted by people with a purely academic affiliation. However, to bridge the relevance gap and to create useful knowledge for practitioners, researchers need to bridge some of the 'assumptional differences' that characterize knowledge creation and utilization activities in research and in practice (Hodgkinson, Herriot, & Anderson, 2001; Van de Ven & Johnson, 2006; Vermeulen, 2007). Starkey and Madan (2001) suggested that the formation of knowledge networks can align the needs of researchers and practitioners. These knowledge networks involve the practitioners from the beginning of the research process (e.g., formulating the research agenda, choosing the topic and mode of research) and make sure dissemination of research findings takes place as an integral part of the actual research process. According to Amabile and colleagues (2001), academic-practitioner collaboration includes:

> framing research questions in a way that will be meaningful for practitioners, gaining access to sites for field research, designing data collection instruments and methods appropriate for today's workforce, and interpreting results accurately within the business context. (Amabile et al., 2001, p. 418)

This implies that practitioners are not only involved in the knowledge creation, but also that the findings of research are located in the right perspective, contextualized, and operationalized in such a way that people in practice can actually implement them, as also stated in the first chapter of this book (Rayner & Cools, Chapter 1).

Second, we would like to call for an increase in the number of *international collaborative studies*. Again, existing networks of style scholars such as ELSIN can play an important role to stimulate this (Evans et al., 2010), both in an informal way and in a more formalized way; this is by the establishment of Research Interest Groups (RIGs; Rayner, 2008a, 2008b). A RIG consists of a small group, team, or partnership working toward a shared goal; this is energizing research activity targeted at realizing greater integration and application of style theories from a multidisciplinary perspective as well as a pragmatic research methodology for use in style research. A RIG offers a deliberate strategic option for paradigm shift by adopting processes associated with theories of social cognition and knowledge management in the functioning of a community of practice (Wenger, McDermott, & Snyder, 2002).

*Contextualization*

Just as people do not live and act in a vacuum, we cannot investigate style in isolation. Different scholars called for taking context into account when studying human behavior as context elements can have subtle and powerful effects on research results (e.g., Chatman & Flynn, 2005; Johns, 2006; Rousseau & Fried, 2001). How people behave in learning environments, their job, and organization do not only depend on their individual (style) differences but also on environmental factors and the interaction between their style and environmental conditions. However, a lot of style research still does not take context into account. Hence, it is important to integrate the context into the research design, forms of measurement, and analyses of data in future cognitive style studies.

In this sense, we would like to call for an increase in the number of field studies and a decrease in the use of student samples (as surrogates for people in real organizations and settings), as this is one potential way to move from a third-person to a second-person perspective (Rosenfeld & Rosenfeld, Chapter 10). In addition, culture (in the broadest sense of the word, that is, nation, organization, institution) can be an important influencing factor in style differences, as stated by different authors in this book (e.g., Zhang & Fan, Chapter 4; Hardaker, Jeffery, & Sabki, Chapter 14; Charlesworth, Chapter 15). Researching with multiple samples, preferably from different countries or cultures, should be encouraged as a basis for enabling replication and cross validation of research findings. Finally, more attention for context also implies more purposeful sampling when conducting empirical style research, thereby moving away from reliance upon the use of convenience samples.

Importantly, enhanced contextualization of style research also implies specifying in the resulting research reports or articles in what context the findings apply and how the results can be used in educational and organizational practice. It is, for instance, not enough to conclude that style differences impact on management behavior, but the research also needs to stipulate in which specific circumstances this was (not) the case and how managers can effectively use the results in their management practice.

## APPLICATIONS OF STYLES

Almost every chapter in this book refers to the importance of acknowledging and constructively using style differences for effective management and education for all, sometimes even listing specific and applicable approaches that can be used in different educational or organizational contexts (see Appendix 1A for an overview). Indeed, if we take ourselves seriously the field of styles research should take its responsibility towards management, organization, and society as a whole (i.e., the three aspects within the series title of this book) and make clear how the results of research can be applied in each of these contexts and in this sense can contribute to making a real difference to people. Style research cannot take place in isolation from applied fields, specific contexts, and settings, and should attempt to play a role in management, organizations, and society. Organizations would benefit from more research into the influence of styles on aspects of intrapersonal development and interpersonal relationships as a way of improving management practice in the workplace. Whetten, Cameron, and Woods (2000) emphasized the importance of intrapersonal self-awareness and thorough analyses of one's strengths and weaknesses as one way of improving people's effectiveness. In this respect, understanding the interplay between stylistic preferences and day-to-day (workplace) behavior is known to be crucial for implementing effective individual development efforts (Berr et al., 2000). In a broader perspective, style research can play an important role in the society as a whole by stimulating respect for diversity and style awareness at all levels of education in order to take people's individuality into account in a constructive and inclusive way.

Accepting the priority for this practitioner focus also implies that we need to stimulate more research in areas of relevance to practice, for instance, looking at the trends towards e-learning, e-pedagogy, and adaptive hypermedia environments (Hardaker et al., Chapter 14; Tsianos, Germanakos, Lekkas, & Mourlas, Chapter 16), personalized, student-centered, inclusive education that respects diversity at all levels (Boyatzis & Mainemelis, Chapter 7; Dunn & Honigsfeld, Chapter 18; Evans & Waring, Chapter 13; Mortimore, Chapter 19; Vanthournout et al., Chapter 6), the internationalization of higher education (Charlesworth, Chapter 15), the increasing importance of understanding the role of individual differences in management (Backhaus, Chapter 17; Sharma & Kolb, Chapter 5) and teaching (Almeida et al., Chapter 8; Kinchin, Chapter 9; Peterson et al., Chapter 11; Rosenfeld & Rosenfeld, Chapter 10; Vermunt, Chapter 12). It is clear that the chapters in this book cover a wide range of timely and highly relevant trends applicable to education and management, while calling for further research in each of these areas. The hope is that we are taking a first step toward a new wave of research which will seek to integrate and improve upon our knowledge and its application of personal and social diversity in the learning context.

## NOTE

1. As the focus of this study was limited (only cognitive styles, two decades, business and management domain, empirical studies selected from 236 top-ranked journals), we are aware that these results cannot be generalized to the whole field of style research (this is, including learning styles, a broader time frame, broader sources). However, we do believe the results are illustrative and give a partial picture of the research and methodological practices that

have shaped the style field. A more elaborate explanation of the selection process of the articles can be found in Armstrong and Cools (2009).

## BIBLIOGRAPHY

Aguinis, H., Pierce, C.A., Bosco, F.A., & Muslin, I.S. (2009). First decade of *Organizational Research Methods*: trends in design, measurement, and data-analysis topics. *Organizational Research Methods, 12,* 69–112.

Amabile, T.M., Patterson, C., Mueller, J., Wojcik, T., Odomirok, P.W., Marsh, M., et al. (2001). Academic-practitioner collaboration in management research: a case of cross-profession collaboration. *Academy of Management Journal, 44,* 418–431.

Armstrong, S.J., & Cools, E. (2009). Cognitive styles and their relevance for business and management: a review of development over the past two decades. In L.F. Zhang & R.J. Sternberg (Eds.), *Perspectives on the Nature of Intellectual Styles* (pp. 253–290). Heidelberg: Springer.

Armstrong, S.J., Peterson, E.R., & Rayner, S.G. (in press). Understanding and defining 'cognitive style' and 'learning style': a Delphi study in an individual differences paradigm. *Learning and Individual Differences.*

Armstrong, S.J., & Rayner, S.G. (2002). Inquiry and style: research verities and the development of a consensual theory? In M. Valcke, D. Gombeir, S.J. Armstrong, A. Francis, M. Graff, J. Hill, et al. (Eds.), *Learning Styles: Reliability & Validity* (pp. 25–36). Proceedings of the 7th Annual ELSIN conference, June 26–28, Ghent University, Department of Education, Ghent, Belgium.

Austin, J., Scherbaum, C.A., & Mahlman, R.A. (2002). History of research methods in industrial and organizational psychology: measurement, design, analysis. In S.G. Rogelberg (Ed.), *Handbook of Research Methods in Industrial and Organizational Psychology* (pp. 3–33). Malden, MA: Blackwell.

Berr, S.A., Church, A.H., & Waclawski, J. (2000). The right personality is everything: linking personality preferences to managerial behaviors. *Human Resource Development Quarterly, 11,* 133–157.

Buelens, M., Van De Woestyne, M., Mestdagh, S., & Bouckenooghe, D. (2008). Methodological issues in negotiation research: a state-of-the-art-review. *Group Decision & Negotiation, 17,* 321–345.

Chatman, J.A., & Flynn, F.J. (2005). Full-cycle micro-organizational behavior research. *Organization Science, 16,* 434–447.

Cools, E. (2009a). A reflection on the future of the cognitive style field: a proposed research agenda. *Reflecting Education, 5,* 19–34.

Cools, E. (2009b). *Research Methodology in the Thinking Styles Field: Practices, Trends and Implications.* Paper presented in the symposium Thinking Styles in Managerial Cognition and Learning: An Integrative Overview (organizers: E. Sadler-Smith & S.J. Armstrong) at the Academy of Management (AoM) conference, August 7–11, Chicago.

Cools, E., Armstrong, S.J., & Sadler-Smith, E. (2010). *Methodological Practices in the Field of Cognitive Styles: A Review Study.* Paper presented at the 15th European Learning Styles Information Network (ELSIN) conference, June 28–30, Aveiro, Portugal.

Creswell, J.W. (2003). *Research Design: Qualitative, Quantitative and Mixed Methods Approaches* (2nd ed.). Thousand Oaks, CA: Sage.

Curry, L. (1983). An organization of learning style theory and constructs. In L. Curry (Ed.), *Learning Style in Continuing Medical Education* (pp. 115–123). Halifax: Dalhouse University.

Curry, L. (2006). *Enabling Life Long Learning at Work and at school: What Should We Do if We Meant It?* Keynote address, Enabling Lifelong Learning in Education, Training and Development, Eleventh Annual Conference of the European Learning Styles Information Network, June 12–14, Oslo, Norway.

Evans, C., Cools, E., & Charlesworth, Z.M. (2010). Learning in higher education—how cognitive and learning styles matter. *Teaching in Higher Education*, 15, 469–480.

Hodgkinson, G.P., Herriot, P., & Anderson, N. (2001). Re-aligning stakeholders in management research: lessons from industrial, work and organizational psychology. *British Journal of Management, 12*, S41–S48.

Johns, G. (2006). The essential impact of context on organizational behaviour. *Academy of Management Review, 31*, 386–408.

Ketchen, D.J., Jr., Boyd, B.K., & Bergh, D.D. (2008). Research methodology in strategic management: past accomplishments and future challenges. *Organizational Research Methods, 11*, 643–658.

Kozhevnikov, M. (2007). Cognitive styles in the context of modern psychology: toward an integrated framework of cognitive style. *Psychological Bulletin, 133*, 464–481.

Lieberman, M.D. (2007). Social cognitive neuroscience: a review of core processes. *Annual Review of Psychology, 58*, 259–289.

Peterson, E.R., Rayner, S.G., & Armstrong, S.J. (2009). Researching the psychology of cognitive style and learning style: is there really a future? *Learning and Individual Differences, 19*, 518–523.

Priola, V., Smith, J.L., & Armstrong, S.J. (2004). Group work and cognitive style: a discursive investigation. *Small Group Research, 35*, 565–595.

Rayner, S. (2006). What next? Developing global research and applied practice in the field of cognitive and learning styles. In L. Lassen, L. Bostrom, & C. Evans (Eds.), *Enabling Lifelong Learning in Education, Training and Development*. Eleventh Annual Conference of the European Learning Styles Information Network (CD-ROM). Oslo, Norway: University of Oslo.

Rayner, S.G. (2008a). Are you researching in style? What about epistemology, paradigm shifts and the RIG? In E. Cools, H. Van den Broeck, C. Evans, & T. Redmond (Eds.), *Style and cultural differences: how can organisations, regions and countries take advantage of style differences? Proceedings of the 13th Annual Conference of the European Learning Styles Information Network* (pp. 95–113). Ghent, Belgium: Vlerick Leuven Gent Management School.

Rayner, S. (2008b). What's a RIG—How will I know it when I see one? *ELSIN Newsletter, an International Forum*, Winter 2008–2009, 2–5. Retrieved from http://www.elsinnews.com at November 15, 2009.

Rayner, S., & Peterson, E.R. (2009). Reaffirming style as an individual difference: toward a global paradigm or knowledge diaspora? In L.F. Zhang & R.J. Sternberg (Eds.), *Perspectives on the Nature of Intellectual Styles* (pp. 107–137). Heidelberg: Springer.

Riding, R.J. (2000). Cognitive style: a strategic approach for advancement. In R.J. Riding & S.G. Rayner (Eds.), *International Perspectives on Individual Differences. Volume 1: Cognitive Styles* (pp. 365–377). Stamford, CT: Ablex.

Riding, R., & Rayner, S. (1998). *Cognitive Styles and Learning Strategies: Understanding Style Differences in Learning and Behaviour*. London: David Fulton.

Rosenfeld, M., & Rosenfeld, S. (2008) Illustrating a new paradigm: from a third-person to a second-person perspective. In E. Cools, H. Van den Broeck, C. Evans, & T. Redmond (Eds.), *Style and cultural differences: how can organisations, regions and countries take advantage of style differences? Proceedings of the 13th Annual Conference of the European Learning Styles Information*

*Network* (pp. 115–128). Ghent, Belgium: Vlerick Leuven Gent Management School.

Rousseau, D.M., & Fried, Y. (2001). Location, location, location: contextualizing organizational research. *Journal of Organizational Behavior, 22,* 1–13.

Sadler-Smith, E. (2009a). Cognitive styles and learning strategies in management education. In S.J. Armstrong & C.V. Fukami (Eds.), *The SAGE Handbook of Management Learning, Education and Development* (pp. 301–324). Thousand Oaks, CA: Sage.

Sadler-Smith, E. (2009b). A duplex model of cognitive style. In L.F. Zhang & R.J. Sternberg (Eds.), *Perspectives on the Nature of Intellectual Styles* (pp. 3–28). Heidelberg: Springer.

Sadler-Smith, E., & Armstrong, S.J. (2009). *Thinking Styles in Managerial Cognition and Learning: An Integrative Overview.* Symposium presented at the Academy of Management (AoM) conference, August 7–11, Chicago.

Scandura, T.A., & Williams, E.A. (2000). Research methodology in management: current practices, trends, and implications for future research. *Academy of Management Journal, 43,* 1248–1264.

Starkey, K., & Madan, P. (2001). Bridging the relevance gap: aligning stakeholders in the future of management research. *British Journal of Management, 12,* S3–S26.

Sternberg, R.J. (1997). *Thinking Styles.* New York: Cambridge University Press.

Van de Ven, A.H., & Johnson, P.E. (2006). Knowledge for theory and practice. *Academy of Management Review, 31,* 802–821.

Vermeulen, F. (2007). "I shall not remain insignificant": adding a second loop to matter more. *Academy of Management Journal, 50,* 754–761.

Wenger, E., McDermott, R., & Snyder, W.M. (2002). *Cultivating Communities of Practice: A Guide to Managing Knowledge.* Boston: Harvard Business School Press.

Whetten, D., Cameron, K., & Woods, M. (2000). *Developing Management Skills for Europe* (2nd ed.). Harlow, UK: Pearson Education.

Zhang, L.F., & Sternberg, R.J. (2005). A threefold model of intellectual styles. *Educational Psychology Review, 17,* 1–53.

Zhang, L.F., & Sternberg, R.J. (Eds.) (2009a). *Perspectives on the Nature of Intellectual Styles.* New York: Springer.

Zhang, L.F., & Sternberg, R.J. (2009b). Intellectual styles: Nehru jacket or solid blue blazer. In L.F. Zhang & R.J. Sternberg (Eds.), *Perspectives on the Nature of Intellectual Styles* (pp. 291–298). Heidelberg: Springer.

# Contributors

**Patrícia Almeida**, PhD, is researcher at the Research Centre for Didactics and Technology in Teacher Education at the University of Aveiro, Portugal. She holds a PhD in science education, having also completed a postdoctorate programme on didactics. Her main research interests are classroom questioning, learning styles, and innovative learning and teaching approaches in science education. Currently she is also interested in linking teaching and research in higher education.

**Kristin Backhaus**, PhD, is an Associate Professor in the School of Business at the State University of New York at New Paltz. She teaches courses in management, leadership, and human resources and was awarded the SUNY Chancellor's Award for Excellence in Teaching in 2009. She has published research in the areas of cognitive styles, employer branding, and organizational attractiveness. Kris conducts corporate training in supervision and is a consultant in the area of employer branding.

**Richard E. Boyatzis**, PhD, is Professor in the Departments of Organizational Behavior, Psychology, and Cognitive Science at Case Western Reserve University and Adjunct Professor at ESADE. He is the author of more than 150 articles and books on leadership, competencies, emotional intelligence, and change from a complexity perspective, including: *The Competent Manager; Primal Leadership* with Daniel Goleman and Annie McKee, in twenty-eight languages; *Resonant Leadership*, with Annie McKee; and *Transforming Qualitative Information*.

**Sarah S. Carne**, PhD, has recently completed her PhD thesis at the University of Auckland, New Zealand. Her thesis explored quality of life and issues relating to adolescent obesity in a predominantly overweight population utilizing a mixed-methods study design. Her areas of interests include obesity research, child and adolescent development, and the impact of the computer age on the field of psychology.

**Zarina M. Charlesworth,** PhD, is a research associate and lecturer at Les Roches-Gruyère University of Applied Sciences and Glion Institute of Higher Education, Switzerland. Building on work experience in European agribusiness and hospitality management, together with an international educational background, her interests are in the management of higher education. Her research focuses on teaching and learning in the international higher education classroom with particular attention on culture.

**Eva Cools,** PhD, earned a KU Leuven master's degree in pedagogical sciences (2000) and graduated as a doctor in applied economics at Ghent University (2007). She works as a postdoctoral research associate within the People and Organization department of Vlerick Leuven Gent Management School, Belgium. She is research officer of the European Learning Styles Information Network (ELSIN). Her current research activities focus upon cognitive styles, person-environment fit, and styles and learning within the context of management education.

**Vincent Donche,** PhD, is assistant professor at the Institute of Education and Information Sciences of the University of Antwerp, Belgium. His research interests are situated on the level of learning and teaching conceptions and related learning and teaching strategies, the development of learning patterns, the impact of counseling interventions on the development of learning patterns in relationship with other individual differences, and the assessment of the quality of learning and teaching style instruments.

**Rita Dunn,** PhD, was professor in the Department of Administrative and Instructional Leadership for over thirty years and director of the Center for the Study of Learning and Teaching Styles at St. John's University, Jamaica, New York. She is the author of over thirty books and hundreds of articles on learning styles. She was the recipient of numerous awards and mentored over 160 doctoral students in her long, productive career.

**Carol Evans,** PhD, is Assistant Director of Learning and Teaching (ITE) at the Institute of Education, London. She is a fellow of the Higher Education Academy, honorary fellow of the School of Education, Durham University and also president of the European Learning Styles Information Network (ELSIN: an international and cross-disciplinary research organization). Her research interests include: improving conditions for learning and enhancing understanding of cognitive and learning styles to inform teaching in higher education.

**Weiqiao Fan,** PhD, obtained his doctorate from the University of Hong Kong. He is currently Associate Professor of psychology in Shanghai Normal University, P.R. China, where he is also the Director of the

Center for Psychological Testing and Assessment. His main research interests include intellectual styles, personality, and career counseling and development. He has published in journals such as *Learning and Individual Differences*, *Educational Psychology*, and *Social and Personality Psychology Compass*.

**Sarah J. Freear** is a University of Auckland psychology graduate. Her research interests include educational psychology, cognitive development in children, dyslexia, and neuroscience.

**Panagiotis Germanakos**, PhD, is Assistant Professor in the Department of Management and MIS, University of Nicosia. He is also Deputy Head in the S.C.R.A.T. research group of the Department of Computer Science, University of Cyprus, and research scientist in the Faculty of Communication & Media Studies, University of Athens. He obtained his PhD from the University of Athens in 2008 and he has several publications, including co-edited books, chapters, articles in journals, and conference contributions (Web: www.media.uoa.gr/~pgerman).

**David Gijbels**, PhD, is assistant professor of learning and instruction at the Institute for Education and Information Sciences of the University of Antwerp, Belgium. His research and development interests focus on the relationship between learning and assessment in higher education and on workplace learning. He is currently coordinator of the special interest group on 'Learning and Professional Development' of the European Association for Research on Learning and Instruction.

**Glenn Hardaker**, PhD, is a Professor of Innovation at the University of Huddersfield, UK, and a national teaching fellow (HEA). His research focus is inclusion, learning, and innovation. Glenn has published numerous articles in journals such as *Long Range Planning*, *European Journal of Innovation Management*, and *International Journal of Inclusive Education*. He is also editor of two international journals, *Multicultural Education and Technology Journal* and *Campus Wide Information Systems*.

**Andrea Honigsfeld**, PhD, is Associate Dean in the division of education at Molloy College, Rockville Centre, NY. She teaches graduate education courses related to cultural and linguistic diversity, linguistics, ESL methodology, and action research. She was the recipient of a doctoral fellowship at St. John's University, where she conducted research on learning styles. She has published extensively on working with English-language learners and/or providing differentiated instruction.

**Annie Jeffery** has extensive experience in educational technology and instructional design, and has undertaken projects into areas such as learning activities, learning object repositories, Web 2.0 tools, and learning taxonomies. Annie is a virtual worlds researcher and educator, and currently teaches two classes at Boise State University in Second Life. Her virtual worlds research interests are in sensory pedagogies, learning styles, and virtual worlds.

**Ian M. Kinchin,** PhD, is Assistant Director of King's Learning Institute at King's College, London, where he actively supports the development of innovative teaching practice across the academic disciplines. His research interests focus on the exploitation of knowledge structures as a tool in curriculum design and in the development of professional expertise, particularly within clinical education. He enjoys listening to the music of Bruce Springsteen and Bob Dylan, and is a fellow of the Society of Biology.

**David A. Kolb,** PhD, is Professor of Organizational Behavior at the Weatherhead School of Management, Case Western Reserve University, US. He received his BA from Knox College and his PhD in social psychology from Harvard University. He is best known for his research on experiential learning and learning styles described in *Experiential Learning: Experience as the Source of Learning and Development.* David has received four honorary degrees recognizing his contributions to experiential learning in higher education.

**Maria Kozhevnikov,** PhD, focuses her research on examining the neural mechanisms of individual differences in cognitive functioning. Maria received her PhD from Technion (Israel) jointly with UC Santa Barbara. Since 2001, she has held faculty positions at the Harvard, Rutgers, and George Mason Universities. In the past two years, she has served as a program director at the US National Science Foundation. Maria is now an Associate Professor at the National University of Singapore and also a Visiting Associate Professor at Harvard Medical School.

**Zacharias Lekkas** is a research assistant and doctoral candidate at the New Technologies Laboratory of the Faculty of Communication and Media Studies of the University of Athens. He holds an MSc in occupational psychology from the University of Nottingham. He is interested in the role of emotions and personality in the fields of decision making, learning, and performance. His work has been published in conferences, journals, and edited books.

**Charalampos Mainemelis,** PhD, is Associate Professor of Organizational Behavior at ALBA Graduate Business School in Athens, Greece, Visiting Professor at the University of Porto, and member of the editorial board of *Academy of Management Review.* His research interests encompass creativity, time, playfulness, and learning. His work has appeared in the *Academy of Management Review, Research in Organizational Behavior, Creativity Research Journal, Management Learning,* and other journals.

**Tilly Mortimore,** PhD, is a senior lecturer in Education Studies and Inclusion at Bath Spa University, teaching undergraduates and running master's programs in SpLD/dyslexia. She researches and writes about dyslexia, learning style, inclusion, and vulnerable learners. Her latest project focuses upon dyslexia and bilingual learners. She has taught in international educational and training contexts and books include *Dyslexia and Learning Style* (2008) and, with Jane Dupree, *Supporting Learners with SpLD/dyslexia in the Secondary Classroom* (2008).

**Valentyna Moskvina,** PhD, has been interested in studying cognitive styles since she was a student at the National University of Kiev, Ukraine. Her doctoral dissertation was devoted to investigating the nature of individual differences in cognition in the broader context of personal life regulation. After moving to the United States in 2000, she has been working as a research associate at the Psychology Department at Rutgers University. Currently, Valentyna is affiliated with Bergen Community College (NJ).

**Costas Mourlas,** PhD, is Assistant Professor in the National and Kapodistrian University of Athens (Greece), Department of Communication and Media Studies since 2002. His current main research interest is in the design and the development of intelligent environments that provide adaptive and personalized context to the users according to their preferences, cognitive characteristics, and emotional state. He has several publications including edited books, chapters, articles in journals, and conference contributions (Web: www.media.uoa.gr/~mourlas).

**Helena Pedrosa De Jesus,** PhD, holds a PhD in Science Education from the University of East Anglia, UK. Currently she is Associate Professor, with Agregação, at the Department of Education, University of Aveiro, Portugal. Her main research interests are classroom based and aim at developing strategies and processes to understand and improve students' learning. The present focus of her research is on questioning and approaches to develop the Scholarship of Teaching and Learning in Higher Education.

**Elizabeth R. Peterson,** PhD, is a senior lecturer in the Psychology Department at the University of Auckland, New Zealand. Her research interests include the psychology of individual differences, the development of educational beliefs and expectations, and cognitive and learning styles.

Most of her research is focused on trying to understand the factors and processes that lead to the development of successful and well-rounded students.

**Stephen Rayner,** PhD, is Professor of Education at Oxford Brookes University, UK. He is an internationally recognized scholar in the field of individual differences in learning, as well as in leadership and the management of inclusive education. Recent research includes the study of international knowledge creation in cognitive style research; examining the construction and use of personalizing pedagogies associated with Web-based learning; evaluating pedagogies and engagement in educationists' professional learning leadership at doctoral level; and investigating academic leadership in the role of the professoriate in the 'UK University'.

**Esther M. Roodenburg** is a graduate of the Australian universities of Melbourne, New England, and Monash, teacher and registered psychologist, lecturer in psychology in the Faculty of Education at Monash University after many years in private practice as a counseling psychologist. She currently undertakes a research program developing a personality-centered cognitive style instrument for psycho-educational assessment.

**John Roodenburg,** PhD, is a graduate of the universities of Melbourne and New England Australia, registered teacher and registered psychologist in Victoria, lecturer in Psychology at Monash University, coordinator of postgraduate educational and developmental psychology courses, deputy director of the Krongold Centre for Exceptional Children. He has a background in teaching, practice of counseling and Educational Psychology in rural settings. His research interests are in psychological assessment of abilities, personality, and cognitive style.

**Melodie Rosenfeld,** PhD, is a lecturer at the Achva Academic College of Education in Israel. Her expertise includes teacher development in the areas of individual differences, special education, and academic writing. She is director of the Pla'ot Program to develop academic learning and self-regulation in first-year college students. She holds an MA from UC Berkeley and a PhD from the University of Utrecht, The Netherlands, on the topic of "developing teacher sensitivity to individual learning differences".

**Sherman Rosenfeld,** PhD, is a science educator at the Weizmann Institute of Science. His expertise and research interests include the professional development of science teachers, project-based learning (PBL), bridging the gap between formal and informal learning, and the design of educational software. He directed the Agam Program for Visual Cognition and is currently the chairperson of a national committee to promote the culture of inquiry across the disciplines from K–12 in Israeli schools.

**A'ishah A. Sabki** is a Senior Lecturer in e-Commerce at the University of Huddersfield, UK. Her research focus is Islamic pedagogy and technology management. In addition, A'ishah is an experienced project manager in implementing e-commerce solutions.

**Garima Sharma** is a doctoral candidate in Organizational Behavior at the Weatherhead School of Management, Case Western Reserve University, US. Garima received her bachelor's in engineering and master's in business administration from India, after which she worked as an internal organizational development consultant for a software consulting firm in India. Her research interests are around experiential learning, corporate social responsibility, and large system change using appreciative inquiry.

**Nikos Tsianos** is a research assistant and doctoral candidate at the Department of Communication and Media Studies of the University of Athens. He holds an MSc in political communication. His main research area is the incorporation of theories from the psychology of individual differences into adaptive educational hypermedia. He has published several articles in conferences, books, and journals, while he has been credited with the best student paper award at the Adaptive Hypermedia 2008 conference.

**Peter Van Petegem**, PhD, is full professor at the Institute of Education and Information Sciences of the University of Antwerp, Belgium. He is chair of the research group EduBROn (www.edubron.be) and of the Center of Excellence in Higher Education (www.ua.ac.be/echo). His research interests focus on the level of learning and teaching strategies, external and internal evaluation of school policies, and evaluation of educational policies.

**Gert Vanthournout** is a PhD student at the Institute of Education and Information Sciences of the University of Antwerp, Belgium. His research interests focus on the development of learning patterns throughout higher education, on the relationship between motivation and learning patterns, and on individual and contextual influences in learning pattern development.

**Jan D. Vermunt**, PhD, is Professor of Teaching and Teacher Education at Utrecht University, The Netherlands. He has published extensively on student learning and higher education teaching, and has developed the Inventory of Learning Styles, a widely used diagnostic instrument to measure patterns in student learning. Later on, his research interests broadened to include phenomena of teacher learning and professional development in different phases of the professional career, often in the context of educational innovation.

**Michael Waring**, PhD, is Director of the MSc (QTS) physical education program in the School of Sport, Exercise and Health Sciences, Loughborough University, UK. He acts as a consultant, advisor, and inspector of learning and teaching in higher education and teacher education within the UK and internationally. His research interests involve the exploration and development of pedagogy in higher education and initial teacher education contexts, including the use of blended learning.

**Mike Watts**, PhD, is Chair in Education in the School of Sport and Education at Brunel University, London. He is head of the Department for Education and responsible for developing teaching, research, and consultancy education at Brunel. His own areas of research interest lie in the learning and teaching of science, in schools and beyond. He is a National Teaching Fellowship of the Higher Education Academy, awarded for his excellence in teaching, and a fellow of the Institute of Physics.

**Li-Fang Zhang**, PhD, is currently Associate Dean in the Faculty of Education at the University of Hong Kong, where she is also Associate Professor. She is the author of over 100 peer-reviewed articles, book chapters, and books. Two of her recent books (with Dr. Robert J. Sternberg) are entitled *The Nature of Intellectual Styles* and *Perspectives on the Nature of Intellectual Styles*. She serves on the editorial board of *Educational Psychology* and that of *Educational Psychology Review*.

# Index